SUSY AND MARK TWAIN

Mrs. Salsbury was born in Bedford, New York, and attended the Ethel Walker School, Simsbury, Connecticut. After graduating from Smith College she studied art abroad and in New York. She exhibited paintings in group shows and was a member of the National Arts Club and the National Society of Women Painters and Sculptors.

She is married to Charles Baker Salsbury, an architect, whom she met when they were students at the Ecole Américaine des Beaux Arts at Fontainebleau. They have two sons and a daughter and have lived in Hartford since 1937.

SUSY AND MARK TWAIN

Family Dialogues

ARRANGED AND EDITED

BY

EDITH COLGATE SALSBURY

HARPER & ROW, PUBLISHERS

NEW YORK

The author makes grateful acknowledgment to the following publishers, authors and authors' representatives for permission to quote from the works named below:

A Lifetime with Mark Twain: The Memories of Katy Leary by Mary Lawton. Reprinted by permission of Harcourt, Brace & World, Inc.

Concerning Cats: Two Tales by Mark Twain with an Introduction by Frederick Anderson. The Book Club of California. Copyright © 1959 by the Mark Twain Company.

Europe and Elsewhere by Mark Twain. Copyright 1923, 1951 by the Mark Twain Company. Reprinted by permission of Harper & Row, Publishers.

George W. Cable: His Life and Letters by Lucy Leffingwell Cable Biklé. Copyright 1928 by Charles Scribner's Sons. Reprinted by permission of the publishers and Lucy Leffingwell Cable Biklé.

Mark Twain: A Biography by Albert Bigelow Paine. 3 volumes. Copyright 1912 by Harper & Brothers; renewed 1940 by Dora F. Paine. Reprinted by permission of Harper & Row, Publishers.

Mark Twain, Business Man edited by Samuel Charles Webster. Little, Brown & Company, 1946. Copyright 1944, 1946 by the Mark Twain Company. Reprinted by permission of Mrs. Samuel Charles Webster.

Mark Twain, Family Man by Caroline Thomas Harnsberger. Citadel Press, 1960. Copyright © 1960 by Caroline Thomas Harnsberger. Reprinted by permission of the author. Acknowledgment is made for permission given by Thomas G. Chamberlain and the Central Hanover Bank and Trust Company, co-trustees of the Estate of Samuel L. Clemens, to quote hitherto unpublished Twain material.

Mark Twain-Howells Letters edited by Henry Nash Smith and William M. Gibson with the assistance of Frederick Anderson. Harvard University Press, 1960. Copyright © 1960 by the Mark Twain Company, copyright © 1960 by Mildred H. and John Mead Howells; copyright © 1960 by the President and Fellows of Harvard College. Reprinted by permission of the Mark Twain Company and William White Howells for the Estate of William Dean Howells.

(*Continued on next page*)

FIRST EDITION

LIBRARY OF CONGRESS CATALOG CARD NUMBER: 65-20437

H-P

This book is for Chas

CONTENTS

ILLUSTRATIONS

The following are grouped in a separate section after page 172.

Sam and Livy Clemens and their daughters
Sam Clemens about the time of his marriage
Olivia (Livy) Langdon
Olivia Lewis Langdon, Livy's mother
Jervis Langdon, Livy's father
Drawing room of the Langdon house
The Jervis Langdon house, Elmira, New York
Olivia Susan (Susy) Clemens, b. 1872
Clara Langdon Clemens, b. 1874
Jane Lampton (Jean) Clemens, b. 1880
Langdon Clemens (1870–1872)
Clara, Jean and Susy Clemens, 1884
Dr. and Mrs. A. R. Jackson with the Clemenses
The Clemens house, Nook Farm, Hartford
George Henry Warner
Lilly Gillette Warner
Susan Lee Warner
Charles Dudley Warner
Harriet Beecher Stowe
Mrs. Stowe's house in Nook Farm
Clara Spaulding, Susy, Livy and Sam Clemens, and Dr. John Brown
John Lewis
Quarry Farm
Susan Langdon Crane
Theodore Crane
Charles Jervis Langdon

The photographs unless otherwise credited are used courtesy of Mark Twain Memorial, Hartford, Connecticut.

ACKNOWLEDGMENTS

I wish to express my appreciation to the Trustees of the Mark Twain Estate for permission to publish, for the first time, portions of letters and literary documents by Samuel L. Clemens and his immediate family. I am also indebted to the Trustees of the Stowe, Beecher, Hooker, Seymour, Day Memorial Library and Historical Foundation for portions of letters by George H. Warner and Elizabeth G. Warner and an unpublished thesis by Katherine Seymour Day; to the Watkinson Library, Trinity College, for a letter by Caroline Dahlweiner; and to the Trustees of the Mark Twain Memorial, Hartford, for a letter by Margaret Warner and excerpts from the records of the Memorial.

I am also grateful to the persons in authority for access to Clemens family manuscripts at the Clifton Waller Barrett Library of American Literature, University of Virginia; the Henry W. and Albert A. Berg Collection, New York Public Library; the Manuscript Room, Boston Public Library; the Manuscript Room, British Museum; the Mark Twain Papers, University of California, Berkeley; the Edward L. Doheny Library, St. John's Seminary, Camarillo, California; the Elmira (New York) College Libraries; the Houghton Library, Harvard College Library; the Stowe, Beecher, Hooker, Seymour, Day Memorial Library and Historical Foundation, and the Mark Twain Memorial, Hartford.

For permitting access to their collections, I thank Mrs. Charles L. Goodspeed, Mrs. Harold F. Whitmore and Mrs. Frances Whitmore

Hartwell. My especial thanks go to Caroline Thomas Harnsberger for allowing me to copy her collection of typescripts of Clemens family letters.

For permission to quote from unpublished letters or manuscripts by persons whose names are in parentheses, I express my appreciation to the following: Kimberly Cheney (Mary Bushnell Cheney), Mrs. John M. Harlan (Evangeline Walker Andrews), Arthur L. Shipman, Jr. (Arthur L. Shipman) and Stanchfield Wright (Clara L. Spaulding).

Two persons, no longer living, gave me inspiration and the benefit of their intimate association with the Clemens family: Miss Ida Langdon of Elmira, New York, Mrs. Clemens' niece, and Miss Katharine Seymour Day, leader for the preservation of Mark Twain's Hartford house.

Many others deserve my gratitude; they include: Merle Eugene Curti, who introduced me, long ago at Smith College, to the pleasure of research, Norman Holmes Pearson, Henry Nash Smith, John C. Parsons, Joseph S. Van Why, Evan Alderson and the staff of the Reference Room, Hartford Public Library. I also wish to express my thanks to Cass Canfield, Elizabeth Lawrence, Margaret Butterfield, Helen Lane, Donald Pace and many others at Harper & Row, Publishers. Practical assistance has been given by Claire Nicoll, Dorothy Tucker, Valborg Proudman, Fay Trowbridge, Kathleen Berggren, Fay Manus and Esther Denson. Two groups of people have patiently helped me for six years: members of my family and the Trustees and staff of the Mark Twain Memorial, Hartford.

Finally, I wish to thank Frederick Anderson, Editor of the Mark Twain Papers, whose encouragement and guidance have made this book possible.

E.C.S.

INTRODUCTION

In 1880, shortly after the birth of his youngest daughter, Jean, Mark Twain wrote to his friend, the Rev. Joseph Twichell:

. . . the baby is five weeks old and—but no more of this, somebody may be reading *this* letter 80 years hence. And so, my friend (you pitying snob, I mean, who are holding this yellow paper in your hand in 1960,) save yourself the trouble of looking further; I know how pathetically trivial our small concerns will seem to you, and I will not let your eyes profane them.

But by 1906 Clemens had decided, "We recognize that there are *no* trivial occurrences in life if we get the right focus on them." The focus on Mark Twain is now more intense than it has ever been because of increasing recognition of his central importance to American literature. Very few people would argue that information about the life of a writer whose works grew so largely out of the occurrences and relationships that made up his life are "pathetically trivial." Although Clemens at least pretended to modesty, he obviously had little doubt in 1880 that his letters as well as his books would be read in 1960. But it is doubtful that even he anticipated how widespread and persistent the interest would become.

This widespread interest has occasionally led to the production of works which do not seem to be the product of careful research or original thought, and few of the biographical studies succeed in realizing the turbulence that marked the character of the author. A conventional narrative biography restricts the biographer to a point of view which controls the variety of his approach to the subject, or to a judicious, but sometimes tepid, recitation of fact. Mrs. Salsbury has adopted a narrative form which lets the principals speak for themselves through quotations from letters, manuscripts, and journals, with only brief transitional or explanatory notes in the voice of the "Narrator." She is able to convey the immediate reactions of Clemens and his associates without intruding her own opinions or judgments. Inevitably this method means that many matters are not touched upon at all and others perhaps less directly relevant to an account of the writer's professional career are examined from several points of view. But the great merit of the method is that it thoroughly explores those episodes and attitudes which were of greatest apparent importance to the Clemens family. The varying accounts give depth and perspective which no single view could achieve and their juxtaposition often reveals that the tranquil and sentimental idyl which the Clemenses created when they characterized their private family life was not always exact.

Previous attempts to deal with the facts of Clemens' life have been largely dependent upon the long, sometimes inaccurate, overpolite, and now outdated biography published by Albert Bigelow Paine in 1912. In *Sam Clemens of Hannibal,* the first volume of a projected biographical series, Dixon Wecter made a fresh start by going to original sources, but because of his death in 1950 the study ends with Samuel Clemens' late adolescence. These were the years of experience from which Mark Twain drew much of the best of his writing, but such a book could not answer the inevitable questions about what kind of a man Samuel Clemens became, what effect he had on those around him, and what influences they in turn exerted.

One of the most informative sources about Clemens in mid-career has never been published in full. Clemens' eldest daughter, Susy, began a biography of her father in 1885 when she was thirteen years old. She continued the project intermittently for a little over a year. This remarkably perceptive and intimate study is the nucleus for *Susy and Mark Twain* and is quoted extensively in Mrs. Salsbury's narrative. Readers of this unique record will concur in Clemens' judgment of later years that Susy's technique resembles that of a painter whose "random dashes on the canvases have developed into portraits" which present "a pretty clear and nicely shaded idea of the several members of this family—including Susy herself." Mrs.

Salsbury has enriched the scope and detail of Susy's portraits by quoting from hundreds of letters and other documents written by the family and their friends. The result is a social document in which the Clemenses' observant and detailed accounts of travel, education, public and domestic affairs, and social activities provide a picture of an entire period from the viewpoint of a family with unusually broad exposure to both American and European life in the later nineteenth century.

Mrs. Salsbury became interested in the history of the family during her work in all phases of the restoration of the Mark Twain house and museum in Hartford, Connecticut. In her research work for the Memorial since 1952 she has uncovered substantial information not previously published about the Clemens family and the Hartford community which she now makes available in entertaining and unusual form in *Susy and Mark Twain*.

FREDERICK ANDERSON
Editor of the Mark Twain Papers

EDITOR'S NOTE

The family, their friends, and their servants tell the story of Susy Clemens and her father, Mark Twain. I have elected to call the dialogists according to the names usually used for them by their contemporaries: Mark Twain and his wife are "Sam" and "Livy," the Rev. Joseph Hopkins Twichell is "Twichell," William Dean Howells is "Howells" and so on. I have assumed the part of the Narrator.

Livy's accidental misspelling and some of her punctuation have been corrected, but not Susy's. As Sam wrote, it was "frequently desperate, but it was Susy's and it shall stand."* Susy's name is spelled with a "y," as she spelled it, and ampersands have been spelled out; brackets serve to indicate editorial clarification. In some cases I have combined two versions of the same story; Sam frequently made on-the-spot notes and, years later, wrote the story with elaborations. In a few cases anecdotes have been shifted chronologically. All chapters except "Before Susy" and "After Susy" commence at the time of Susy's birthday, March 19th. Reference notes for each chapter will be found at the end of the book, as well as a bibliography, biographical directory and an index.

EDITH COLGATE SALSBURY

---

* [Clemens, Samuel L.] *Mark Twain's Autobiography*. Albert Bigelow Paine, ed., II, 66.

BEFORE SUSY

1835–1872

NARRATOR: Susy's life closely parallels an era in the life of a house, the house which was the setting for her family's happiest years. Both were creations reflecting the powerful influence of Sam Clemens, known the world over as Mark Twain. The house is in Hartford, Connecticut, and my close association with its restoration has led me to put down in words, "mainly stolen from books, tho' credit given,"[1]* the story of Susy Clemens and her family. Susy's "Biography" of Sam gives us a broad picture of the years preceding her birth. Sam introduces Susy and comments on her work.

SAM: When Susy was thirteen, and was a slender little maid with plaited tails of copper-tinged brown hair down her back, and was perhaps the busiest bee in the household hive, by reason of the manifold studies, health exercises, and recreations she had to attend to, she secretly, and of her own motion, and out of love, added another task to her labors—the writing of a biography of me.[2]

SUSY: Papa was born in Missouri. His mother is Grandma Clemens (Jane Lampton Clemens) of Kentucky. Grandpa Clemens was of the F.F.V.'s of Virginia.

SAM: Without doubt it was I that gave Susy that impression. I cannot imagine why, because I was never in my life much impressed by grandeurs which proceed from the accident of birth.

SUSY: Clara and I are sure that papa played the trick on Grandma,

* Superior numbers refer to Reference Notes, page 401.

about the whipping, that is related in "The Adventures of Tom Sawyer": "Hand me that switch." The switch hovered in the air, the peril was desperate—"My, look behind you, Aunt!" The old lady whirled around and snatched her skirts out of danger. The lad fled on the instant, scrambling up the high board fence and disappeared over it.

SAM: Susy and Clara were quite right about that.

SUSY: And we know papa played "Hookey" all the time. And how readily would papa pretend to be dying so as not to have to go to school!

SAM: These revelations and exposures are searching, but they are just. If I am as transparent to other people as I was to Susy, I have wasted much effort in this life.

SUSY: Grandma couldn't make papa go to school, so she let him go into a printing-office to learn a trade. He did so, and gradually picked up enough education to enable him to do about as well as those who were more studious in early life.

SAM: It is noticeable that Susy does not get overheated when she is complimenting me, but maintains a proper judicial and biographical calm. It is noticeable, also, and it is to her credit as a biographer, that she distributes compliment and criticism with a fair and even hand.[3]

SUSY: Papa was about twenty years old when he went on the Mississippi as a pilot. Just before he started on his tripp Grandma Clemens asked him to promise her on the Bible not to touch intoxicating liquors or swear, and he said "Yes, mother, I will," and he kept that promise seven years when Grandma released him from it.

SAM: Under the inspiring influence of that remark, what a garden of forgotten reforms rises upon my sight.[4]

SUSY: After papa had been a pilot on the Mississippi for a time, Uncle Orion Clemens, his brother, was appointed Secretary of the State of Nevada, and papa went with him out to Nevada to be his secretary. Afterwards he became interested in mining in California; then he reported for a newspaper and was on several newspapers. Then he was sent to the Sandwich Islands. After that he came back to America and his friends wanted him to lecture so he lectured. Then he went abroad on the Quaker City, and on board that ship he became equainted with Uncle Charlie (Mr. C. J. Langdon, of Elmira, New York). Papa and Uncle Charlie soon became friends, and when they returned from their journey Grandpa Langdon, Uncle Charlie's father, told Uncle Charlie to invite Mr. Clemens to dine with them at the St. Nicholas Hotel, in New York. Papa accepted the invitation and went to dine at the St. Nicholas with Grandpa and there he met mamma (Olivia Lewis Langdon) first. But they did not meet again until the next August, because papa went away to California, and there wrote "The Inocense Abroad."

SAM: I will remark here that Susy is not quite correct as to that next meeting. That first meeting was on the 27th of December, 1867, and the next one was at the house of Mrs. Berry, five days later. Miss Langdon had gone there to help Mrs. Berry receive New Year guests. I went there at ten in the morning to pay a New Year call. I had thirty-four calls on my list, and this was the first one. I continued it during thirteen hours, and put the other thirty-three off till next year.

SUSY: Mamma was the daughter of Mr. Jervis Langdon, (I don't know whether Grandpa had a middle name or not) and Mrs. Olivia Lewis Langdon, of Elmira, New York. She had one brother and one sister, Uncle Charlie (Charles J. Langdon) and Aunt Susie (Susan Langdon Crane). Mamma loved Grandpa more than any one else in the world. He was her idol and she his; I think mamma's love for grandpa must have very much resembled my love for mamma. Grandpa was a great and good man and we all think of him with respect and love. Mamma was an invalid when she was young, and had to give up study a long time.

SAM: She became an invalid at sixteen, through a partial paralysis caused by falling on the ice, and she was never strong again while her life lasted.[5]

SUSY: Papa wrote mamma a great many beautiful love letters when he was engaged to mamma, but mamma says I am too young to see them yet; I asked papa what I should do for I didn't (know) how I could write a Biography of him without his love letters, Papa said that I could write mamma's opinion of them, and that would do just as well. So I'll do as papa says, and mamma says she thinks they are the loveliest love letters that ever were written, she says that Hawthorne's love letters to Mrs. Hawthorne are far inferior to these.[6]

SAM: She [Livy] is small. There isn't much of her, but what there is, assays as high as any bullion that ever I saw.[7]

SUSY: Soon papa came back East and papa and mamma were married.

SAM: It sounds easy and swift and unobstructed, but that was not the way of it. It did not happen in that smooth and comfortable way. There was a deal of courtship. There were three or four proposals of marriage and just as many declinations.[8]

SUSY: Mamma (and papa) were going to board first in Buffalo and grandpa said he would find them a good boarding-house. But he afterwards told mamma that he had bought a pretty house for them, and had it all beautifully furnished, he had also hired a young coachman, Patrick McAleer, and had bought a horse for them, which all would be ready waiting for them, when they should arrive in Buffalo; but he wanted to keep it a secret from "Youth," as grandpa called papa. What a delightful surprise it was! Grandpa went down to Buffalo with mamma and papa. And when they drove up to the house, papa said he thought the landlord of such a boarding-house must charge a great deal to those who wanted to live there. And when the secret was told papa was delighted beyond all degree. Mamma has told me the story many times, and I asked her what papa said when grandpa told him that the delightful boarding-house was his home, mamma answered that he was rather embariesed and so delighted he didn't know what to say.[9]

NARRATOR: The Rev. Joseph Hopkins Twichell of Hartford, who had officiated at their wedding with the Rev. Thomas K. Beecher of The Park Church, Elmira, came with his wife, Harmony, to spend the night.

SAM: I went after them with the carriage at 3.40 PM . . . and from that till dinner time (at 5.) we showed them elaborately over the house, and made Twichell wipe his feet and blow his nose before entering each apartment (so as to keep his respect up to an impressive attitude,)—and we listened to their raptures and enjoyed the same—and I told them the story of what happened to Little Sammy in Fairy Land when he was hunting for a Boarding House, and they enjoyed *that*. But I never let them near that drawing room till they thought they had seen all the glories of the palace— till after dinner, in fact, for I wanted to have the gas ablaze and the furniture-covers removed. It looked magnificent! I think they will give a good account.[10]

NARRATOR: Sam reveled in being master-of-the-house.

SAM: You can't think what a carver I have become. I hardly ever have to take hold of a chicken by the leg, now. And I look mighty imposing too, at the head of my table, with my big fork, my carving-knife and my glove-stretcher about me. (I use the glove-stretcher to hold the chicken while I get out the stuffing—Livy is keeping her eyes shut till I tell her she may look and see what I am to do with the glove stretcher.)[11]

LIVY: Isn't he a funny Youth?[12]

SUSY: About six months after papa and mamma were married grandpa died; it was a terrible blow on mamma, and papa told Aunt Sue he thought Livy would never smile again, she was so broken hearted. Mamma couldn't have had a greater sorrow than that of dear grandpa's death, or any that could equal it exept the death of papa. Mamma helped take care of grandpa during his illness and she couldn't give up hope till the end had realy come.[13]

After grandpapa's death mamma and papa went back to Buffalo; and three months afterward dear little Langdon was born.[14]

SAM: He was prematurely born. We had a visitor in the house and when she was leaving she wanted Mrs. Clemens to go to the station with her. I objected. But this was a visitor whose desire Mrs. Clemens regarded as law. The visitor wasted so much precious time in taking her leave that Patrick had to drive in a gallop to get to the station in time. . . . The streets . . . were paved with large cobblestones and had not been repaired since Columbus's time. Therefore the journey to the station was like the Channel passage in a storm. The result to Mrs. Clemens was a premature confinement, followed by a dangerous illness.[15]

SUSY: Mamma named him Langdon after grandpapa, he was a wonderfully beautiful little boy, but very, very delicate. He had wonderful blue eyes, but such a blue that mamma has never been able to describe them to me so that I could see them clearly in my mind's eye. His delicate health was a constant anxiety to mamma, and he was so good and sweet that that must have troubled her too, as I know it did. . . .

Soon after little Langdon was born (a year) papa and mamma moved to Hartford to live. Their house in Buffalo reminded them too much of dear grandpapa, so they moved to Hartford soon after he died.

SAM: Susy is right. Our year and a half in Buffalo had so saturated us with horrors and distress that we became restless and wanted to change, either to a place with pleasanter associations or with none at all. . . .

When we could endure imprisonment no longer, Mrs. Clemens sold the house and I sold my one-third interest in the newspaper [Buffalo *Express*], and we went to Hartford to live.[16]

NARRATOR: Sam and Livy both had friends in Hartford. Livy had visited Alice Hooker, John and Isabella Beecher Hooker's daughter and Harriet Beecher Stowe's niece; Sam had made many friends since his first visit to Hartford in 1868 to arrange for the publication of *The Innocents Abroad* with Elisha Bliss of the American Publishing Company. They leased the Hookers' house on the corner of Forest and Hawthorne streets. Livy commented, "You'd know this house was built by a Beecher. It's so queer."[17]

The house was in an area known as Nook Farm, a colony of literary and artistic people which had been founded by John Hooker and his brother-in-law, Francis Gillette. It was a progressive group: Isabella was an early suffragist and Gillette conducted a station of the Underground Railway in his barn. Neighbors included Harriet Beecher Stowe, Charles Dudley Warner, editor of the Hartford *Courant*, and his wife, Susan, the best amateur pianist in Hartford, and Charles' brother, George, whose wife was Gillette's daughter. Sam and Livy liked Hartford; Sam wrote, "You do not know what beauty is if you have not been here."[18]

Shortly after moving, Sam left on a lecture tour to pay off debts incurred in Buffalo. Livy, who was pregnant, wanted to build and, with Lilly Warner, she walked all around Nook Farm looking at land. Lilly and George Warner had started to build and they wanted the Clemenses to consult their architect, Edward Tuckerman Potter. Sam came home in January, and early in March they went to Elmira, to Mother Langdon's, where Livy planned to have her second child.

SUSY'S FIRST YEAR

1872–1873

NARRATOR: Susy's birth was recorded with very little fanfare; Sam and Livy were worried about Langdon's health; he was not developing normally.

SUSY: (About a year and five months) after Langdon was born I was born, and my chief occupation then was to cry, so I must have added greatly to mamma's care.[1]

SAM: Olivia Susan Clemens was born at the Langdon homestead in Elmira, N.Y., 19th March, 1872 and was named for her grandmother and her aunt Susan Crane.[2]

I have no news save of the household. The new baby flourishes, and groweth strong and comely apace. She keeps one cow "humping herself" to supply the bread of life for her—and Livy is relieved from duty (Livy is very inefficient in some respects.) Langdon has no appetite, but is brisk and strong. His teeth don't come—and neither does his language.[3]

NARRATOR: Sam and Livy and Sam's mother had a brief vacation in Cleveland with one of Sam's *Quaker City* friends, Mrs. Abel Fairbanks. "Mother" Fairbanks, Sam said, "was the most refined, intelligent, and cultivated lady in the ship, and altogether the kindest and best. She sewed my buttons on, kept my clothes in presentable trim, fed me on Egyptian jam, (when I behaved,) lectured me awfully on the quarter-deck on moonlit promenading evenings, and cured me of several bad habits."[4] While in Cleveland, Sam wrote Susy for the first time.

SAM: My Dear Daughter: Your grandmother Fairbanks joins your mother and me in great love to yourself and your brother Langdon.

We are enjoying our stay here to an extent not expressible save in words of syllables beyond your strength. Part of our enjoyment is derived from sleeping tranquilly right along, and never listening to see if you have got the snuffles afresh or the grand duke upstairs has wakened and wants a wet rag. And yet no doubt *you*, both of you, prospered just as well all night long as if you had had your father and mother's usual anxious supervision. Many's the night I've lain awake till 2 oclock in the morning reading Dumas and drinking beer, listening for the slightest sound you might make, my daughter, and suffering as only a father can suffer, with anxiety for his child. Some day you will thank me for this.

Well, good bye to you and to all the loving ones who are trying to supply the paternal place.—My child be virtuous and you will be happy. Yr father Saml L. Clemens.[5]

NARRATOR: They returned to Elmira May 14th.

SAM: We arrived last night from Cleveland. . . . We find Langdon enjoying a heavy cough. . . . He is as white as alabaster and is weak; but he is pretty jolly about half the time. The new baby is as fat as butter, and wholly free from infelicities of any kind.[6]

NARRATOR: Susy continues in her "Biography."

SUSY: At last it was time for papa to return to Hartford, and Langdon was real sick at that time, but still mamma decided to go with him, thinking the journey might do him good. But after they reached Hartford he became very sick.[7]

SAM: I was the cause of the child's illness. His mother trusted him to my care and I took him for a long drive in an open barouche for an airing. It was a raw, cold morning, but he was well wrapped about with furs and, in the hands of a careful person, no harm would have come to him. But I soon dropped into a reverie and forgot all about my charge. The furs fell away and exposed his bare legs. By and by the coachman noticed this, and I arranged the wraps again, but it was too late. The child was almost frozen. I hurried home with him. I was aghast at what I had done, and I feared the consequences.

SUSY: His trouble prooved to be diptheeria. He died about a week after mamma and papa reached Hartford.[8]

SAM: Tonsilitis or something of the sort set in, and he did not get any better. . . . There it was pronounced diphtheria, and of course he died [June 2nd].[9]

Susy: He was burried by the side of grandpa at Elmira, New York.[10]

Livy: I feel so often as if my path was to be lined with graves.[11]

Susy: After that, mamma became very very ill, so ill that there seemed great danger of death, but with a great deal of good care she recovered.[12]

Sam: We have replied to none of the many letters of condolence we received, writing was so painful.[13]

Narrator: Langdon's death put a damper on building plans, but the George Warners continued to urge Sam and Livy to consult their architect.

George: I want immensely to get that house for Potter.[14]

Lilly: The Clemens come at 7 tonight. I'll do all in my power . . . to get the house for Mr. P. Langdon's death postpones buying land . . . perhaps seeing our house begun will start them up. If . . . the builders begin now perhaps we will get in by New Years.[15]

Narrator: On their return to Hartford, Sam, Livy and Susy went, for a month, to Fenwick Hall at Saybrook, on the Connecticut shore.

Sam: Our Susy is doing famously *here*, but the case was different in Hartford, the moment the warm weather set in. We had to pack our trunks mighty suddenly, the 5th of July and rush down here—and none too soon, for the succeeding week wilted Hartford children like a simoon. This place is on the Sound, 2 hours from Hartford, and is delightfully cool and comfortable—never an hour of heat, day or night. . . .

Susy is bright and strong and we love her so that no sacrifice seems too much to make for her; though I feel that we *must* look up a less expensive article of condensed milk for her.[16]

Narrator: At the shore, Sam occupied himself with his only invention that was ever to make any money, "a *self-pasting scrap-book* —good enough idea if some juggling tailor does not come along and ante-date me a couple of months, as in the case of the elastic vest-strap."[17] He was making plans to go abroad.

Sam: Mrs. Langdon will reach here in a day or two [August 11th], and she and Livy will remain till cool weather—but I sail in the Scotia, Aug. 21st for Europe—England, rather—to be gone several months. If I find I am to be away very long, shall return by and by and take Livy over. I confine myself to England and Scotland.[18]

NARRATOR: Sam's trip was ostensibly to see his English publisher, gather material for a new travel book and to lecture. Actually he was beginning his long battle for copyright. He was immediately homesick for Livy and Susy.

SAM: Livy darling, I have little or nothing to write, except that I love you and think of you night and day, and wonder where you are, and what you are doing, and how the Muggins comes on, and whether she ever speaks of me—and whether Mother [Mrs. Langdon] is cheerful and happy. I hope and trust and pray that you are all well and enjoying yourselves—but I can't say that I have been enjoying myself, greatly, lost in a vast ship where our 40 or 50 passengers flit about in the great grim distances like vagrant spirits. But latterly our small clique *have* had a somewhat better time of it, though if one is absent there can be no whist.

I have given the purser a ten-dollar telegram of 3 words to send to you from Queenstown, and also my journal in 2 envelopes— and now I'll rush and give him this—consider, my dear, that I am standing high on the stern of the ship, looking westward, with my hands to my mouth, trumpet fashion, yelling across the tossing waste of waves, "I LOVE YOU, LIVY DARLING! ! !"

NARRATOR: Arriving in London, he was swept into a round of social activity.

SAM: Livy darling, I was getting positively uneasy until this morning [September 11th] when I got your two first letters (one dated Aug. 20 and one Aug. 28). I was going to telegraph you to day, to ask what the matter was. But now I am all right. You are well, Mother is with you and the Muggins is jolly and knows what her hands are made for. I would like very much to see you all just now.

Confound this town, time slips relentlessly away and I accomplish next to nothing. Too much company—too much dining—too much sociability.[19]

LIVY: I am so *very* anxious to have Mr. Clemens do his very best, and I believe he will, I think. England is a subject that he will get inspired over—I do miss him so much and yet I am contented to have him away, because I think it is just the work that he should be at now. . . . I am without my natural protector . . . my Susy does comfort me so wonderfully, in the absence of her Father and brother—sometimes the desire is almost stronger than I can bear to see the dear little son and daughter together, and I feel sure that I shall have that joy someday.[20]

SAM: I came here to take notes for a book, but I haven't done much but attend dinners and make speeches. I have had a jolly good time, and I do hate to go away from these English folks; they make a stranger feel entirely at home, and they laugh so easily that it is a comfort to make after-dinner speeches here. I have made hundreds of friends.[21]

NARRATOR: Joaquin Miller, Californian poet, was living in London; he described Sam: "He was shy as a girl, although time was already coyly flirting white flowers at his temples, and could hardly be coaxed to meet the learned and great who wanted to take him by the hand."[22]

Sam arrived home November 26th; Mrs. Langdon stayed on to celebrate his birthday and then returned home to Elmira. Sam wrote her how much they missed her and told her they wanted Sue and Theodore Crane to come to visit. He wrote: "The *little* Susy needs them, too. She has a marvelous cold—as bad a one as I ever had myself, I think. It pulls her down at a wonderful rate. She is nothing now but skin and bones and flesh."

He also commented on the Henry Ward Beecher scandal, which for some months had had Nook Farm and the Beechers themselves divided in bitter camps. Henry, pastor of the Plymouth Church in Brooklyn, New York, preached a doctrine of love and perfectionism, a radical departure from Calvinism. In 1871 gossip was circulated by Susan B. Anthony that Beecher had committed adultery with a Mrs. Tilton, and, while Sam was in England, Victoria Woodhull, spectacular advocate of free love, spiritualism and feminism, published the story. Francis D. Moulton served as intermediary between the Tiltons and Beecher. Isabella Beecher Hooker joined the feminist camp and was ostracized by Nook Farm. Beecher, eventually, after a trial where no verdict was reached, was exonerated by a council of Congregational ministers.

SAM: How stands Elmira on the Beecher Scandal? Miss Catherine Beecher tells us that Mr. Moulton *did* go after a MS., to Mr. Beecher, and expecting that he "would be mad," took a pistol with him. The poor old soul was in considerable trouble, evidently, and fully appreciated the damaging effect of *one* statement in the Woodhull arraignment being a *fact*. She was sorry a sweeping assertion of the untruth of the said arraignment would not do

—because of that unlucky pistol business. However, she said Beecher didn't give up the paper. The Twichells now tell us that a full year ago the Tiltons (both the he one and the she one) gave to Mr. Beecher an absolute denial of all these slanders, and that that paper is still in Mr. B.'s possession.

Very well, then. The Twichells say, with us, that that paper ought at once to be printed. Whoever feels uncertain about the truth or falsehood of those slanders (and I would extremely like to know who feels certain) is suffering shame and defilement, and is continuing to carry a filthy subject in his mind, to his further defilement, when possibly the Beecher party are all the while able to sweep away his doubts and purify his mind with a breath. *I* think the silence of the Beechers is a hundred fold more of an *obscene publication* than that of the Woodhulls—and the said silence is a thousand-fold more potent in convincing people of the truth of that scandal than the evidence of fifty Woodhulls could be. *Silence has given assent* in all ages of the world—it is a law of *nature,* not ethics—and Henry Ward Beecher is as amenable to it as the humblest of us. You will find presently that the general thought of the nation will gradually form itself into the verdict that there is *some* fire somewhere in all this smoke of scandal.

NARRATOR: Sam had made copious notes in England for another travel book and he settled down to work on December 2nd.

SAM: I went to work on my English book yesterday and turned out 36 pages of satisfactory manuscript, but the baby kept me awake so much last night that today I find the inspiration is vanished and gone, right in the middle of my subject.[23]

NARRATOR: They had a family reunion with Sam's brother and his wife.

LIVY: We took dinner last night with Orion and Mollie and had an exceedingly pleasant time. They are very cozily situated— Yesterday was the anniversary of their wedding.[24]

SAM: Every day he [Orion] was the most joyous and hopeful man that ever was, I think, and also every day he was the most miserable man that ever was.[25]

She [Mollie] was a good woman and was greatly liked. Her vanity was pretty large and inconvenient, but she had a practical side, too.[26]

NARRATOR: Orion had come to Hartford to work first for Elisha Bliss of the American Publishing Company, Sam's publisher. He changed jobs frequently. Sam and Livy, and others, found Mollie and Orion Clemens difficult. Sam reported on their welfare to his mother.

SAM: Your eldest son and daughter are exceedingly cosily situated, and Orion is as happy as a martyr when the fire won't burn.

Wish you all a Merry Christmas and many happy returns. I have been aggravating the baby by showing her another baby in a handglass whom she can't find behind it.[27]

NARRATOR: Early in January, Sam and Livy decided on the lot they would buy in Nook Farm. Their choice had lain between the Gillette lot on the west side of Forest Street and land on Farmington Avenue belonging to Franklin Chamberlin which included a knoll overlooking the river. The deed was signed on January 16th. They paid $10,000 for a parcel of land which began on Farmington Avenue 350 feet west of the corner of Forest Street. It was bounded on the south by Gillette's land and on the west by the river.

LIVY: Mr. Chamberlin let us have the low land for less than $9 a foot—but in measuring the land there proved to be more of the bank than Mr. C. thought, so that by taking a hundred and thirteen (I believe) of the table land seventy five did not bring us to the flat land, so Mr. C. sold us the rest of the bank for $50 a front foot.[28]

Mr. Clemens seems to glory in his sense of possession; he goes daily into the lot, has had several falls trying to lay off the land by sliding around on his feet.[29]

NARRATOR: Samuel Webster, whose mother was the daughter of Sam's sister, Pamela, later remarked on winter in Nook Farm.

SAMUEL WEBSTER: When Uncle Sam and Aunt Livy dropped in on the neighbors in the winter he would pull Livy on a sled. There was a sociability about the life. People went in and out of each others' houses without ringing the bell.[30]

LIVY: The other night Mr. Clemens drew me on a sled over to Mr. Chas. Perkins—we had a real good time—there was a stool tied onto the sled so that it made a comfortable seat.[31]

For three days the ice has covered the trees, and they have been glorious. We could do nothing but watch the beauty outside; if you looked at the trees as the sun struck them, with your back toward the sun, they were covered with jewels. If you looked toward the sun it was all crystal whiteness, a perfect fairy-land.

Then the nights were moonlight, and that was a great beauty, the moon giving us the same prismatic effect.[32]

SAM: . . . when a leafless tree is clothed with ice from the bottom to the top— ice that is as bright and clear as crystal; when every bough and twig is strung with ice-beads, frozen dew-drops, and the whole tree sparkles cold and white, like the Shah of Persia's diamond plume. Then the wind waves the branches and the sun comes out and turns all those myriads of beads and drops to prisms that glow and burn and flash with all manner of colored fires, which change and change again with inconceivable rapidity from blue to red, from red to green, and green to gold—the tree becomes a spraying fountain, a very explosion of dazzling jewels; and it stands there the acme, the climax, the supermost possibility in art or nature, of bewildering, intoxicating, intolerable magnificence. One cannot make the words too strong.[33]

NARRATOR: Charles W. Burpee, Hartford historian, wrote about Sam's architect.

CHARLES W. BURPEE: Mr. Clemens selected his architect with great care. He chose Edward Tupperman [Tuckerman] Potter of New York, eminent in his profession (a brother of Bishop Potter) and a builder of churches as well as residences. He was a quaint gentleman, very much suited to association with the Literary Colony of Nook Farm. Generally he carried a good-sized cotton umbrella under his arm. . . Rather large of stature and benevolent of countenance, one would take him for a dreamy philosopher, but his mind was stored with a wealth of literature and also of music. He could compose beautiful sonnets and he could set them to music in a way which would have brought him fame had he not been wedded to his own art.[34]

NARRATOR: Susy was thriving this winter of '72 to '73, and she had a playmate, Margaret Warner, George's and Lilly's daughter, who was nicknamed Daisy and was a few months older than Susy. Sam, too, had many friends and had been elected a member of a literary group, the Monday Evening Club. His first paper was on "The License of the Press." Howell Cheney, president, many years later described the club.

HOWELL CHENEY: The Club has a constitution which, probably instigated by Horace Bushnell in the year 1869, was written by the Reverend Charles S. Henry and James Hammond Trumbull.

NARRATOR: Trumbull was known as the most learned man who had ever lived in Hartford. Sam said he could swear in twenty-seven different languages.

HOWELL CHENEY: It started with the practice of laying upon the table at each meeting a book in which were to be recorded the subjects the members would like to have discussed. Of course the essayist paid little attention to this and chose his subject out of his own experience.[35]

Each host was the presiding officer of the evening, and each essayist, in perfect confidence of the fellowship of the Club, opened his heart and discussed the articles of his personal faith and interests.[36]

SAM: Those were the brighest minds in Hartford—and indeed they were very superior minds.[37]

NARRATOR: A club member described Sam.

ARTHUR L. SHIPMAN: He acted with one or two present as if there were a hundred. . . . I am inclined to think that he acted and spun his tales in talk for the mere tickling of his own creative instinct. Clemens loved to play with his own picture painting and he acted out his stories because his imagination moved more effectively thereby. The presence of others gave him the necessary stimulus. When he didn't have the physical presence of sympathizers, he found that response in imagination with his readers-to-be.[38]

LIVY: Mr. Clemens was never so good and lovable as he is now, we never were so happy together it seems to me—He is *perfectly brim full* of work, says he never worked with such perfect ease and happiness in his life—He is going to New York the last of next week to deliver some lectures, he delivers two or three in New York and two or three in Brooklyn, he was seduced into it by the large prices they offer him, half the gross proceeds which will probably be five and six hundred dollars a night—Now that we have bought the lot he feels anxious to make all the money that he can, but knows that he will make more in the long run by writing than by lecturing, but it is a great temptation to him when they offer him such enormous prices—but he will only lecture six or seven times—It is splendid to see him so heartily love his work, he begrudges every moment's interruption.[39]

NARRATOR: A trip to England for the whole family was being planned for the summer. In the meantime Sam and Charles Dudley Warner were writing *The Gilded Age,* having been goaded by their wives into providing more entertaining novels than those recently published.

SAM: [We wrote alternately] in the superstition that we were writing one coherent yarn, when I suppose, as a matter of fact, we were writing two *in*coherent ones.[40]

WARNER: Mark and I are writing a novel, and can so nearly see the end of it that it is safe to speak of it. No one here, except our wives, knows anything of it. We conceived the design early in the winter, but were not able to get seriously at work on it till some time in January. If there is any satire on the times in it, it won't be our fault, but the fault of the times. We have hatched the plot day by day, drawn out the characters, and written it so that we cannot exactly say which belongs to who; though the different styles will show in the chapters. This may be a good feature, giving the reader relief, and it may be it will only bother him. It is rather a novel experiment.

We hope to get it ready for the press before Clemens goes to England.

WHITELAW REID: Mark was in prodigious feather over the prospects of the book. He was going to take a copy of the manuscript over to England with him, so as to publish simultaneously on both sides of the ocean.

SAM: Some people think I have no head for business . . . but this is a lie . . . We think a pretty good deal of this novel I can tell you; even the paper it is written on cost eleven dollars.[41]

SUSY'S SECOND YEAR

1873–1874

NARRATOR: Susy was very gay and lively on her first birthday.

SAM: Susy began to talk a little when she was a year old. If an article pleased her, she said *"Like* it—awnt (want) it—hab (have) it—take it"—and took it, unless somebody got in ahead and prevented.[1]

NARRATOR: On March 22nd Sam bought another strip of land from Chamberlin to enlarge his lot. He paid $1,000 for a wedge-shaped strip of land which increased his frontage on Farmington Avenue by twenty feet.

There were incessant conferences with architect and builder. Both Potter and Sam were imaginative men and many of their pet idiosyncrasies were to be reflected in the design of the house. They changed their minds with great rapidity.

SAMUEL WEBSTER: At the last moment, just as the ground was about to be broken, it was discovered that it would be necessary to cut down one of the trees. Everything was held up, the site was studied anew, the prospective house was moved several feet away and the tree was spared.[2]

MRS. LANGDON: Saml is hard at work, and Livy is very busy getting ready to leave her house for the summer . . . and I am going to take her home with me for a visit of two or three weeks before she goes to England.[3]

NARRATOR: Sam wrote Livy in Elmira.

SAM: Livy darling, I have finished trimming and revamping all my

MS, and to-day [April 26th] we began the work of critically reading the book, line by line and numbering the chapters and working them in together in their appropriate places. It is perfectly
fascinating work. All of the first eleven chapters are mine, and
when I came to read them right straight along without breaking,
I got really interested. . . .

We both think this is going to be no slouch of a novel, as
Solomon said to the Hebrew Children.

Dined with Warner yesterday—at home today—lunch with
Twichell noon tomorrow. The kitties are very frisky, now. They
and the old cat sleep with me, nights, and have the run of the
house. I wouldn't take thousands of dollars for them. Next to a
wife whom I idolise, give me a cat—an *old* cat, with kittens. How
is the Muggins, now, by the way. It is very melancholy here, but I
don't notice it. I'm pretty sad, but I'm used to it—it can't phaze
me. I'm an old hand at grief. Grief makes me hump myself when
I'm alone, but that is taking advantages. When my family is
around I am superior to it.

But I am not grieving tonight, honey. I've pegged away all day
till this hour and done a big day's work, and I feel as gay as a
hymn.

Got a French version of the Jumping Frog—fun is no name
for it. I am going to translate it *literally*, French construction and
all (apologising in parenthesis where a word is too many for me)
and publish it in the Atlantic as the grave effort of a man who
does not know but what he is as good a French scholar as there
is—and sign my name to it, without another word. It will be tooth-
some reading.

Goodbye my darling, I love you and I love the muggins.—It
is bed time, now—I got to go down and roust out the cats.[4]

NARRATOR: Sam, Livy, Susy, Nellie, the nursemaid, and Livy's Elmira
friend, Clara Spaulding, sailed on the S.S. *Batavia* on May 17th.
Sam described Clara Spaulding as Livy's "playmate and schoolmate from the earliest times . . . mentally, morally, spiritually,
and in all ways, a superior and lovable personality."[5]

SUE CRANE: Miss Clara Spaulding had long desired to go abroad.
Mrs. Clemens desired her company, for there had never been
any break in the friendship beginning in early girlhood—Mr.
Spaulding, with large means was happy to send the daughter to
whom he was devoted.

It proved to be one of the experiences where friends can travel many months together, with increasing devotion.[6]

SAM: The ship was casting off, with that hubbub and confusion and rushing of sailors, and shouting of orders and shrieking of boatswain whistles, which marked the departure preparations. . . . Mrs. Clemens, Clara Spaulding, little Susy, and the nurse-maid were all properly garbed for the occasion. We all had on our storm-rig, heavy clothes of somber hue, but new and designed and constructed for the purpose, strictly in accordance with seagoing etiquette; anything wearable on land being distinctly and odiously out of the question.[7]

LIVY: From New York for two days we had perfectly lovely weather, there was no more motion than there is on the Jersey City ferry boat—Monday afternoon we had a hail storm. Nellie was a little sick but Clara and I were not a particle sick—Tuesday afternoon it began to be pretty rough and Clara and I were both sick and Nellie was very sick. . . . Susy staid in her basket in the Capt.'s chart room all day—Nellie lying on the sofa there, but Mr. Clemens taking the main care of her, she slept most of the day, when she was awake played in her basket. . . . Capt. Morland is just about perfection, he has done everything that he possibly could to make us comfortable and to make things pleasant for us, he and Clara take long walks on the deck together—I do not know hardly what we should do if it was not for his chart room, the baby goes there early in the forenoon and stays until her bed time. It crowds Capt. Morland very much but he insists that it does not—He grows more and more delightful the better one knows him—We would not come back with any one else, on any account, if it is possible to come with him.

The table is very good indeed, but we lack appetites somewhat, we can eat fruit and they have plenty of that, *delicious* oranges . . . all the fruits that can now be procured and we can have them, any hour of the day . . . in fact I do not think from my experience that one needs to bring any thing to eat with them. . . .

Little Susy was not very well for a day or two after we left N.Y., but now she is well. She eats *very* heartily. We hardly give her the bottle before it will be entirely empty—she has never eaten so since she was born.[8]

NARRATOR: They went directly to London and settled down at the Langham Hotel in Portland Place for a gay season.

SAM: We have a luxuriously ample suite of apartments . . . 3rd floor, our bedroom looking straight up Portland Place and our parlor having a noble array of great windows looking out upon both streets (Portland Place and the crook that joins it to Regent Street.)[9]

LIVY: Our apartments are perfectly delightful, I expected to find them rather barren looking but was very happily disappointed— Our food is excellent, delicious bread and butter and everything palatable, we do feel so cosy and comfortable as we sit down to our meals.

Susy's lower gums are very much swollen and she is a little worried today [May 31st].[10]

SAM: Livy and the Modoc are well. . . . The Modoc is able to stand alone, now. She is getting into a habit, of swearing when things don't suit. This gives us grave uneasiness.[11]

Susy never had but one nick-name . . . and only kept that one a year. That was "Modoc," (from the cut of her hair.) This was at the time of the Modoc war in the lava beds of northern California.[12]

NARRATOR: Joaquin Miller had just written his *Life Among the Modocs*. As in many instances, Sam's memory was at fault. He recalled later that Susy acquired several nicknames.

LIVY: Little Susy is very well indeed, she creeps all about the room, eats meat and potato for her breakfast every morning and is as fat and hearty as possible—Nellie takes care of her now nights. I am out so much that I need my unbroken sleep.[13]

SAM: Indeed, the baby seems to have unfailing, robust health. She is on her feet all her waking hours, and always busy—generally in matters that would fare better without her help. She says a few trifling words in broken English.[14]

NARRATOR: All the great vied to entertain Sam and his charming ladies. Years later, names were meticulously recorded by Susy in her "Biography" of Sam.

SUSY: He met . . . Mr. Charles Kingsley, Mr. Henry M. Stanley, Sir Thomas Hardy grandson of the Captain Hardy to whom Nellson said "Kiss me Hardy," when dying on shipboard, Mr. Henry Irving, Robert Browning, Sir Charles Dilke, Mr. Charles Reade, Mr. William Black, Lord Houghton, Frank Buckland, Mr. Tom Hughes, Anthony Trollope, Tom Hood, son of the poet—and mamma and papa were quite well equanted with Dr. Macdonald and family, and papa met Harrison Ainsworth.[15]

CLARA SPAULDING: I remember a delightful luncheon that Charles Kingsley gave for Mr. Clemens; also an evening when Lord Dunraven brought Mr. Home, the medium, Lord Dunraven telling many of the remarkable things he had seen Mr. Home do. I remember I wanted so much to see him float out of a seven or eight story window, and enter another, which Lord Dunraven said he had seen him do many times. But Mr. Home had been very ill, and said his power had left him. My great regret was that we did not see Carlyle, who was too sad and ill for visits.

LIVY: It is perfectly discouraging to try to write. There is so much to write about that it makes me feel as if it was no use to begin.[16]

NARRATOR: Livy became quite worn out so they left for a rest in Edinburgh.

SAM: In the train on the way from London to Edinburgh . . . [Susy] developed a rather lame talent for crowing like a rooster.[17]

We carried no letters of introduction; we hid ourselves away in Veitch's family hotel in George Street and prepared to have a comfortable season all to ourselves. But by good fortune this did not happen. Straightway Mrs. Clemens needed a physician, and I stepped around to 23 Rutland Street to see if the author of *Rab and His Friends* was still a practicing physician. He was. He came, and for six weeks thereafter we were together every day, either in his house or in our hotel. . . .

His was a sweet and winning face—as beautiful a face as I have ever known. Reposeful, gentle, benignant—the face of a saint at peace with all the world and placidly beaming upon it the sunshine of love that filled his heart. Dr. John was beloved by everybody in Scotland; and I think that on its downward sweep southward it found no frontier.[18]

DR. BROWN: I am attending the wife of Mark Twain. His real name is Clemens. She is a quite lovely little woman, modest and clever, and she has a girlie eighteen months old, her ludicrous miniature —and such eyes![19]

LIVY: I have been having a very lazy day [August 2nd] lying on the sofa and just resting most of the day—Mr. Clemens has gone out now for a little walk, it is a bright beautiful evening—

Susy trots all about the room of course she is not at all steady

on her feet as yet but she enjoys it just as much apparently—
I say to her "Susy shoo the flies" and she makes her little hands
go and says "Sh! Sh! Sh!" She has watched with the greatest
interest two or three flies that have been on the window and
would laugh when they would fly—she grows more and more
interesting and entertaining all the time—She says baby very
distinctly—The other day her father bought her a very pretty
picture of a kitten and we asked her to say cat, she says "tat," she
says "kitty" quite distinctly—Every picture or anything that she
particularly admires she says something nearly like "puddle,"
every time she comes into the room she points to the picture on
the wall and says "puddle." [20]

NARRATOR: Sam made an important purchase in Edinburgh: a
carved oak mantelpiece, which had been removed from a castle
belonging to the Mitchell-Innes family. The mantel and overmantel measured twelve feet from floor to ceiling; dolphins supported
the pillars and in the center of the overmantel was an elaborately
carved escutcheon, with symbols of the arts including a lyre and
a mask. The enormous piece was crated and sent home to grace
the library in the new house.

SAM: Susy and the Doctor had a good deal of romping together.
Daily he unbent his dignity and played "bear" with the child.
I do not now remember which of them was the bear but I think
it was the child. There was a sofa across a corner of the parlor
with a door behind it opening into Susy's quarters and she used
to lie in wait for the Doctor behind the sofa—not lie in wait but
stand in wait; for you could only get just a glimpse of the top of
her yellow head when she stood upright. According to the rules
of the game she was invisible and this glimpse did not count. I
think she must have been the bear, for I can remember two or
three occasions when she sprang out from behind the sofa and
surprised the Doctor into frenzies of fright, which were not in
the least modified by the fact that he knew that the "bear" was
there and coming.[21]

> And now from out my veiling lids
> I caught a flash of sunlit hair,
> But kept the secret to myself. I knew the game.
> A bear was lurking there, I knew it well,
> And knew its ways. All stealthily it crept
> In shadow and concealment of the forest—

(Which others thought a sofa of the horse-hair type)
The golden splash betraying all its progress as it came—
Until it gained the nearest point of vantage:
Then—out it burst upon me with a roar, and I
Collapsed in fright—which was my part to play.[22]

[Dr. Brown] had two names for her—"Little wifie" and "Megalo-pis," for her large eyes seemed to him to warrant that sounding Greek epithet. When Susy is an old friendless woman and reads this page, let her remember that she has one thing to be proud of and grateful for—Dr. John Brown loved her and petted her.[23]

Livy: This afternoon [August 6th] at three o'clock Dr. Brown is coming to take us for a drive; he is the most charming old gentle-man and I believe grows more and more so all the time—Being in bed and lying about on the sofa I had worn a net every time that he saw me, the other day he said to me "I hope you do not put one of those horrid things (meaning the false hair extras) on the top of your head when you go out.[24]

Sam: Our books have come—a rare thing we have been on the track of for ten days—got it at last—the famous "Abbottsford Edition" of Scott's works—12 huge volumes elaborately illus-trated. Pretty scarce book.[25]

Narrator: With his love for exotic clothes, Sam was in his element in Scotland.

Sam: I had my clothes . . . colored tartan. . . . I stuck a big feather in my cap too, and the people would follow me for miles . . . some of the best judges in Scotland said they had never seen a High-land costume like mine. What's more, one of those judges fined me for wearing it—out of mere envy, I suppose.[26]

Narrator: Livy worried about money.

Livy: It is real hard to have the exchange so heavy—think of taking $3000 and only having $2500 when you get here—If I was *sure* our house would not exceed $20 or $25,000 I would spend more here, because we shall want the things when we get into our new house.[27]

Narrator: They went to Ireland the end of August and Livy wrote her mother.

Livy: We had a very disagreeable trip from Glasgow to Belfast. We were all except Mr. Clemens wretchedly sick, Susy and all. I think we suffered more in that one day than in the ten days crossing the Atlantic.

We reached Belfast about eight in the evening and before we had finished our supper a Mr. Finley, son-in-law to the Mr. Russel that we stopped with near Melrose, called. He was a delightful man and did do every thing he possibly could to make our stay in Belfast pleasant.

NARRATOR: Mr. Finley introduced them to a family named Ritchie who entertained them lavishly at their large house, having, according to Livy, an "abundance of servants—two grown men and a half-grown boy waited on the table."

LIVY: I hardly know how we should have gotten along if it had not been for the kindness of these people for the hotel food was unbearable, we could not eat it, it is the first time that we have had really bad fare. . . . We make friends in every place that we very much dislike to leave behind us, it makes me really sad when I think that I am not likely ever again to see Dr. and Miss Brown—they were so good to us and I did so truly love and admire them. . . . Dr. Brown gave Susy a very pretty pin, it is a cairngorm stone, which is a Scotch stone, brilliant and about the value of an amethyst—she is to have it when she is married and I am to wear it until then—

I do wish you could see the little thing she is as happy as the day is long trots all about the room saying Mama, mama, papa, papa, babe, babe.—There is a glass to the floor in the parlor that we now have and she goes up to it and kisses the baby in it—

We are having exceedingly pleasant times and yet I shall be more than glad when we start for home—eight weeks from last Sat. we sail. The 25th of Oct. . . . Charlie [Langdon] must be sure and be in New York, we want to see him and we want to use him—Mr. Clemens would be in the insane asylum if he had to see about getting our trunks through the custom house. So if Charlie would not feel it a real imposition (even if he would I want him to come just the same) I want him to meet us in New York and help us— . . . don't let him fail us for we shall really *need* him—tell him we will pay his expenses.[28]

NARRATOR: They went to Paris for two weeks, where they bought furnishings for the new house. In October Sam lectured in London and it was a complete triumph; Livy, who was pregnant, wanted to go home.

LIVY: I am blue and cross and homesick. I suppose what makes me feel the latter is because we are contemplating to stay in

London another *month*. There has not one sheet of Mr. Clemens's proof come yet, and if he goes home before the book [*The Gilded Age*] is published here he will lose his copyright. And then his friends feel that it will be better for him to lecture in London before his book is published, not only that it will give him a larger but a more enviable reputation. I would not hesitate *one moment* if it were simply for the money that his copyright will bring him, but if his reputation will be better for his staying and lecturing, of course he ought to stay. . . . The truth is, I can't bear the thought of postponing going home.[29]

NARRATOR: They sailed October 21st; Sam wrote Dr. Brown on ship-board.

SAM: The first three days were stormy, and wife, child, maid, and Miss Spaulding were all sea-sick 25 hours out of the 24, and I was sorry I ever started.[30]

We have plowed a long way over the sea, and there's twenty-two hundred miles of restless water between us now, besides the railway stretch. And yet you are so present with us, so close to us, that a span and a whisper would bridge the distance.[31]

NARRATOR: Home less than a week, Sam sailed back to London to lecture for two months and protect the copyright of *The Gilded Age*, which was published in London in December. He took Charles Warren Stoddard with him as secretary.

SAM: I am *hoping* to be back in 20 days, but I have *so much* to go home to and enjoy with a jubilant joy, that it seems hardly possible that it can ever come to pass in so uncertain a world as this.[32]

Livy darling, it is 2 in the morning here, and about 9 in the evening in Hartford, or half past 8. I am imagining you to be in the parlor, and the Modoc gone to bed. You are sitting by the table and the Warners are about to go home in the snow—and then you will go to bed too.—Well, I wish I were there with you. Here, Stoddard and I have been talking and keeping a lonely vigil for hours—but I won't talk of it any more. It is *so* unsatisfying. I want *you*—and nobody else. I do love you so.[33]

NARRATOR: The first Charles Dudley Warner house was on Hawthorne Street diagonally across from the Hooker house. It was the garden of this house which was the setting for Warner's *My Summer in a Garden*. Spring, 1874, was a busy season: Sam was supervising the new house, lecturing only occasionally and enjoying his family and visitors.

SAM: There isn't enough money in America to hire me to leave you [Livy] for one day.[34]

The Modoc has just tumbled down again and smashed some more furniture—and herself. I hear an angel sing, maybe, but there's other times I prefer.[35]

NARRATOR: A memorable gathering occurred in early spring when Thomas Bailey Aldrich and his wife, William Dean Howells and James R. Osgood came to Hartford to visit the Clemenses and the Warners. Sam was not fond of Mrs. Aldrich.

SAM: She is one of those people who are profusely affectionate, and whose demonstrations disorder your stomach. You never believe in them; you always regard them as fictions, artificialities, with a selfish motive back of them. Aldrich was delightful company, but we never saw a great deal of him because we couldn't have him by himself.[36]

When it came to making fun of a folly, a silliness, a windy pretense, a wild absurdity, Aldrich the brilliant, Aldrich the sarcastic, Aldrich the ironical, Aldrich the merciless, was a master.[37]

Thomas Bailey Aldrich has said fifteen hundred if not fifteen thousand things as brilliant as the things Talleyrand said, which are labelled "French Wit."[38]

MRS. ALDRICH: As our train moved slowly into the station at Springfield, we saw on the platform Mark Twain and Charles Dudley Warner, waiting to join their guests, and go with them the rest of the short journey. Mark Twain was then in his golden dawn; he had friends in crowds; he had married the woman he loved, and fame had become a tangible asset. With the same slow and lengthened utterance that had made the old man at his lecture ask, "Be them your natural tones of eloquence?"—with his waving, undulating motion as he came towards us he said, "Well, I reckon I am prodigiously glad to see you all. I got up this morning and put on a clean shirt, and feel powerful fine. Old Warner there did n't do it, and is darned sorry—said it was a lot of fuss to get himself constructed properly just to show off, and that that bit of a red silk handkerchief on the starboard side of his gray coat would make up for it; and I allow it has done it."

NARRATOR: On arrival in Hartford, they were met at the station by Patrick with the carriage.

MRS. ALDRICH: Patrick McAleer was accompanied by "George,"

who was both butler and guardian spirit of the house. George had been the body servant of an army general, and was of the best style of the Southern negro of that day. With much formality we were presented to him by Mr. Clemens, who said: "George came one day to wash windows; he will stay for his lifetime. His morals are defective; he is a gambler—will bet on anything. I have trained him so that now he is a proficient liar—you should see Mrs. Clemens's joy and pride when she hears him lying to the newspaper correspondent, or the visitor at the front door."[39]

SAM: Mrs. Clemens discharged him every now and then, but she was never able to get him to pack his satchel. He always explained that "You couldn't get along without me, Mrs. Clemens, and I ain't going to try and get along without you." He had faults, but his worship of her was perfect, and made the rest of us blind to them.[40]

NARRATOR: This was Howells' first visit to Hartford. Sam had met him for the first time in the office of James T. Fields, editor of the *Atlantic Monthly,* in 1869. Howells reviewed *The Innocents Abroad* in December of that year. When he read the review, Sam is reported to have said, "I felt like the woman who was so glad her baby had come white.[41]

HOWELLS: It seems to me quite an ideal life. They [Warner and Mark Twain] live very near each other, in a sort of suburban grove, and their neighbors are the Stowes and Hookers, and a great many delightful people. They go in and out of each other's houses without ringing, and nobody gets more than the first syllable of his first name—they call their minister *Joe* Twichell. I staid with Warner, but of course I saw a good deal of Twain, and he's a thoroughly great fellow. His wife is a delicate little beauty, the very flower and perfume of *ladylikeness,* who simply adores him—but this leaves no word to describe his love for her.[42]

In the good-fellowship of that cordial neighborhood we had two such days as the aging sun no longer shines on in his round. . . . Clemens was then building the stately mansion in which he satisfied his love of magnificence as if it had been another sealskin coat, and he was at the crest of the prosperity which enabled him to humor every whim or extravagance.[43]

SUSY'S THIRD YEAR

1874–1875

NARRATOR: At about the time of her birthday, Susy acquired a new nursemaid, Rosina Hay, a young German girl. Rosa was to become, like George, Patrick and others, one of a devoted group who were so important to the family way of life and to the development of the children. She was a Lutheran, had a lovely sense of humor and an easy, cordial laugh. She had good sense and great courage.

The house was progressing rapidly and creating much comment; there was a news story in March.

HARTFORD DAILY TIMES: Most of the residents of Hartford know that Mr. Samuel L. Clemens, otherwise known as "Mark Twain," is building a residence on Farmington Avenue, a short distance east of the stone bridge on that thoroughfare. Many of the readers of *The Times,* doubtless have had at least an external view of the structure, which already has acquired something beyond a local fame; and such persons, we think, will agree with us in the opinion that it is one of the oddest looking buildings in the State ever designed for a dwelling, if not in the whole country. From an inspection of the building, now fast approaching completion, we are able to give the following description of it:

It is located on a lot of ground some 612 feet by 400, just west of Forest Street, being on the south side of Farmington Avenue. It is of brick, and three stories in height, fronting easterly. The extreme length of the building is 105 feet 4 inches; its extreme width 62 feet 4 inches. On the west side there is an octagonal tower 48 or 50 feet in height; while at the extreme ends, north and south, of the house, there are towers of less height.

NARRATOR: The tallest tower, which was topped by a semicircular porch or deck, opened off the billiard room, as did the south tower. The decks offered delightful views of the lawns and the river. The north tower had a smaller deck opening off Sam's and Livy's bedroom.

HARTFORD DAILY TIMES: On the first floor there is to be a parlor, drawing-room or library, dining room and bedrooms. The drawing-room on the rear of the south end of the building, is to open into a semi circular conservatory.[1]

NARRATOR: The Clemenses called the parlor the drawing room, and the drawing room the library. The design of the conservatory had been invented by Harriet Beecher Stowe, and most of the houses in Nook Farm had such an area.

HOWELLS: The plants were set in the ground, and the flowering vines climbed up the sides and overhung the roof above the silent spray of a fountain companied by callas and other water-loving lilies. There, while we breakfasted, Patrick came in from the barn and sprinkled the pretty bower, which poured out its responsive perfume in the delicate accents of its varied blossoms.[2]

HARTFORD DAILY TIMES: The dining-room, at the rear, on the north end of the house, has one feature we do not recollect to have seen in any other building, and that is a window directly above a fire-place.

NARRATOR: Sam liked the idea of watching the flames leap to meet the falling snowflakes.

HARTFORD DAILY TIMES: On the second floor there will be a study, nursery, sewing-room and boudoir, house-keeper's room, servants' bedroom, and numerous bath-rooms. On the third floor there will be a billiard-room, artists' friends' room, toilet and two servants' rooms. . . . There are no less than five balconies about this building, beside that of the west tower. A veranda will run around the south end and the east front of the ground floor of the building, with an extensive covered projection or porte-cochère (drive-way for carriages) on the east.[3]

NARRATOR: The report was not accurate, but the description generally reflected the ebullient character of the architecture. One of the reasons the building was considered "odd" was that the service wing was on the street (north) and the principal living rooms opened to the southwest. When questioned as to why the kitchen was on Farmington Avenue, Sam replied, "So the servants can see the circus go by without running out into the front yard."[4]

The veranda, called sometimes "the deck" but generally the *ombra,* meaning "shade" in Italian, was to become a favorite family spot for eating, relaxing and entertaining. A Viennese author, Friedrich Eckstein, visiting Warner at this time commented on the *ombra.* "In the back of the house, was a white-washed open porch, fashioned after a 'Hurricane Deck,' the top-most deck of the Mississippi steamers, which plays a special part in Mark Twain's 'Life on the Mississippi.'

"Nostalgic memories of his youth caused Mark Twain to make this arrangement. There he used to go to and fro, clad in white linen, as was his custom, or peacefully lie on a deck chair facing the park."[5]

HARTFORD DAILY TIMES: The rooms will all be finished in black walnut and oak, except the nursery and bathrooms, in which butternut will be used. The main hall-way of the building, open from the first floor to the third, is 15 by 25 feet; and this gives promise of being a very fine portion of the structure.[6]

NARRATOR: The whole family was fascinated with the house, but Livy's time was drawing near; in April they went to Elmira to await the new baby.

SAM: This town is in the interior of the State of New York—and was my wife's birth-place. We are here to spend the whole summer. Although it is so near summer, we had a great snow-storm yesterday, and one the day before. This is rather breaking in upon our plans, as it may keep us down here in the valley a trifle longer than we desired. It gets fearfully hot here in the summer, so we spend our summers on top of a hill [at Quarry Farm] 6 or 700 feet high, about two or three miles from here—it never gets hot up there.[7]

NARRATOR: Years later, Ida Langdon, Susy's cousin, described Quarry Farm.

IDA LANGDON: Quarry Farm was then a cottage-like house that stood . . . on the crest of East Hill. From its vine-hung porch there was a wide view across the roofs and spires of Elmira to the distant ranges of the Pennsylvania hills. Behind it valleys and wood- and farm-lands rolled away into deep country.[8]

SAM: Mrs. Clemens is pretty strong, and so is the "little wifie" barring a desperate cold in the head—the child grows in grace and beauty marvellously. I wish the nations of the earth would combine in a baby show and give us a chance to compete.[9]

Indeed I *am* thankful for the wifey and the child, and if there is one individual creature on all this footstool who is more thoroughly and uniformly and unceasingly *happy* than I am I defy the world to produce him and *prove* him. In my opinion he don't exist. I was a mighty rough, coarse, unpromising subject when Livy took charge of me, four years ago, and I may *still* be to the rest of the world, but not to her. She has made a very creditable job of me.[10]

NARRATOR: Clara Langdon Clemens was born June 8th.

SAM: She was named for Miss Clara Spaulding, of Elmira, a very especial friend of her parents.

When she was an hour and 4 minutes old, she was shown to Susy. She looked like a velvet-headed grub worm squirming in a blanket—but no matter, Susy admired. She said, in her imperfect way, "Lat bay (baby) got boofu' hair"—So Clara has been commonly called "Bay."[11]

[She is] the great American Giantess—weighing 7¾ pounds. We had to wait a good long time for her, but she was full of compensation when she *did* come.

The Modoc was delighted with it, and gave it her doll at once. There is nothing selfish about the Modoc. She is fascinated with the new baby. The Modoc rips and tears around out doors, most of the time, and consequently is as hard as a pine knot and as brown as an Indian. She is bosom friend to all the ducks, chickens, turkeys and guinea hens on the place. Yesterday as she marched along the winding path that leads up the hill through the red clover beds to the summer-house, there was a long procession of these fowls stringing contentedly after her, led by a stately rooster who can look over the Modoc's head. The devotion of these vassals has been purchased with daily largess of Indian meal, and so the Modoc, attended by her bodyguard, moves in state wherever she goes.[12]

HOWELLS: It was immensely kind of you to pause in your blissful consciousness of that new little girl of yours and acknowledge that my trivial story existed. Thank Mrs. Clemens for me, and tell (her) how glad I am that she has another girl—boys wear out their clothes so fast; and in the present diversity of boys' and men's costumes, you cannot roll up the paternal trowsers so as to make them fit.[13]

NARRATOR: Sam was writing *The Adventures of Tom Sawyer*, working from breakfast till five in the afternoon, in an isolated spot where only the blowing of a horn at the house could disturb him in an emergency.

SAM: Susie Crane has built the loveliest study for me, you ever saw. It is octagonal, with a peaked roof, each octagon filled with a spacious window, and it sits perched in complete isolation on top of an elevation that commands leagues of valley and city and retreating ranges of distant blue hills. It is a cosy nest, with just room in it for a sofa and a table and three or four chairs—and when the storms sweep down the remote valley and the lightning flashes above the hills beyond, and the rain beats upon the roof over my head, imagine the luxury of it! It stands 500 feet above the valley and 2½ miles from it.[14]

NARRATOR: All the family recognized the delightful relationship between Sue Crane and Sam. Years later Clara Clemens recalled that: "Aunt Sue, for whom my elder sister was named, was the one person I have ever seen who appeared to be continually above and beyond the hurts inflicted by human existence. Father sometimes called her Saint Sue, and she returned the compliment by baptizing him Holy Samuel, though with a strong touch of humor in her tone of voice whenever she used this title. Aunt Sue adored Father's little bursts of temper and would laugh at him most heartily. Often he laughed with her, altering his vehement mood instantaneously to one of childlike mirth. These sudden changes from shadow to light, and from light to shadow, were perhaps one of Father's real charms, for the human race likes surprises."[15]

A family-group photograph was taken that summer and Sam sent one to Dr. Brown.

SAM: The group represents the vine-clad carriageway in front of the farm-house. On the left is Megalopis sitting in the lap of her German nurse-maid. I am sitting behind them. Mrs. Crane is in the center. Mr. Crane next to her. Then Mrs. Clemens and the new baby. Her Irish nurse stands at her back. Then comes the table waitress, a young negro girl, born free. Next to her is Auntie Cord (a fragment of whose history I have just sent to a magazine). She is the cook; was in slavery more than forty years.[16]

NARRATOR: Sam said that Auntie Cord called Livy the " 'Queen o' de Magazines,'—which was indefinite but sounded fine."[17]

SAM: The self-satisfied wench, the last of the group, is the little baby's American nurse-maid. In the middle distance my mother-in-law's coachman (up on errand) has taken a position unsolicited to help out the picture. No, that is not true. He was waiting there a minute or two before the photographer came. In the extreme background, under the archway, you glimpse my study.[18]

From the Bay's first birth-day till some weeks had passed, her chances were uncertain. She could live on nothing but breast milk, and her mother could not furnish it. We got Mary Lewis, the colored wife of the colored lessee of Quarry Farm to supply it a couple of weeks, but the moment we tried to put her on prepared food she turned blue around her mouth and began to gasp. We thought she would not live 15 minutes. Then we got Maggie O'Day from Elmira, who brought her blind child with her and divided up her rations—not enough for the two; so we tried to eke out the Bay's supply with prepared food, and failed.—She turned blue again and came near perishing.

We never tried prepared food any more. Next we got Lizzie Botheker, and had to pay her worthless husband $60 to let her come, besides her wages of $5 per week.

Next we got Patrick's wife (our coachman) Mary McAleer, to furnish milk for the Bay.

Lastly we got Maria McLaughlin, wife of a worthless Irishman.[19]

No. 1 was a mulatto, No. 2 was half American, half Irish, No. 3 was half German, half Dutch, No. 4 was Irish, No. 5 was apparently Irish, with a powerful strain of Egyptian in her. This one ended the procession,—and in great style too.

It has always been held that mother's milk imparts to the child certain details of the mother's make-up in permanency—such as character, disposition, tastes, inclinations, traces of nationality and so on. Supposedly, then, Clara is a hybrid, a polyglot, a person of no particular country or breed, a General Member of the Human Race, a Cosmopolitan.

She got valuable details of construction out of those other contributors, no doubt . . . but it was the mighty Egyptian that did the final work and reared upon it the imposing superstructure. There was never any wet-nurse like that one—the unique, the sublime, the unapproachable! She stood six feet in her stockings, she was perfect in form and contour, raven-haired, dark as an Indian, stately, carrying her head like an empress. She had the martial port and stride of a grenadier, and the pluck and strength of a battalion of them. In professional capacity the cow was a poor thing compared to her, and not even the pump was qualified to take on airs where she was. She was as independent as the flag, she was indifferent to morals and principles, she disdained company, and marched in a procession by herself. She was as healthy as iron, she had the appetite of a crocodile, the stomach of a cellar, and the digestion of a quartz-mill. Scorning the adamantine law that a wet-nurse must partake of delicate things only, she devoured anything and everything she could get her hands on, shoveling into her person fiendish combinations of fresh pork, lemon pie, boiled cabbage, ice cream, green apples, pickled tripe, raw turnips, and washing the cargo down with freshets of coffee, tea, brandy, whiskey, . . .—anything that was liquid; she smoked pipes, cigars, cigarettes, she whooped like a Pawnee and swore like a demon; and then she would go up stairs loaded as described and perfectly delight the baby with a banquet which ought to have killed it at thirty yards, but which only made it happy and fat and contented and boozy. No child but this one ever had such grand and whole-some service. The giantess raided my tobacco and cigar department every day; no drinkable thing was safe from her if you turned your back a moment; and in addition to the great quantities of strong liquors which she bought down town every day and con-sumed, she drank 256 pint bottles of beer in our house in one month, and that month, the shortest one of the year. These things sound impossible, but they are facts. She was a wonder, a portent, that Egyptian.[20]

NARRATOR: In August Sam and Livy and the children went to visit Sam's mother at Pamela Moffett's in Fredonia, New York. It was very hot, and the children *and* Sam were fretful; Livy bore the brunt of it all.

SAM: I brought Mrs. Clemens back from her trip in a dreadfully broken-down condition—so by the doctor's orders we unpacked the trunks sorrowfully to lie idle here another month instead of going at once to Hartford and proceeding to furnish the new house which is now finished. We hate to have it go longer desolate and tenant-less, but cannot help it.[21]

NARRATOR: In September they went to New York for ten days to buy carpets and furnishings for the house, which continued to arouse much comment. Charles W. Burpee, Hartford historian, inter-viewed the architect.

CHARLES W. BURPEE: Mr. Potter was required to get some suggestion of a steamboat into the Clemens house. If one will inspect the south portion of the house, which was the front of it according to Mr. Clemens's idea, he will see how the conception was carried out. The mind can be led easily to perceive the pilot-house and the deck. The beloved billiard-room was in the pilot-house. In general, it can be said that the whole style of the house was Mark Twain. No one ever saw anything like it before, or ever will again.[22]

SAM: Livy wore herself out buying carpets and furniture in New York—that and the journeys "fixed" her. But she will rest up now, I hope.[23]

I *am* the gladdest man. Livy would be another, if the house were finished, but it isn't—full of carpenters yet, on the lower floor. We have thrown down an old carpet or two and are living on the second floor. We sleep in Ma's bedroom; eat in the nursery and use my study for a parlor. Rosa and Susy sleep in Livy's private sitting room which opens out of the nursery on the east front. We have gas, now, in these apartments, and water in Ma's and little Susy's bathroom—so we are pretty comfortable, and Margaret's cookery goes ahead of anything we have had at the best table in New York. . . .

The stable is all done, and is exceedingly handsome. The house and grounds are not to be described, they are so beautiful. Patrick and family occupy large handsome rooms in the stable. I don't think I ever saw such a bewitching place as ours is.[24]

NARRATOR: Livy wrote a letter home to which Sam added a post-script.

LIVY: We are perfectly delighted with everything here and do so want you all to see it.

SAM: Livy appoints me to finish this; but how can a headless man perform an intelligent function? I have been bullyragged all day by the builder, by his foreman, by the architect, by the tapestry devil who is to upholster the furniture, by the idiot who is putting down the carpets, by the scoundrel who is setting up the billiard-table (and has left the balls in New York), by the wildcat who is sodding the ground and finishing the driveway (after the sun went down), by a book *agent*, whose body is in the back yard and the coroner notified. Just think of this thing going on the whole day long, and I a man who loathes details with all his heart! But I haven't lost my temper, and I've made Livy lie down *most* of the time; could anybody make her lie down *all* the time?[25]

NARRATOR: The circular balconies, opening off the billiard room, were favorite retreats for Livy and Sam.

LIVY: The atmosphere is very hazy, and it makes the autumn tints even more soft and beautiful than usual. Mr. Twichell came for Mr. Clemens to go walking with him; they returned at dinner-time, heavily laden with autumn leaves.

SAM: Twichell came up here with me to luncheon after services, and I went back home with him and took Susy along in her little carriage. We have just got home again, middle of afternoon, and Livy has gone to rest and left the west balcony to me. There is a shining and most marvelous miracle of cloud-effects mirrored in the brook; a picture which began with perfection, and has momently surpassed it ever since, until at last it is almost unendurably beautiful. . . .

There is a cloud-picture in the stream now whose hues are as manifold as those in an opal and as delicate at the tintings of a sea-shell. But now a muskrat is swimming through it and obliterating it with the turmoil of wavelets he casts abroad from his shoulders.

The customary Sunday assemblage of strangers is gathered together in the grounds discussing the house.[26]

HARTFORD DAILY TIMES: The novelty displayed in the architecture of the building, the oddity of its internal arrangement, and the fame of its owner, will all conspire to make it a house of note for a long time to come.[27]

ALDRICH: It is apparently a comfortable little shanty. Cosy, and all that sort of thing.[28]

NARRATOR: The house and the babies were much photographed.

HOWELLS: Mrs. Howells thanks you ever so much for the fotographs. We both admire the babies, who seem to have behaved uncommonly well under fire of the fotographer, and to have come out seriously charming. We think they and the house the prettiest in the world.[29]

NARRATOR: Sue and Theodore Crane came to see the new house.

SAM: I have an admirable billiard table up stairs and am prepared to take pupils. I have taught Theodore the rudiments. . . . The house is still imperceptibly progressing.

NARRATOR: Sam and Livy are worried about the baby, who continued to have feeding problems. This was the Mary McAleer stage in the procession of wet nurses.

SAM: The "bay" had another of those spells . . . and turned blue and white and scared everybody. Cause—a spoonful of cow's milk. She will experiment no more. Patrick's wife will sleep in the house and board her night and day hereafter till she quits school.[30]

NARRATOR: Sam bought a typewriter and experimented on it writing to Orion.

SAM: I AM TRYING TO GET THE HANG OF THIS NEW F
FANGLED WRITING MACHINE, BUT AM NOT MAKING
A SHINING SUCCESS OF IT, HOWEVER THIS IS THE
FIRST ATTEMPT I EVER HAVE MADE, & YET I PER-
CEIVETHAT I SHALL SOON & EASILY ACQUIRE A FINE
FACILITY IN ITS USE. I SAW THE THING IN BOS-
TON THE OTHER DAY & WAS GREATLY TAKEN WI:TH
IT. SUSY HAS STRUCK THE KEYS ONCE OR TWICE,
& NO DOUBT HAS PRINTED SOME LETTERS WHICH DO
NOT BELONG WHERE SHE PUT THEM.
THE HAVING BEEN A COMPOSITOR IS LIKELY TO BE
A GREAT HELP TO ME,SINCE O NE CHIEFLY NEEDS
SWIFTNESS IN BANGING THE KEYS.THE MACHINE COSTS
125 DOLLARS.THE MACHINE HAS SEVERAL VIRTUES
I BELIEVE IT WILL PRINT FASTER THAN I CAN WRITE.
ONE MAY LEAN BACK IN HIS CHAIR & WORK IT. IT
PILES AN AWFUL STACK OF WORDS ON ONE PAGE.
IT DONT MUSS THINGS OR SCATTER INK BLOTS AROUND.
OF COURSE IT SAVES PAPER.

SUSY IS GONE,
NOW, & I FANCY I SHALL MAKE BETTER PROGRESS.
WORKING THIS TYPE-WRITER REMINDS ME OF OLD
ROBERT BUCHANAN, WHO, YOU REMEMBER, USED TO
SET UP ARTICLES AT THE CASE WITHOUT PREVIOUS-
LY PUTTING THEM IN THE FORM OF MANUSCRIPT.I
WAS LOST IN ADMIRATION OF SUOH MARVELOUS
INTELLECTUAL CAPACITY.[31]

NARRATOR: Susy depended on the servants as well as on her father for entertainment and instruction.

SAM: [When Clara was born] this circumstance set a new influence at work upon Susy's development. Mother and father are but two —to be accurate, they are but one and a tenth—and they do their share as developers; but along a number of lines certain other developers do more work than they, their number being larger and their opportunities more abundant—i.e. brothers and sisters and servants.[32]

NARRATOR: The new year saw Sam working on *Tom Sawyer*. Livy wore herself out with sick babies, guests and furnishing the house. She brought the children up to observe the Sabbath and a daily prayer hour; Susy was very conscious of the implications.

SAM: Her religious activities began to develop rapidly. Many of her remarks took cast from this interest.

She was found in the act of getting out her water colors one Sunday to make vari-colored splotches and splashes on paper— which she considered "pictures." Her mother said:

"Susy, you forget it is Sunday."

"But mamma, I was only going to paint a few pictures for Jesus, to take up with me when I go."

Her aunt Sue used to sing a hymn for her which ended—

"I love Jesus because he first loved me."

Susy's mother sang it for her months afterward, ending it as above, of course. But Susy corrected her and said:

"No, that is not right, mamma—it is because he first loved *Aunt Sue.*" (The word "me" rather confused her.)

NARRATOR: She included Jesus in many activities.

SAM: One day on the *ombra* Susy burst into song, as follows:

"Oh Jesus are you dead, so you cannot dance and sing!"

The air was exceedingly gay—rather pretty, too—and was accompanied by a manner and gestures that were equally gay and chipper. Her mother was astonished and distressed. She said:

"Why Susy! Did Maria teach you that dreadful song?"

"No, mamma, I made it myself all out of my own head. *No*-body helped me."

She was plainly proud of it, and went on repeating it with great content.[33]

NARRATOR: Mrs. Langdon gave each of the babies a silver set; she added flat silver on Christmas and birthdays.

LIVY: Clara's *beautiful* silver set came yesterday—It is just as exquisite as it can be. When Susy's and Langdon's came we thought that nothing could be prettier, but Clara's I think is—The mug is such a rare, unusual shape—Clara was exceedingly pleased when we showed it to her. She handled it and was very much inclined to bang the mug with the spoon but of course that she was not allowed to do—Susy too was very much interested—I had to get out her silver set so that she could look at hers at the same time—her napkin ring she has not seen yet I shall keep it until her birthday.[34]

SUSY'S FOURTH YEAR

1875–1876

NARRATOR: There was a gala party on March 19th, 1875.

SAM: This is Susy's birth-day. Lizzie brought her in at 8:30 this morning (before we were up) hooded with a blanket, red curl-papers in her hair, a great red japonica in one hand (for Livy) and a yellow rose-bud nestled in violets (for my buttonhole) in the other—and she looked wonderfully pretty. She delivered her memorials and received her birth-day kisses. Livy laid her japonica down to get a better "holt" for kissing—which Susy presently perceived, and became thoughtful: then said sorrowfully, turning the great deeps of her eyes upon her mother: "Don't you care for you wow?"

Right after breakfast we got up a rousing wood fire in the main hall (it is a cold morning).[1]

HARTFORD COURANT: And a charming haunt it is, with its wide hall, finished in dark wood under a panelled ceiling, and full of easy-chairs, rugs, cushions, and carved furniture that instantly invite the guest to lounge in front of the big fire-place. . . . Over the fire-place, through a large plate-glass suggesting Alice's Adventures, a glimpse is had of the drawing-room, luminous with white and silver and pale blue; and on another side, between a broad flight of stairs and a chiselled Ginevra chest drawn against the wall, the always open library door attracts one's steps.[2]

SAM: [We] illuminated the place with a rich glow from all the globes of the newell chandelier, spread a bright rug before the fire, set a circling row of chairs (pink ones and dove-colored) and in the midst a low invalid-table covered with a fanciful cloth and laden with the presents—a pink azalea in lavish bloom from Rosa; a gold inscribed Russia-leather bible from Patrick and Mary; a gold ring (inscribed) from "Maggy Cook;" a silver thimble (inscribed with motto and initials) from Lizzie; a rattling mob of Sunday clad dolls from Livy and Annie, and a Noah's Ark from me, containing 200 wooden animals such as only a human being could create and only God call by name without referring to the passenger list. Then the family and the seven servants assembled there, and Susy and the "Bay" arrived in state from above, the Bay's head being fearfully and wonderfully decorated with a profusion of blazing red flowers and overflowing cataracts of lycopodium. Wee congratulatory notes accompanied the presents of the servants. I tell you it was a great occasion and a striking and cheery group, taking all the surroundings into account and the wintry aspect outside.[3]

NARRATOR: Lizzie was Livy's maid whom they had brought back from England; she helped with the children. Annie was Sam's niece, Pamela Clemens Moffett's daughter, who was visiting the Clemenses.

LIVY: My dear Mother I wish you could have been here on Susy's birthday. We did have such a good time—Mr. Clemens wrote Charlie about it—there was one thing that he did not mention—there was a knit doll on the table for "Bay," for Susy to give to her. When Susy took it up—I said, "that is Susy's, for her to give to "Bay"—she took it right over to baby, did not even stop to look at it, and said "here Bay, dolly for you"—Then she had three pieces of molasses candy put in a white napkin in a fanciful way on her silver plate—I proposed that it should be broken up and passed around, so Lizzie broke it into little pieces and Susy passed it to everybody, me first, then Cousin Annie, then the servants, (Mr. C. was not just that moment present)—She had one pretty good sized piece for herself—after she had taken just a little suck of hers, Patrick came in. I said "Susy aren't you going to pass Patrick a piece of candy" thinking that she would pass him the plate which still had her Father's piece on it—but instead she handed him her piece, he took it and she was turning away satisfied without any, but Patrick broke hers and took only a little, giving back the rest— Tonight she was so loving and sweet and said "Mamma you're so good to me, dear Mamma" and talked about her birthday, and wanted me to make it again, seemed to think that I could make the dolls—I told her that I could only make her paper dolls—

Mother I hope you will not get tired of my writing all these particulars and think I am silly, but you know Susy is so large a part of my life and I am so *desperately* fond of her—although I only told her once who the different gifts were from and all in the first excitement and confusion—she remembered several hours afterward that you gave her the napkin ring—Clara continues to grow in loveliness—

I went to church this morning—President Porter from Yale College preached, the sermon did not touch me. I like Mr. Twichell's preaching better. Of course it was good and I doubt not the fault lay much with me but he did not stir me at all.[4]

NARRATOR: Susy began to imitate Sam. They took a spring walk one day.

SAM: She was drawing a baby carriage with 2 dolls in it, one with a straw hat on. The hat kept falling off and delaying the procession while Susy picked it up. Finally I dropped behind the carriage and said, "Now go on—if it falls off again, I'll pick it up." Nearly 2 days afterward, she said to her English nurse, Lizzie Wills:

"Lizzie, can you talk like papa? When my dolly's hat fell, papa said, 'I-f i-t f-a-l-l-s o-f-f a-g-a-i-n, I—l-l p-i-c-k i-t u-p.'"

Considering that she had probably never heard my drawling manner of speech imitated, this was not bad—nor reverent, either.[5]

NARRATOR: There were no plans to go to the farm this summer.

SAM: We have determined to try to sweat it out, here in Hartford, this summer, and not go away at all. That is Livy's idea, not mine; for I can write ten chapters in Elmira where I can write one here. I work *at* work here, but I don't accomplish anything worth speaking of.—Livy *wants* to go to Cleveland, but she can't. To carry the household would be like moving a menagerie; and to leave it behind would be like leaving a menagerie behind without a keeper. You mustn't suppose I am not *trying* to work.—Bless you I peg away all the time. I allow myself few privileges, but when one is in the *workaday world,* there's a million interruptions and interferences. I can't succeed except by getting clear out of the world on top of the mountain at Elmira.[6]

NARRATOR: Livy worried constantly about Susy's health; she dreaded the hot weather because it made Susy very irritable.

Sam was invited to participate in a spelling bee in the chapel of the Asylum Hall Church. He opened the bee with a speech.

SAM: I don't see any use in spelling a word right—and never did. I mean I don't see any use in having a uniform and arbitrary way of spelling words. We might as well make all clothes alike and cook all dishes alike. Sameness is tiresome; variety is pleasing. I have a correspondent whose letters are always a refreshment to me; there is such a breezy, unfettered originality about his orthography. He always spells "kow" with a large "K." Now that is just as good as to spell it with a small one. It is better. It gives the imagination a broader field, a wider scope. It suggests to the mind a grand, vague, impressive new kind of cow.[7]

NARRATOR: Sam was spelled down; "cauldron" instead of "chaldron." It was a question of the dictionary in authority.

On July 5th Sam wrote Howells that Susy was "down with a fever."[8] They decided they must get the children out of Hartford.

SAM: We spent the summer of '75 at the seaside at Newport, and the children used to sleep a couple of hours every day under umbrellas on the rocks within six feet of the wash of the waves, and that made them strong and hearty.[9]

NARRATOR: They stayed at a hotel called Bateman's Point, which was on Ocean Drive between Castle Hill Avenue and Winans Avenue. There, they met some Hartford neighbors, the Nathaniel Shipman family.

SAM: It was a comfortable boarding-place, well stocked with sweet mothers and little children, but the male sex was scarce.[10]

ARTHUR L. SHIPMAN: That summer, every afternoon Mr. Clemens played ball with us and after we were tired, he sat under the trees and talked with us. I can still see in my mind's eye Mr. Clemens urging me to throw the balls just as hard as I could, and he caught them very well, his red hair all standing on end.[11]

Mr. Clemens never tried to come down to our level as boys . . . for he was one of us. Like all boys he would have been peculiarly sensitive to any condescension and would have resented it. But he was a boy with us and we were "comfortable" with him. When he sat under an orchard tree with us, we never realized that anyone outside our own crowd was there.

I remember one morning when he started to play ball with me. He liked games of dexterity, especially baseball. This morning we began to have a catch when, suddenly, with that strange intensity he had, he tried his best to knock me over. He threw and threw with all his might and kept at it. And I threw back with all my strength! His hair—it was light brown then—stuck up and he was the picture of intensity, all afire.[12]

NARRATOR: Sam also entertained himself in a broken-down alley playing tenpins with equipment that reminded him of the old billiard tables in western mining camps. After he had figured out how to win with balls and pins that functioned in an eccentric fashion, he would invite a stranger to play and sit back and hilariously watch the poor man suffer.

He finished *Tom Sawyer*. He wrote later that he thought it was at Bateman's Point that "I told [Henry] Irving and Wills, the playwright, about the whitewashing of the fence by Tom Sawyer, and thereby captured a chapter on cheap terms; for I wrote it out when I got back to the hotel while it was fresh in my mind.[13]

They returned to Hartford and their usual busy life. It had been a year of many literary matters: *Sketches* had been published, *Tom Sawyer* was approaching the proofreading stage and Sam wrote an amusing skit, "A Literary Nightmare," inspired by his version of the popular jingle called streetcar poetry which children and adults were reciting all over the world.

> Conductor, when you receive a fare,
> Punch in the presence of the passenjare!
> A blue trip slip for an eight-cent fare,
> A buff trip slip for a six-cent fare,
> A pink trip slip for a three-cent fare.
> Punch in the presence of the passenjare!

> CHORUS

> Punch, brothers! Punch with care!
> Punch in the presence of the passenjare![14]

SAM: I question if I can write . . . intelligently for Susy is in the study with me and requires pretty constant attention.[15]

HOWELLS: Clemens had appointed himself, with the architect's connivance, a luxurious study over the library in his new house . . . with its carved and cushioned arm-chairs.[16]

The house was the design of that most original artist, Edward Potter, who once, when hard pressed by incompetent curiosity for the name of his style in a certain church, proposed that it should be called the English violet order of architecture; and this house was so absolutely suited to the owner's humor that I suppose there never was another house like it.[17]

NARRATOR: In October Livy and Sam planned a trip to Boston.

SAM: Mrs. C. said the other day, "We will go to Cambridge if we have to walk; for I don't believe we can ever get the Howellses to come here again until we have been there." I was gratified to see that there was one string, anyway, that could take her to Cambridge. But I will do her the justice to say that she is always wanting to go to Cambridge, independent of the selfish desire to get a visit out of you by it. I want her to get started, now, before children's diseases are fashionable again, because they always play such hob with visiting arrangements.[18]

NARRATOR: They had a delightful visit in Boston, which included luncheon at Craigie House with Longfellow. Sam, as usual, said and did things for which Livy scolded him. He wrote Howells.

SAM: I "caught it" for letting Mrs. Howells bother and bother about her coffee when it was "a good deal better than we get at home." I "caught it" for interrupting Mrs. C. at the last moment and losing her the opportunity to urge you not to forget to send her that MS when the printers are done with it.—I caught it once more for personating that drunken Col. James. I caught it (like everything for confessing, with contrition) for mentioning that Mr. Longfellow's picture was slightly damaged; and when, after a lull in the storm, I confessed, shame-facedly, that I had privately suggested to you that we hadn't any *frames* and that if you wouldn't mind hinting to Mr. Houghton, etc., etc., etc., the madam was simply speechless for the space of a minute. Then she said:

"How *could* you, Youth! The idea of sending Mr. Howells, with his sensitive nature, upon such a repulsive er—"

"Oh, *Howells* won't mind it! You don't know Howells. Howells is a man who—"

She was gone. But George was the first person she stumbled on in the hall, so she took it out of George. I was glad of that, because it saved the babies.[19]

NARRATOR: Livy's thirtieth birthday was celebrated in November.

SAM: Livy Darling,—Six years have gone by since I made my first great success in life and won you, and thirty years have passed since Providence made preparation for that happy success by sending you into the world. Every day we live together adds to the security of my confidence that we can never any more wish to be separated than we can imagine a regret that we were ever joined. You are dearer to me to-day, my child, than you were upon the last anniversary of this birthday; you were dearer then than you were a year before; you have grown more and more dear from the first of those anniversaries, and I do not doubt that this precious progression will continue on to the end.

Let us look forward to the coming anniversaries, with their age and their gray hairs, without fear and without depression, trusting and believing that the love we bear each other will be sufficient to make them blessed.

So, with abounding affection for you and our babies I hail this day that brings you the matronly grace and dignity of three decades![20]

NARRATOR: Livy and Sam made much of Christmas: the house was decorated with garlands and wreaths, there were mounds of presents and, always a special effort by Sam, usually a last-minute effort, but it brought that undefinable, poignant, delightful sense of Christmas which only he could bring. One year he wrote Susy a Christmas letter.

SANTA CLAUS, WHOM PEOPLE SOMETIMES CALL THE MAN IN THE MOON: My dear Susy Clemens: I have received and read all the letters which you and your little sister have written me by the hand of your mother and your nurses; I have also read those which you little people have written me with your own hands—for although you did not use any characters that are in grown peoples' alphabet, you used the characters that all children in all lands on earth and in the twinkling stars use; and as all my subjects in the moon are children and use no character but that, you will easily understand that I can read your and your baby sister's jagged and fantastic marks without any trouble at all. But I had trouble with those letters which you dictated through your mother and the nurses, for I am a foreigner and cannot read English writing well. You will find that I made no mistakes about the things which you and the baby ordered in your *own* letters—I went down your chimney at midnight when you were asleep and delivered them all myself—and kissed both of you, too, because you are good children, well-trained, nice-mannered, and about the most obedient little people I ever saw. But in the letters which you dictated there were some words which I could not make out for certain, and one or two small orders which I could not fill because we ran out of stock. Our last lot of kitchen-furniture for dolls has just gone to a very poor little child in the North Star away up in the cold country above the Big Dipper. Your mama can show you that star and you will say: "Little Snow Flake" (for that is the child's name) "I'm glad you got that furniture, for you need it more than I." That is, you must *write* that, with your own hand, and Snow Flake will write you an answer. If you only spoke it she wouldn't hear you. Make your letter light and thin, for the distance is great and the postage very heavy.

There was a word or two in your mama's letter which I couldn't be certain of. I took it to be "trunk full of doll's clothes." Is that it? I will call at your kitchen door about nine o'clock this morning to inquire. But I must not see anybody and I must not speak to anybody but you. When the kitchen door bell rings George must be blindfolded and sent to open the door. Then he must go back to the dining-room or the china closet and take the cook with him. You must tell George he must walk on tiptoe and not speak— otherwise he will die some day. Then you must go up to the nursery and stand on a chair or the nurse's bed and put your ear to the speaking-tube that leads down to the kitchen and when I whistle through it you must speak in the tube and say, "Welcome, Santa Claus!" Then I will ask whether it was a trunk you ordered or not. If you say it was, I shall ask you what *color* you want the trunk to be. Your mama will help you to name a nice color and then you must tell me every single thing in detail which you want the trunk to contain. Then when I say "Good bye and a Merry Christmas to my little Susy Clemens," you must say "Goodbye, good old Santa Claus, I thank you very much and please tell that little Snow Flake I will look at her star tonight and she must look down here—I will be right in the West bay-window; and every fine night I will look at her star and say, 'I know somebody up there and *like* her, too.'" Then you must go down into the library and make George close all the doors that open into the main hall, and everybody must keep still for a little while. I will go to the moon and get those things and in a few minutes I will come down the chimney that belongs to the fireplace that is in the hall—if it is a trunk you want—because I couldn't get such a thing as a trunk down the nursery chimney, you know.

People may talk if they want, until they hear my footsteps in the hall. Then you tell them to keep quiet a little while till I go back up the chimney. Maybe you will not hear my footsteps at all—so you may go now and then and peep through the dining-room doors, and by and by you will see that thing which you want, right under the piano in the drawing-room—for I shall put it there. If I should leave any snow in the hall, you must tell George to sweep it into the fireplace, for I haven't time to do such things. George must not use a broom, but a rag—else he will die some day. You must watch George and not let him run into danger. If my boot should leave a stain on the marble, George must not holy-stone it away. Leave it there always in memory of my visit; and whenever you look at it or show it to anybody you must let it remind you to be a good little girl. Whenever you are naughty and somebody points to that mark which your good old Santa Claus's boot made on the marble, what will you say, little Sweetheart?

Goodbye for a few minutes, till I come down to the world and ring the kitchen door-bell. Your loving Santa Claus.

Palace of St. Nicholas in the Moon, Christmas Morning.[21]

NARRATOR: In March Howells brought his son, John, six years old, to spend two nights with the Clemenses.

HOWELLS: We had a really charming visit, not marred by anything. The Clemenses are whole-souled hosts, with inextinguishable money, and a palace of a house . . . and we met all the pleasant people whose acquaintance I made last year, except the [Charles Dudley] Warners who are now up the Nile.[22]

I took John with me, and as his mother had prepared his mind for the splendors of the Twain mansion, he came to everything with the most exalted fairy-palace expectations. He found some red soap in the bathroom. "Why, they've even got their soap painted!" says he; and the next morning when he found the black serving-man getting ready for breakfast, he came and woke me. "Better get up, papa. The *slave* is setting the table." I suppose he thought Clemens could have that darkey's head off whenever he liked.[23]

SUSY'S FIFTH YEAR

1876–1877

NARRATOR: March 19th found the household absorbed in a dramatic venture; Sam had agreed to play the lead, Peter Spuyk, in *The Loan of a Lover*, a benefit for a local organization. Michael Bennett Leavitt, a theatrical manager and promoter for fifty years, commented on Hartford as a theater center.

M. B. LEAVITT: Hartford was a veritable Mecca for Thespians. The puritanical spirit which formerly existed throughout New England found no harbor here. Among the many distinguished theatrical people who lived there were William Gillette, Otis Skinner, Charles B. Dillingham, Lew Dockstader, Bruce Edwards, Sher. C. Campbell, William Raymond Sill, Francis Carlyle, Henry Woodruff, Maud Granger, and others.[1]

NARRATOR: James T. Fields, editor of the *Atlantic*, came to Hartford to lecture and stayed with the Clemenses while Sam was rehearsing. His wife recorded his visit in her diary.

MRS. FIELDS: He found Mrs. Clemens quite ill. They had been in New York, where he had given four lectures, hoping to get money for Dr. Brown. He had never lectured there before without making a great deal of money. This time he barely covered his expenses. He was very interesting and told J. the whole story of his life. They sat until midnight after the lecture, Mark drinking ale to make him sleepy. He says he can't sleep as other people do; his kind of sleep is the only sort for him—three or four hours of good solid comfort—more than that makes him ill; he can't afford to sleep all his thoughts away. . . .

He and his wife have wretched health, poor things! And in spite of their beautiful home must often have rather a hard time. He is very eccentric, disturbed by every noise, and it cannot be altogether easy to have care of such a man. It is a very loving household, though Mrs. Clemens's mother, Mrs. Langdon, hardly knows what to make of him sometimes, it is quite evident.

NARRATOR: A few days later Fields came back to Hartford with his wife to see the play; they went directly to the theater from the station.

MRS. FIELDS: It is a pretty play, and the girl's part, Gertrude, was well done by Miss Helen Smith; but Mr. Clemens's part was a creation. I see no reason why, if he chose to adopt the profession of actor, he should not be as successful as [Joseph] Jefferson in whatever he might conclude to undertake. It is really amazing to see what a man of genius can do besides what is usually considered his legitimate sphere.[2]

LILLY WARNER: Mr. Clemens was inimitable as a slow young dutchman.[3]

MRS. FIELDS: Afterward we went with Mr. Hammersley to the Club for a bit of supper—this I did not wish to do, but I was overruled of course by the decision of our host. . . . It was after twelve o'clock when we finally reached Mr. Clemens's house. . . .

The house is a brick villa, designed by one of the first New York architects, standing in a lovely lawn, which slopes down to a small stream or river at the side. In this spring season the blackbirds are busy in the trees and the air is sweet and vocal. Inside there is great luxury. Especially I delight in a lovely conservatory opening out of the drawing-room [library]. . . .

He believed his wife would have retired, as she is very delicate in health; but there she was, expecting us, with a pretty supper-table laid. When her husband discovered this, he fell down on his knees in mock desire for forgiveness. His mind was so full of the play, and with the poor figure he felt he had made in it, that he had entirely forgotten all her directions and injunctions. She is very small, sweet-looking, simple, finished creature, charming in her ways and evidently deeply beloved by him. . . .

Although we had already eaten supper, the gentlemen took a glass of lager beer to keep Mrs. Clemens company while she ate a bit of bread after her long anxiety and waiting.

NARRATOR: The Fieldses met Susy and Clara the next morning.

MRS. FIELDS: Their two beautiful baby girls came to pass an hour with us after breakfast—exquisite, affectionate children, the very fountain of joy to their interesting parents.[4]

NARRATOR: Susy's blond beauty was a piquant contrast to Clara's black hair and light coloring. She was delicate in personality as well as coloring and charming to observe.

SAM:

. . . THE LITTLE FORM

In slip of flimsy stuff all creamy white,
Pink-belted waist with ample bows,
Blue shoes scarce bigger than the house-cat's ears—
Capering in delight and choked with glee.[5]

MRS. FIELDS: Returning to lunch, I found our host and hostess and eldest little girl in the drawing-room [library]. . . .

He proceeded to speak of his Autobiography, which he intends to write as fully and simply as possible, to leave behind him. His wife laughingly said she should look it over and leave out objectionable passages. "No," he said, very earnestly, almost sternly, "*you* are not to edit it—it is to appear as it is written, with the whole tale told as truly as I can tell it. I shall take out passages from it, and publish as I go along in the *Atlantic* and elsewhere, but I shall not limit myself as to space, and at whatever age I am writing about, even if I am an infant, and an idea comes to me about myself when I am forty, I shall put that in. Every man feels that his experience is unlike that of anybody else, and therefore he should write it down. He finds also that everybody else has thought and felt on some points precisely as he has done, and therefore he should write it down." . . .

At five, the hour appointed for dinner, I returned to the drawing-room [library], where our host lay at full length on the floor, with his head on cushions in the bay-window, reading, and taking what he called "delicious comfort." . . .

He is forty years old, with some color in his cheeks and a heavy light-colored moustache, and overhanging light eyebrows. His eyes are grey and piercing, yet soft, and his whole face expresses great sensitiveness. He is exquisitely neat also, though careless, and his hands are small, not without delicacy. He is a small man, but his mass of hair seems the one rugged-looking thing about him. I thought in the play last night that it was a wig.

NARRATOR: During the night Susy came down with a sore throat and a high fever. Sam and Livy were worried; their guests found the household very disturbed when they came down in the morning.

MRS. FIELDS: When I did go to the drawing-room, however, I found Mr. Clemens alone. He greeted me apparently as cheerfully as ever, and it was not until some moments had passed that he told me they had a very sick child upstairs. From that instant I saw, especially after his wife came in, that they could think of nothing else. They were half-distracted with anxiety. Their messenger could not find the doctor, which made matters worse. However, the little girl did not really seem very sick, so I could not help thinking they were unnecessarily excited. The effect on them, however, was just as bad as if the child were really very ill.[6]

NARRATOR: The family doctor was Cincinnatus Taft; he and his wife and their daughter Laura, were great friends of the Clemenses. Helen Post Chapman, a neighbor, described Dr. Taft.

HELEN POST CHAPMAN: Almost everyone had the same doctor. Could anyone ever forget Dr. C. A. Taft? He was a large, powerful man with a long white beard and white hair, and the biggest heart in the world. He was a homeopathist and distributed among his patients little white pellets that always made us well. He had a contract with some large families naming a specified sum for medical attention throughout the year. It was a gamble whether he would win with few calls or whether you would win with much illness. One always felt better for seeing him and in the winter he was especially good to look at in a large sealskin coat and cap.[7]

MRS. FIELDS: The messenger was hardly dispatched the second time before Jamie and Mrs. Clemens began to talk of our getting away in the next train, whereat he (Mr. C.) said to his wife, "Why didn't you tell me of that?" etc., etc. It was all over in a moment, but in his excitement he spoke more quickly than he knew, and his wife felt it. Nothing was said at the time, indeed we hardly observed it; but we were intensely amused and could not help finding it pathetic, too, afterward, when he came to us and said he spent the larger part of his life on his knees making apologies, and now he had got to make an apology to us about the carriage. He was always bringing the blood to his wife's face by his bad behavior, and here this very morning he had said such things about that carriage! His whole life was one long apology. His wife had told him to see how well we behaved (poor we!), and he knew he had everything to learn.

He was so amusing about it . . . yet at bottom I could see it was no laughing matter to him. He is in dead earnest, with a desire for growth and truth in life, and with such a sincere admiration for his wife's sweetness and beauty of character, that the most prejudiced and hardest heart could not fail to fall in love with him. She looked like an exquisite lily as we left her. So white and delicate and tender! Such sensitiveness and self-control as she possesses are very very rare.[8]

LILLY WARNER: Susy Clemens was taken with diphtheria, this morning [Saturday, April 22]—but does not seem very sick . . . she has had several touches of it.[9]

NARRATOR: On May 4th, Sam wrote Howells that he would go to Boston on the 8th but that Livy couldn't go, "because Susy is just recovering from about the savagest assault of diphtheria a child ever *did* recover from."[10]

SAM: When our children were little she nursed them through long nights of sickness, as she had nursed her father. I have seen her sit up and hold a sick child upon her knees and croon to it and sway it monotonously to and fro to comfort it, a whole night long, without complaint or respite. But I could not keep awake ten minutes at a time. My whole duty was to put wood on the fire. I did it ten or twelve times during the night, but had to be called every time, and was always asleep again before I finished the operation, or immediately afterward.[11]

NARRATOR: In June they went to Elmira.

SAM: We are perched on a hill-top that overlooks a little world of green valleys, shining rivers, sumptuous forests and billowy uplands veiled in the haze of distance. We have no neighbors. It is the quietest of all quiet places, and we are hermits that eschew caves and live in the sun.[12]

NARRATOR: Livy answered a long letter from Dr. Brown.

LIVY: Indeed I was a happy woman to see the familiar handwriting. I do hope that we shall not have to go so long again without a word from you. I wish you could come over to us for a season; it seems as if it would do you good, you and yours would be so very welcome.

We are now where we were two years ago, on the farm on the

top of a high hill where my sister spends her summers. The children are grown fat and hearty, feeding chickens and ducks twice a day, and are keenly alive to all the farm interests. . . .

I wish that you could see them. Susy is very motherly to the little one. Mr. Clemens is hard at work on a new book [*The Adventures of Huckleberry Finn*] now. He has a new book of sketches recently out, which he is going to send to you in a few days; most of the sketches are old, but some few are new. . . .

You ask if Clara is "queer and wistful and commanding," like your Susy. We think she is more queer . . . perhaps more commanding, but not nearly so wistful in her ways as "your Susy."[13]

SAM: I started a record of our children's sayings, last night [August 8th]. Which reminds me that last week I sent down and got Susy a vast pair of shoes of a most villainous pattern, for I discovered that her feet were being twisted and cramped out of shape by a smaller and prettier article. She did not complain, but looked degraded and injured. At night her mamma gave her the usual admonition when she was about to say her prayers—to wit:

"Now, Susy—think about God."

"Mamma, I can't, with those shoes."[14]

Susy's mother read to her the story of Joseph. The killing of the kid to stain the garment with blood was arrived at in due course and made deep impression. Susy's comment, full of sympathy and compassion, was: *"Poor little kid!"*—This is probably the only time, in 4000 years, that any human being has pitied that kid—everybody has been too much taken up with pitying Joseph, to remember that that innocent little animal suffered even more violently than he, and is fairly entitled to a word of compassion. I did not suppose that an unhackneyed (let alone an original) thought could be started on an Old Bible subject, but plainly this is one.[15]

NARRATOR: Susy was not always good-tempered.

SAM: From early babyhood until she was 3½ years old, she was addicted to sudden and raging tempests of passion. Coaxing was tried; reasoning was tried; diversion was tried; even bribery; also deprivations of various kinds; also captivity in a corner; in fact, *every*thing was tried that ever had been tried with any child —but all to no purpose. Indeed the storms grew more frequent. At last we dropped every feature of the system utterly and resorted to flogging. Since that day there has never been a better child. We had to whip her once a day, at first; then three times a week; then twice, then once a week; then twice a month. She is nearly 4½ years old, now, and I have only touched her once in the last 3 months. "Spare the rod and spoil the child" was well said—and not by an amateur, I judge.[16]

SUSY: Our very worst nautinesses were punished by being taken to the bath-room and being whipped by the paper cutter.[17]

NARRATOR: Clara's turn came for her first spanking.

SAM: About a fortnight ago Bay got what may be called her first thrashing. Her mother took both children gravely to the bed-chamber to punish them. It was all new to Bay and the novelty of it charmed her. Madam turned Susy across her lap and began to spat her (very lightly). Bay was delighted with the episode. The[n] *she* was called for and came skipping forward with jovial alacrity and threw herself across her mother's lap as who should say, "My, but ain't these good times!" The spat descended sharply, and by the war-whoop that followed, one perceived that the Bay's ideas about the festivities had changed. The madam could not whip for laughing and had to leave the punishment but half performed.[18]

Bay did not mind the electric shocks from the bell-buttons, on cold mornings, but they frightened Susy. Bay . . . would hold Japanese fire-works in her fingers till they flashed and spit and sputtered all away—but when the angry volume of sparks began to storm around Susy's hand, she would presently back down and let go.[19]

SUSY: Clara's reputation as a baby was always a fine one, mine exactly the contrary. One often related story concerning her brave-ness as a baby and her own opinion of this quality of hers is this. Clara and I often got slivers in our hands and when mama took them out with a much dreaded needle, Clara was always very brave, and I very cowardly. One day Clara got one of these slivers in her hand, a very bad one, and while mama was taking it out, Clara stood perfectly still without even wincing; I saw how brave she was and turning to mama said "Mama isn't she a brave little thing!" presently mamma had to give the little hand quite a dig with the needle and noticing how perfectly quiet Clara was about it she exclaimed, Why Clara! you *are* a brave little thing! Clara responded "No bodys braver but God!"

SAM: I take pride in Clara's remark . . . because it shows that . . . her fireside teachings were already making her a thinker—a thinker and also an observer of proportions. I am not claiming any credit for this. I furnished to the children worldly knowledge and wisdom, but was not competent to go higher, and so I left their spiritual education in the hands of the mother.[20]

NARRATOR: Home again in September, there were the usual crowds of visitors. Bret Harte came to stay for a long time and he and Sam worked on *Ah Sin* in the loft of the stable. "Mother" Fairbanks wrote asking if Susy was still orthodox in her theology and if Clara still looked like one of Doré's heads. Nook Farm neighbors continued to drop in at all hours.

SAM: One day Livy and Mrs. Lilly Warner were talking earnestly in the library; Susy interrupted them several times; finally Livy said, very sharply,—"Susy, if you interrupt me again, I will send you instantly to the nursery!" Five minutes later, Livy saw Mrs. W. to the front door; on her way back she saw Susy on the stairs, and said, "Where are you going, Susy?" "To the nursery, Mamma." "What are you going up there for, dear?—don't you want to stay with me in the library?" "You didn't speak to me *right*, Mamma." Livy was surprised; she had forgotten that rebuke; she pushed her inquiries further; Susy said, with a gentle dignity that carried its own reproach, "You didn't speak to me *right*, Mamma." She had been humiliated in the presence of an outsider. Livy felt condemned. She carried Susy to the library, and argued the case with her. Susy hadn't a fault to find with the justice of the rebuke, but she held out steadily against the *manner* of it, saying gently, once or twice, "But you didn't speak to me *right*, Mamma." She won her cause; and her mother had to confess that she *hadn't* spoken to her "right."

We require courteous speech from the children at all times and in all circumstances; we owe them the same courtesy in return; and when we fail of it we deserve correction.[21]

NARRATOR: Susy puzzled over many problems.

SAM: Several times her mother said to her, "There, there, Susy, you mustn't cry over little things."

This furnished Susy a text for thought. She had been breaking her heart over what had seemed vast disasters—a broken toy; a picnic canceled by thunder and lightning and rain; the mouse that was growing tame and friendly in the nursery caught and killed

by the cat—and now came this strange revelation. For some unaccountable reason these were not vast calamities. Why? How is
the size of calamities measured? What is the rule? There must be
some way to tell the great ones from the small ones; what is the
law of these proportions? She examined the problem earnestly and
long. She gave it her best thought from time to time for two or
three days—but it baffled her—defeated her. And at last she gave
up and went to her mother for help.[22]

"Mamma, what *is* LITTLE things?"

"Papa, how will brother Langdon know us, in heaven?—it is
so long that he has been there; and he was such a little fellow."

"Mamma, what is it all for?" . . .

"I find there are a great many things that I don't understand,
mamma."[23]

It seemed a simple question—at first. And yet before the answer
could be put into words, unsuspected and unforseen difficulties
began to appear. They increased; they multiplied; they brought
about another defeat. The effort to explain came to a standstill.
Then Susy tried to help her mother out—with an instance, an
example, an illustration. The mother was getting ready to go
downtown, and one of her errands was to buy a long-promised toy
watch for Susy.

"If you forgot the watch, mamma, would that be a little thing?"

She was not concerned about the watch, for she knew it would
not be forgotten. What she was hoping for was that the answer
would unriddle the riddle and bring rest and peace to her perplexed little mind.

The hope was disappointed, of course—for the reason that the
size of a misfortune is not determinable by an outsider's measurement of it but only by the measurements applied to it by the person
specially affected by it. The king's lost crown is a vast matter to
the king but of no consequence to the child. The lost toy is a great
matter to the child but in the king's eyes it is not a thing to break
the heart about. A verdict was reached but it was based upon the
above model and Susy was granted leave to measure her disasters
thereafter with her own tape-line.[24]

NARRATOR: Frank D. Millet came to stay with the Clemenses while
he painted Sam's portrait. The children loved him and included
him in their prayers with all the members of the household. Sam
called the group the "Holy Family."

SAM: One day Susy asked her mamma to read to her. Millet said—
"I'll read to you, Susy."
Susy said with a grave sweet grace and great dignity—
"I thank you, Mr. Millet, but I am a little more acquainted with
mamma, and so I would rather she would do it."[25]

NARRATOR: Susy and Clara were much interested in their neighbor,
Harriet Beecher Stowe, whose mind had begun to show evidence
of senility.

SAM: In those days she made as much use of our grounds as of her
own. . . . Among the colonists of our neighborhood the doors always stood open in pleasant weather. Mrs. Stowe entered them at
her own free will, and as she was always softly slippered and
generally full of animal spirits, she was able to deal in surprises,
and she liked to do it. She would slip up behind a person who
was deep in dreams and musings and fetch a war whoop that
would jump that person out of his clothes. And she had other
moods. Sometimes we would hear gentle music in the drawing-
room and would find her there at the piano singing ancient and
melancholy songs with infinitely touching effect.

Her husband, old Professor Stowe, was a picturesque figure. He
wore a broad slouch hat. He was a large man, and solemn. His
beard was white and thick and hung far down on his breast. His
nose was enlarged and broken up by a disease which made it look
like a cauliflower. The first time our little Susy ever saw him she
encountered him on the street near our house and came flying
wide-eyed to her mother and said, "Santa Claus has got loose."[26]

NARRATOR: Livy and Sam celebrated their seventh wedding anniversary February 2nd; she wrote her mother.

LIVY: Your lovely, beautiful exquisite gift came today! I never was
more surprised or more delighted in my life—Mother, how did
you come to do it? I never *dreamed* of your giving me a gift on my
wedding day, and then such a wonderfully beautiful gift.

Mr. Clemens and I drank a little wine out of the glasses for
dinner, he using the claret glass, I the sherry—Then I had the
finger bowl and Susy and Clara both had their dear little fingers
washed in it too. . . .

This morning when I went into the nursery, I said to Susy, "This
is my wedding day, Susy, seven years ago today I was married."
"Why are you *married* mamma?" "Yes, I am married."—"Who to,
to me?" "No, to Papa." "*Oh* to Papa." Indicating by the tone of

voice that it was all right if it was Papa, that there would be no breaking up of the family.[27]

NARRATOR: Shortly after Valentine's Day, Susy dictated a letter to Frank Millet.

SUSY: Dear Mr. Millet Bay and I has both got valentines, I have a sun fan and a German book and bay's got a new carriage—Papa teached me that tick, tick—my Grandfather clock was too large for the shelf so it stood 90 years on the floor. Mr. Millet is that the same clock what is in your picture—Dear Mr Millet I give you my love. I put it on my heart to get the love out. The little Kittye is in Bays Carrage my love and Susy Clemens Write me a little note.[28]

SUSY'S SIXTH YEAR

1877–1878

NARRATOR: Susy, at five, was becoming more and more entrancing to her father.

SAM: She was born free of selfishness—a thing I was not glad of, for a little of it is not only valuable, but a *necessary* quality in every rightly-constructed human creature—but Bay had a noble share, and has divided up with her in the most generous way—so both are just about rightly equipped, now. Susy has an unusually penetrating mind, a charitable spirit, and a sterling great heart. It is curious, (and there's a pang in it, too,) to see so little a creature struggling to sound the great deeps of thought with her brief plummet, and groping among the mighty mysteries of life with her poor little farthing candle.[1]

The other evening, after the children's prayers, Mrs. Clemens told Susy that she must often think of Jesus and ask him to help her to overcome bad impulses. She said—

"I do think of him, mamma. Every day I see his cross on my Bible, and I think of him then—the cross they crucified him on—it was too bad—*I was quite sorry.*"

NARRATOR: She invented games for Bay.

SAM: While we were at dinner, the children came down from the nursery as usual to spend the hour between six and seven. They were in the library and the folding doors were open. Presently I heard Susy tell the Bay to lie down on the rug before the fire—which Bay did. Then Susy came into the dining room, turned, ran back, hovered over Bay and said—

"Now, Bay, you are a little dead baby you know, and I am an angel come down to take you up to heaven. Come, now, get up —give me your hand—now we'll run—that's to pretend to be flying, you know. Ready now—now we're flying."

When they came flying by the dinner table, something there attracted the Bay's attention and she suddenly stopped but Susy ran on, full of enthusiasm. She brought up behind a chair by a door and cried out—

"Come on, Bay—here's heaven!"—then put her hand on the door knob and said,—"See!—*here's* Jesus!"[2]

NARRATOR: Sam wrote Mrs. Fairbanks of his plans to superintend rehearsals of *Ah Sin*.

SAM: I suppose I shall remain in Washington and Baltimore till the middle of May, if things seem to require it, and I am depending upon Livy's going with me—but she doubtless won't, because she would find it burdensome to take the children, and—you catch her leaving them behind! . . . it ain't any use of trying to get Livy to sleep apart from Susy a night. That is one of those impossible things, you know.[3]

NARRATOR: As the children grew older, it became obvious that they needed a room for study and play so Sam gave up his study, which adjoined the nursery on the second floor. He tried working in a room in the loft in the carriage house, and then he tried a rented room in an office building downtown, but neither was satisfactory. The billiard room was the answer.

HOWELLS: It was pretty cold up there in the early spring and late fall weather with which I chiefly associate the place, but by lighting up all the gas-burners and kindling a reluctant fire on the hearth we could keep it well above freezing. Clemens could also push the balls about, and, without rivalry from me, who could no more play billiards than smoke, could win endless games of pool, while he carried points of argument against imaginable differers in opinion. Here he wrote many of his tales and sketches, and for anything I know some of his books. I particularly remember his reading me here his first rough sketch of *Captain Stormfield's Visit to Heaven*, with the real name of the captain, whom I knew already from his many stories about him.

We had a peculiar pleasure in looking off from the high windows on the pretty Hartford landscape, and down from them into the tops of the trees clothing the hillside by which his house stood. We agreed that there was a novel charm in trees seen from such advantage, far surpassing that of the farther scenery.[4]

NARRATOR: Sam and Livy enjoyed the balconies off the billiard room.

LIVY: Mr. Clemens and I are sitting on the west balcony out of the billiard room, it is warm and pleasant, but Mr. Clemens has a terrible cold in the head—As I look down to the stream I see our four ducks—we have also six little ducks—the old duck has a nest in the duck house and is pretending to set, but it seems to me she is always on the river.[5]

NARRATOR: The ducks were a temptation to the small boys of the neighborhood, one of whom was William Lyon Phelps.

PHELPS: I was shooting with a schoolmate, George Peters. We became separated in the woods along the banks of Hog River. Suddenly I saw, sweeping around a bend in the stream, a flock of white ducks, which I supposed to be wild. I let them have both barrels, killing two and mortally wounding three. Attracted by the report, George came up, and was overcome with horror. I fully expected him to be envious of my wonderful good luck; but instead of that, he cried, "What have you done? Those are Mark Twain's prize ducks. If you are caught, he will put you in jail. Run for your life!"

My flush of joy turned to the icy sweat of fear. . . .

The next morning I read in the Hartford newspaper a prominently displayed notice from Mark Twain, offering a substantial financial reward for the apprehension of the "miscreant" who had killed his white ducks. Here I was, a criminal, sought by the police, with a price set on my head. For several months I avoided Hog River and was in terror.[6]

NARRATOR: Despite small boys, there were many peaceful days.

LIVY: We are having a wonderfully restful Sunday morning. We neither of us went to church. . . .

The children have been out gathering wild flowers and have brought me such a beautiful lot. I am going down now pretty soon to arrange them.[7]

NARRATOR: Sam continued to record Susy's remarks.

SAM: Susy had a present of a new parasol, and hit Bay a whack with it—to see if it was substantial, perhaps. Rosa the nurse took it away from her and put it in the blue room. Susy was vastly frightened and begged Rosa not to tell on her, but her pleadings failed. In the evening Susy said, with earnestness, "Mamma, I begged, and *begged* Rosa not to tell you—*but all in vain.*"[8]

She was thoughtful and considerate of others—an acquired quality, no doubt. No one seems to be born with it. One hot day . . . her mother borrowed her fan several times (a Japanese one, value five cents), refreshed herself with it a moment or two, then handed it back with a word of thanks. Susy knew her mother would use the fan all the time if she could do it without putting a deprivation upon its owner. She also knew that her mother could not be persuaded to do that. A relief must be devised somehow; Susy devised it. She got five cents out of her money box and carried it to Patrick and asked him to take it downtown (a mile and a half) and buy a Japanese fan and bring it home. He did it—and thus thoughtfully and delicately was the exigency met and the mother's comfort secured. It is to the child's credit that she did not save herself expense by bringing down another and more costly kind of fan from upstairs, but was content to act upon the impression that her mother desired the Japanese kind—content to accomplish the desire and stop with that, without troubling about the wisdom or unwisdom of it.[9]

NARRATOR: They went to Elmira about June 7th.

SAM: We had to remain at Mother's in Elmira until yesterday [June 13th], to let our youngest have a run of fever and get back her strength. But we are housed here on top of the hill, now, where it is always cool, and still, and reposeful and bewitching.[10]

NARRATOR: Sam wrote 400 pages of *The Prince and the Pauper* and then laid it aside. He finished the play, *Simon Wheeler, Detective,* and took it to New York, stopping in Hartford on the way. In New York he attended the opening of *Ah Sin.*

LIVY: Youth Darling—We are all well and have had a most delightful Sunday, it would have been entirely perfect if you had been here —I made wreaths and crowns of Golden rod for the children this morning—This afternoon Susy and I had rather a sad time because she told me a lie—she felt very unhappy about it—This evening after her prayer I prayed that she might be forgiven for it, then I said "Susy don't you want to pray about it and ask for your self to be forgiven?" She said "Oh one is enough"—Good night darling I will not write more for this may not reach you.

NARRATOR: Sam wrote to Susy.

SAM: Susy dear, you and Rosa and Bay must keep a sharp lookout on the young birdlings up at the pond and see them begin life. They are ready to fly, now. Keep the squirrel supplied with nuts, if he comes around. If you have a very fine sunset, put a blanket over it and keep it till I come. Aunt Sue will give you one. I saw a lovely sunset yesterday, reflected in the water of New Jersey marshes. It was a beautiful, still evening—no sound but just one cow singing and some frogs—(frosches).

There are some bells close here and a man who rings chimes. That man will die some day, and then he will wish he had behaved himself. I saw a cat yesterday, with 4 legs—and yet it was only a yellow cat, and rather small, too, for its size. They were not *all* fore legs—several of them were hind legs; indeed almost a majority of them were. Write me. Papa.[11]

NARRATOR: Sam sent dolls to the children with explanatory notes. Clara's was addressed to "Miss Clara Botheker Clemens."

SAM: Bay Clemens, I have bought two bath tubs and two dolls and sent them by express—they are for you and Susy. One of the dolls is named Hosannah Maria and is in quite delicate health. She belongs to you.—She was out driving and got rained on, and caught a very severe cold. It settled on her mind. When she had partly recovered, she caught a new cold, which paralyzed the sounding-board of her ears and the wobbling nerve of her tongue. She has never heard or spoken since. I have consulted the best physicians. They say constant and complicated bathing will fetch her. Papa.

Susy dear, *Your* doll is named Hallelujah Jennings. She early suffered a stroke of some sort, and since that day all efforts of the best physicians have failed to take the stiffening out of her legs. —They say incessant bathing is the only thing that can give her eventual relief. Her child, Glory Ann Jennings, is sickly and must never be bathed. She cries a good deal in a quiet way, but if you pinch her face together you can vary the expression and make her smile, after a sickly fashion.—Hosannah Maria's child (named Whoop-Jamboree) is similar. I send the children with their mothers. I kiss you all. Papa.

LIVY: Today [July 29th] I had the baby all undressed but her little under shirt—she said, "Oh if Susy see me she will say I am all legged."

Tonight I was reading to her [Susy] that ever interesting story in Rollo, "Little Girl, *little girl*, you have left the gate open" etc. when I read about the rooster I asked her if she would like to sleep up on a high pole, she said, "No, for the world, I wouldn't"—once afterward during our conversation she used that expression "for the world"—I spoke about our riding on the clouds the[y] were so beautiful as we sat looking at them, she said in quite a fretful voice, "there isn't any chair up there on the clouds"—Susy worked a long time today printing the letters to send to you, at first she seemed to think that she was going to print the entire letter to you in a few minutes—but after she found how difficult it was she worked faithfully on it.[12]

SAM: She [Susy] informed a visitor that she had been in a church only once, and that was the time when Clara was "crucified" (christened).[13]

NARRATOR: Sam taught the Bay what he called "the catechism." He began, "Who is a hard lot?" She answered, "Papa." Varying degrees of "hard-lot" questions followed, involving members of the household. Then came, "Who is the hardest lot in the civilized world?" The answer was "Mamma." To the final query, "Who is the confoundedest hardest lot in the entire universe?" the Bay was taught to answer, "Me."[14]

There was a frightening near-accident that summer at the farm. Sam wrote about it to Howells and his wife.

SAM: My Dear Howellses; I thought I ought to make a sort of record of it for future reference; the pleasantest way to do that would be to write it to somebody; BUT that somebody would let it leak into print, and that we wish to avoid. The Howellses would be safe—so let us tell the Howellses about it.

Day before yesterday was a fine summer day away up here on the summit. Aunt Marsh [Mrs. Jervis Langdon's twin sister] and Cousin May Marsh were here visiting Susie Crane and Livy at our farm house. By and by mother Langdon came up the hill in the "high carriage" with Nora the nurse and little Jervis (Charley Langdon's little boy)—Timothy the coachman driving. Behind these came Charley's wife and little girl in the buggy, with the new, young, spry gray horse—a high-stepper. Theodore Crane arrived a little later.

The Bay and Susy were on hand with their nurse, Rosa. I was on hand, too. Susie Crane's trio of colored servants ditto—these being Josie, housemaid; Aunty Cord, cook, aged 62, turbaned, very tall, very broad, very fine every way (see her portrait in "A True Story Just as I Heard It" in my Sketches;) Chocklate (the laundress,) (as the Bay calls her—she can't say Charlotte), still taller, still more majestic of proportions, turbaned, very black, straight as an Indian—age, 24. Then there was the farmer's wife (colored) and her little girl, Susie [Lewis].

Wasn't it a good audience to get up an excitement before? Good excitable, inflammable (combustible) material?

Lewis was still down town, three miles away, with his two-horse wagon, to get a load of manure. Lewis is the farmer (colored.) He is of mighty frame and muscle, stocky, stooping, ungainly, has a good manly face and a clear eye. Age about 45—and the most picturesque of men, when he sits in his fluttering work-day rags, humped forward into a bunch, with his aged slouch hat mashed down over his ears and neck. It is a spectacle to make the broken-hearted smile.

Lewis has worked mighty hard and remained mighty poor. At the end of each whole year's toil he can't show a gain of fifty dollars. He had borrowed money of the Cranes till he owed them $700—and he being conscientious and honest, imagine what it was to him to have to carry this stubborn, hopeless load year in and year out.

Well, sunset came, and Ida the young and comely (Charley Langdon's wife) and her little Julia and the nurse Nora, drove out at the gate behind the new gray horse and started down the long hill—the high carriage receiving its load under the porte cochère. Ida was seen to turn her face toward us across the fence and intervening lawn—Theodore waved good bye to her, for he did not know that her sign was a speechless appeal for help.

The next moment Livy said, "Ida's driving too fast down hill!" She followed it with a sort of scream, "Her horse is running away!"

We could see two hundred yards down that descent. The buggy seemed to fly. It would strike obstructions and apparently spring the height of a man from the ground.

Theodore and I left the shrieking crowd behind and ran down the hill bareheaded and shouting. A neighbor appeared at his gate —a tenth of a second too late!—the buggy vanished past him like a thought. My last glimpse showed it for one instant, far down the descent, springing high in the air out of a cloud of dust, and then it disappeared. As I flew down the road, my impulse was to shut my eyes as I turned them to the right or left, and so delay for a moment the ghastly spectacle of mutilation and death I was expecting.

I ran on and on, still spared this spectacle but saying to myself

"I shall see it at the turn of the road; they never can pass that turn alive." When I came in sight of that turn I saw two wagons there bunched together—one of them full of people. I said, "Just so— they are staring petrified at the remains."

But when I got amongst that bunch, there sat Ida in her buggy and nobody hurt, not even the horse or the vehicle. . . . Ida was pale but serene. As I came tearing down she smiled back over her shoulder at me and [I] said, "Well, you're alive yet, *aren't* you?" . . . A miracle had been performed—nothing less.

You see, Lewis,—the prodigious, humped upon his front seat, had been toiling up, on his load of manure; he saw the frantic horse plunging down the hill toward him, on a full gallop, throwing his heels as high as a man's head at every jump. So Lewis turned his team diagonally across the road just at the "turn," thus making a V with the fence—the running horse could not escape that but must enter it. Then Lewis sprang to the ground and stood in this V. He gathered his vast strength and with a perfect Creedmoor aim he seized the gray horse's bit as he plunged by and fetched him up standing!

It was down hill, mind you; ten feet *further* down hill neither Lewis nor any other man could have saved them, for they would have been on the abrupt "turn," then. But how this miracle was ever accomplished at all, by human strength, generalship and ac- curacy, is clear beyond my comprehension—and grows more so the more I go and examine the ground and try to believe it was actually done. I know one thing, well; if Lewis had missed his aim he would have been killed on the spot in the trap he had made for himself, and we should have found the rest of the remains away down at the bottom of the steep ravine.

Ten minutes later Theodore and I arrived opposite the house, with the servants straggling after us, and shouted to the distracted group on the porch, "Everybody safe!"

Believe it? Why how *could* they? They knew the road perfectly. We might as well have said it to people who had seen their friends go over Niagara.

However, we convinced them; and then, instead of saying some- thing, or going on crying, they grew very still—words could not express it, I suppose.

Nobody could do anything that night, or sleep, either; but there was a good deal of moving talk, with long pauses between—pictures of that flying carriage, these pauses represented—this picture intruded itself all the time and disjointed the talk.

But yesterday evening late, when Lewis arrived from down town he found his supper spread, and some presents of books there, with very complimentary writings on the fly-leaves, and certain very complimentary letters, and more or less greenbacks of dignified denomination pinned to these letters and fly-leaves,—and one said, among other things, (signed by The Cranes) "We cancel $400 of your indebtedness to us," etc., etc.

(The end whereof is not yet, of course, for Charley Langdon is west and will arrive ignorant of all these things to-day.)

The supper-room had been kept locked and imposingly secret and mysterious until Lewis should arrive; but around that part of the house were gathered Lewis's wife and child, Chocklate, Josie, Aunty Cord and our Rosa, canvassing things and waiting impatiently. They were all on hand when the (avalanche came) curtain rose.

Now Aunty Cord is a violent Methodist and Lewis an (fanatic) implacable Dunker-Baptist. These two are inveterate religious disputants. The revealments having been made, Aunty Cord said with effusion—

"*Now* let folks go on saying there ain't no God! Lewis, the Lord sent you there to stop that horse."

Says Lewis—

"Then who sent the *horse* there in sich a shape?"

But I want to call your attention to one thing. When Lewis arrived the other evening, after saving those lives by a feat which I think is the most marvelous of any I can call to mind—when he arrived, hunched up on his manure wagon and as grotesquely picturesque as usual, everybody wanted to go and see how he looked.—They came back and said he was beautiful. It was *so,* too—and yet he would have *photographed* exactly as he would have done any day these past 7 years that he has occupied this farm.

P.S.—Our little romance in real life is happily and satisfactorily completed. Charley has come, listened, acted—and now John T. Lewis has ceased to consider himself as belonging to that class called "the poor."

It has been known, during some years, that it was Lewis's purpose to buy a thirty-dollar silver watch some day, if he ever got where he could afford it. To-day Ida has given him a new, sumptuous gold Swiss stem-winding stop-watch; and if any scoffer shall say "Behold this thing is out of character," there is an inscription within, which will silence him; for it will teach him that this wearer aggrandizes the watch, not the watch the wearer.

I was asked, beforehand if this would be a wise gift, and I said "Yes, the very wisest of all; I know the colored race, and I know that in Lewis's eyes this fine toy will throw the other more valuable testimonials far away into the shade. If he lived in England, the Humane Society would give him a gold medal as costly as this watch, and nobody would say: 'It is out of character.'

"If Lewis chose to wear a town clock, who would become it better?"

Lewis has sound common sense, and is not going to be spoiled. —The instant he found himself possessed of money, he forgot himself in a plan to make his old father comfortable, who is wretchedly poor and lives down in Maryland. His next act, on the spot, was the proffer to the Cranes of the $300 of his remaining indebtedness to them. This was put off by them to the indefinite future, for he is not going to be allowed to pay that at all, though he doesn't know it.

A letter of acknowledgment from Lewis contains a sentence which raises it to the dignity of literature:

"But I beg to say, humbly, that inasmuch as divine providence saw fit to use me as an instrument for the saving of those presshious lives, the honner conferd upon me was greater than the feat performed."

That is well said.[15]

HOWELLS: *Can't* I use that story in the Club about your Elmira life-preserver? As you tell it, I think it's one of the most impressive things I've ever read.[16]

NARRATOR: In Hartford, in the fall, Sam discovered that Susy was very nearsighted.

SAM: I discovered the defect by accident. I was half-way up the hall stairs one day at home, and was leading her by the hand, when I glanced back through the open door of the dining-room and saw what I thought she would recognize as a pretty picture. It was "Stray Kit," the slender, the graceful, the sociable, the beautiful, the incomparable, cat of cats, the tortoise-shell, curled up as round as a wheel and sound asleep on the fire-red cover of the dining-table, with a brilliant stream of sunlight falling across her. I exclaimed about it, but Susy said she could see nothing there, neither cat nor table-cloth. The distance was so slight—not more than twenty feet perhaps—that if it had been any other child I should not have credited the statement.[17]

NARRATOR: Autumn in Hartford always signaled the revival of Sam's and Twichell's Saturday walk to Bartlett's, sometimes called Talcott's, Tower. Katy Leary, who before long was to become a family fixture, described this pastime.

KATY: Mr. Twichell and Mr. Clemens was just devoted to each other, and Mr. Twichell used to influence him a great deal, I think—more than anybody else, except Mrs. Clemens. They used to have the grandest times together, tellin' stories and laughing, and every fall when Mr. Clemens got back from Elmira, he and Mr. Twichell (Joe and Sam, they called themselves) used to take a long walk together. They'd walk right up Talcott Mountain. 'Twas a ten-mile walk and they'd rig themselves all up good and walk out there and back to that old mountain every fall. Mr. Clemens said they'd have to take that long walk at least once a year, just to see if they was holdin' their own.[18]

NARRATOR: Sam was working on his "Autobiography" and made an interesting comparison of the cost of living in 1877 with that in Missouri forty years earlier, which emphasizes the luxurious life in Hartford.

SAM: At first my father owned slaves, but by and by he sold them and hired others by the year from the farmers. For a girl of fifteen he paid twelve dollars a year and gave her two linsey-wolsey frocks and a pair of "stogy" shoes—cost, a modification of nothing; for a negro woman of twenty-five, as general house servant, he paid twenty-five dollars a year and gave her shoes and the afore-mentioned linsey-wolsey frocks; for a strong negro woman of forty, as cook, washer, etc., he paid forty dollars a year and the customary two suits of clothes; and for an able-bodied man he paid from seventy-five to a hundred dollars a year and gave him two suits of jeans and two pairs of "stogy" shoes—an outfit that cost about three dollars. But times have changed. We pay our German nursemaid $155 a year; Irish housemaid, $150; Irish laundress, $150; negro woman, a cook, $240; young negro man, to wait on door and table, $360; Irish coachman, $600 a year, with gas, hot and cold water, and dwelling consisting of parlor, kitchen, and two bedrooms, connected with the stable, free.[19]

NARRATOR: The Christmas season lacked the usual sparkle for Sam and Livy; their thoughts were occupied with the tragic Whittier dinner which had taken place on December 17th. Sam had been invited to make a speech at a dinner held in Boston in honor of Whittier's birthday. He improvised a ludicrous scene in which a California miner encountered three disreputable tramps who claimed to be Longfellow, Emerson and Holmes. The venerable poets, who were all present, were quoted and misquoted to the accompaniment of cards and liquor, and the results were disastrous, at least in the eyes of Sam and of Howells, who had introduced him.

SAM: My sense of disgrace does not abate. It grows. . . .

   It seems as if I must have been insane when I wrote that speech and saw no harm in it, no disrespect toward those men whom I reverenced so much.[20]

   I haven't done a stroke of work since the *Atlantic* dinner; have only moped around. . . . How could I ever have—

   Ah, well, I am a great and sublime fool. But then I am God's fool, and all His work must be contemplated with respect.[21]

NARRATOR: There was cheerful news about the scrapbook in the new year.

SAM: The Scrap-Book is booming, now, and promises to kill all the other Scrap-books in the world. . . . The firm [Slote] are as charmed as if they had found the philosopher's stone. They have declined a liberal English offer for exclusive right on a royalty. So one of the firm will go to London and take up permanent residence, within a month, and proceed to Scrap-Book the Eastern hemisphere. They have secured 14 eligible feet in the Paris Exposition and another member of the firm will remain there and Scrap-book the French. It seems funny that an invention which cost me five-minutes' thought, in a railway car one day, should in this little while be paying me an income as large as any salary I ever received on a newspaper. My royalty on each book is very trifling—so the sales are already very great.[22]

SUSY'S SEVENTH YEAR

1878–1879

NARRATOR: Excitement was at high pitch in March; the whole family was going to Europe; Livy's friend, Clara Spaulding, was to accompany them.

SAM: We are now to retire for a fortnight into the study and adjoining bedroom while workmen box up the furniture and carpets of the rest of the house and put the place into the state of (eruption) desolation meet for our two-years' absence from it. . . .

Why do we go to Germany . . . ? Because the only chance I get here to work is the 3 months we spend at the farm in the summer. A nine months' annual vacation is too burdensome. I want to find a German village where nobody knows my name or speaks any English, and shut myself up in a closet 2 miles from the hotel, and work every day without interruption until I shall have satisfied my consuming desire in that direction. Livy and the children and Miss Clara [Spaulding] may learn the language, for occupation, with our nurse Rosa and some tutors for teachers.[1]

Our plan is to leave for Elmira March 25. We have taken 2 staterooms in the Holsatia, which sails for Hamburg April 11. . . . We shall leave nobody here but Patrick and the horses.[2]

NARRATOR: Sam described himself in a facetious application for a passport made to his friend, Bayard Taylor, United States Minister to Berlin, who was traveling to Europe on the same ship.

SAM: Meine Beschreibung ist vollenden: Geborn 1835; 5 Fuss 8½ inches hoch; weight doch aber about 145 pfund, sometimes ein wenig unter, sometimes ein wenig oben; dunkel braun Haar und rhotes Moustache, full Gesicht, mit sehr hohe Oren and leicht grau prachtvolles strahlenden Augen und ein Verdammtes gut moral character. Handlungkeit, Author von Bücher.[3]

SUE CRANE: Mr. and Mrs. Clemens, the children and nurse, Rosa, arrived at mother's in town [Elmira] on March 29, 1878 . . . as a farewell before the journey to both mothers and friends. Mr. C. alone went to Fredonia to see his mother.[4]

NARRATOR: The *Holsatia* started out by anchoring in the bay because of the storm.

HOWELLS: When I parted from you, that dismal day in New York, I saw that the weather was capable of anything.[5]

SAM: Noisy cabin—shrieking children—the ceaseless metallic clatter of that old cracked kettle of a piano and the thunder and pounding of the screw, with an occasional avalanche of crashing crockery as the ship lurches, this is the afternoon hell in this ship daily. But the piano is the special hell—how it racks one's head.

Until it stops—then you think the scream-voiced boy is it.

There goes the B's crying baby. Now a guffaw of beastly laughter. Now the little Spanish boy is hurled headlong down into our gangway by a lurch of the ship and fetches up with a heavy bang and pile of books and rubbish tumble down.[6]

Mother dear, having no other paper convenient, I use the bill of fare. You can see by the articles underlined, (Roman punch, roast chicken, jelly and salad,) what portion of it Livy and Clara partook of this evening. And even this little is a bigger meal than they have ventured upon before for several days. But I have had an inexhaustible appetite and have tried to make up for them. It has been all kinds of a voyage—calm, smooth seas, then rough seas, then middling—and so on. On the 17th we had heavy seas, then easy ones, then rough again; then brilliant sunshine, then black skies, with thick driving storms of rain, hail, sleet and snow—sunshine again, followed by more snow, hail, rain and sleet—and so on, all day long; we sighted an ice-berg in the morning and a water-spout in the afternoon. To-day a lurch of the ship threw a passenger against an iron railing and they think he has a rib broken. The girls are worn out with the rolling and tumbling of the ship, and starved out too, since they eat nothing. But they'll be all right 2 days hence, when we reach Plymouth.

The children get along splendidly, though the Bay swears at the weather sometimes.

We like the vessel very much. She is a good sea-boat, and has a delightful old Captain, who thinks Miss Clarence (as he calls Clara Spaulding) is my daughter. We have an unusually pleasant lot of passengers—mostly Germans.[7]

LIVY: Here we are at the end of our voyage and we find ourselves most charmingly situated in Hamburg—we are greatly surprised to find it such a beautiful city. . . .

When we arrived at the hotel they were expecting us, Mr. Clemens having sent a dispatch from Plymouth . . . our rooms were all in readiness, a nice large room with small dark room adjoining for Rosa and the children, three single beds in the two rooms—and next to these a single room for Clara, for Mr. Clemens and me a parlor with an alcove to it, in which stand two single beds and two wash stands.[8]

SAM: Huge parlor and bedroom. Silk quilts and top beds. Parlor vast—looks out on great paved space before the stately railroad station. Two red silk sofas; 4 tables; writing desk; 12 chairs. Polished floor with rugs.

Three large windows; 2 large mirrors; 2 candelabra with 3 candles each against the walls; 2 with 4 each before the mirrors.

In Europe they use safety matches and then entrust candles to drunken men, children, idiots, etc., and yet suffer little from fires, apparently. The idea of an open light in one of our houses makes us shudder.

NARRATOR: They were much entertained with the German stoves.

SAM: "Who is buried here?"

"Nobody."

"Then why the monument?"

"It is not a monument. It is a stove."

We had reverently removed our hats. We now put them on again. Stove 8 ft. high—female bust in a circle in the side midway —3½ ft. by 2¼—very ornamental, around the top.[9]

LIVY: I never tasted more palatable food than they have here— Yesterday afternoon we took a carriage and drove about the town —The homes that are just about us are as pretty as any [I] think I ever saw—some of them look like palaces and the grounds about them are extremely inviting, I marvel that we hear so little of the beauties of Hamburg. Mr. George Warner is the only person that

I ever heard speak enthusiastically of the city—I supposed it was a sea port town with no especial attractions, and I think it is the finest city I was ever in. . . .

As I write Mr. Clemens is lying on the sofa reading a German book. Clara is upstairs . . . the children are in bed, Rosa has just been in to bring something—Rosa has been *absolutely perfect* ever since we left home—My greatest anxiety just at present is the fear that the children will be utterly spoiled by the admiration that they receive—they had much more attention than anyone on the ship, from gentlemen, ladies, servants and all—Several gentlemen and ladies spoke to Mr. Clemens and me about them saying they were much the best children on the ship. I have had quite a long serious talk with Rosa tonight about the children and told her, when she possibly could to ask people not to talk so to them and when she could not, to turn it in some way, saying that they tried to be good children, etc.

Rosa says that almost everyone on the street will stop and say, "Oh what pretty children." Now, of course, the children do not understand, because it is spoken in German, but they soon will—

It is so chilly here that we are still wearing our seal skins—the children are rather tired and cross but Susy's cold is better.[10]

SAM: Poor Susy! From the day we reached German soil, we have required Rosa to speak German to the children—which they hate with all their souls. The other morning in Hanover, Susy came to me (from Rosa, in the nursery) and said, in halting syllables, "Papa, wie viel Uhr ist es?"—then turned, with pathos in her big eyes, and said, "Mamma, I wish Rosa was made in English."[11]

HOWELLS: I hope that by this time Mrs. Clemens is all well of her cold, and that poor Susy is more reconciled to Rosa's composition.[12]

NARRATOR: They went to Mannheim and Frankfort-on-the-Main.

SAM: What a paradise this is! What clean clothes, what good faces, what tranquil contentment, what prosperity, what genuine freedom, what superb government.[13]

Bought a couple of gorgeously dressed horrors in castle museum to start a portrait gallery of my ancestors with. Paid $1.25 for the male portrait and $2.50 for the lady. The gentleman has a most self-satisfied smirk, but if he had known he would be sold to a base untitled Republican a hundred years later for $1.25 would it have taken some of the tuck out of that smirk?

And this fair young creature with her lavish finery and her hair in a druggist's mortar shape with a bed of roses on top—what has become of her graces in these hundred years? Very likely the gallants praised this picture and said it was destined to grow in value and fame with the century like the works of the old masters, and by and by be within the purse-reach of none but kings and successful brewers. And now she goes for $2.50.[14]

NARRATOR: They settled down at the Schloss Hotel, Heidelberg.

SAM: From this airy perch among the shining groves we look down upon Heidelberg Castle, and upon the swift Neckar, and the town, and out over the wide green level of the Rhine valley—a marvelous prospect. We are in a cul de sac formed of hill-ranges and river: we are on the side of a steep mountain; the river at our feet is walled, on its other side, (yes, on both sides,) by a steep and wooded mountain-range which rises abruptly aloft from the water's edge; portions of these mountains are densely wooded; the plain of the Rhine, seen through (the mouth of the opening of) the mouth of this pocket, has many and peculiar charms for the eye.

Our (big) bedroom has two great glass bird-cages (enclosed balconies) one looking toward the Rhine Valley and sunset, the other looking up the Neckar-cul de sac, and naturally we spend nearly all our time in these—when one is sunny the other is shady. We have tables and chairs in them; we do our reading, writing, studying, smoking and suppering in them.[15]

LIVY: We have a large bedroom with two large glass enclosed balconies opening out of it, which we use as parlor and Mr. Clemens' and my sleeping room, opening from this, is a comfortable sized room for the children and Rosa. Clara's room is a single bedroom on the opposite side of the hall. We get these three rooms and three meals a day for each of us, for a little less than $250. a month. . . . The first afternoon that we were here, the children went out to the stables and got acquainted with two dogs and some little puppies, some ponies—they came in as full of the animals as they would at the farm—the landlord's little girl has some dogs that are harnessed and draw her, and they have a promise of a ride after them—it is just the place for the children.

This morning was our first breakfast . . . a little after nine Mr. Clemens went down to order it—Beef steak, eggs, potatoes, etc.— he came back in a few minutes and said that with our arrangement we could not have meat for breakfast, that we could have rolls and butter, coffee and honey. . . . When Mr. Clemens begins to work we shall make some different arrangement for he must have a heartier breakfast.[16]

SAM: It must have been a noble genius who devised this hotel. Lord, how blessed is the repose, the tranquillity of this place! Only two sounds: the happy clamor of the birds in the groves and the muffled music of the Neckar tumbling over the opposing dikes. It is no hardship to lie awake awhile nights, for this subdued roar has exactly the sound of a steady rain beating upon a roof. It is so healing to the spirit; and it bears up the thread of one's imaginings as the accompaniment bears up a song.[17]

NARRATOR: Susy dictated a letter to her aunt, Sue Crane.

SUSY: I know a lot of German; everybody says I know a lot. I give you a million dollars to see you, and you would give two hundred dollars to see the lovely woods that we see.[18]

LIVY: The children are so perfectly happy here. They are out nearly all day long. Their appetites are most excellent—

Yesterday Rosa was in the castle grounds with the children, two ladies one English the other German sitting on a seat spoke to them, after a little asked their name, where they were from etc., etc. then she said, "Clemens, why could that be Mark Twain?"— Rosa told them that it was, then the lady said to Susy, "I wish you would tell your papa that I have enjoyed his books very much"— No one in the hotel knows who Mr. Clemens is—we are having as quiet a life as we could possibly desire—The ladies asked the children if they could not sing some English songs, so they sang "Grandfathers Clock," "I Have a Savior," "Ring the Bells of Heaven" and Rosa said she saw tears in one of the ladies eyes. . . .

As I write Mr. Clemens is writing Mr. Howells—Rosa is talking German as fast as she can to the children—She is very faithful in the matter talks no English to them and Susy is picking up a great deal of German—I shall try next week to get them a teacher.[19]

SAM: The hotel grounds join and communicate with the Castle grounds; so we and the children loaf in the winding paths of those leafy vastnesses a great deal, and drink beer and listen to excellent music.[20]

[Susy] noticed that the Schloss gardens were populous with snails creeping all about everywhere. One day she found a new dish on her table and inquired concerning it and learned that it was made of snails. She was awed and impressed and said, "Wild ones, mamma?"[21]

Drat this German tongue, I never shall be able to learn it. I think I could learn a little conversational stuff, maybe, if I could attend to it, but I found I couldn't spare the time. I took lessons two weeks and got so I could understand the talk going on around me, and even answer back, after a fashion. But I neither talk nor listen, now, so I can't even understand the language any more. Mrs. Clemens is getting along fast, and Miss Spaulding and our little Susy talk the devilish tongue without difficulty. But the Bay scorns the language. The nurse and the governess blandish around her in vain. She maintains the calm and persistent attitude of not caring a damn for German. There is a good deal of character in the Bay—such as it is.[22]

There is one disease which is sure to affect everybody at some time or other during his life, and that is the disease which prompts a man to learn a foreign language. I escaped that infection for a long time—the major part of my life, in fact; but I did not escape it entirely. I had learned a smattering of Chinese, one or two Indian dialects and some other kindred classic languages, but nothing serious. The serious part came later. I went to Germany . . . with an evil instinct that I could learn the German language. I know better now. I went to work at it, worked hard and hopefully, fought a good, honest fight with it, but the German language had been in the business longer than I have and it came out ahead.[23]

LIVY: Clara sits by me writing her Mother and Mr. Clemens sits the other side of the table reading Mr. Warner's Adirondack Sketch, he is perfectly convulsed with laughter—This evening Clara and I will read it—Tomorrow Mr. Clemens goes to work he has been making notes ever since we left home, so he has a good deal of material to work from. . . . I have secured a young lady to be with them, the children—three hours a day. She begins tomorrow morning—She has taught in an English School. . . . I liked her appearance very much indeed.[24]

NARRATOR: Susy dictated to Livy a letter to Grandma Langdon.

SUSY: We have rided after a big dog, that shakes hands. We have got some new spring hats—It's lots of pictures here of the view 'at we have bought and may be we will send you one—It's beautiful buttercups and daisys and blue flowers and every thing—

We take our dinner and our breakfast and our supper down stairs—One day I tried "Tell me daisy ere I go" with a daisy—you pick off the leaves from the daisy—

One day this week we went out on some little donkeys, it was a woman leaded us and Rosa stood on the other side—they had some little red saddles on their backs—We went to the Wolf's-bannen, it was some fishes there and some chickens—the donkeys belonged to the woman that led them.

We go every night to get goat's milk, there are little young goats and me and baby can lift them—After we walk over there we drink a glass of the goat's milk—its a little baby over there as light as a feather—I tend the baby and I hold it—there are dogs there and pigs there. . . .

I must tell you Grandmamma how Clara and I earn money every day by being quiet every morning so my mamma can sleep—She gives us each 5 fennigs every morning that we don't make a noise.

Grandmamma I guess I must go and close the letter—Grandmamma I want you to write me—good bye I'll say yours lovingly Susy.[25]

LIVY: The children went on Tuesday of this week to the fair in the town, there were booths built each side of the street and everything sold in them, then there were places where they had little carriages and wooden horses on a large round platform, and the children got in these carriages or on these horses and then the entire platform went round and round, the children enjoyed it immensely. . . . They brought home a rabbit that cost .25 cts. that was their most expensive purchase. The rabbit was Clara's—Susy had a horse . . . the children are so happy and we are all so happy.[26]

SAM: I have waited for a "call" to go to work—I knew it would come. Well, it began to come a week ago; my note-book comes out more and more frequently every day since; three days ago I concluded to move my manuscripts over to my den. *Now* the call is loud and decided at last. So to-morrow I shall begin regular, steady work, and stick to it till the middle of July or August 1st, when I look for Twichell; we will then walk about Germany two or three weeks and then I'll go to work again (perhaps in Munich).[27]

NARRATOR: Livy wrote to her mother.

LIVY: Yesterday was Clara's birthday and she and Susy had a very happy time—In the morning the gifts were arranged on one of the balconies. When we came up from breakfast we all went out there—There were two books, a little donkey with a red saddle such as the children have had a ride on—a slate, a very pretty doll from Rosa. When you make it cry its head and arms move—a doll

from aunt Clara—a little doll's nursing bottle—a little egg from
the governess that opened and had inside it a stork that had
brought a baby—the whole thing was not more than two and
a half or three inches long—Susy and Clara each had a cup from
Rosa—Susy had a little doll—Rosa and the chambermaid each
gave the baby a large bouquet of flowers—The landlord's daughter
brought up a large dish of strawberries for them.

In the afternoon I had the donkeys to take them up to the King's
Seat, a high hill near us. The hill is 1200 feet higher than the
[Quarry] farm house, and the hill [is] much steeper. The roads are
made in such a way as to be very easy—Rosa and the woman who
owns the donkeys and a man walked with the children—the rest of
us rode—

The children had their supper—bread and butter and straw-
berries up there and about 5½ we started for the hotel, having had
a delightful afternoon.[28]

NARRATOR: Clara had a turn at dictating.

CLARA: I've got a clock. I want to tell her 'at I've got some money in
my porte-monaie—say 'at we seen the little puppies and the little
kitties. We seen Uno and Naro and the cross dog (Uno and Naro
means Juno and Nero) Well we been down to the kitchen—Well
now we will say we seen everything nice—and I had my birthday
my German birthday—and we found a beautiful egg and a beautiful beautiful birthday—We went down to the goats milk and we
seen the dear little baby—I want to say 'at Susy's been sick and 'at
Susy lie down this morning and went to sleep—She is much better
now—now we ride on the donkeys.[29]

LIVY: Susy asks almost daily for a letter. She feels sure that you
[Mrs. Langdon] or her aunt Sue will write her—

How I wish that we could see you all—I am glad our home is
in America. I enjoy it as much as possible here but I should not
like to think of living here always, of this being my home—I would
rather live just where I do than any place that I know of—and I
only hope that we shall always have money enough so that we
can continue to live there.

NARRATOR: The financial policies of the Rutherford B. Hayes administration were causing concern at home.

LIVY: Sue's letter which we rec'd last night which spoke of the mutterings and threatenings in the air worried us somewhat—we have
seen the same things in the papers and Mr. Clemens feels that bad
times are likely to come—I do hope that evil will be averted but

it does seem with the large force organized in the West as if there was great danger—

I do hope the government will be aroused to *do* something. . . .

Yesterday I told Clara not to do something and she said "Why?" I said "because Mamma says so"—she says "that isn't any *why*."³⁰

NARRATOR: Susy dictated a letter to Livy.

SUSY: We've been to a nice picnic there were woods and every thing in it—And we've been to the fair—we went on some donkeys, we had some donkeys and we went on them to the woods—and came back in the carriage.

I saw some women having some great big faggots, the little boy helping them gather them—The little boy had a great long stick to knock down the dead twigs from the trees so that he could gather them—they were very large faggots and the women had round cushions to put on their heads and then they put the faggots on the cushions—I found a nest Grandmamma out doors with my teacher. She said if I didn't break it she was going to bring it some eggs and a stuffed humming bird and the next morning she brought them. Now Grandmamma I *must* get a letter and If I don't get a letter pretty soon I don't know what I shall do.³¹

LIVY: I am exceedingly pleased with the progress that Susy is making in German. She chatters away with almost as much ease as she does in English—this morning the children with flowers would run by the side of the carriage, we bought one rose bud. Susy then asked me in English if that was all I wanted, turned to the little boy and apparently with as much ease as she had spoken to me in English told him in German that we had enough—

Yesterday, she came in from the nursery where the governess had been reading her a story in German, she began telling it to me giving it in English until she reached the most exciting part and then dropped into German—I thought when she had progressed so far as to do that she was certainly doing well.³²

SAM: For some little time . . . Clara was rich in given-names drawn from the surnames of the nurses, and was taught to string them together as well as her incompetent tongue would let her, as a show-off for the admiration of visitors, when required to "be nice and tell the ladies your name." As she did it with proper gravity and earnestness, not knowing there was any joke in it, it went very well: "Clara Lewis O'Day Botheker McAleer McLaughlin Clemens."³³

Two or three times lately, I have heard Bay make a mild protest under a certain head, but I paid no attention and straightway forgot the matter. Perhaps I ought to speak of it, now, however, for the guidance of her home-correspondents. When Jervis's letter was read to her, to-day, I heard her say, with the former gentle protest in her tone, "Cousin Jervis only calls me Clara Clemens—it isn't *half* of my names." You see, you will have to ring in those wet nurses to satisfy Bay.[34]

NARRATOR: They all went to Baden-Baden, August 1st, to meet Twichell.

LIVY: It is so delightful to have Mr. Twichell with us, he is to remain six weeks—we shall dislike to have the time draw near for his going—he and Mr. Clemens will start off walking tomorrow or Tuesday . . . into the Black Forest for a day and a half and then they go to Heidelberg and up the Neckar for a week—we go with a *good* Courier . . . to Strasbourg for a day to see the Cathedral and from there to Zurich on Lake Zurich where we shall probably remain until the Gentlemen come to us—a week or ten days.[35]

Last Monday night Mr. Twichell and Mr. Clemens joined us after their Black Forest and Neckar trip, of course we were desperately glad to get them back. . . .

Thursday about two o'clock we started on our trip to the top of the Rigi, we went for nearly an hour in a boat then took an open car in which we were pushed by a steam engine up the mountain. . . . Mr. Clemens and Mr. Twichell walked up. . . . When we reached the top the rain was pouring and the wind blowing a perfect gale. . . . We went to our rooms took a glass of wine, lay down and I had a nap before the gentlemen came. . . .

After the gentlemen had gotten on dry clothes (Mr. Clemens lay in bed while his pants were dried) we had our supper—The hotel is a beautiful one away up there on the top of the mountains . . . after supper we tried to get warm at the stove but there were too many people . . . so after a little we went to our room. Mr. Clemens got in bed to get warm, we brought all the candles into one room, so that we might have a little cheerful look to things—Mr. Twichell wrote, Mr. Clemens read, Clara sewed. I held a book and pretended to read but most of the time talked to Clara. . . .

The wind blew very *very* hard all night, about four in the morning the trumpet blew for us all to get up and see the sun rise. Such a spectacle as it is to see the people get up and come out frozen to death to watch for the sun.[36]

NARRATOR: Livy, Clara and the children stayed at Ouchy, near Lausanne, on Lake Geneva while the men went off on the second, and longer, stage of their walking trip on which *A Tramp Abroad* was largely based. Susy dictates.

SUSY: My dear Grandmamma I am having a beautiful time now playing and throwing stones in the watter—When Mamma was at church this morning, there came a big boat along. I didn't know 'at there was music on it and so I went and asked Rosa if there was music on it and she said, "yes" I heard music somewhere and I didn't know where it was—

Once while we were at Interlaken we went up on a boat, Aunt Clara and Mamma and I to see the Geerbach falls they are most the wonderfullest falls in Switzerland—dear Grandmamma, I was lifted up in the air because Mamma couldn't walk so far and so we went—

When we came down from seeing the falls, we saw some women singing at the end of the station, and I gave them a frank—Dear Grandmamma I think I must close the letter except that I am going to print a little.[37]

SAM: Twichell and I did a good deal of tramping together among the mountains and had a good time. I seem to have walked the rheumatism out of myself. . . . He and I walked to Martigny to Chamonix and Mont Blanc.

NARRATOR: The family met Sam in Lausanne.

SAM: Livy and Clara and the children are out shopping, and Rosa is packing trunks for Venice . . . a day or two ago Livy and I drove . . . [to Chamonix] in a two-horse carriage and remained a day—9 hours' drive thither and 9 hours back. It tired Livy out and she went to bed early last night—but she is out shopping again today. At Chamouny [Chamonix] she ascended part of a mountain in a chair borne by men, and then walked to an ice-cavern in the great glacier below the Grandes Mulets, and back again. . . . We had *perfect* weather and some marvelous Alpine spectacles, both by daylight and full-moonlight. Clara had charge of the children while we were gone. They entertained her—sometimes with philosophical remarks and sometimes with questions which only the Almighty could answer. Susy said, "Aunt Clara, if the horses should run away and mamma be killed, would you be my mamma?" "Yes, for a little while, Susy, till we got to Elmira—but you wouldn't want your mamma to be killed by the horses, of course?"—"Well,—

—I wouldn't want her *to go in that WAY*, but I would like to have you for my mamma." There's discrimination for you!

Another time, Susy asked Aunt Clara if she wouldn't like to be God. Clara could not make her understand that there were reasons why she would prefer to reserve her decision in that matter.

Susy persecuted Clara with questions as to how God *could* build all these people out of dust "and make them stick together."

You must understand that Susy's thinkings run nearly altogether on the heavenly and the supernatural; but Bay's mind is essentially worldly. Bay says she does not want to go to heaven—prefers Hartford. The other day she had a private conference with Clara, and said, impressively: "Aunt Clara, I am going to tell you something. Papa gives me a good deal of trouble lately."

"Why, *Bay!*"

"Yes, he does, Aunt Clara; papa is a good deal of trouble to me. He interrupts me when I am busy; and he wants me to get in bed with him—and I can't do that with jelmuls" (gentlemen;) I don't like jelmuls."

"Why Bay, you like Uncle Theodore, don't you?"

"O yes, but *he* ain't a jelmul, he's a *friend*."

The other day I gave Bay a small gold ring. Afterward she said to Clara: "It was very delicate in papa to give me that ring."

We can't quite make out what she meant by that stately word, unless she meant that it was a "delicate attention" on my part.[38]

LIVY: Here we are in a little town [Chambéry], nearly on the border between France and Italy, where we have stopped to break our journey into Italy. . . .

We go tomorrow to Turin and on Tuesday to Milan where we shall stay two or three days and then on to Venice. . . .

Oh how different this town is on Sunday from any American town—such quantities of idlers standing about—such an aimless look about everybody. . . . Oh how I do dislike the French—and I am more and more thankful that I am an American—I believe the old puritan education brings better men and women, than any of these looser methods—perhaps they were too severe, but they certainly leaned toward the wiser course.[39]

NARRATOR: They all enjoyed Venice.

LIVY: Here we are in Venice. . . . It is so fascinating, so thoroughly charming. . . .

We left Bellagio Wednesday morning . . . it rained almost all the time that we were in the boat and part of the time there was quite a heavy sea. . . .

Last night [Sunday, September 29th] . . . Mr. [Gedney] Bunce, a cousin of Mr. Ned Bunce, an artist called and he staid until after eleven. . . .

. . . calls again last night [Monday] until nearly eleven—out tonight and calls until after eleven—three appointments for to-morrow—we are worse pushed than [in] Hartford.[40]

NARRATOR: Clara takes a turn at dictating her experience with the St. Mark's pigeons.

CLARA: I went out walking and I buyed some corn, and I holded my hand out and they all flied on it and pickted my hand, and then I leaned over for them to pick my hand and instead picking my hand they flied upon my back—I went in a Gondaler yesterday to ride—

We got in the Gondaler and then when we was there, we got out and we rided in a carriage and then when we was to the house we got out and we went into the grass (sea weed) and into the sand and we found some shells and some live creatures and then we went in the carriage again and drove to the gondaler and then we drove home—

I love Grandmamma very much and I like to see her—

Clara Langdon Lewis O'Day Bocketer Placklick Lewis Bay Clemens—that is my really name.[41]

SAM: In Venice they were on the water in the gondola most of the time, and were great friends with our gondolier.[42]

NARRATOR: Livy writes for Susy.

SUSY: Dear Grandmamma My Mamma came near not having any little children any more—We got lost in a bad street, Rosa looked in every corner but she couldn't find the house—pretty soon she asked somebody but they didn't understand her, she asked some-body else but they didn't know—and then she said "Susy if we don't find our way in this street we have to go without looking tonight—first Rosa cried and then Bay cried—then she turned that street and she found her house—and the next time I'll ask a gondalier and he'll take me to our hotel.[43]

LIVY: We find altogether too much social life in Venice for our comfort. . . .

We have had a most delightful week going about among the pictures, and some of them have been such a great delight to us that we shall leave them with real regret. . . .

This week too I have done a good deal of shopping. . . . We have bought several most beautiful pieces of wood carving and I am very anxious to see them in our house—There is now standing in the room a carved chest that I have bought for our hall, and on it are standing a number of little odds and ends that I am going to put inside of it—then it will be shipped to Liverpool where it will await us—We have ordered made a cabinet of drawers for the bay window in the Library to stand where that little stand with books has always been. Then we found a most wonderful old carved bedstead that was a great beauty—that we got for our room.[44]

SAM: It was this . . . old elaborately carved black Venetian bedstead—the most comfortable bedstead that ever was, with space enough in it for a family, and carved angels enough surmounting its twisted columns and its headboard and footboard to bring peace to the sleepers, and pleasant dreams.[45]

LIVY: I found an old apron in one of these shops, it was very heavy silk tapestry with flowers woven on it . . . I found that there was a little child's apron and two large sleeves that all belonged together—it will make plenty of stuff to cover a large chair and will I think be very pretty.[46]

NARRATOR: They met a delightful couple named Chamberlain from Concord, Massachusetts, friends of Ralph Waldo Emerson's. Mr. Chamberlain was an artist, and they planned to meet again in Rome. The Clemenses went next to Florence.

LIVY: We are enjoying so very much our stay in Italy and it seems to me that we are getting more and more into the spirit of the thing. . . .

Bay informed us this morning that she spoke four languages, English—German—French and Italian. . . .

. . . we had to go to a wine store and lay in some wine—(I don't let the children drink any water without some wine in it and we also drink wine, with our luncheon and dinner) we get the wine much cheaper by buying it outside of the hotel. . . .

Florence is much more restful than Venice, because we have no social demands—and one ought to know no one when they are visiting picture galleries. . . .

This Italy does tempt money so out of one's pocket—almost everything we see here is singularly pretty.[47]

We have enjoyed Rome immensely and wish so very much that we were going to spend three months here.[48]

SAM: Spent all day in [Elihu] Vedder's lofty studio, and the evening with him and another artist spinning yarns and drinking beer in a quiet saloon. Big row in the street but no bloodshed.[49]

LIVY: Yesterday morning we went to Mr. Vedder's studio, he certainly has immense genius, he had such a large amount of pictures and such infinite variety of subjects—we did enjoy the morning so very much—I felt as if I could spend two thousand dollars there if I had it to spend.

NARRATOR: Sam, eventually, bought Vedder's "Young Medusa" for $250. They met the Chamberlains again; Livy sent her mother charming pencil sketches of herself and Sam.

LIVY: I am going to send you in this [letter], a sketch that Mr. Chamberlain made of Mr. Clemens and me one evening when Mr. Clemens was reading aloud and the rest of us were working—he does not do heads at all, but does other things extremely well.[50]

SAM: In Rome and Florence they [the children] had long daily tramps, for Rosa is a famous hand to smell out the sights of a strange place.[51]

NARRATOR: Sam was very proud of his skill as a courier.

SAM: Now *I* brought the tribe through from Rome, myself. We never had so little trouble before. The next time anybody has a courier to put out to nurse, I shall not be in the market.[52]

Left [Florence] at 10:45 for Bologna. . . . Leave the omnibus-driver a franc to bring the conductor of the train out there to me. Made him understand I wanted a first-class compartment to myself and had five in my party—for future cash. All right. Omnibus-driver also took my luggage into waiting-room and brought the ticket taker to me. Gave *him* two francs and he flew around with many winks and brought the conductor again and both winked that all was right. The former took my five through tickets and sent a fat porter to get them viséd. Then allowed our tribe to pass through to the train without tickets. Found the conductor right outside on the qui vive, who helped me carry my luggage, put us into a compartment and fastened the door. Presently the fat porter came with my tickets and I gave *him* a franc. The conductor allowed nobody to look in all the way, not even a ticket puncher.

Had a mighty smooth trip of it. Gave the conductor five francs. Total cost nine francs. If I had had a courier I should have had to take care of him, pay him ten francs wages and twelve francs fare.

From Rome to Florence I paid the conductor five francs and had a heap of attention. Once he kept the train waiting for me at a station.

Am a shining success as a courier, so far, by the use of francs.[53]

NARRATOR: On the way to Munich, they spent a night in Trent, Austria.

SAM: . . . where the confounded hotel had not received our message, and so at that miserable hour, in that snowy region, the tribe had to shiver together in fireless rooms while beds were prepared and warmed, then up at 6 in the morning and a noble view of snow-peaks glittering in the rich light of a full moon while the hotel-devils lazily deranged a breakfast for us in the dreary gloom of blinking candles; then a solid 12 hours pull through the loveliest snow-ranges and snow-draped forest—and at 7 P.M. we hauled up, in drizzle and fog, at the domicile which had been engaged for us ten months before.

NARRATOR: Fräulein Dahlweiner's pension, la Karlstrasse, had been recommended by Charles Dudley Warner.

SAM: Munich did seem the horriblest place, the most desolate place, the most unendurable place!—and the rooms were *so* small, the conveniences so meagre, and the porcelain stoves so grim, ghastly, dismal, intolerable! So Livy and Clara (Spaulding) sat down forlorn, and cried, and I retired to a private place to pray. By and by we all retired to our narrow German beds; and when Livy and I finished talking across the room, it was all decided that we would rest 24 hours then pay whatever damages were required, and straightway fly to the south of France.[54]

. . . as I was dropping to sleep I discovered that my pet detestation was in the house—a cuckoo clock.[55]

But you see, that was simply fatigue. Next morning the tribe fell in love with the rooms, with the weather, with Munich, and head over heels in love with Fräulein Dahlweiner. We got a larger parlor—an ample one—threw two communicating bedrooms into one, for the children, and now we are entirely comfortable. The only apprehension, at present, is that the climate may not be just right for the children, in which case we shall *have* to go to France, but it will be with the sincerest regret.[56]

Our bedroom window looked upon a court; all sorts of occupations were carried on under it. At 5:00 A.M., they sawed wood and split it there; at 6:00 a professional carpet beater began to add his whackings; at 7:00 some boiler-makers reinforced the carpet beater—now think of all those noises going at once! . . . Clara Spaulding's bed has tumbled down twice. Her window shade has to be put up with a step ladder, and gotten down in the same way. To our morning noises was soon added, (in the hall) the barking of a Spitz dog at 7:30. The fact is, there was but one thing we took solid and healing comfort in, and that was our gentle young colored girl who waits on our table. But alas, day before yesterday she fell in the cistern and the color all came off.

We require her to fall in every day, now. We have clean table linen, now. Clara's bed and window shade are to be fixed today. I shall invite the Spitz to supper this evening and tomorrow he will know more about the Sweet By and By than he does now.

So we are all right. . . . We are contented, and pretty happy. We think the world of the Fräulein, and would not be willing to live elsewhere in Munich than under her motherly wing.[57]

While it occurs to me, I must tell you Susy's last. She is sorely badgered with dreams; and her stock dream is that she is being eaten up by bears. She is a grave and thoughtful child. . . . Last night she had the usual dream. This morning she stood apart (after telling it,) for some time, looking vacantly at the floor, and absorbed in meditation. At last she looked up, and with the pathos of one who feels he has not been dealt by with even-handed fairness, said "But Mamma, the trouble is, that I am never the *bear,* but always the person."

It would not have occurred to me that there might be an advantage, even in a dream, in occasionally being the eater, instead of always the party eaten, but I easily perceived that her point was well taken.[58]

Susy backed her good judgment in matters of morals with conduct to match—even upon occasions when it caused her sacrifice to do it . . . the pair [she and Clara] were troublesomely quarrelsome. Punishments were tried as a means of breaking up this custom—these failed. Then rewards were tried. A day without a quarrel brought candy. The children were their own witnesses— each for or against her own self. Once Susy took the candy, hesitated, then returned it with a suggestion that she was not fairly

entitled to it. Clara kept hers, so here was a conflict of evidence—
one witness *for* a quarrel and one against it. But the better witness
of the two was on the affirmative side and the quarrel stood proved
and no candy due to either side. There seemed to be no defense
for Clara—yet there was and Susy furnished it; and Clara went
free. Susy said, "I don't know whether she felt wrong in *her* heart
but I didn't feel right in *my* heart."

It was a fair and honorable view of the case and a specially
acute analysis of it for a child of six to make. There was no way to
convict Clara now, except to put her on the stand again and review
her evidence. There was a doubt as to the fairness of this pro-
cedure, since her former evidence had been accepted and not
challenged at the time. The doubt was examined and canvassed
—then she was given the benefit of it and acquitted; which was
just as well, for in the meantime she had eaten the candy anyway.[59]

LIVY: The children have gone out with Rosa and their governess to
try on their little dark dresses. Susy's is to be dark brown and
Clara's dark blue trimmed with red. . . . I like the way that the
children's teacher begins and I hope she will prove to be just what
we desire—they have begun their reading lessons this morning.
I hope by Spring they will read German as well as they speak it.[60]

SAM: Our little family arrived at Fräulein Dahlweiner's on time—
where the rooms had been engaged for us ten months before. That
was not all of it: we arrived *exactly* on time—on the very day and
by the very train as planned out by Mrs. Clemens ten months
before.[61]

CLARA SPAULDING: You don't know how blessed we are in our Jour-
neyings, and what a rare good time we are having. It seems as if
some one person in the party must be the owner of Aladdin's lamp.
We said, at first, we will stay three months in Heidelberg and
study German, our lamp was rubbed and our plans carried out—
then we said we will travel through Switzerland staying a week
or two in the principal places. This also was carried out. Then we
planned our Italian trip and I think we all feared we would not be
able to accomplish as much as we desired to see, but the trip was
a grand success from first to last, and we even reached Munich on
the very day that we said we wanted to when arranging our trip
two months before—And now that we are here the same good
luck seems to be following us. We wanted teachers for German

and drawing, and Mr. Clemens wanted a room about twenty minutes walk from the house. A friend of Mrs. Warner's whom Livy went to see knew of just the right teacher for the children and her sister who was very nice would be very glad to come to Livy for two hours a day, and when I asked her if she knew any German family who could take care of me for five hours and give me my dinner, she knew just the place for me, and tomorrow I am to begin. Mr. Clemens has secured a room and expects soon to go to work. Our drawing teacher is the same as engaged, and we are all prepared for a hard winter's work.[62]

NARRATOR: Sam had trouble starting work in his new quarters; he couldn't find his Swiss notebook.

SAM: I was about to write to my publisher and propose some other book, when the confounded thing (the note-book) turned up, and down went my heart into my boots. But there was now no excuse, so I went solidly to work, tore up a great part of the MS. written in Heidelberg—wrote and tore up, continued to write and tear up —and at last, reward of patient and noble persistence, my pen got the old swing again! Since then I am glad that Providence knew better what to do with the Swiss note-book than I did.[63]

CLARA SPAULDING: The children are so good and sweet. I feel very matronly with them, for I play so often that I am their mamma— they come to my door so often in the morning and say "Good morning Mamma." I never saw such good little travelers as they are—they so rarely fret, and are so happy and good natured.[64]

SAM: This morning (November 30th) when Bay discovered that this is my birth-day, she was greatly troubled because she had provided no gift for me—repeated her sorrow several times. Finally she went off musing to the nursery and presently returned with her newest and chiefest treasure, a large toy-horse and said, "You shall have this horse for your birth-day, papa." I accepted it with many thanks. After an hour she was racing up and down the room with the horse when Susy said,—

"Why Clara! You gave that horse to papa, and now you've tooken it back again."

Bay.—"I never give it to him for *always;* I give it to him for his *birth-day.*"[65]

I broke the back of life yesterday and started down-hill toward old age. This fact has not produced any effect upon me that I can detect.

I suppose we are located here for the winter. I have a pleasant work-room a mile from here where I do my writing. The walk to and from that place gives me what exercise I need, and all I take. . . . Livy and Miss Spaulding are studying drawing and German, and the children have a German day-governess. I cannot see but that the children speak German as well as they do English.[66]

Susy repeated a little German stanza about the "Vöglein;" I read it from the book, and with deliberation and emphasis, to correct her pronunciation—whereupon, the Bay, in shattered English, corrected *me*. I said I had read it right, and asked Susy if I hadn't. She said:

"Yes, papa, you did—but you read it so *'stinctly* that that 'fused Bay."[67]

Susy often translates Livy's orders to the servants. I cannot work and study German at the same time; so I have dropped the latter, and do not even read the language, except in the morning paper to get the news.

We have all pretty good health, latterly, and have seldom had to call the doctor.—The children have been in the open air pretty constantly for months now.[68]

LIVY: Clara has been brought in to me now for the second time from the nursery she is so full of mischief that Rosa often gets to her wits ends with her. . . . She has the meekest way when she is brought to me, (her Aunt Clara calls her the pious fox) and as she stands before me smiling a deprecatory smile and with her eyes cast down, occasionally looking at me out of the corner of them, I think she is the prettiest most bewitching culprit in the world.[69]

NARRATOR: The Christmas season with all its delightful German manifestations was at hand giving but one direction to the children's thoughts.

SUSY: The reindeer is a very swift animal. One reindeer travelled 400 miles in two hours. This was regarded as extraordinary. When the reindeer was done, he died.

SAM: . . . [Susy's first story] which her governess could not have put into a page. . . . Now this expresses the whole process of thought in literature, the putting of this and that together and drawing a conclusion.[70]

NARRATOR: Sam took dictation from Susy.

SUSY: I really don't know which I shall tell first—One night Rosa said, and everybody said, 'at Santa Claus was coming before

Christmas and let everybody see; Rosa said she was afraid Santa Claus wouldn't come to us, because we wasn't German; Mamma and everybody said 'at they thought Santa Claus wouldn't come; when Mamma sat down to the table, when she was eating her dessert, we heard a knock on the door and Fräulein Dahlweiner came in; after her, Santa Claus. He came in with a cloth bag, and he said, "Nock ein Sack!" (i.e. "Another bag!")—He took a bundle out, and that bundle had candies in it; after, came out two dollies; and then it came out some gold nuts and some apples. And some switches came out. Erhat gesagt, (He said,) "Wenn du nicht brav bist, denn gibt es 'was!" ("When or *if* you ain't good, you'll catch it!") He had a big muffle over his head; he kept covering it up, he didn't like anybody to see his face. I looked into his face, *hard,*— and he laughed, when he went away he said, "Ich hab' viele ünnadige Knaben dass ich in Wasser nein werfen muss . . . und nieder 'naüs nehmen" (I've lots of bad boys whom I've got to throw in the water and pull out again,)—and then he said good-bye, and went. That is all,—of Santa Claus.

NARRATOR: She added a postscript for her cousin, Julie, Charley Langdon's daughter.

SUSY: I want you to tell Julie about Santa Claus. I am glad about Santa Claus, that he *came,* because Julie was always saying there wasn't any Santa Claus or anybody that came that way, and brings children things.[71]

NARRATOR: Their landlady wrote to Charles Dudley Warner.

FRÄULEIN CAROLINE DAHLWEINER: Mrs. Clemens and the family is now more than a mounth in my Pension, and I am truly happy to have it. . . . I thank you hundert tousend times for this reccoman-dation.

We have this year a very cold snowy Winder—Mrs. Clemens sais to me she like Munick very muck. How nice the Children— they have been a little unwell. . . . Mrs. Clemens is very buissee now for Chrismas trees, just came a large one.[72]

SAM: On scores of street corners in the snow are groves of Christmas trees for sale and the toy and other shops are crowded, and driving a tremendous trade. . . .

In the week [Christmas] a prodigious audience of parents and children in the big theater. A curtain hung across the middle of the stage from right to left. In front a lady with a lot of eager children around her on stools. She asks what familiar story from folklore she shall read. They clap their eager hands and name a story. She reads; they applaud, or laugh, or are grieved—all well drilled and natural—and as she finishes the curtain slowly rises and displays in tableau an exquisite picture from the story. The children in the audience get so carried away that they applaud, shout, cry and make comments aloud.[73]

LIVY: It is astounding to see how much they make of Christmas. In sight of our windows there are two places where country women have established themselves with their evergreen trees for Christmas trees—and as we drive along the street every third or fourth corner has from ten to fifty trees all fastened into wooden boards . . . and you can't look out of the window any time during the day without seeing from one to four persons passing with their Christmas trees—they are passing all the time—the poor woman with her very small one that (judging by what I paid for one) probably does not cost her over ten or fifteen cents—all the way up to the rich gentleman who brings his servant, selects one and the servant carries it off on his shoulders—Young boys and girls who have got a little too old for the mystery of it—go and buy theirs themselves and carry them home themselves. *Everybody* here has their Christmas tree, they are to be bought all the way from one foot high up to twenty feet.[74]

SAM: Take it by and large, it was a very happy and abundant sort of Christmas which we had here. Livy gave me a noble great copy of the "Reinicke Fuchs," nearly as big as the Faust, and containing the original Kaulbach illustrations.[75]

Things go on just as usual, so there is nothing important to report. I have written 900 pages of manuscript on my book [*A Tramp Abroad*], therefore it is half done; Livy and Clara Spaulding have learned half of the German language together, so they are half done; the children have learned how to speak German, drink beer and break the Sabbath like the natives, so they are half done. We are all a half-way lot, like the rest of the world; but we are progressing toward the great goal, Completion, Perfection,—which has also another name, the Unattainable. We have been here nine weeks, and according to Livy's plans we remain here nine weeks longer; if it were a perfectly reputable place as to health I would like to stay here six months longer, for it is very pleasant—even the dirt now that we are used to it and don't mind seeing it caked around. It is the greatest country for Art and dirt in the world; they have all kinds of Art and all kinds of dirt; there is more dirt than Art, of course, because the dirt has had the longer start and more people have devoted themselves to learning how to make it and make it right; but Art is coming, Art is progressing here all the time: this very year there is to be a prodigious international Art Exhibition here which will astonish the world—and if they follow it up with a dirt exhibition their fortune is made.[76]

LIVY: Mr. Clemens and I have read almost every evening the [German] lesson for the next day together, we have had a great deal of sport over it.

NARRATOR: Livy heard disturbing news from her mother about George Griffin, their colored butler, being out of work.

LIVY: I am so very sorry for George, Mother, and I wish that you would send us his address—he was faithful to us and the things that tried us in him were his childishnesses which I think he was not responsible for—We expect to take him back, in fact it seems as if the house would not be at all natural without him and I should feel badly to think of his suffering in any way—He was so careful in many ways not to give me trouble, would remain at home when it was his night to go out if he felt that I needed him etc. etc.—

When we came away he said he could get work at the Allyn House or the United States Hotel at any time that he wanted it, he ought now to work there simply for his board if he cannot do better, until we come back. . . .

Write me anything new that you hear of George please Mother dear—One of the great objections to our leaving home was the fact that we in that way threw three people out of work—however we keep some busy here so perhaps it is in a measure balanced.[77]

NARRATOR: Sam wrote Mrs. Langdon.

SAM: It has been snowing with a perfect fury for four hours and a half. During the past hour the customary Sunday noon crowds of people have been thinning out; and now, although I have six streets and a big pleasure-square in sight, there are not 15 people in view. The snow is falling so densely that it makes the trees in the square look spectral. . . .

I've got the airs for my music box selected at last, thanks to goodness,—been 5 months at it. If I ever get the thing home I'll give you some musical chords which you will say are the softest and sweetest you ever heard. The sounds are more suggestive of

the violin or a combination of violins (softly played) than anything else.—I had never seen a box of the sort before. It is to play
10 tunes and cost $400. It is small in size,—comparatively speak-
ing,—but it has virtues of large dimensions.

NARRATOR: Sam had ordered the music box in Geneva.

SAM: We are packing. Our plan is to leave for Paris next Thursday
at 6.40 AM, arriving at Strasburg at 5.30 PM and going on to Paris
the next day. We were in a good deal of a sweat about the plague
for some time, and it still promises to sweep the whole world this
year, but our physician says one need have no present fear about
it.

We send a power of love to you all—and thank goodness it
doesn't have to go through the custom house. They would charge
duty on it, and break it all to pieces in the bargain.[78]

NARRATOR: The children were very proud of their German.

SAM: Susy announced, to-day, that she . . . could read any German
book. "And if I can read German books, I can read German
papers, too, can't I?" She had the "Allgemeine Zeitung" in her
hand, ready to begin. I was obliged to dash her spirits by saying
I didn't believe *any*body could read a German newspaper.

However, if the children are a trifle mistaken as to their ability
to read German, they certainly speak it as well as they do English,
and as glibly and prettily.[79]

LIVY: We expect to leave here a week from this week Thursday
(Feb. 27th) going to Paris where we shall remain until Mr.
Clemens has finished his book. We hope not more than three
months but it may be more than four—He is working very hard
now and it is bad for him to be interrupted but we don't like to
spend the Spring months here. . . .[80]

We left the hotel [in Strasbourg] the next morning at six o'clock,
the children were always so good, never a cry or anything unpleasant although they had to be wakened at such unreasonable
hours.[81]

NARRATOR: They did not like the first Paris hotel and Sam didn't like
Paris. They moved shortly to the Normandy in the rue de l'Échelle.

SAM: Ten squatty, ugly arm-chairs, upholstered in the ugliest and
coarsest conceivable scarlet plush; two hideous sofas of the same—
uncounted armless chairs ditto. Five ornamental chairs, seats covered with a coarse rag, embroidered in flat expanse with a confusion of leaves such as no tree ever bore, six or seven a dirty

white and the rest a faded red. How those hideous chairs do swear at the hideous sofa near them! This is the very hatefulest room I have seen in Europe.

Oh, how *cold* and raw and unwarmable it is!

France has neither winter, nor summer, nor morals. Apart from these drawbacks it is a fine country.[82]

LIVY: Mr. Clemens and I went to call this afternoon [Sunday, March 3rd] on Mr. Millet [the painter], the young lady that he is to marry and her mother and sister—we had a perfectly charming time. I liked the young lady that he is to marry very much indeed and he is just as lovable as ever—his house is so very artistic and his studio was filled with interesting things that he had brought from the East with him . . . it was such an interesting visit—he has been doing such fine work lately—it was altogether a most restful visit—Paris and the world seemed brighter and happier after we came away from there. They are to be married the eleventh of this month—Mr. Clemens is to be one of the witnesses to sign the marriage paper—and then we both go to the wedding breakfast— they sail that same day for England—Mr. Millet takes some of his pictures for exhibition in London, he has a studio and will work there for two months. . . .[83]

Mr. Clemens is to have his studio to work in—so he will get to work again next Wednesday—he will be nearly and I hope, quite through his book in that time.

NARRATOR: They had disturbing news of the business world from home and Livy wrote, "I am sorry that business looks so badly I hope there may be a change for the better."[84] Sam wrote news of the family to his mother-in-law.

SAM: Things go along just the same, mother dear. There is no change. I still catch cold and am pestered with rheumatism, and as a consequence my work lags and drags and mostly stands still. Livy has pains in the back of her neck, and the old ones in her spine, but she keeps up her studies and other activities with spirit. The children have French colds which can't be told from German ones by people ignorant of the language. Rosa has a horrible cold. —Clara Spaulding has the twin to it. She studies hard, and has got into the new language so deeply now that the French can't understand her French and we can't understand her English. But she and Livy will get over this transition stage presently. . . . I must take care of the children, now, as Livy and Clara are out and Rosa has gone to dinner. I will write a letter which Susy proposes to dictate to you.—As follows:

SUSY: I've got a new governess, and we play school with the dollies, and play Schwartzpeter, and read stories, and jump rope, and we sang to her; we sang "Kommt ein Vogel" and "Hänselein willst du tantzen." We went over to a little baby here in the hotel and we played Blind Man's Puff, and played hoop and I knocked myself on the nose.—and then I think we went back in a few minutes. Charles is a little French boy with brass buttons; he rides us up in the lift; and me and Clara was playing ball a minute ago; and Queen Victoria was in Paris day before yesterday, but I didn't see her. I'll say that I'll close the letter, now.[85]

SAM: One day Livy and Clara Spaulding were exclaiming over the odd, queer ways of the Europeans. Susy looked up from her work of doll-dressing and said, "Well, mamma, don't you reckon we seem queer to *them?*"[86]

NARRATOR: The Clemenses had many friends in Paris: Aldrich, Gedney Bunce, the Hjalmar Boyesens, Turgenieff, Richard Whiteing, Edwin A. Abbey, as well as Frank Millet. Sam's sight-seeing was unorthodox; he once went up in a balloon. He did a lot of reading on Joan of Arc and the Reign of Terror and made publishing arrangements with Bernhard Tauchnitz.

SAM: Tauchnitz called the other day—a mighty nice old gentleman. He paid me 425 francs for the Innocents—I think he paid me about 6 or 700 fr. for Tom Sawyer (it being new); he is going to print Roughing It by and by and has engaged advance sheets of my new book. Don't know what he will pay for the two latter—I leave that to him—one can't have the heart to dicker with a publisher who won't steal.[87]

NARRATOR: Paris continued to be cold and dreary.

SAM: The children are well, and as good as they can be, except that Bay will lie,—which is rather a grace than a defect—and besides it makes her conspicuous in a family like this. They speak German glibly—the rest of us can't. You won't ever catch me fooling around any more foreign languages—particularly as I don't intend to wander off to any more foreign lands till after I'm dead. Livy's health is very good, and wood is very high—3 francs a basket— plain, ungilded firewood—five dollars a day is what it costs us— and when I first saw the bill here I thought it was for carved furniture, but no,—sir, it was for firewood, and glad I am we

didn't arrive here when it was cold weather.—Livy sends a world
of love to you ["Mother" Fairbanks] and all sorts of affectionate
remembrances and to think that the basket only holds 6 sticks, too,
and at 3 francs the basket that makes it ½ a franc the stick, and no
ornamentation at all on it but just plain ordinary wood such as we
get from Charley Warner's wood-pile nights at home for absolutely nothing; and she wishes you were here, so she could show
you how much French and German she and Clara have still to
learn, and I'll be hanged if I don't honestly believe that if we had
been here in the January cold snap we should have had to turn our
entire income into wood and then eat the ashes, for at 3 francs a
basket you see yourself how it would mount up, and how soon a
person would bust or freeze if he did not turn the thermometer the
other way.[88]

We burn fires—I am miserably tired of it. But the children are
booming—the climate suits them exactly.[89]

SUSY'S EIGHTH YEAR

1879–1880

NARRATOR: By the time Susy's birthday came around in March, the
family had settled down into a daily, Parisian routine: lessons for
the children, lessons and sight-seeing for Livy and Clara and work
for Sam. As usual, there were many visitors, but Sam found time
every day to play with the children and watch them grow up. He
cherished every word they said and delighted in recalling anecdotes about them.

SAM: [Susy] was a magazine of feelings, and they were of all kinds
and of all shades of force; and she was so volatile, as a little child,
that sometimes the whole battery came into play in the short
compass of a day. She was full of life, full of activity, full of fire,
her waking hours were a crowding and hurrying procession of
enthusiasms, with each one in its turn differing from the others in
origin, subject and aspect. Joy, sorrow, anger, remorse, storm, sunshine, rain, darkness—they were all there: they came in a moment,
and were gone as quickly. Her approval was passionate, her dis-
approval the same, and both were prompt. Her affections were
strong, and toward some her love was of the nature of worship.
Especially was this her attitude toward her mother.[1]

We found that Susy had about ceased from praying. The matter
was inquired into. She answered, with simplicity: "I hardly ever
pray, now; when I want anything, I just leave it to Him—He
understands."

The words, without her voice and manner, do not convey her
meaning. What she meant, was, that she had thought the thing all

out, and arrived at the conclusion that there was no obstructing vagueness or confusion between herself and God requiring her to explain herself in set words;—when she felt a want, He knew it without its being formulated, and could be trusted to grant or wisely withhold as should be best for both parties; and she was conscious of the impropriety and the needlessness of bothering Him with every little craving that came into her head.[2]

[She] was shy of crowds of strangers, and hung back in the shelter of the party whenever we arrived at a new town and its big inn; but Bay always marched far in the lead and alone, and tramped up the steps and invaded those hotels with the air of a proprietor taking possession.—Bay is not without a certain degree of pride in her fortitude.[3]

LIVY: Susy grows sweet and womanly all the time and Clara is the same rowdy as ever—sweet tempered, but very hard to make any impression on.[4]

SAM: In Paris, when my day's writing, on the 6th floor, was done, I used to slip quietly into our parlor on the 2nd floor, hoping to have a rest and a smoke on the sofa before dinner was brought up; but I seldom succeeded, because the nursery opened into the parlor, and the children were pretty sure to come in for something and discover me—then I would have to take a big chair, place a child on each arm of it, and spin them a story.

Whenever Bay discovered me she always called out (without any preliminary by-your-leave) "Susy, *Come!*—going to have a story!" Without any remark to me she would go and get a magazine, perch herself on the chair-arm, seek out a suggestive picture, (Susy taking perch on the other arm, meantime), then say, "We're ready, papa."

The tough part of it was, that every detail of the story had to be brand-new—invented on the spot—and it must *fit the picture*. They wouldn't have the story that already belonged to the picture, nor any part of it, nor even any idea that was in it; they were quick to discover when I was borrowing a suggestion from the book, and then they would immediately shut down on that irregularity. Sometimes they would take such a strong fancy to one particular picture that I would have to build an entirely new story upon that picture several evenings in succession. Their selections were pretty odd, too sometimes. For instance, in the back part of a "Scribner's Monthly" they once found an outline figure which

Page the artist had drawn to show the just proportions of the human frame. . . . The chances of getting anything romantic, adventurous and heroic out of so sterile a text as that, seemed so remote, that I tried to divert them to a more promising picture; but no, none but this one would answer. So I bent myself to my task; and made such a thrilling and rattling success of it that I was rewarded with the privilege of digging a brand-new story out of that barren text during the next *five ensuing evenings*. I wore that poor outline devil's romantic-possibilities entirely out before I got done with him. I drowned him, I hanged him, I pitted him against giants and genii, I adventured him all through fairy-land, I made him the sport of fiery dragons of the air and the pitiless monsters of field and flood, I fed him to the cannibals. The cross-bars which intersected him were the iron gratings of a dungeon in one story, the web of a gigantic spider in another, the parallels of latitude and meridians of longitude webbing a vast and helpless denizen of the wandering comets—and so on; for it was rigidly required of me that those cross-bars be made to play a big and essential role in every yarn.

In all my inventions for the children . . . I have always had one formidable difficulty to contend with—any villains *must not lie*. This hampered me a good deal. The blacker and bloodier and viler I painted the villain of my tale, the more the children delighted in him, until he made the mistake of telling a lie—then down he went, in their estimation. Nothing could resurrect him again; he simply had to pack up and go; his character was damaged beyond help, the children wouldn't have him around, any longer.

Sometimes I tried to cover up, or slide over, or explain away, one of these lies which I had blundered into, but this was lost time, for Susy is an alert critic. I was calmly proceeding, one evening: "But the moment the giant invited him, the grasshopper whispered in Johnny's ear that the food was poisoned; so Johnny said, very politely, "I am very much obliged to you indeed, sir, but I am not hungry—." "Why *papa!* he told a *lie!*" (Confound that blunder! I said to myself—I must try to get Johnny out of this scrape.) "Well, you see, Susy, I reckon he didn't think what he was saying, and—." "But papa, it couldn't *be*—because he had just said, that very minute, that he was *so* hungry!" "Yes, that is true—yes, that *is* so—well, I think perhaps he was heedless, and just came out with the first thing that happened in his mind, and—." "O, no, papa, he wasn't ever a heedless boy; it wasn't like him to be heedless; you know how wise he always was—why night before last, you remember"—(this was a *continued* story, which lasted over a week)—"when all those fairies and enchanted creatures tried their very best, a whole day, to catch him in some little carelessness so they could get power over him, they never *could*—no, as long as this story has gone on, papa, there never was such a wise boy before—he *couldn't* be heedless, papa." "Well, Susy, I reckon he was so weary, so kind of tired out—." "Why papa, he *rode* all the way, on the eagle, and he had been sound asleep all the whole day in the gold and ivory bed, with his two lions watching him and taking care of him—Why how *could* he be tired, papa, and be so strong?—You know the other night when his whale took him to Africa he went ashore and walked all day and all night, and wasn't a bit tired—and you know that other time when—." "Yes, yes, you are right, Susy, and I was wrong; he couldn't have been tired—but he never intended any wrong; I'm sure he didn't mean what he said; for—." "Then it *was* a lie, papa! if he didn't mean what he said."

Johnny's days of usefulness were over; he was up a stump, and I had to leave him there. The children are good listeners, generally; they do not interrupt—to criticise—until somebody lies. Then the interruptions come thick and fast.—They will put up with all inconsistencies in my people cheerfully but that solitary *one;*—that even the blackest scoundrel should lie, is out of character, inconsistent, inexcusable; and the children are bound to call him to the strictest account every time.

They did not get this prejudice from me.[5]

NARRATOR: Livy took dictation.

SUSY: Today I have been in the Champs Elysee. We rid in the four white goats' wagon. We saw up there some ships up in the air and people in them that went up and down—Then once we went with Mr. Bunce in a garden, and I went in a ship over the water and first we saw some lions and bears but not very big lions—and pretty soon we saw a polar bear and we'd throw bread down and he'd open his mouth and catch it—and we saw some storks alive storks—and something like storks with long legs and something pink I think they came from Egypt—and we saw some turkeys one a beautiful white one with his tail spread out. Oh I meant peacocks and I said turkeys—We saw some big white things I think they were donkeys and we saw some black bears—then we saw some kind of pigs not the other kind of pigs but I think they called them wild pigs—and there were three elephants but we didn't see those—and got caught in the rain storm and we staid in a little house and Rosa wondered when we would get out—Mr. Bunce went for a carriage and pretty soon it got pleasanter. . . .

And the children jump rope and play hoop out there in the Champs Elysee and the Tuileries both.—Some little children in Tuileries garden that were jumping rope asked me to jump rope with them, but Mamma didn't allow me to jump rope because I had colds and I'd get heated—but we couldn't understand the children and the children couldn't understand us and they teased and teased for us to do it and asked Rosa if we could do it but Rosa said "no"—and I think the children thought that Rosa didn't like us to be with the children and so they took me in the rope and swinged the rope over but I wouldn't jump—so I went to Rosa and asked her what I should do—and Rosa asked an English nurse to tell them that my mamma doesn't want me to—and that's all about those children—And our teacher when we're good all the week gives us a picture and now I must shut my letter.[6]

SAM: I wish this eternal winter would come to an end. Snow-flakes fell today [May 7th], and also about a week ago. Have had rain almost without intermission for two months and one week. Have had a fire every day since September 10 and have now just lighted one.[7]

LIVY: I shall be glad when the time comes to leave Paris and how I should hate to bring up the children here—I am afraid it would take more strength of mind than I possess to draw the line where it ought to be drawn—I am glad we live in Hartford. . . .

Susy said something that showed her wisdom, this morning. I said to her, "Susy why *don't* you speak German to me all the time," she said, "Well Mamma, I don't always know what to do. I think when you have company you wouldn't like to have me speak German to you"—I thought that showed a fine instinct, she felt undoubtedly that there would be something like showing off in speaking German before those who were speaking English— Of course I encouraged the sentiment—

Our French teacher was broken hearted over the death of Prince Louis Napoleon, it was *very* touching to hear her talk about him, tell about the things he used to do here in Paris when he was a little bit of a boy—I said, "Oh I should think all Paris would mourn for him"—She said, "Well, if you think that, you don't know the French people, they are the most cultivated and at the same time the most barbarous people on the face of the earth—they have no gratitude toward their monarchs. . . ."

Miss Mary Dunham stopped here with us for two days on her way to Switzerland where she was to join her cousins. . . . It was so delightful to have a visit with her it was like a bit of Hartford —She is so lovely. . . .

We hope now to go away from here week after next if the illustrations are finished for the book. . . .

I hope to teach the children myself next Winter—I have had such a long play time that I ought to be ready and able to do some good work. . . .

I have today a great longing to get back to my settled ways, there seems no good bottom here—every thing seems sandy and uncertain.[8]

We live in such a perfect whirl of people these days, that it seems utterly impossible to do anything, I wish that I had put down the names of the people that have been here for the last two months, but I think every day, well, this will be the last, we shan't have as many again.[9]

NARRATOR: They were all looking forward to leaving Paris, whose spring had proved to be an unusually dismal one. They were going to Belgium, Holland and England, but Livy, mentally, was planning life in Hartford. Mrs. Langdon wrote offering a thousand dollars for spending abroad.

LIVY: I think that you are the very best Mother in the world, how could you offer me that thousand dollars! . . .

We have no need of it now Mother. I do hate to settle our house without decorating it—the white walls are not pleasant and it seems as if now, when it is all torn up, was such a good time to finish the inside.

I don't think I shall do anything in England except try to get some ideas, for I am afraid it might greatly increase the expense to carry home things (paper etc.) and have duty to pay—So when we get home we will talk it over and, if it then seems best to decorate it and you feel at that time that you have a thousand dollars that you desire to part with, I think a thousand dollars would do all to the house that we should care to have done—and I should be very glad to accept it—although I feel like a pig, mother, to contemplate accepting it at all—you are so more than generous to us, so lavish with us in every way. We do appreciate it and thank you so much for it.[10]

I have still over three hundred dollars left, part of that is the Christmas money—I am going to get some stained glass with that when we get to London—Mr. Clemens suggested that I reserve it to pay the duties with, now wasn't that like a man? . . .

We are taking particular comfort now because Mr. Clemens is not going to work any more until he gets home, and it is so nice to feel that he is at leisure. . . .

Mother dear you will have to spend next Christmas with us, won't you? I should like it so much if the whole family would spend it with us—Charlie and Ida—Sue and Theodore and the children—What a gay time we would have—you and Ida and Sue talk it over.[11]

NARRATOR: They left Paris on July 10th for Brussels, which Sam termed "a dirty, beautiful (architecturally), interesting town."[12] They went to Antwerp.

SAM: . . . went on board flagship Trenton, dined that evening [July 13th] with Consul Stewart and some officers of the Trenton and the Alliance. Took the family and breakfasted on board the Trenton, Monday, 14th. Admiral Rowan arrived during the meal. I smoked on the Admiral's side of the deck, not knowing it was sacred, by naval etiquette.[13]

LIVY: What a trip we have had through Belgium and Holland. . . .

At Haarlem . . . took a carriage and drove out to see a Dutch farm; and what an astounding sight it was, we went first into the dairy part of the farm and the dairy woman showed us about. . . . While we were looking about there, the eldest daughter from the great house came down to the dairy house—She was a wholesome hearty girl of fifteen. She rolled the children on the hay, talked German with them, English with us, Dutch with the dairy woman and also spoke French and a little Italian—then she took us and showed us her horse, the animals on the place, peacocks, pheasants, rabbits, doves—chickens and goats and some creatures which I did not know . . . we were taken out into the field to see the great handsome cows—then into the beautiful woods near the great house . . . then into the house to speak with her father and mother—this we hesitated about doing, but she insisted and she was one of the girls that it seems impossible to refuse—so bright and hearty and enthusiastic—When we went to get into the carriage, her two younger sisters went with her and us—one ten and one three years old—to see us off. . . .

We enjoyed some of the pictures at the Hague very much— when I went to get photographs of some of those that I particularly admired, I found a beautiful etching of one of the pictures . . . and no photograph that gave the least idea of the picture. . . . The etching was very expensive, twenty dollars, but I decided if Mr. Clemens liked it that we would get it. . . . Mr. Clemens went to see it and liked it, so we possess the etching—it is an etching of Rembrandt's Night Watch. . . .

Susy has little arithmetic lessons with buttons, adding and subtracting with the buttons etc.—yesterday I said to her "Susy, next Winter we will study arithmetic together"—She said "Oh Mamma I know arithmetic, I have learned all the buttons"—She is an old thoughtful little thing as compared with Clara, who is as sweet as possible but seems to have no mind.

NARRATOR: They arrived in London July 20th.

LIVY: We reached here this morning having crossed the Channel in the night—We had a comfortable passage, very smooth sea, none of us were sea sick, but crossing the Channel is not pleasant at the best—The children slept and today Clara seems as bright as ever, but Susy looks somewhat worn—

Our courier proved to be *perfect,* we had no care whatever, he managed everything so splendidly—We have wished during all those days that we had had him last Fall we should have had so much more pleasure in our Switzerland and Italian trip. . . .

We find ourselves so *very comfortably* housed here, "The Brunswick House Hotel," Hanover Square.[14]

NARRATOR: London was a round of brilliant affairs; they spent a week with Reginald Cholmondeley at "Condover," and Sam talked with Darwin. They saw something of Henry James.

LIVY: Clara went in to dinner with Mr. Henry James; she enjoyed him very much. I had a little chat with him before dinner, and he was exceedingly pleasant and easy to talk with. I had expected just the reverse, thinking one would feel looked over by him and criticized. Mr. Whistler, the artist, was at the dinner, but he did not attract me.[15]

NARRATOR: They spent the night of August 21st at the Washington Hotel in Liverpool and sailed on the *S.S. Gallia* the next day. Sam wrote Dr. Brown on shipboard.

SAM: During all the 15 months we have been spending on the continent, we have been promising ourselves a sight of you as our latest and most prized delight in a foreign land—but our hope has failed, our plan has miscarried. One obstruction after another intruded itself, and our short sojourn of three or four weeks on English soil was thus frittered gradually away, and we were at last obliged to give up the idea of seeing you at all. It is a great disappointment, for we wanted to show you how much "Megalopis" has grown (she is 7 now) and what a fine creature her sister is, and how prettily they both speak German.[16]

NARRATOR: The children had a gay time on the ship.

SAM: She [Susy] made a failure . . . when she was at sea on a voyage —age 7½. . . . A group of ladies and gentlemen began to question her as to her relationships, and one lady who felt herself on the track of a relationship with Mrs. Clemens's mother, asked Susy what her grandmama's name was before she was married—which brought out this grave slander, uttered with tranquil simplicity— "My grandmama has never been married."[17]

NARRATOR: Charley Langdon came from Elmira to cope with the trunks. The Hartford *Courant* reported on their arrival.

HARTFORD COURANT: The only thing about Mark Twain that seems natural is his drawl. That is as nasal and as deliberate as ever. His hat, as he stood on the deck of the incoming Cunarder Gallia, yesterday [September 2nd], was of the pattern that English army officers wear in India, and his suit of clothes was such as a merchant wears in his store. He looks older than when he went to Germany, and his hair has turned quite gray.

His wife returned with him, and his brother-in-law came on board at Quarantine. "So," as Mark Twain said, "I shall le—t hi—m ta—ke ca—re of my lug—gage and fi—ght it ou—t with the cus—tom house offic—ers." . . .

Mr. Clemens had twenty-two freight packages and twelve trunks weighing on his mind, and he went away to get his brother-in-law to look after them. He goes to Elmira to-day to spend the remainder of the season and to finish his new book.[18]

CUSTOM'S INSPECTOR: "Oh, chalk his baggage, of course! Don't you know it's Mark Twain and that he'll talk all night?"[19]

SUE CRANE: They arrived here September 3, 1879. On September 10, both Mr. and Mrs. C. went to Fredonia, leaving the children at the farm.[20]

NARRATOR: Sue Crane's memory must have erred for Sam wrote his mother:

SAM: We had a charming visit with you—Susy wants to go back and "stay forever."[21]

We have been to Fredonia; we have finished our visit here in the valley with Mother Langdon; to-day we depart with bag and baggage to the serene hill-top. Consequently this is a busy day. Livy is viewing designs and instructing an artist who is making ready to fresco the Hartford house, Rosa is packing trunks, and I am bracing myself for the serious work of answering some thirty letters. During some hours, now, I shall be steadily declining—I always decline, and keep on declining, on these correspondence-clearing occasions.

I have to decline to lecture; and to furnish autographic "sentiments;" and to write articles for periodicals; and to read and give a "candid opinion" upon manuscripts submitted by strangers—and so on, and so on. This goes on, week in and week out, and is almighty irksome and monotonous. I went to Europe mainly to get rid of my inane, brain-softening letter-answering.[22]

NARRATOR: Sam usually singled out letters from children and from English admirers for special treatment. His interest in his own children absorbed him more and more as they began to emerge from the nursery.

SAM: When Susy was six months along in her eighth year, she did something one day in the presence of company which subjected her to criticism and reproof. Afterward, when she was alone with her mother, as was her custom she reflected a little while over the matter. Then she set up what I think—and what the shade of Burns would think—was a quite good philosophical defense: "Well, mamma, you know I didn't see myself and so I couldn't know how it looked."

In homes where the near friends and visitors are mainly literary people—lawyers, judges, professors and clergymen—the children's ears become early familiarized with wide vocabularies. It is natural for them to pick up any words that fall in their way; it is natural for them to pick up big and little ones indiscriminately; it is natural for them to use without fear any word that comes to their net, no matter how formidable it may be as to size. As a result, their talk is a curious and funny musketry-clatter of little words, interrupted at intervals by the heavy-artillery crash of a word of such imposing sound and size that it seems to shake the ground and rattle the windows. Sometimes the child gets a wrong idea of a word which it has picked up by chance and attaches to it a meaning which impairs its usefulness—but this does not happen as often as one might expect it would. Indeed, it happens with an infrequency which may be regarded as remarkable. As a child, Susy had good fortune with her large words and she employed many of them. She made no more than her fair share of mistakes. Once when she thought something very funny was going to happen (but it didn't) she was racked and torn with laughter, by anticipation. But apparently she still felt sure of her position, for she said, "If it had happened I should have been transformed (transported) with glee."[23]

Bay is a sturdy little character . . . precious little sentiment, no nonsense. She is sensitive, and can be deeply hurt; I think she must have been five years old before we discovered this fact—at least before we realized it. This, I think, was because she had the power of concealing all but the big hurts: a power born of her high pluck and fortitude. Pluck and fortitude have been marked features of her character from the beginning; they were born in her—they had to be educated into Susy, who has them, now, in a pretty considerable degree but was born destitute of them. When Bay used to toddle out to feed the fowls, they would swarm around her, and all over her, a greedy, struggling horde, and trip her up or buffet her down—which she enjoyed—but Susy used to fly.[24]

Under mamma's teachings and Bay's example, Susy is making most gratifying progress. Last week she allowed a tooth to be pulled, and was as steady and tranquil about it as any grown person could have been; yet the forceps slipped off it three or four times before the doctor achieved success. . . .

Both of the children are sweet, gentle, humane, tractable, and lovable creatures, with sharply marked and differing characters. Susy is intellectual, a deep thinker, is analytical, and a reasoner —is a philosopher, too. We had always looked upon Bay as a mere and dear little animal; but lately we are beginning to suspect that she has a mind, and that she is deep, and thinks out problems, in privacy and keeps the results to herself. We shall see, by and by. These children are selfish and hightempered, naturally—but they have been so long and so diligently taught to keep these two gifts under the governance of a taut rein, that they do not show out very frequently.[25]

SUE CRANE: October 10th of '79 they started for Hartford, to take up the busy life.[26]

SAM: Nine months of the year were spent in the house which we built in Hartford, Connecticut.[27]

CLARA: When I first became aware of things, a street car drawn by one horse passed our house on the large avenue bounding our private drive. The horse was too tired and the car too small to make much noise, and so we seemed to live in the arms of nature during the lovely New England winters.[28]

HELEN POST CHAPMAN: We usually bought tickets by way of saving a fare, red at three cents a ride for school children and yellow at seven cents a ride for grown ups. These tickets were collected from the box and used over and over again until they were too soiled and worn to handle.

In the winter these cars were heated by a stove in one end and made warmer by straw on the floor. When there was snow they were replaced by conveyances on runners. One resembled an old Fifth Avenue omnibus, the others looked like Noah's Ark on runners.[29]

LIVY: We are all well, the children have slight colds in their heads but they are not at all sick with them—they are happy to be at home and think everything is so nice—The other night Susy gave me quite a reproof—I said to Mr. Clemens "I am low," he turned to Susy and said "Susy why do you let Mamma get low?" She said "Mamma I don't see how you can be low now you have come back to your beautiful home."

NARRATOR: Unpacking the European purchases and settling the household exhausted Livy, who was pregnant. They gave up the plan to redecorate the house that fall.

LIVY: I am getting on very well indeed, but . . . I don't believe you [Mrs. Langdon] know what it is to get a house going that has stood empty for eighteen months. . . . *Everything, everywhere* in confusion—I have felt a good many times during these days that if it were not for the children I would give up housekeeping —but when I remember the sense of being taken care of which I had . . . I feel that I must give the same sense to the children

—What an intense love of home I always had as a young lady—
now surely I ought to be able to do for my children what you
did for me.[30]

NARRATOR: The Hartford social season was in full swing; Mrs.
Samuel Colt gave a large party the latter part of November.

LIVY: We had a pleasant time at Mrs. Colt's. I enjoyed it and Mr.
Clemens enjoyed it *exceedingly*—it was nice to see him so enthusiastic . . . instead of a thousand invitations there were nearer
fifteen hundred and . . . it was estimated that there were nine
hundred present—there were a good many guests from New
York, Boston, Philadelphia, Newport and of course neighboring
cities like New Haven etc.—There was not the least sense of
crowd except about the drawing room doors where the singing
quadrille was being danced—Sixteen young ladies and gentlemen
dressed in fancy costume, with powdered hair formed two quad-
rilles dancing to their own singing which was the Mother Goose
melodies—"Where are you going to my pretty maid," "How does
my lady's garden grow," "Bo-Peep," "Sing a Song of Sixpence,"
"Little Mary quite Contrary" etc. etc.—it was exceedingly pretty
to see them.[31]

NARRATOR: Livy started lessons with the children in Sam's old
study, now called the schoolroom.

LIVY: It has been a rainy day [December 8th] here, this morning
I taught the children for nearly two hours, perhaps it lacked a
few minutes of two hours—They are so delightful to teach for
they enjoy it so very much, it is the pleasantest work I do—
When I get in from the kitchen they have the chairs all ready
and are eager to begin—their only anxiety during the lesson is
lest it shall be too short—First we have a reading lesson in
German—3 or 4 pages of the German reader then Geography—
a short lesson in that, then mental arithmetic, then they make
numbers in their copy books . . . in the middle of the lessons
somewhere we have bean bags or gymnastics, and one day they
. . . sewed a little—I do enjoy my forenoons with them so very
much.[32]

Susy learns her lessons very nicely—they are good children
and I do take much comfort with them this Winter.

NARRATOR: She did not "take comfort" in everything she felt called
upon to be and do.

LIVY: I told Mr. Clemens the other day, that in this day women

must be everything, they must keep up with all the current literature, they must know all about art, they must help in one or two
benevolent societies—they must be perfect mothers—they must
be perfect housekeepers and graceful, gracious hostesses, they
must know how to give perfect dinners, they must go and visit
all the people in the town where they live, they must always be
ready to receive their acquaintances—they must dress themselves
and their children becomingly and above all they must make their
houses *"charming"* and so on without end—then if they are not
studying something their case is a hopeless one.[33]

NARRATOR: Sam resumed his billiard evenings.

LILLY WARNER: I had the nicest evening with Livy—Saturday—
the last half with her alone, as it was Billiard evening, except for
a call from the Woods, people I like. How lovely their house is
now.[34]

NARRATOR: There were games in the library, too.

SAM: We were diligent in the chase, and the library was the hunt-
ing-ground—"jungle," by fiction of fancy—and there we hunted
the tiger and the lion. I was the elephant, and bore Susy or Clara
on my back—and sometimes both—and they carried the guns
and shot the game. George, the colored ex-slave, was with us then,
first and last he was in our service 18 years, and was as good as
he was black—servant in the matter of work, member of the
family in the closer ties and larger enthusiasms of play. He was
the lion—also the tiger; but preferably tiger, because as lion
his roaring was over-robust, and embarrassed the hunt by scaring
Susy.

He was handsome, well built, shrewd, wise, polite, always good-
natured, cheerful to gaiety, honest, religious, a cautious truth-
speaker, devoted friend to the family, champion of its interests,
a sort of idol to the children and a trial to Mrs. Clemens—not in
all ways but in several. For he was as serenely and dispassionately
slow about his work as he was thorough in parts of it; he was
phenomenally forgetful; he would postpone work any time to join
the children in their play if invited, and he was always being
invited, for he was very strong, and always ready for service as
horse, camel, elephant or any other kind of transportation required; he was fond of talking, and always willing to do it in
the intervals of work—also willing to create the intervals; and
finally, if a lie could be useful to Mrs. Clemens he would tell it.

That was his worst fault, and of it he could not be cured. He placidly and courteously disposed of objections with the remark— "Why, Mrs. Clemens, if I was to stop lying you couldn't keep house a week."[35]

NARRATOR: *A Tramp Abroad* was almost finished.

SAM: I am revising my MS. I did not expect to like it, but I do. I have been knocking out early chapters for more than a year now, not because they had not merit, but merely because they hindered the flow of the narrative; it was a dredging process. Day before yesterday my shovel fetched up three more chapters and laid them, reeking, on the festering shore-pile of their predecessors, and now I think the yarn swims right along, without hitch or halt. I believe it will be a readable book of travels. I cannot see that it lacks anything but information.[36]

NARRATOR: Susy and Clara were often tempted to stray from Livy's admonitions, but when Sam suggested some "dazzling enterprise," Susy would say, "But papa, you know mamma does not allow us to do that."

SAM: One day a neighbor of ours whose children never obey her except when it suits them, begged Susy and Bay to come in and see her (they were in her grounds.) They declined, and said mamma had told them (at some time or other) not to go into a house without her permission—thus intimating their knowledge that although the command had not lately been repeated, it was still in force and must be respected until it was distinctly abrogated. This ought to have compelled this lady's admiration; on the contrary she heedlessly set herself to work to *persuade* the children to come in, against their consciences—saying *she* would take all the responsibility, etc., and at last won their reluctant acquiescence; she took all this trouble to undermine a foundation of obedience which had been laid at such protracted and painstaking cost. I never can think of this outrage and keep my temper. However, at the end of two minutes she found that the children were so full of doubts and misgivings and so ill at ease that they were far from enjoying themselves—so she let them go. This lady is one of the noblest and loveliest spirits in the land, but she is no more fitted to govern children than she is to govern the Indians.[37]

NARRATOR: Visitors from all parts of the world continued to pour into Hartford.

HENRY DRUMMOND: I had a delightful day at Hartford. . . . Called on Mark Twain, Mrs. Harriet Beecher Stowe, and the widow of Horace Bushnell. I was wishing A——— had been at the Mark Twain interview. He is funnier than any of his books, and to my surprise a most respected citizen, devoted to things esthetic, and the friend of the poor and struggling.[38]

NARRATOR: Sam wrote his mother early in January.

SAM: I have been so busy I could not well write, and Livy has been too sick to write. We are very sorry to hear you have been suffering so. We supposed you were much better. I would have written long ago if I had not supposed you were getting along well. I have been buried in my book all this time, doing my best to get it done, and meantime Livy has been running down and getting weak, in consequence of overwork in re-arranging the house. . . .

We got the things safely that came from Fredonia, and they happened to be just the articles the children were longing for.[39]

Am waiting for Patrick to come with the carriage. Mrs. Clemens and I are starting (without the children) to stay indefinitely in Elmira. The wear and tear of settling the house broke her down, and she has been growing weaker and weaker for a fortnight. All that time . . . I have been fighting a life-and-death battle with this infernal book and *hoping* to get done some day. I required 300 pages of MS, and I have written near 600 since I saw you [Howells]—and tore it all up except 288. This I was about to tear up yesterday and begin again when Mrs. [Mary Beecher] Perkins came up to the billiard room and said, "You will never get any woman to do the thing necessary to save her life by mere *persuasion*; you see you have wasted your words for three weeks; it is time to use *force*; she *must* have a change; take her home and leave the children here."

I said, "If there is one death that is painfuller than another, may I get it if I don't do that thing."[40]

SUSY'S NINTH YEAR

1880–1881

NARRATOR: *A Tramp Abroad* was published six days before Susy's birthday. The spring was a pleasant one, and they all continued to enjoy the European purchases.

CLARA: One of the early miracles in my life was a huge music-box Father bought. . . . Could such a thing really be true? A great brown case of polished wood that resembled a coffin, and out of it floated the most enthralling melodies and harmonies. . . . The "Pilgrim's Chorus" from "Tannhäuser" and the "Lohengrin Wedding March" were our favorites. Well do I remember Father's delight over the joyful amazement expressed by us all.

We were pleased when our parents made a trip to New York, because they usually returned with an acquisition to the home that some one could enjoy. We had a pair of very large black horses, and the instant we heard the tramp of their feet on the hard road leading to our house from the street, we rushed to the window and watched the approach of the victoria, lit up by sidelights, for it was generally early evening when our parents returned.

The servants in the kitchen also heard the patter of feet, and George would arrive, hastily putting on his coat. . . .

Sometimes, on evenings when Father and Mother returned from New York and the weather was bitterly cold, George served supper for them on a small table in front of the fire in the library. . . . Once Father drew from his pocket two little silver watches, one for my elder sister, Susy, and one for me. Susy poured out streams of words expressing her delight, but I stood dumb, staring at my father. Such a chill of rapture rushed down my spine that I could not speak. Finally he said, addressing me by a pet name he often used:

"Well, Bay, are you disappointed?"

"Oh no! but it is too beautiful!"

"It won't be in a few days," he answered, with twinkling eyes.

As a matter of fact, though, I never broke or even bruised that watch.[1]

NARRATOR: The children received another gift in March.

LIVY: George brought them today a beautiful great maltese cat, about a year old that his wife raised—it is a splendid creature and is getting wonted already.[2]

NARRATOR: Sam reported on feline activities to Howells.

SAM: Last night, when I went to bed, Mrs. Clemens said, "George didn't take the cat down to the cellar—Rosa says he has left it shut up in the conservatory." So I went down to attend to Abner (the cat.) About 3 in the morning Mrs. C. woke me and said, "I do believe I hear that cat in the drawing-room—what did you do with him?" I answered up with the (satisfaction) confidence of a man who has managed to do the right thing for once, and said, "I opened the conservatory doors, took the library off the alarm, and spread everything open, so that there wasn't any obstruction between him and the cellar." Language wasn't capable of conveying this woman's disgust. But the sense of what she said, was, "He couldn't have done any harm in the conservatory—so you must go and make the entire house free to him and the burglars, imagining that he will prefer the coal-bins to the drawing-room. If you had had Mr. Howells to help you, I should have admired but not been astonished, because I should know that *together* you would be equal to it; but how you managed to contrive such a stately blunder all by yourself, is what I cannot understand."

So, you see, even *she* knows how to appreciate our gifts.[3]

NARRATOR: George and Abner put on an entertainment for Susy and Clara.

SAM: [George] had a mysterious influence over animals—so the children believed. He conferred a human intelligence upon Abner the tom cat—so he made *them* believe. He told them he had instructed Abner that four pressures of the button was his ring, and he said Abner would obey that call. The children marveled, and wanted it tried. George went to the kitchen to set the door open, so that Abner could enter the dining room; then we rang for him, and sure enough he appeared. The children were lost in astonishment at Abner's promptness and willingness, for they had not noticed that there was something about the humping plunge of his entrance that was suggestive of assistance from behind. Then they wondered how he could tell his ring from the other rings— could he count? Probably. We could try experiments and draw conclusions. Abner was removed. Two pressures brought no Abner, it brought Rosa; three brought some one else; five got no response, there being no such ring in the list; then, under great excitement No. 4 was tried once more, and once more Abner plunged in with his suspicious humping impulse. That settled it; Abner could count, and George was the magician that had expanded his intelligence.[4]

NARRATOR: Lessons continued.

LIVY: The children are so good and well and happy—we have such happy times at our lessons every day.... If we get through with the lessons before half past twelve I read to them. We have just finished the first one of the Franconia stories and are nearly half through "Alice in Wonderland."[5]

NARRATOR: In May, Hartford society was preparing for a week-long Grand Bazaar to be held the first week in June ... for the benefit of the Union for Home Work. Sam had prevailed upon Mrs. Thomas K. Beecher to contribute some of her entertaining figures made from roots of trees and shrubs collected in the Chemung County hills at Elmira. When the "Jabberwocks," as he called them, arrived in Hartford, he lined them up, much to the children's delight, on the piano in the drawing room. He relayed his own delight to Mrs. Beecher.

SAM: I have arranged your Jabberwocks and other devils in procession according to number and rank on the piano in the drawing-room, and in that subdued light they take to themselves added atrocities of form and expression, and so make a body's flesh crawl with pleasure. There is a compulsory fascination about them which has drawn me in there every half hour all day; every time I go they look more intelligent, more alive, more suggestive of a convention of Consciences met together to play roots on their poor human proprietors; (see my late Atlantic article.) If I come down at midnight (with my usual dose of hot-Scotch stowed) I shall very easily be able to imagine I see them climbing about the furniture, bearing their rigid tails on high and inspecting everything with their critical brass eyes. I tell you they are different creatures now from what they were this morning. Then, they were desiccated vague imitations of the familiar works of God, and soulless; *now*, they are real creatures out of Wonderland, secretly alive, natural, proper, and ungrotesque to eyes used to them in the world they came from—and so they take the fiction all out of the Jabberwock and I recognize and accept him as a fact.

You have had a genuine inspiration; you have wrought it out, not lamely, but to perfection. It is the most ingenious thing of this generation. I shall hate to see any of these enchanting monsters go out of the house; they grow so in grotesque grace, hour by hour; and the more of them there are in a group the happier is the effect. Make more—don't leave a root unutilized in Chemung County. But don't go to the last limit—that is, don't breathe actual life into them; for I know (if there is anything in physiognomy and general personal appearance), that they would all vote the Democratic ticket, every devil of them. . . .

These things shan't be fooled away at this fair; they've got to be sold at auction, and I mean to be the auctioneer.[6]

NARRATOR: Sam did serve as auctioneer the last night of the fair.

HARTFORD COURANT: Mr. George G. Sill acted in the capacity of auctioneer at the south end of the hall and Mr. Samuel L. Clemens at the north. The latter gentleman, after successfully disposing of a number of articles in Booth J, generously offered to dispose of the booth itself and all the people in it, including himself, but as no satisfactory offers were made, the lot was withdrawn.[7]

NARRATOR: They went to the farm June 15th. Jane Lampton Clemens, always called Jean, was born July 26th.

SAM: I have been up all night helping to receive Miss Clemens, who arrived perfectly sound but with no more baggage than I had when I was on the river. I will go to bed, now—merely adding that (it is a girl again and) mother and child are doing quite well and the latter weighs about 7 pounds. That is a pretty big one—for us. . . .

The new baby is thoroughly satisfactory, as far as it goes; but we did hope it was going to be twins. We were alarmed about Mrs. Clemens during 2 or 3 days, but she seems to be coming along all right, now. . . .

We all vote that the baby is the prettiest and perfectest little creature we have turned out yet. Susy and Bay could not worship it more if it were a cat—and the same formula will fit my case.

MRS. HOWELLS: Let me have the pleasure of congratulating you on your new daughter. What is her name, who is she most like, and why didn't you *tell* me! I am always in the wrong as to your intentions it seems.[8]

SAM: (She is "most like"—well, say an orange that is a little mildewed in spots.) No—I discover you don't mean complexion, but *who* is she most like? That is easily answered: Mrs. Crane says, Livy; Livy says, my mother; Bay Clemens says, me; Susy Clemens says, Bay; *I* think she looks most like a successful attempt to resemble nobody. Take your choice.[9]

NARRATOR: Sam thanked Mrs. Howells for sending some hair tonic that Livy wanted.

SAM: The box came yesterday, and I enclose check—at least I *mean* to, though one of the hardest things in this life to remember is to enclose a thing—even a dog—in the letter one is writing. It most always goes in another envelop, half an hour later, tottering under a load of profanity which runs it aground at the postoffice for insufficient postage. The hair restorer (is that what it is?) is very welcome, indeed, and Mrs. Clemens is greatly obliged. It is in good time, for Mrs. Clemens is abed yet and can't go to restoring till she is up; the baby was born well fixed on top; and the thing *I* need is something that will make the hair come out.[10]

Susy was sick all day, up stairs, but was brought down to her mother's bedside this evening for a few minutes. Mamma said, "I have missed you so—have you missed me, Susy?" Susy remained silent, and weighed the matter, with the conscientious desire to frame a reply which should convey the exact truth, no more, no less. When she had got it thought out and *knew* she knew how the matter stood in her mind and feelings, then this modern young George Washington who cannot lie, said: "Well—no—I had Aunt Sue and Rosa with me all the time; and they talked; and papa read to me a good deal—no, I did not miss you, Mamma." It was very sweetly and simply said: the *manner* of it could wound no one. Mamma said afterward that the *fact* broke her heart a little, at the moment, but that at the same time she respected and honored the child for her dauntless truthfulness. (Now mamma shouldn't have had any pang at all; for she knew Susy loved her to desperation, and did not miss her for the mere reason that her mind had been kept occupied with other things all the time. She has taught Susy to speak the absolute truth, unembroidered and ungilded; and Susy doesn't know how to tell any other kind of a truth.)[11]

For some months Bay has been bribed to not quarrel with Susy —at 3 cents a day. Conversation to-day:

Bay. "Mamma, you owe me for two days."

Mamma. "Bay, you have not seen Susy for 2 days—she has been sick in bed."

Bay. "Why Mamma, don't you count that?"[12]

We often *commend* the children, of course, when they have been good, but never in such a way as to make them vain and boastful. We *never* tell to other people the fine things they have said or done when they are within hearing—as less wise and extraordinary parents are so given to doing; and although they *are* beautiful, we are particular not to mention that fact in their presence. But the other day, when Susy's tooth was pulled, Bay overheard some of the praises of her fortitude; and consequently has been aching to have a tooth pulled herself, ever since. She has been trying daily (but without success) to convince us all that one of her teeth is loose. But yesterday when Susy developed *two* decidedly loose teeth, poor Bay gave it up in despondency and despair; it was no use to try to buck against such odds as that.[13]

Hay-cutting time was approaching and Susy and Clara were counting the hours, for the time was big with a great event for them; they had been promised that they might mount the wagon and ride home from the fields on the summit of the hay mountain. This perilous privilege, so dear to their age and species, had never been granted them before. Their excitement had no bounds. They could talk of nothing but this epoch-making adventure now. But misfortune overtook Susy on the very morning of the important day. In a sudden outbreak of passion she corrected Clara—with a shovel or stick or something of the sort. At any rate, the offense committed was of gravity clearly beyond the limit allowed in the nursery. In accordance with the rule and custom of the house, Susy went to her mother to confess and to help decide upon the size and character of the punishment due. It was quite understood that as a punishment could have but one rational object and function— to act as a reminder and warn the transgressor against transgressing in the same way again—the children would know about as well as any how to choose a penalty which would be rememberable and effective. Susy and her mother discussed various punishments but none of them seemed adequate. This fault was an unusually serious one and required the setting up of a danger signal in the memory that would not blow out nor burn out but remain a fixture there and furnish its saving warning indefinitely. Among the punishments mentioned was deprivation of the hay-wagon ride. It was noticeable that this one hit Susy hard. Finally, in the summing up, the mother named over the list and asked, "Which one do you think it ought to be, Susy?"

Susy studied, shrank from her duty, and asked, "Which do you think, mamma?"

"Well, Susy, I would rather leave it to you. *You* make the choice yourself."

It cost Susy a struggle and much and deep thinking and weighing—but she came out where anyone who knew her could have foretold she would:

"Well, mamma, I'll make it the hay wagon, because, you know, the other things might not make me remember not to do it again, but if I don't get to ride on the hay wagon I can remember it easily."[14]

NARRATOR: Jean's birth gave Sam an opportunity to pursue a favorite hobby.

SAM: Dear Grandma—I arrived pretty short, and have not had a chance to make anything yet over and above a most scanty and inadequate living; so I am not able to send anything to testify to my love for you . . . and do homage to your birthday, but a mere lock of my hair—heaven knows I wish it were more, but I am short even in hair; if even this little had been taken from my bang I should miss it this cold weather—but it is back hair and easier spared. I offer my love and loving duty. Jean Clemens.[15]

NARRATOR: Twichell received news of the baby.

SAM: Concerning Jean Clemens, if anybody said he "didn't see no p'ints about that frog that's any better'n any other frog," I should think he was convicting himself of being a pretty poor sort of observer. . . . I will not go into details; it is not necessary; you will soon be in Hartford, where I have already hired a hall; the admission fee will be but a trifle.

It is curious to note the change in the stock-quotation of the Affection Board brought about by throwing this new security on the market. Four weeks ago the children still put Mamma at the head of the list right along, where she had always been. But now:

Jean
Mamma
Motley   ⎫
Fraulein ⎬ Cats
Papa   ⎭

That is the way it stands, now. Mamma is become No. 2; I have dropped from No. 4, and am become No. 5. Some time ago it used to be nip and tuck between me and the cats, but after the cats "developed" I didn't stand any more show.

I've got a swollen ear; so I take advantage of it to lie abed most of the day, and read and smoke and scribble and have a good time. Last evening Livy said with deep concern, "O dear, I believe an abscess is forming in your ear."

I responded as the poet would have done if he had had a cold in the head—

> "'Tis said that abscess conquers love,
>   But O believe it not."

This made a coolness. . . .

Well, we are all getting along here first-rate; Livy gains strength daily . . . the baby is five weeks old and—but no more of this; somebody may be reading *this* letter 80 years hence. And so, my friend (you pitying snob, I mean, who are holding this yellow paper in your hand in 1960,) save yourself the trouble of looking further; I know how pathetically trivial our small concerns will seem to you, and I will not let your eye profane them. No, I keep my news; you keep your compassion. Suffice it you to know, scoffer and ribald, that the little child is old and blind, now, and once more toothless; and the rest of us are shadows, these many, many years. Yes, and *your* time cometh![16]

NARRATOR: Sam was much in demand for bedtime stories.

SAM: My little girls—Susy, aged eight, and Clara, six and a half—often require me to help them to go to sleep, nights, by telling them original tales. They think my tales are better than paregoric, and quicker. While I talk, they make comments and ask questions, and we have a pretty good time.

NARRATOR: Stories about a cat family were worked up into an elaborate tale.

SAM: Once there was a noble big cat, whose Christian name was Catasauqua—because she lived in that region—but she did not have any surname, because she was a short-tailed cat—being a Manx—and did not need one. It is very just and becoming in a long-tailed cat to have a surname, but it would be very ostentatious, and even dishonorable, in a Manx. Well, Catasauqua had a beautiful family of catlings; and they were of different colors, to harmonize with their characters. Cataraugus, the eldest, was white, and he had high impulses and a pure heart; Catiline, the youngest, was black, and he had a self-seeking nature, his motives were nearly always base, he was truculent and insincere.

NARRATOR: Catasauqua's home burned (luckily it was heavily insured); she built a new one and "had money left to add a gaudy concatenation of extra improvements with."

SAM: Yes, behind the house she constructed a splendid large catadrome, and enclosed it with a caterwaul about nine feet high, and in the center was a spacious grass-plot. . . . for cat-fights, and other free exhibitions; and for ball-games—three-cornered cat, and all that sort of thing; a lovely spot, lovely. Yes, indeed; it had a hedge of dainty little catkins around it, and right in the centre was a splendid great categorematic in full leaf. . . .

NARRATOR: Inside the house there were many innovations: catcalls instead of bells, catamounts instead of elevators, civet cats in the kitchen instead of sieves, and two ash-cats to keep the stove clean. On the roof there was "an alert and cultivated pole-cat to watch the flag-pole and keep the banner a-flying."

SAM: The front garden was a spectacle of sublime and bewildering magnificence.—A stately row of flowering catalpas stretched from the front door clear to the gate, wreathed from stem to stern with the delicate tendrils and shining scales of the cat's foot ivy, whilst ever and anon the enchanted eye wandered from congeries of lordly cat-tails and kindred catapetalous blooms too deep for utterance, only to encounter the still more entrancing vision of cat-nip without number and without price, and swoon away in ecstasy unutterable, under the blissful intoxication of its too too fragrant breath![17]

NARRATOR: In this atmosphere of elegance, Catiline and Cataraugus studied their little books called catechisms, earned "a little circus-money by building cat's-cradles"[18] . . . called each other names like Catapult and Catso and "spat and clawed and fought until they dimmed away and finally disappeared in a flying fog of cat-fur."[19]

Make-believe cats were forgotten when tragedy struck one of their own kittens.

SAM: When Motley, the kitten, died, some one said that the thoughts of the two children need not be inquired into, they could be divined: that Susy was wondering if this was the *end* of Motley, and had his life been worth while; whereas Clara was merely interested in seeing to it that there should be a creditable funeral.[20]

NARRATOR: The felines were not the only pets; they had a coach dog named Jip at this time. Sam found much entertainment in the animals when he wasn't at work; he was finishing up his book.

SAM: I wrote the first half of the climax chapter of "The Little Prince and the Little Pauper" three days ago. Another week's work will finish that book. It would be nearly finished now, but I was stopped by an ear-ache. The story will contain only two thirds as much matter as Tom Sawyer, unless I change my mind and elaborate one portion of it a little more than I have done—but that would be at the expense of the dramatic strength and I judge I won't do it.[21]

IDA LANGDON: The long day of writing usually had been uninterrupted, but when Mark Twain was at work on *The Prince and the Pauper* there were frequent gatherings on the Study steps that did perhaps amount to interruptions, but welcome ones. The children . . . would come trouping silently into the "quiet zone" maintained around the little octagon late in the afternoon. If he were ready for them he would call out (sometimes they were not just on the spot, and he blew a horn for them) and in breathless excitement, they would gather around him to hear the newest chapter of this story that they passionately loved. Its characters were real to them, their fortunes and misfortunes of vital concern. They poured out suggestions to which Mark Twain listened with intense interest, certainly at times with considerable amusement. I do not know how many of them he adopted, but some I am sure, for this was, in his own words, "a yarn for youth," and here was an audience whose reactions he felt were of first-rate importance to him.[22]

NARRATOR: One day, Livy interviewed a young Irish girl, Katy Leary, who had applied for a position as housemaid; it was an historic occasion.

KATY: I was settin' in the library waiting, and this wonderful, wonderful woman appeared, and she startled me with all her beauty— she was like an angel, almost. She wore a white silk dress and her hair was perfectly plain, you know, combed down plain and done in a coil; but her face and her manner was wonderful, and I felt like she was something from another world.[23]

NARRATOR: Katy was hired, and immediately endeared herself to the whole family.

SAM: Katy was a potent influence, all over the premises. Fidelity, truthfulness, courage, magnanimity, personal dignity, a pole-star for steadiness—these were her equipment, along with a heart of Irish warmth, quick Irish wit, and a good store of that veiled and shimmering and half-surreptitious humor which is the best feature of the "American" brand—or of any brand, for that matter.[24]

NARRATOR: Sam and the older children went back to Hartford in October, leaving Livy and the baby in Elmira for a little longer. They stopped at the Gilsey House in New York for three days, where purchases were made at Schwartz's toy store which included a fish pond game, a checkerboard and a game of Authors. Mark Twain was the subject of one of the Authors cards. He also bought Livy a seal paletot and muff trimmed with silvery unplucked Beaver.[25]

There was great excitement in Hartford, for Grant came to push the election of Garfield for President. There was a big parade, and Sam wrote Livy about the decorations at their house.

SAM: I found Mr. Beals hard at work in the rain with his decorations. With a ladder he had strung flags around our bedroom balcony, and thence around to the porte-cochère, which was elaborately flagged; thence the flags of all nations were suspended from a line which stretched past the greenhouse to the limit of our grounds. Against each of the two trees on the mound, half-way down to our gate, stands a knight in complete armor. Piles of still-bundled flags clutter up the ombra (to be put up), also gaudy shields of various shapes (arms of this and other countries), also some huge glittering arches and things done in gold and silver paper, containing mottoes in big letters. I broke Mr. Beals's heart by persistently and inflexibly annulling and forbidding the biggest and gorgeousest of the arches—it had on it, in all the fires of the rainbow, "The Home of Mark Twain," in letters as big as your head. Oh, we're going to be decorated sufficient, don't you worry about that, madam.

NARRATOR: Sam made a speech at the gathering which welcomed Grant to Hartford.

SAM: I am among those deputed to welcome you to the sincere and cordial hospitalities of Hartford, the city of the historic and revered Charter Oak, of which most of the town is built.[26]

SUSY: What a wonderful man [Grant], to fight five years—he must be scratched up a good deal.[27]

NARRATOR: Sam wrote his mother.

SAM: Jean got the stockings and is much obliged; Mollie wants to know whom she most resembles, but I can't tell; she has blue eyes and brown hair, and three chins, and is very fat and happy; and at one time or another she has resembled all the different Clemenses and Langdons, in turn, that have ever lived.

Livy is too much beaten out with the baby, nights, to write, these times; and *I* don't know of anything urgent to say, except that a basket full of letters has accumulated in the 7 days that I have been whooping and cursing over a cold in the head—and I must attack the pile this very minute.[28]

NARRATOR: Susy joined Livy and Howells as an editor of *The Prince and the Pauper*.

"MOTHER" FAIRBANKS: I know the school and the teachers where he has learned to do the fine work of that book—I put myself again in the home that holds him. I recall the little audiences . . . (when the book was in manuscript) Livy on one side of the fire, and those honest little critics, Susy and Clara perched on your arm-chair—and I your foster-mother, trying to be critical, yet always pleased.[29]

SAM: I have two stories, and by the verbal agreement they are both going into the same book; but Livy says they're not, and by George I. she ought to know. She says they're going into separate books, and that one of them is going to be elegantly gotten up, even if the elegance of it eats up the publisher's profits and mine too.

I anticipate that publisher's melancholy surprise when he calls here Tuesday. However, let him suffer; it is his own fault. People who fix up agreements with me without first finding out what Livy's plans are take their fate into their own hands.

I said *two* stories, but one of them is only half done; two or three months' work on it yet. I shall tackle it Wednesday or Thursday; that is, if Livy yields and allows both stories to go in one book, which I hope she won't.[30]

NARRATOR: It was this year that Miss Lilly Gillette Foote became a household fixture at the Clemenses; she was no stranger to Nook Farm, having spent much time in her teens with her cousin, Mrs.

George Warner. Her sister, Harriet, lived with the Charles Dudley
Warners. Lilly was responsible for the children's formal education
and eventually prepared Susy for Bryn Mawr.

SAM: Mrs. Clemens and I, and Miss Foote the governess, were in our
respective degrees of efficiency and opportunity trainers of the
children—*conscious and intentional* ones—and we were reinforced
in our work by the usual and formidable multitude of unconscious
and unintentional trainers, such as servants, friends, visitors, books,
dogs, cats, horses, cows, accidents, travel, joys, sorrows, lies,
slanders, oppositions, persuasions, good and evil beguilements,
treacheries, fidelities, the tireless and everlasting impact of charac-
ter-forming exterior influences which begin their strenuous assault
at the cradle and only end it at the grave. Books, home, the school
and the pulpit may and must do the *directing*—it is their limited
but lofty and powerful office—but the countless outside unconscious and unintentional trainers do the real work, and over them
the responsible superintendents have no considerable supervision
or authority.

Conscious teaching is good and necessary, and in a hundred
instances it effects its purpose, while in a hundred others it fails and
the purpose, if accomplished at all, is accomplished by some other
agent or influence. I suppose that in most cases changes take place
in us without our being aware of it at the time, and in after life we
give the credit of it—if it be of a creditable nature—to mamma, or
the school or the pulpit.[31]

Bay and Susy *taught themselves to read English, without help
or instruction from anybody, and without knowing the alphabet,* or
making any attempt *to spell* the words or divide them into syllables.[32]

Bay (who has never been allowed to meddle with English alpha-
bets or books lest she would neglect her German), collared an English juvenile-poem book sent her from London . . . and *now,* 10 or
12 days later . . . she reads abstruse English works with astounding
facility! Nobody has given her an instant's assistance. Susy has
learned to read English during these same 10 or 12 days, but she
is 8 yrs old, and besides she can't read it as glibly as Bay.[33]

They both read fluently, now, but they make no attempts at
spelling; neither of them knows more than half the letters of the
alphabet. They read wholly by the *look* of the word. . . . The
reason they have learned to read English and are so fond of it, is,

I think, because they were long ago forbidden to meddle with English . . . till they should be far advanced in German. Forbidden fruits are most coveted, since Eve's time.[34]

NARRATOR: There was a caller in the billiard room in the fall.

SAM: Dwight Buell, a jeweler, called at our house and was shown up to the billiard-room—which was my study; and the game got more study than the other sciences. He wanted me to take some stock in a type-setting machine. He said it was at the Colt's Arms factory, and was about finished. I took $2,000 of the stock. I was always taking little chances like that, and almost always losing by it, too. Some time afterward I was invited to go down to the factory and see the machine. I went, promising myself nothing, for I knew all about type-setting by practical experience, and held the settled and solidified opinion that a successful type-setting machine was an impossibility, for the reason that a machine cannot be made to *think*, and the thing that sets movable type *must* think or retire defeated. So, the performance I witnessed did most thoroughly amaze me. Here was a machine that was really setting type, and doing it with swiftness and accuracy, too. Moreover, it was distributing its case at the same time. The distribution was automatic; the machine fed itself from a galley of dead matter and without human help or suggestion, for it began its work of its own accord when the type channels needed filling, and stopped of its own accord when they were full enough. The machine was almost a complete compositor; it lacked but one feature—it did not "justify" the lines. This was done by the operator's assistant.

I saw the operator set at the rate of 3,000 ems an hour, which, counting distribution, was but little short of four casemen's work. William Hamersley was there. He said he was already a considerable owner, and was going to take as much more of the stock as he could afford. Wherefore, I set down my name for an additional $3,000. It is here that the music begins.

NARRATOR: The typesetting machine was the invention of a man named James W. Paige. Sam was fascinated by Paige and his machine.

SAM: He is a poet; a most great and genuine poet, whose sublime creations are written in steel.[35]

KATY: Well, now I'll tell you about the typesetting machine. That's a long story. Mr. Clemens' heart was just set on that, he believed in it so. He was expecting such wonderful things from it. Why, he thought he could buy all New York. He was asking how much it would take to buy all the railroads in New York, and all the newspapers, too,—buy everything in New York on account of the typesetting machine. He thought he'd make millions and own the world, because he had such faith in it. That was Mr. Clemens' way.[36]

SAM: I don't need to do anything to protect the $5000 invested in that machine; it is safe, there, and is very much the best investment I have ever had. I want an opportunity to add to it—that is how I feel about it.[37]

NARRATOR: Sam celebrated his forty-fifth birthday.

SAM: I stand to-day on the mid-summit of life and am for the first time looking down upon the country beyond, while the sun in the zenith has begun to tilt westward toward his setting.[38]

NARRATOR: Katy described Thanksgiving festivities.

KATY: Thanksgiving was most as wonderful as Christmas. Mrs. Clemens always had all the people to a great dinner that day— people that wasn't very well off, poor people—not her own friends specially. Then in the evening the Warners would have a great dinner (and the Twichells used to go over to the Warners for that).[39]

NARRATOR: Twichell's son and namesake loved the Warner parties.

YOUNG JOE TWICHELL: . . . first of all . . . are the Thanksgiving dinners at Uncle Charley Warner's house. After the service at the church we would all meet there. There would be two tables' full of kids alone, as well as a table of grownups. There were always interesting people there, besides the neighborhood families. . . . After dinner, everyone would get together in the library . . . one person would hold forth for a while—Uncle Charley or Mark Twain or my father —then the conversational ball would be passed round.

After dinner . . . we would walk through the woods to the Clemens' house and play charades in the evening.[40]

KATY: Then on their way back Mr. Twichell and his wife and the nine little Twichells used to stop at our house and then we used to play charades.

The dining table was always loaded with all the candy that there was—about ten dishes of candy—set all around the table near the edge, just where the little Twichells could reach up their hands to get it and there was the little Twichells' hands going around that table as fast as they could go until all the candy was gone. They'd empty all them dishes in no time![41]

NARRATOR: And then Christmas.

KATY: The Christmases they used to have was something wonderful. The way they used to make everybody happy! Baskets and packages all over the place. Mrs. Clemens would be fixing baskets in the Billiard Room [mahogany room] off the library (they always used to do the Christmas things there) and she used to do up about fifty baskets herself. She always had a crowd of people, children and old people and grown-up people, too, depending on her and she fixed them up wonderful baskets with a big turkey and cans of peas and tomatoes and vegetables and then, oh, a bottle of wine and a great big box of candy, and nuts and raisins, and then there was always some stockings and underwear and a few pretty things, too. She used to give every one of them a present, individual-like, extra. She knew, it seems to me, just what each person wanted most and she shopped for weeks before Christmas, doing up all those things and having all those baskets ready, and then when Christmas morning come, if it was cold and snow on the ground, Mr. Clemens would start out to distribute the things. He'd put on his big fur overcoat, take the sleigh and the two children with him, Susy and Clara, and they'd start early in the morning with them great baskets. The children would read the names and then Mr. Clemens would lift out the baskets and Patrick would take them into the house.

Mr. Clemens looked just like Santa Claus, you know, with that great big fur coat with a white fur collar on it, and he and the children had such fun over it.[42]

CLARA: Katy was so devoted to "her family" that her praise of everything connected with it was always extravagant, many times to the point of little or no veracity.[43]

The day before Christmas was always spent in a somewhat fatiguing way by my sisters and me. We drove around with the coachman while he delivered Christmas packages that went to the poor. Great baskets with the feet of turkeys protruding below blankets of flowers and fruit. Wrapped up in mufflers and snugly tucked in a fur robe, we children drove far out into the country in an open sleigh, tingling with delight at the sound of the bells.[44]

KATY: Then Mrs. Clemens, she'd have presents besides for everyone in the house, and a great big tree for the children and their stockings hung up the night before, and really a wonderful Christmas for them all.[45]

CLARA: At this time my sisters and I were obliged to retire at an early hour every evening, not excepting Christmas Eve. Therefore, by eight o'clock we were in bed, launched on a long night of wakefulness, while mother started on a night of work down in the "mahogany room." Two of us, Jean and I, slept in the nursery, and my elder sister, Susy, occupied a little blue room adjoining. But, on Christmas Eve, Susy crept into bed with me and we listened for the mysterious sounds that would betray the presence of fairies in the schoolroom.

"Ah, there they are! rattling paper, subdued voices. A dull thud; something falls. I wonder what it is? If only it isn't broken! Oh, Susy, listen to that heavy thing they are dragging across the floor! What on earth can that be? I'll die if I can't find out soon. How many hours yet? If only we could sleep!"

Finally all became still in the schoolroom. The fairies must have gone. Not a sound. The forms left behind are motionless, speechless. . . .

By and by, Susy whispered to me, "Let's take *one* little peek through the door. With a tiny bit of light from the bathroom we might get an idea of the shapes without seeing anything."

It didn't take me long to say "Yes."

Opening the door a few inches, and by means of a dim ray of light, we saw—

"Oh dear! Shut the door quick! We must not look. That's wicked. What do you suppose that huge black thing can be? It seems to fill the room. Come, let's try to go to sleep." Of course that was impossible.

Eventually 6 A.M. came and we rang for the nurse to build a fire in the schoolroom and help us dress with as little washing as possible. And now the door opens wide! . . .

At last each makes a rush for her own table, scattering ribbons, papers, and ejaculations with vehement haste. . . . The big object seeming to fill the center of the room turns out to be a lovely upright piano. Can it be true? . . .

Father and Mother always rose very late on Christmas morning, having spent most of the night up. So we were well acquainted with our presents, and had even written several letters of thanks, before our parents appeared. They inspected their gifts, which were down in the drawing-room and callers from the neighborhood began to arrive.

Father, however, always drew a sigh of relief when the holidays were over. The reason was that they included social festivities that were sometimes a burden to him, particularly if he happened to be in the mood of writing; and this mood, he was wont to declare always attacked him when some "mentally dead people brought their corpses with them for a long visit."[46]

NARRATOR: After Christmas, there were three near-tragedies, known as "The Three Days."

SAM: Clara had diphtheria, and her crib was in our bedroom, which was on the second floor; over the crib was built a tent of blankets, into which projected the pipe of a steaming apparatus which stood upon the floor. Mrs. Clemens left the room for a little while, and presently Rosa entered on an errand, and found a conflagration; the alcohol lamp had set fire to the tent and the blankets were blazing. Rosa snatched the patient out and put her on the bed, then gathered up the burning mattress and blankets and threw them out of the window. The crib itself had caught fire; she smothered that detail. Clara's burns were very slight, and Rosa got no burns, except on her hands.

That was the First Day. The next morning Jean, the baby, was asleep in her crib in front of a vigorous wood fire in the nursery on the second floor. The crib had a tall lawn canopy over it. A spark was driven through the close-webbed fire-screen and it lit on the slant of the canopy, and presently the result was a blaze. After a little a Polish servant-woman entered the nursery, caught sight of the tall flame, and rushed out shrieking. That brought Rosa from somewhere, and she rescued the child and threw the burning mattress and bedding out of the window. The baby was slightly burnt in several spots, and again Rosa's hand suffered, but otherwise no harm was done. Nothing but instant perception of the right thing to do, and lightning promptness in doing it could save the children's lives, a minute's delay in either case would have been fatal; but Rosa had the quick eye, the sane mind and the prompt hand, and these great qualities made her mistress of the emergency.

The next day was the Third Day, and completed the series. The barber came out daily from town to shave me. His function was performed in a room on the first floor—it was the rule; but this time, by luck, he was sent up to the schoolroom, which adjoined the nursery, on the second floor. He knocked; there being no response, he entered. Susy's back was visible at the far end of

the room; she was deep in a piano lesson, and unconscious of
other matters. A log had burned in two, the ends had fallen
against the heavy woodwork which enclosed the fireplace and
supported the mantel piece, and the conflagration was just beginning. Five minutes later the house would have been past saving. The barber did the requisite thing, and the danger was over.
So ended what in the family history we call "the Three Days,"
and aggrandize them with capital letters, as is proper.[47]

KATY: If ever they were sick she would get them out of the nursery
and bring them right in to her own bed, and Mr. Clemens—well,
he'd have to go into another room. . . . Oh, the children! They
use to *love* to be sick, because they loved to be taken into their
mother's room. She had a great large bed. . . . It was an old
Dutch [Venetian] bed, four-poster, and there was four little smiling, fat cherubs. . . . They use to have them taken down and put on
the bed with them. (They'd come off the posts—unscrew, you
know.) They was delighted with that, and delighted to be sick, too,
just to be in their mother's room—that is, if they wasn't too sick.[48]

NARRATOR: About the first of February a young woman came to call
on Sam and the relationship with the Karl Gerhardts began.

SAM: Livy and Clara Spaulding and I were at breakfast, at 10 A.M.,
and I was in an irritable mood, for the barber was up stairs waiting and his hot water getting cold, when the colored George
returned from answering the bell and said—

"There's a lady in the drawing room wants to see you."

"A book agent!" says I, with heat. "I won't see her; I will die
in my tracks first."

Then I got up with a soul full of rage, and went in there and
bent scowling over that person, and began a succession of rude
and raspy questions—and without even offering to sit down. . . .

And this was her tale, and her plea—diffidently stated, but
straightforwardly; and bravely, and most winningly simply and
earnestly. . . .

Mr. Karl Gerhardt, who works in Pratt & Whitney's machine
shops, has made a statue in clay, and would I be so kind as to
come and look at it, and tell him if there is any promise in it?
He has none to go to and he would be so glad.

NARRATOR: Sam, disclaiming any knowledge of sculpture, became
enchanted with young Mrs. Gerhardt and promised to go to see
her husband's work.

SAM: Patrick and I hunted up the place . . . the girl saw us driving up, and flew down stairs and received me. Her quarters were the second story of a little wooden house—another family on the ground floor. The husband was at the machine-shop, the wife kept no servant; she was there alone. She had a little parlor, with a chair or two and a sofa; and the artist-husband's hand was visible in a couple of plaster busts, one of the wife, the other of a neighbor's child; visible also, in a couple of water colors of flowers and birds; an ambitious unfinished portrait of the wife in oils; some paint-decorations on the pine mantel; and an excellent human ear, done in some plastic material at 16.

Then we went into the neat kitchen, and the girl flew around, with enthusiasm and snatched rag after rag from a tall something in the corner, and presently there stood the clay statue, life size— a graceful girlish creature, (life size) nude to the waist, and holding up a single garment with one hand—the expression attempted being a modified scare—she was interrupted when about to enter the bath.

NARRATOR: To Sam's amazement, she said she had been the model, posing nights and Sundays.

SAM: Well, sir, it was perfectly charming, this girl's innocence and purity—exhibiting her naked self, as it were, to a stranger and alone, and never once dreaming that there was the slightest in-delicacy about the matter. And so there wasn't, but it will be many a long day before I run across another woman who can do the like and show no trace of self-consciousness.

NARRATOR: She told Sam of her husband's passionate interest in art and their longing to find a way for him to have lessons. When Gerhardt came in from work, Sam found him to be "as simple, and natural, and as beautiful in spirit as his wife was."

SAM: I went home enchanted. Told Livy and Clara [Spaulding] all about the paradise down yonder where those two enthusiasts are happy with a yearly expense of $350. Livy and Clara went there next day and came away enchanted.

NARRATOR: Charles Dudley Warner and Sam arranged for J. Wells Champney, the portrait painter, and John Quincy Adams Ward, the sculptor, to come to Hartford to give an opinion of Gerhardt's work. Champney said the statue seemed to him "an extraordinary performance for an untrained hand"; Ward said, "it is full of crudities, but it is full of genius, too."

SAM: Well, you see, that's all *we* wanted. After Ward was gone Livy came out with the thing that was in my mind. She said, "Go privately and start the Gerhardts off to Paris, and say nothing about it to anyone else."

So I tramped down this morning [February 21st] in the snow-storm—and there was a stirring time.[49]

As I was starting out at the front door, with Gerhardt beside me and the young wife dancing and jubilating behind, this latter cried out impulsively, "Tell Mrs. Clemens I want to hug her— I want to hug you both!"[50]

LIVY: Mr and Mrs Gerhardt start for New York today [February 28th] and for Paris on Saturday—every time we see them we are more in love with them, they seem like story book people—he is mature and fine. She is young and charming and with quick intuitions—They are just the people to have experiences.[51]

SUSY'S TENTH YEAR

1881–1882

NARRATOR: Three days before Susy's ninth birthday, Sam bought more land from Chamberlin.

SAM: To-day we bought Mr. Chamberlin's greenhouse and 100 feet of land adjoining our east line (to stop Mr. C. from building a dwelling house there); we have also set architect and builder to work to tear down our kitchen and build a bigger one; in June we shall tear out the reception room to make our front hall bigger; and at the same time the decorators will decorate the walls and ceilings of our whole lower floor.[1]

NARRATOR: There are two versions of how this land purchase happened. According to Sam, he heard chopping one morning when he was shaving. He stepped out on the balcony opening off his bedroom and called out:

> Woodman spare that tree,
> Forego, forego thy hacks,
> And list, oh list, to me,
> Lay down thy gory axe.[2]

According to Chamberlin, he ordered a little deliberate chopping to trick Sam into buying the strip of land for $12,000. Lilly Warner wrote George that Livy was "radiant" over the purchase; Lilly thought "the deceiver" had "won his game."[3]

In June the whole family went to the Montowese House at Branford on the Connecticut shore. Business matters, which included the Kaolatype, an engraving process Sam had bought, and house remodeling, were left in the hands of Charley Webster, who had married Sam's niece, Pamela Clemens Moffett's daughter.

SAMUEL WEBSTER: Mark Twain brought my father on from Fredonia to take charge of the Kaolatype, which was losing money at an alarming rate—but he was soon acting as Mark Twain's general business manager. It seemed like a good move to him although he had been doing very well in Fredonia.[4]

NARRATOR: Mark Twain started at once to unload instructions, plans and bright ideas on his new helper. In August the family had a tiresome trip to Elmira.

SAM: Broke an axle eight hours from New York and twenty-five miles from home lay still and roasted two hours. . . .[5]

Carrying Jean up and down in the car, on that red-hot 12-hour trip, has disabled me with lumbago. . . .

Jean is mighty fat and hearty, but she is forever asleep, up here in this strong brisk mountain air; consequently we don't see a great deal of her. She bore that hard journey in the bravest way; didn't break out into any hard cries, but only mourned and complained in a gentle and most pathetic way, while she boiled slowly to death in her own sooty and pasty perspiration. Susy and Bay uttered no complaints, of course—their mother taught them patient endurance long ago. Poor Susy was so worn out that I couldn't even entertain her by showing her how the ties had been torn and smashed by the broken axle. She was indifferent to that stirring spectacle. I tried to gaudify the interest of my topic by explaining to her that we all came within less than three-quarters of a hair's-breadth of going to smash and destruction, but she only responded, with indifference, "But as long as we didn't, papa, what does it amount to?—let us get in the car again."[6]

NARRATOR: Work was progressing at the Hartford house; Sam was in constant touch with Webster.

SAM: Charley, don't order soapstones or anything without consulting your aunt Livy—an order from me, unendorsed by her, ain't sufficient.[7]

NARRATOR: He wrote to his mother.

SAM: The baby is a beauty—there is no question about that. Other pretty babies become mighty commonplace when they are brought into her presence; I could furnish you evidence outside the family to prove that. And everybody remarks her strong resemblance to you.—It is a remark which has been made so often that it doesn't attract attention any more.—Susy offered some advice yesterday (through her Aunt Sue, for she recognized the impropriety of presuming to advise her own mother.) It was, that Jean be not punished when she does wrong: then she will not know she has done wrong; and if she does not know she is doing wrong, she commits no sin.—She was entirely serious about it.[8]

NARRATOR: They had tried to get Herbert Lawrence to decorate the house, but he was abroad; he had recommended La Farge or Louis Comfort Tiffany. Tiffany was employed, but when they returned October 2nd, nothing was finished.

SAM: We are in our carpetless and dismantled home, living like a gang of tramps on the second floor. . . . We have pulled down the kitchen and rebuilt it, adding twenty feet to it, and have lowered the ground in front of the greenhouse, and also carried the drive-way a hundred feet further to the east (down-townwards) before it enters the Avenue. Excellent improvements.[9]

The house is full of carpenters and decorators; whereas, what we really need here, is an incendiary. If the house would only burn down, we would pack up the cubs and fly to the isles of the blest [Sandwich Islands], and shut ourselves up in the healing solitudes of the crater of Haleakala and get a good rest; for the mails do not intrude there, nor yet the telephone and the tele-graph. And after resting, we would come down the mountain a piece and board with a godly, breech-clouted native, and eat poi and dirt and give thanks to whom all thanks belong, for these privileges, and never house-keep any more.

I think my wife would be twice as strong as she is, but for this wearing and wearying slavery of house-keeping. However, she thinks she must submit to it for the sake of the children; whereas, I have always had a tenderness for parents too, so, for her sake and mine, I sigh for the incendiary. When the evening comes and the gas is lit and the wear and tear of life ceases, we want to keep house always; but next morning we wish, once more, that we were free and irresponsible boarders.[10]

NARRATOR: Sam had trouble with his language.

SAM: All through the first ten years of my married life I kept a constant and discreet watch upon my tongue while in the house, and went outside and to a distance when circumstances were too much for me and I was obliged to seek relief. . . .

But at last an accident exposed me. I went into the bathroom one morning to make my toilet and carelessly left the door two or three inches ajar. It was the first time that I had ever failed to take the precaution of closing it tightly. I knew the necessity of being particular about this, because shaving was always a trying ordeal for me, and I could seldom carry it through to a finish without verbal helps. . . . I had no extraordinary trouble with my razor on this occasion and was able to worry through with mere mutterings and growlings of an improper sort. . . . Then I put on a shirt. My shirts are an invention of my own. They open in the back and are buttoned there—when there are buttons. This time the button was missing. My temper jumped up several degrees in a moment and my remarks rose accordingly, both in loudness and vigor of expression. But I was not troubled, for the bathroom door was a solid one and I supposed it was firmly closed. I flung up the window and threw the shirt out. It fell upon the shrubbery where the people on their way to church could admire it if they wanted to; there was merely fifty feet of grass between the shirt and the passer-by. Still rumbling and thundering distantly, I put on another shirt. Again the button was absent. I augmented my language to meet the emergency and threw that shirt out of the window. I was too angry—too insane—to examine the third shirt, but put it furiously on. Again the button was absent, and that shirt followed its comrades out of the window. Then I straightened up, gathered my reserves, and let myself go like a cavalry charge. In the midst of that great assault my eye fell upon that gaping door and I was paralyzed.

It took me a good while to finish my toilet. I extended the time unnecessarily in trying to make up my mind as to what I would best do in the circumstances. I tried to hope that Mrs. Clemens was asleep but I knew better. I could not escape by the window. It was narrow and suited only to shirts. At last I made up my mind to boldly loaf through the bedroom with the air of a person who had not been doing anything. I made half the journey successfully. I did not turn my eyes in her direction, because that would not be safe. . . . I had to stop in the middle of the room. I hadn't the strength to go on. . . . You know how it is when you are convinced that somebody behind you is looking steadily at you. You *have* to turn your face—you can't help it. I turned mine. . . .

Against the white pillows I saw the black head—I saw that young and beautiful face; and I saw the gracious eyes with a something in them which I had never seen there before. They were snapping and flashing with indignation. I felt myself crumbling; I felt myself shrinking away to nothing under that accusing gaze. I stood silent under that desolating fire for as much as a minute, I should say—it seemed a very, very long time. Then my wife's lips parted and from them issued—*my latest bathroom remark.* . . . In my life time I had never heard anything so out of tune, so inharmonious, so incongruous, so ill suited to each other as were those mighty words set to that feeble music. I tried to keep from laughing, for I was a guilty person in deep need of charity and mercy. I tried to keep from bursting, and I succeeded—until she gravely said, "There, now you know how it sounds."

Then I exploded; the air was filled with my fragments and you could hear them whiz. I said, "Oh, Livy, if it sounds like that, God forgive me, I will never do it again!"

Then she had to laugh herself. Both of us broke into convulsions and went on laughing until we were physically exhausted and spiritually reconciled.

The children were present at breakfast . . . and the mother made a guarded remark about strong language; guarded because she did not wish the children to suspect anything—a guarded remark which censured strong language. Both children broke out in one voice with this comment: "Why, mamma, papa uses it!" I was astonished. I had supposed that that secret was safe in my own breast and that its presence had never been suspected. I asked, "How did you know, you little rascals?"

"Oh," they said, "we often listen over the balusters when you are in the hall explaining things to George."[11]

Susy: Papa uses very strong language, but I have an idea not nearly so strong as when he first married mamma. A lady acquaintance of his is rather apt to interupt what one is saying, and papa told mamma that he thought he should say to the lady's husband "I am glad your wife wasn't present when the Deity said Let there be light."

Sam: Of course I made the remark which she has quoted . . . I am still as much as half persuaded that if that lady mentioned had been present when the Creator said "Let there be light" she would have interrupted him and we shouldn't ever have got it.[12]

NARRATOR: Sam had been guilty of using strong language in the hall on other than George. He had recently had a telephone put in, one of the first in Hartford. He said it was "the *first* one that was ever used in a private house in the world."[13] A year or so earlier, he had refused to buy stock from Alexander Graham Bell.

SAM: There was a young fellow there. . . . He was with Graham Bell and was agent for a new invention called the telephone. He believed there was great fortune in store for it and wanted me to take some stock. I declined. I said I didn't want anything more to do with wildcat speculation.[14]

KATY: It was shortly after the telephone invention that I went to Hartford. They just put it in about that time and it made Mr. Clemens so mad—"just to hear the damned thing ring," he said. Yes, that telephone used to make Mr. Clemens wild, because he would hear all right, but he couldn't give his message out good. It wasn't very good service them days, and he used to fight the telephone girls all the time. He'd say:

"Why, damn it, are you all asleep down there? If you don't give me better service you can send somebody right up here now and pull this thing out. I won't have this damned thing in the house—it's a nuisance!"[15]

NARRATOR: Sam kept a weekly chart on how the telephone was operating, and he wrote the telephone company.

SAM: The time is coming very soon when the telephone will be a perfect instrument, when proximity will no longer be a hindrance to its performance, when, in fact, one will hear a man who is in the next block just as easily and comfortably as he would if that man were in San Francisco.

KATY: One day he tried to call up Mrs. Dr. Taft. He could not hear plainly and thought he was talking to central. "Send down here and take this d[amned] thing out of here," he said; "I'm tired of it." He was mad, and using a good deal of bad language. All at once he heard Mrs. Dr. Taft say, "Oh, Mr. Clemens, good morning." He said, "Why, Mrs. Taft, I have just come to the telephone. George, our butler, was here before me and I heard him swearing as I came up. I shall have to talk to him about it."

Mrs. Taft often told it on him.[16]

NARRATOR: As the children grew older, Susy's and Clara's personalities continued to show marked differences which were intensely interesting to Sam and Livy and the neighbors.

SAM: It would seem that we set down Susy's remarks because they were wise, Clara's because they were robustly practical, and Jean's because they happened to be quaintly phrased.[17]

Some one said Susy was of mind, Clara of matter—a generalization justified by appearances of the time, but unjust to Clara. . . . In her early years Clara quite successfully concealed some of the most creditable elements of her make-up. Susy was sensitive, shrinking; and in danger timid; Clara was not shrinking, not timid, and she had a liking for risky ventures. Susy had an abundance of moral courage, and kept it up to standard by exercising it.[18]

NARRATOR: Susy worried about things.

SAM: Once . . . she came to her mother's room when her sister Jean was a baby and said Jean was crying in the nursery and asked if she might ring for the nurse. Her mother asked, "Is she crying hard?"—meaning cross, ugly.

"Well, no, mamma. It is a weary, lonesome cry."[19]

For a week, her mother had not been able to go to the nursery, evenings, at the child's prayer hour. She spoke of it—was sorry for it and said she would come to-night and hoped she could continue to come every night and hear Susy pray, as before. Noticing that the child wished to respond but was evidently troubled as to how to word her answer, she asked what the difficulty was. Susy explained that Miss Foote (the governess) had been teaching her about the Indians and their religious beliefs, whereby it appeared that they had not only a god but several. This had set Susy to thinking. As a result of this thinking she had stopped praying. She qualified this statement—that is, she modified it—saying she did not now pray "in the same way" as she had formerly done. Her mother said. "Tell me about it, dear."

"Well, mamma, the Indians believed they knew, but now we know they were wrong. By and by it can turn out that we are wrong. So now I only pray that there may be a God and a heaven —or something better."

I wrote down this pathetic prayer in its precise wording. . . . Its untaught grace and simplicity are a child's but the wisdom and the pathos of it are of all the ages that have come and gone since the race of man has lived and longed and hoped and feared and doubted.[20]

NARRATOR: Sam went to Montreal the end of November to protect *The Prince and the Pauper* copyright; he wrote Livy on her birthday.

SAM: The longer I know you, the more and more I esteem and admire and honor you for your rare wisdom, your peculiar good sense, your fortitude, endurance, pertinacity. Your justice, your charity, kindliness, generosity, magnanimity, your *genuine* righteousness and your unapproachable excellence in the sublime and gracious offices of motherhood. Many wives call out love—that is common—but very few such honor and admiration. . . .

I offer you as a birthday present, the fact that only three profane expressions have issued from my lips *or existed in my heart* (which is the *great* thing) since the event of the 8th of last August. Of course I mean in waking hours: (curiously enough, or *not* curiously, I don't know which) there is no change in my dreams: in my dreams I still do swear like the very army in Flanders.[21]

NARRATOR: He sent a rebus letter to the children.

SAM: There,—that's for the children—was not sure that they could read writing; especially Jean, who is strangely ignorant in some things.[22]

NARRATOR: *The Prince and the Pauper* was published in December in America and England; it was dedicated "To Those Good-Mannered and Agreeable Children, Susy and Clara Clemens."

SAM: The proof-reading on the P & P cost me the last rags of my religion.[23]

"MOTHER" FAIRBANKS: It is just a lovely book, and I am as happy as if I had written it myself. . . .The book is your masterpiece in fineness—"The Innocents" was your bulletin—"The Prince and the Pauper" your specimen. Now, what comes next? There is time for another.[24]

SUSY: One of papa's latest books is "The Prince and the Pauper" and it is unquestionably the best book he has ever written, some people want him to keep to his old style, some gentleman wrote him, "I enjoyed Huckleberry Finn immensely [Susy was writing in 1885] and am glad to see that you have returned to your old style." That enoyed me that enoyed me greatly, because it trobles me to have so few people know papa, I mean really know him, they think of Mark Twain as a humorist joking at everything; "And with a mop of reddish brown hair which sorely needs the

barbars brush a roman nose, short stubby mustache, a sad care-
worn face, with maney crow's feet," etc. That is the way people
picture papa, I have wanted papa to write a book that would
reveal something of his kind sympathetic nature, and "The Prince
and the Pauper" partly does it. The book is full of lovely charming ideas, and oh the language! It is *perfect*. I think that one
of the most touching scenes in it, is where the pauper is riding
on horseback with his nobles in the "recognition procession" and
he sees his mother oh and then what followed! How she runs
to his side, when she sees him throw up his hand palm outward,
and is rudely pushed off by one of the King's officers, and then
how the little pauper's consceince troubles him when he remem-
bers the shameful words that were falling from his lips, when she
was turned from his side "I know you not woman" and how his
grandeurs were stricken valueless, and his pride consumed to
ashes. It is a wonderfully beautiful and touching little scene,
and papa has described it so wonderfully. I never saw a man
with so much variety of feeling as papa has; now the "Prince and
the Pauper" is full of touching places, but there is most always
a streak of humor in them somewhere. Now in the coronation—
in the stirring coronation, just after the little king has got his
crown back again papa brings that in about the Seal, where the
pauper says he used the Seal "to crack nuts with." Oh it is so
funny and nice! Papa very seldom writes a passage without some
humor in it somewhere, and I don't think he ever will.[25]

SAM: I had half a dozen of my books printed on China paper for
Susy and Bay and Koto ([Edward] House's adopted Japanese
daughter) and two or three other especial friends. Don't you
let me forget to hand that book to Koto; for I had her in mind
all the time I was ordering those special copies, and I should feel
even more ridiculous than usual if I forgot it now.[26]

NARRATOR: Edward H. House was a newspaperman whom Sam
had known years before. He had lived in Japan, taught there and
edited a paper there. The Clemenses all adored his adopted
daughter, the child of an Englishman and a Japanese woman.
House was interested in doing a dramatization of *The Prince and
the Pauper*.

The children were busy about Christmas; they were making
doll's clothes for a doll to be sent to Allie Webster, Charley's
daughter. Sam, after a particularly trying session with the tele-

phone, composed a Christmas message for Alexander Graham Bell.

SAM: It is my heart-warm and world-embracing Christmas hope and aspiration that all of us, the high, the low, the rich, the poor, the admired, the despised, the loved, . . . the hated, the civilized, the savage, . . . may eventually be gathered together in a heaven of everlasting rest and peace and bliss, except the inventor of the telephone.[27]

NARRATOR: Tiffany's interior decoration was not completed until February, but its progress was watched with admiration and impatience by all. Silver and gold stenciling decorated the ceilings and walls of the drawing room, where the predominant color was salmon, and the library, which was peacock blue. The lower half of the hall walls was paneled in mahogany stenciled in silver. The upper half was red with gold and black stenciling. At the stair landing, halfway to the second floor, the color changed to black and gold on olive green. This color scheme was carried throughout the halls to the third floor. Brilliant Tiffany stained glass and ceramic tiling added sparkling color. Over the fireplace in the library was a Tiffany brass plaque bearing Emerson's motto: "The ornament of a house is the friends who frequent it."

SAM: To us our house was not unsentient matter—it had a heart and a soul and eyes to see us with, and approvals and solicitudes and deep sympathies; it was of us, and we were in its confidence, and lived in its grace and in the peace of its benediction. We never came home from an absence that its face did not light up and speak out its eloquent welcome—and we could not enter it unmoved.[28]

SUSY'S ELEVENTH YEAR

1882–1883

NARRATOR: Sam's mother visited the family for several weeks at the time of Susy's birthday. She was planning to move to Keokuk with Orion and Mollie.

KATY: She used to visit us—she came twice to Hartford, and she used to tell Susy about going to dancing school and how the dancing master always danced with her, because she was the prettiest girl and the best dancer. She looked like Mr. Clemens—he resembled her very much. She was tall and slim and straight and had her face shaped just like Mr. Clemens'. Nice blue eyes—very clear and sharp. Her name was Jane Lampton. She was celebrated for her beauty, they said, able to dance all night and all day, as I told you. I suppose a good many of the things that made Mark Twain famous come from her—his sense of humor, too.[1]

NARRATOR: In April Sam went off with James R. Osgood of the firm of Houghton, Osgood & Company, his publisher, to gather more material for *Life on the Mississippi*. He wrote from "½ way to Memphis."

SAM: Good bye, my darling Livy and kiss everybody but Jean for me. Saml. P.S. Well, Jean too.[2]

NARRATOR: The river had not lost any of its charm.

SAM: I had myself called with the four o'clock watch, mornings, for one cannot see too many summer sunrises on the Mississippi. They are enchanting. First, there is the eloquence of silence; for a deep hush broods everywhere. Next, there is the haunting sense of loneliness, isolation, remoteness from the worry and bustle of the world. The dawn creeps in stealthily; the solid walls of black forest soften to gray, and vast stretches of the river open up and reveal themselves; the water is glass-smooth, gives off spectral little wreaths of white mist, there is not the faintest breath of wind, nor stir of leaf; the tranquillity is profound and infinitely satisfying. Then a bird pipes up, another follows, and soon the pipings develop into a jubilant riot of music. You see none of the birds; you simply move through an atmosphere of song which seems to sing itself. When the light has become a little stronger, you have one of the fairest and softest pictures imaginable. You have the intense green of the massed and crowded foliage near by; you see it paling shade by shade in front of you; upon the next projecting cape, a mile off or more, the tint has lightened to the tender young green of spring; the cape beyond that one has almost lost color and the furthest one, miles away under the horizon, sleeps upon the water a mere dim vapor, and hardly separable from the sky above it and about it. And all this stretch of river is a mirror, and you have the shadowy reflections of the leafage and the curving shores and the receding capes pictured in it. Well, that is all beautiful; soft and rich and beautiful; and when the sun gets well up, and distributes a pink flush here and a powder of gold yonder and a purple haze where it will yield the best effect, you grant that you have seen something that is worth remembering.[3]

Susy: Dear Papa—we all miss you very much, Jean calls for you almost every day, and mamma is very lonesome without you. Miss Murry has ben here, and she can play on the piano beaytifully, she played some pieces from Patience, and some of Scots. song. This morning Clara and I walked to Church with aunt Clara, and back with aunt Alice [Day], the sermon was very good, and the organist did not play so badly. Just the day you went away Katy, Clara and I went to take a long walk, after awhile we went to a little boat near the river. Clara was Capt. first and I was Dr. I found an old pail and fild it with water, gave it to Katy (who was a passenger). We found an old cloth to and cleaned out the boat a little. After awhile we went home, and we thought we had had a very nice time.

Today mamma went to see Mrs. Warner and so we hope to see Daisy soon. We are lerning to play Eucher now, and we like it very much, today played with mamma, Rosa, Katie, Clara and

Jaurge. We went to the mucical last Friday and we enjoyed it very much, I managed to get through with my pieces without one mistake. Dear papa you need not answer me my letter becouse I no you have not nearly enough time.[4]

CLARA: One of our neighbors, Mrs. Charles Dudley Warner, wife of the noted author . . . did a great deal to further Susy's and my interest in music. She used to give musicales four or five times during the winter, and often employed Susy and me to pass the cakes.

Once when I . . . had studied piano for a year, Mrs. Warner asked me to play two little Schumann pieces at one of her "grand" affairs. . . . I wore a wonderful brown velvet dress with a pale-blue bow at the neck, and . . . when I finished playing a great many people clapped and laughed very hard. I wondered why they laughed so much; I hadn't made any mistakes in the pieces and my dress surely was beautiful. Susy tried to comfort me by saying it was just a bad habit of grown people to laugh at children—there was nothing funny about me at all.[5]

NARRATOR: Livy watched for letters from Sam.

LIVY: I hoped for a dispatch or letter today. I wonder if you have reached New Orleans safely—I surely hope so.

We are all well. The house seems pretty dull and quiet with no one in it, particularly after the children go to bed. But it is a pleasant change after the rush that we have been in—however I should like you to enjoy it with me.

Good night I love you and am so glad that you are having such a good time.[6]

NARRATOR: Sam was looking forward to meeting "Uncle Remus."

SAM: Mr. Joel Chandler Harris ("Uncle Remus") was to arrive from Atlanta at seven o'clock Sunday morning; so we got up and received him. We were able to detect him among the crowd of arrivals at the hotel-counter by his correspondence with a description of him which had been furnished us from a trustworthy source. He was said to be undersized, red-haired, and somewhat freckled. He was the only man in the party whose outside tallied with this bill of particulars. He was said to be very shy.[7]

We spent yesterday afternoon and last night at Mr. Cable's house. Uncle Remus was there, but was too bashful to read; so the children of the neighborhood flocked in to look at him (and were grievously disappointed to find he was white and young) and I read Remus' stories and my own stuff to them, and Cable read from the Grandissimes and sketches.

NARRATOR: On May 6th Sam was on his way back up the river.

SAM: We had a rattling nice storm yesterday afternoon: strong wind, blue-black sky, crawly white waves, vast sheets of driving rain, superb bursts of lightning, and a most inspiring cannonade of big thunder. And after it a couple of rainbows and the level rays of the sinking sun turned the Natchez hills into a kind of green-tinted conflagration. It was the kind of effect we get out of the low afternoon sun at home; and I thought of it shining on you loved ones at dinner and pouring upon Emmaline and the gold walls of the library.[8]

NARRATOR: Emmeline (variously spelled) was the water color portrait of the head of a young girl which Sam had bought in Milan in 1878.

He made a nostalgic visit to Hannibal.

SAM: Alas! everything was changed in Hannibal—but when I reached Third or Fourth street the tears burst forth, for I recognized the mud. It at least was the same—the same old mud—the mud that Annie Macdonald got stuck in.[9]

Livy darling, I am desperately homesick. But I have promised Osgood, and must stick it out; otherwise I would take the train at once and break for home. . . .

Now I am under way again, upon this hideous trip to St. Paul, with a heart brimming full of thoughts and images of you and Susy and Bay and the peerless Jean.[10]

I have mightily enjoyed the children's letters, and even *Jean's* letter—(where she blotted a word for you). Well, I haven't seen any lady who is your equal—"taken by and large," as the sailors say—and none whom I could ever love half as well as I do you.[11]

NARRATOR: Home the end of May, Sam found everyone well; the children were bursting with activity.

SAM: Patrick rode horseback with the children in the forenoons; in the afternoons he drove them out, with their mother; Susy never on the box, Clara always there, holding the reins in the safe places and prattling a stream. . . . The children had a deep admiration for Patrick, for he was spanking driver, yet never had an accident. . . .

Patrick was apt to be around when needed, and this happened . . . when he was sorely needed indeed. On the second floor of the stable there was a large oat-bin, whose lid shut with a spring. It had a couple of feet of oats in it. Susy, Clara, and Daisy Warner climbed into it, the lid fell and they were prisoners, there in the dark. They were not able to help themselves, their case was serious, they would soon exhaust the air in that box, then they would suffocate.

Our house was not close by; Patrick's house was a part of the stable, but between it and the stable were thick walls, muffled screams could not bore through them. We at home in the house were comfortable and serene, not suspecting that an awful tragedy was imminent on the premises. Patrick arrived from down town and happened to step into the carriage house instead of passing along to his own door, as had been his purpose. He noticed dull cries, but could not at once tell whence they proceeded— sounds are difficult things to locate. A stupider man would have gone outside, and lost his head, and hunted frantically everywhere but in the right place; a few minutes of this would have answered all tragic purposes. But Patrick was not stupid; he kept his head and listened, then moved when he had reached a conclusion.

It was not Susy that arranged that scrape, it was Clara; Susy was not an inventor of adventures, she was only an accommodating and persuadable follower of reckless inventors of such things, for in her gentle make-up were no nineteen second-hand nationalities and the evil energies of that Egyptian volcano. Susy took, in its turn, each step of the series that led up to the scrape, but she originated none of them, it was mainly Clara's work, the outcome of her heredities. . . .

It is pitiful, those frightened little prisoners struggling, pushing and screaming in the swelter and smother of that pitch-dark hole.[12]

NARRATOR: Clara had been given a new nickname by Jean.

SAM: She calls Susy and Clara "Guck and Ben." We have dropped "Bay" and adopted "Ben," in consequence. . . .

Ben had a birth-day party of 67 children, 8th of June.[13]

NARRATOR: Clara's party led to quarantine.

SAM: Our packing is all finished, today, and a special car engaged to transport our family to Elmira N.Y. for the summer—but now a horrible rash appears upon the body of the baby!—and there is much scarlet fever in the town. The child has been pretty sick during several days; consequently we are now all of a sudden become unspeakably alarmed. The doctor cannot tell, yet, whether this rash is only heat or the other dreadful thing.[14]

NARRATOR: It was scarlet fever.

SAM: Jean . . . was a prisoner some weeks. It delayed our journey to Elmira by six weeks, and delayed "Life on the Mississippi" more than twice as long.[15]

I had to telegraph and countermand the order for special sleeping car; and in fact we all had to fly around in a lively way and undo the patient preparations of weeks—rehabilitate the dismantled house, unpack the trunks, and so on. A couple of days later, the eldest child was taken down with so fierce a fever that she was soon delirious—not scarlet fever, however. Next, I myself was stretched on the bed with three diseases at once, and all of them fatal. But I never did care for fatal diseases if I could only have privacy and room to express myself concerning them.

We gave early warning, and of course nobody has entered the house in all this time but one or two reckless old bachelors—and they probably wanted to carry the disease to the children of former flames of theirs. The house is still in quarantine [July 3rd] and must remain so for a week or two yet—at which time we are hoping to leave for Elmira.[16]

NARRATOR: Sam was one of Jean's nurses.

SAM: Jean is skinning, now; and of course this is a time of great solicitude. For two weeks and a half, now, Rosa, Livy and I have been Jean's nurses; and nobody else but the doctor allowed in that part of the house—and nobody allowed to enter the front door. I have written no letters, attended to no business, not even matters of the vastest importance.[17]

NARRATOR: They were able to go to the farm by the end of July.

SAM: Jean is nearly well, at last. She has been having a rough teething time for a fortnight, and is a skeleton with the complexion of a ghost now.[18]

NARRATOR: They stayed late at the farm that year, Sam working on *Life on the Mississippi.*

SAM: I've rushed in here [*Century* office], with 30 minutes to spare before rushing for the Hartford train. . . . Arrived [New York City] yesterday evening [September 28th] with my whole tribe and 2 cats, from the summer vacation. Shall reach Hartford this evening. A week hence, we shall be all straightened up, there.[19]

The weather turned cold, and we had to rush home, while I still lacked thirty thousand words. I had been sick and got delayed. I am going to write all day and two-thirds of the night until the thing is done or break down at it. The spur and burden of the contract are intolerable to me. I can endure the irritation of it no longer.[20]

KATY: At the top of the house was the famous Billiard Room where Mr. Clemens used to do all his writing (and I did the dusting!), and where we used to fight over them precious manuscripts of his. . . .

He had a table there, you know, and Mrs. Clemens used to go up and dust that table every morning and arrange his manuscript and writing.[21]

SAM: I went to work at nine o'clock yesterday morning [October 29th], and went to bed an hour after midnight. Result of the day . . . 9,500 words. So I reduced my burden by one third in one day. It was five days work in one. I have nothing more to borrow or steal; the rest must all be writing. It is ten days work, and unless something breaks, it will be finished in five.[22]

NARRATOR: The book finished, the relays of visitors commenced.

SAM: Cable has been here, creating worshipers on all hands. He is a marvelous talker on a deep subject. I do not see how even Spencer, could unwind a thought more smoothly or orderly, and do it in cleaner, clearer crisper English. He astounded Twichell with his faculty.[23]

NARRATOR: Susy and Clara resumed classes with Miss Bridges, their governess during a year which Miss Foote spent abroad. Sam wrote Chatto & Windus, his London publishers, for "some maps which our governess wants and has not been able to obtain here. . . ."

He further indicated: "Outline Maps, printed on drawing paper, the size of each Map being 14½ by 11½ inches.

"There are 24 of these Outline Maps published, and of them I want the following.

"1 each of 'World in Hemispheres, Chart of World, British Isles, Australia, West India Islands, Oceania, South America.

"2 each of Europe, North America, Asia and Africa."[24]

He wrote Howells "the latest" about the children.

SAM: The children's governess [Miss Bridges] required them to set down the names of such celebrities as they could recall. You have here the result.

NARRATOR: Sam wrote the note on a sheet of ruled paper which contained the children's lists of "Famous Men" and "Famous Women." He labeled this sheet "Clara's." Her "Famous Men" were: "Columbus, Mr. Clemens, Mr. Millet, Henry Hudson, Mr. Dickens"; her "Famous Women": "Queen Isabella, Mrs. Stowe, Miss Bridges." A similar sheet was labeled "Susy's List," and her "Men" were: "Longfellow, Papa (Mark Twain), Columbus, Teneson, Ferdinad." Her "Famous Women" were, with help from an adult hand: "Boadicea, Bloody Mary, Mrs. Lisy Champtney [the wife of the painter, J. Wells Champney], Isabella."

SAM: Susy was 11, Clara 9. Mrs. Harriet Beecher Stowe was our nearest neighbor; that accounts for her appearance among the renowned. I suppose fathers are usually great men to their children; so I may not in fairness charge this couple with lifting me among the elect with designs upon me slanting toward candy. But I am not so sure about Miss Bridges's case. She being the governess, (it is possible that) Clara's promotion of her has a suspicious look about it. It seems to me to smell of flattery.

The Millet referred to is Frank W., the artist. His promotion was prompted by love, and is above criticism.[25]

KATY: Mr. Clemens always took part in everything and he helped everybody and he was just so good to the children. He was charming with them. He loved all children and they loved him and used to abuse him, too (that is, Susy and Clara did). They used to sit on his lap and pull his hair and pull him all over the house, you know, and he was always ready to crawl on his hands and knees or lie on his back or do anything to make them laugh. . . .

"Now, papa, you've got to do so-and-so this evening."

"All right," he'd say, "we'll play horse or anything you like." So he'd get down on his knees and she'd [Clara] get up on his back and pull his hair for the lines—and pull it good and hard, too, I can tell you.[26]

NARRATOR: Storytelling continued apace in the library.

SUSY: He does tell perfectly delightful stories. Clara and I used to sit on each arm of his chair and listen while he told us stories about the pictures on the wall.[27]

SAM: Susy and Clara—one on each side of me—selecting hickory nut kernels for me—"That's a good one." They beguiled me into many an indigestion and loss of sleep.[28]

Along one side of the library . . . the bookshelves joined the mantelpiece—in fact, there were shelves on both sides of the mantelpiece. On these shelves and on the mantelpiece stood various ornaments. At one end of the procession was a framed oil-painting of a cat's head; at the other end was a head of a beautiful young girl, life size—called Emmeline, because she looked just about like that—an impressionist water-color. Between the one picture and the other there were twelve or fifteen of the bric-à-brac things . . . also an oil-painting by Elihu Vedder, "The Young Medusa." Every now and then the children required me to construct a romance—always impromptu—not a moment's preparation permitted—and into that romance I had to get all that bric-à-brac and the three pictures. I had to start always with the cat and finish with Emmeline. I was never allowed the refreshment of a change, end for end. It was not permissible to introduce a bric-à-brac ornament into the story out of its place in the procession.

These bric-à-bracs were never allowed a peaceful day, a reposeful day, a restful Sabbath. In their lives there was no Sabbath; in their lives there was no peace; they knew no existence but a monotonous career of violence and bloodshed. In the course of time the bric-à-brac and the pictures showed wear. It was because they had had so many and such tumultuous adventures in their romantic career.[29]

CLARA: Father never showed the least sign of being bored when my sister Susy and I clambered upon his knee, begging for a "long" story. This entertainment usually took place in the room we called the library, which was our living-room. In the large fireplace large logs blazed almost continuously, for in spite of furnace heat this room was often cold, owing to winds that howled about the windows during the winter season. The library as well as the dining-room faced a small river and wooded ravine. Seated in a large armchair in front of the fire, with my sister and me in his lap, Father would start a story about the pictures on the wall. Passing from picture to picture, his power of invention led us into countries and among human figures that held us spellbound. He treated a Medusa head according to his own individual method, the snakes being sometimes changed to laurel leaves that tickled joy in Medusa's hair and inspired thoughts of victory. If the colored butler, George, interrupted the tale by announcing a caller, or a meal ready to be served, our hearts sank and did not rise until Father returned to the tales of the pictures. He must have had unflinching patience and I have sometimes wondered if my mother did not send in the butler on imaginary errands to protect him against too much discomfort from the insatiable demands of his tiny auditors.

There was a beautiful conservatory off the library and the scent from the plants brought reality to some of the tropical scenes described by Father. One day a snake came wriggling into the room across the rugs straight for our chair. He must have gotten in from the conservatory, but how he found his way there we never guessed. Father dropped us both to the floor and seizing a pair of tongs from the fireplace lifted the snake in the air and precipitated him through a door in the bay window that faced the wooded ravine. This incident relieved Father from any further oratory that afternoon.[30]

SAM: Jean is incomparably sweet, and good, and entertaining. Sits in my lap, at the fag-end of dinner, and eats "Jean-quum" (crumbs,) and messes up the table with "Jean shawt" (salt,) puts "Jean fum" (plums—i.e. grapes) in the "Jean himble-bo" (finger-bowl,) and says "Naughty George—ve'y naughty George," when George brushes off her salt. Won't consent that she is mamma's blessed Miss Jane—no, is "*Papa* besshy Mish Chain."[31]

KATY: The children never spoke English in the nursery—they always spoke German, 'cause Mrs. Clemens wanted them to be able to talk it good before they got over there.[32]

NARRATOR: Jean had a German nursemaid named Elise.

SAM: . . . a sweet and innocent and plump little creature, with peachy cheeks; a clear-souled little maiden and without offense, notwithstanding her profanities, and she was loaded to the eyebrows with them. She was a mere child. She was not fifteen yet. She was just from Germany and knew no English. She was always scattering her profanities around, and they were such a satisfaction to me that I never dreamed of such a thing as modifying her. For my own sake, I had no disposition to tell on her. Indeed, I took pains to keep her from being found out. I told her to confine her religious expressions to the children's quarters, and urged her to remember that Mrs. Clemens was prejudiced against piety on week days. To the children, the little maid's profanities sounded natural and proper and right because they had been used to that kind of talk in Germany, and they attached no evil importance to it. . . . The trial of that little creature's life was the children's hair. She would tug and strain with her comb, accompanying her work with her misplaced pieties. And when finally she was through with her triple job she always fired up and exploded her thanks toward the sky, where they belonged, in this form: "Gott sei Dank! Ich bin schon fertig mit'm Gott verdammtes Haar!" (I believe I am not quite brave enough to translate it.)[33]

CLARA: I remember long conversations Father and Susy used to have about the value or significance of certain words. . . . In one instance my sister wished to use the word "humans" for the sake of brevity in a poetic line, and Father said there was no such word. My sister thought it well, then, to invent it.[34]

SAM: She is growing steadily into an admirably discriminating habit of language. Yes, and into the use of pretty large words, too, sometimes—as witness: The night before, I referred to some preference expressed by Jean. Susy wanted at once to know *how* she expressed it—inasmuch as Jean knows only about a dozen words. I said, "Why she spoke up, with marked asperity, and exclaimed, 'Well, Mr. Clemens, you may support that fallacy, if native perversity and a fatuous imagination so move you; but the exact opposite is my distinct and decided preference!' "

Susy's grave eyes stood wide open during this speech; she was silent a moment to let it soak home, then said in a tone of absolute conviction, "Well, papa, that *is* an exaggeration!"[35]

CLARA: There was rarely an hour when something of his genius did not shine forth. Even when surrounded by comforts and luxuries, he never sank into their clutches. He did not become "comfortable" to the detriment of his intellect and soul. Both were continually on fire. Not even in sleep could I imagine his mind completely at rest. Wherever he was, he created a world of energized thought. The force in his personality, resulting from an ever-productive brain and a Latin temperament, electrified some people to a certain false brilliancy which only belonged to them in his presence. Those who were habitually stupid became intelligent, and those who were brilliant became super-brilliant. Sparks started by Father grew to flames in their passage from brain to brain. Although a very small child, when guests like Nansen, the explorer, Sir Edwin Arnold, or eminent actors, Edwin Booth and Henry Irving among them, graced our hearthstone, I remember feeling that the dynamic figure of Mark Twain did not pale by their side.[36]

NARRATOR: One day, Mrs. Taft, the doctor's wife, came with a little autograph book which she wanted Sam to sign before she sent it to some friends abroad. He decided that even a fraction of that distant world should know that he could write "pretty able poetry."

SAM   QUESTION AND ANSWER

Who shooteth folk with wit's keen shaft,
                              Mrs. Taft?

Whose clear head maketh mine seem daft,
                              Mrs. Taft?

Who aye compassion had for my sad craft,
                              Mrs. Taft?

And o'er my humor wept when others laughed,
                              Mrs. Taft?

Who into shams drives blade unto the haft,
                              Mrs. Taft?

But heartening cheer to merit aye doth waft,
                              Mrs. Taft?

Whose heart doth keep the wine of life on draft—
Good-fellowship—to be by all the thirsty quaffed,
                              Mrs. Taft?

What answer answereth this whole raft?—
                              MRS. TAFT![37]

NARRATOR: The busy life included festive dinner parties during which Clara later recalled that she and Susy used to sit on the stairs and listen to the gaiety.

CLARA: We got into this habit because we used to hear so many peals of laughter in the distance that we would run to discover the cause of all the mirth. Almost always it turned out that Father was telling a funny story.[38]

NARRATOR: One of Sam's favorite stories was about an old beggar woman he encountered in Horta.

SAM: When she saw me she drifted out and held out her hand. Such friendliness in a strange land touched me, and I seized it. I shook it cordially, and said:

"Madame, I do not know your name, but this act has graven your—your—peculiar features upon my heart, and there they shall remain while that heart continues to throb."[39]

CLARA: We used to announce to each other, "Father is telling the beggar story; they must have reached the meat course."[40]

NARRATOR: Sam told how the beggar woman kept on kissing her palm to him and curtsying and how he persisted in misunderstanding her.

SAM: This unhappy woman loves me: I cannot reciprocate; I cannot love a foreigner; I cannot love a foreigner as homely as she is. . . . I cannot love her, but this wildly beautiful affection she has conceived for me must not go unrewarded—it *shall* not go unrewarded. And so I said, "I will read to her my poetic paraphrase of the Declaration of Independence."[41]

CLARA: When he discovered that his children were taking their turn at having jokes about him, he laughed as much as if we had been very witty.[42]

NARRATOR: The dinner parties were grand affairs.

KATY: We had soup first, of course, and then the beef or ducks, you know, and then we'd have wine with our cigars, and we'd have sherry, claret, and champagne, maybe. . . . We'd always have crème de menthe and most always charlotte russe, too . . . we always had our ice cream put up in some wonderful shapes— like flowers or cherubs, little angels—all different kinds and different shapes and flavors, and colors—oh, everything lovely![43]

NARRATOR: Grace King, author of *Memories* of a *Southern Woman of Letters,* frequently visited in Nook Farm.

GRACE KING: The courses filed past our plates—it was the day of innumerable courses and the portentous array of forks and knives by each plate. Not a delicacy, not a luxury, in the way of eating, was missing from the menu.[44]

NARRATOR: The guests and children were not the only ones who enjoyed the stories.

KATY: George was always very grand and he just adored Mrs. Clemens. He thought there wasn't anybody in the world like Mrs. Clemens; but even so, she couldn't stop him from laughing out at the dinner parties when they were telling stories and having them good jokes. Mrs. Clemens used to take George to task very often about this. If Mr. Clemens or any gentleman was there at dinner and they was telling jokes, if there was anything very funny to laugh at, George would be the first one to laugh! He'd laugh right out loud, before Mrs. Clemens or anybody. He'd laugh right out loud before anybody could stop him—that colored laugh that was kind of loud. He'd laugh before he could even get his handkerchief out and put it up to his mouth to stop the laugh. He couldn't wait until he got to the pantry to roar.[45]

CLARA: When only members of the family were seated at table, however, he preferred listening to the conversation to passing them food. He explained that the intellectual inspiration he received in the dining-room saved him from the bad effects of life in the inferior atmosphere of the kitchen.[46]

KATY: George and I was always great friends, even if he was black and I was white.[47]

CLARA: She and the butler used to fight in such picturesque language that Father often threatened to put them in print. Yet, in spite of the descriptive names they called each other when quarreling, they were at other times the best of friends. A chief cause for discord was the question as to which one did the most work and served the family best. Nothing short of death could really settle that argument, but Father closed it once for a short period. He stepped between them and said, "You are both far too clever to do much work." They weren't expecting any such blow and fell into silence.[48]

NARRATOR: There were times when George acted as peacemaker.

SAM: He was invaluable; for his large wisdoms and his good nature made up for his defects. He was the peace-maker in the kitchen— in fact the peace-keeper, for by his good sense and right spirit and mollifying tongue he adjusted disputes in that quarter before they reached the quarrel-point. The materials for war were all there. There was a time when we had a colored cook—Presbyterian; George—Methodist; Rosa, German nurse—Lutheran; Katy, American-Irish—Roman Catholic; Kosloffska, Pole, wet-nurse— Greek Catholic; "English Mary," some kind of a non-conformist; yet under George's benignant influence and capable diplomacy it was a Barnum's Happy Family, and remained so.[49]

CLARA: George was a great addition to the family and afforded Father almost as much amusement as Father did George.[50]

SAM: There was nothing commonplace about George. He had a

remarkably good head; his promise was good, his note was good he could be trusted to any extent with money or other valuables; his word was worth par, when he was not protecting Mrs. Clemens or the family interests or furnishing information about a race horse to a person he was purposing to get a bet out of; he was strenuously religious, he was deacon and autocrat of the African Methodist Church; no dirt, no profanity, ever soiled his speech, and he neither drank nor smoked. . . . He was well and creditably known to the best whites in the town, and he had the respect and I may say the warm friendly regard of every visiting intimate of our house. Added to all this, he could put a lighted candle in his mouth and close his lips upon it. Consider the influence of a glory like that upon our little kids in the nursery. To them he was something more than mortal; and to their affection for him they added an awed and reverent admiration.[51]

SUSY'S TWELFTH YEAR

1883–1884

NARRATOR: Susy's birthday was celebrated very quietly; the whole place was quarantined for scarlet fever.

SAM: Mrs. Clemens and I got home from New York last night, where we had been since Monday morning . . . we are in a good deal of a flurry here. One of the coachman's children is dying and since midnight Mrs. Clemens has been rather alarmingly ill.[1]

Patrick, the coachman, has seven children and they began to entertain the scarlet fever sometime in January, and have treated it one at a time, and each took the customary six weeks to it, till four or five of them had worried it through, when the supply ran out, owing to some oversight. During several months there was no communication between the house and the stable except by speaking tubes. During several days two of the children lay so near death that the news of their departure was expected hourly.[2]

Clara Spaulding arrived on a visit, and Susy gave her a full and animated account of these momentous and marvelous things. Aunt Clara said:

"Why, considering how very low, those two were, it seems next to miraculous that they got well. But they *did* get well?"

"Yes—both of them." Then, after a pause—pensively: *"It was a great disappointment to us."*

Aunt Clara was astounded—in fact pretty nearly paralyzed; but she didn't "let on"—only said—

"Why?"

"Well, you know, aunt Clara"—another pause—grave deliberation, to get her thought into form—"Well, you see, aunt Clara, we've never had any experience of a funeral."

"Oh, I see. But you—you didn't want the children to die?"

"Well, no—not that, exactly. But—in case they did die—well,—they—we—well, you know, we've never had a funeral."

"Still, it was scarlet fever, and you wouldn't have been allowed to attend it."

"No—I suppose Mamma wouldn't have let us. But then, you know, we could have observed it."

It was the éclat of the thing—the pomp, and solemnity and commotion. That is what Susy was after.[3]

She was entirely serious about the matter; explained that she was not desiring the death of the children, at all, but in as much as the hope of their death had been held out all this time, she could not well help feeling a sense of disappointment and even injury. . . . As a general thing her speeches sound about forty-five years old, and are prodigiously entertaining; but Clara is a perfectly natural child, with nothing remarkable about her; and the same may be said of Jean. Jean can speak a good [sic] of English, and does it; she could speak German also, if she would, but as a general thing she won't.[4]

Livy has been sick a bed for a month or two, with a procession of diseases passing through her: first, diphtheria, then a couple of days of peculiarly vindictive fever; then a week of quinsy; then several minor things, representing citizens on foot and in carriages, whose technical names I have forgotten.[5]

NARRATOR: Sam wanted to take her to Elmira to recuperate.

SAM: There is not much to say about Mrs. Clemenses case. I am not sure that she is any further ahead than she was. . . . She has no disease, now, but then she has no appetite. Consequently she gains no strength, but stands still; that is, lies still, mainly. However, as soon as she shall be able to travel on a mattress, I shall take her to Elmira, N.Y., and see if her mother can nurse her back to health.[6]

NARRATOR: Livy would not leave the children.

SAM: Your loving letter touched Livy deeply (both of us, indeed,) and did her more good than all the day's medicines. I know, and she knows, that a fortnight under the home roof, with the home faces around, and the home affections and tendernesses shining out of them, would bring healing and health to Livy quicker than all other cures combined; and for a while, it was our dream to try it the moment she should be strong enough to travel; but now that Livy's strength has really begun to dribble perceptibly back, she is afraid to venture: for it would be small benefit to her if the children were along; and to leave them behind in this town whose death-rate has been for months just double what it ought in reason to be, is a thing which she can contemplate and HAS contemplated—contemplating is easy—but at the same time is a thing which you and I know she isn't ever going to do. For a while I actually thought she *would;* but when I saw by the paper this morning that the Hartford death-list for the month of March reached the startling and disgraceful figure of 89, I no longer wanted her to venture away and risk the children here. We shall not forget your generous words and your loving invitation, nor let our appreciation of it fall dim or lose value; but I believe, with Livy, whose judgement is always good in such matters, that she had better stand to her post, now, and do the best she can in the circumstances, until the time for the summer flight shall arrive.[7]

LIVY: Susy was quite sick the other night with sore throat and fever and I was very thankful that I was here. There is so much Scarlet fever about that it makes me anxious about the children. . . .

I am a *great deal stronger* than I was a week ago.[8]

SAM: She is able to creep down stairs now, with my help, but will not get back her strength for six months yet. I could shave her with her shoulder blades; she has no more flesh than one of those old-fashioned hoop skirts. I am sure I never have seen so emaciated a person.[9]

LILLY WARNER: Livy is doing well now [April 21st], under a nurse's care, and the sweet soft air of these good days.[10]

Daisy is as well as a kitten—and as happy—now out walking with her "Clicky [presumably Clara] Clemens."

Livy is better and better—and the Gerhardt baby, over in Paris, a month old, is named Olivia for her.[11]

NARRATOR: Howells, from Europe, wrote about the Gerhardts.

HOWELLS: We saw the Gerhards in Paris. I took a fiacre and drove literally hell-wards to the region of the Boulevard d'Enfer, near which they live, and found the little woman preparing asparagus for their dinner in his studio. There was a stove in the middle of the room, a lounge-bed for the nurse and baby at one side, and a curtained corner where I suppose the Gerhards slept. It was as primitive and simple as all Chicopee, and virtuous poverty spoke from every appointment of the place. Gerhard was off at work somewhere, but the next day they both came to see us at our hotel, and Mrs. Howells took a great liking to them. . . . He seems to be a man of delicate and refined genius; the little medallion which he exhibited of you in the Salon was full of this, and seized your best points; it was artfully concealed from the public in the catalogue as the portrait of "M. Marc Swain," but it was favorably noticed by the critics.— You are those poor little people's god—I don't know but they'd like me to write you with the large G.[12]

NARRATOR: Dissatisfied with his publisher, Sam decided to go into business for himself.

SAM: I proposed to be my own publisher now and let young [Charley] Webster do the work. . . .

I erected Webster into a firm—a firm entitled Webster and Company, Publishers—and installed him in a couple of offices at a modest rental on the second floor of a building somewhere below Union Square.[13]

NARRATOR: *Life on the Mississippi* was published in May; Sam went to Montreal on copyright business. Livy wrote him.

LIVY: We are all well. Katy seems just like herself now. Jean has had a very naughty cry this evening and needed you here very much to rap on the nursery door—my rapping was not the least use. She needed a whipping, but I was too cowardly to give it to her. I have had to give her one little spatting today and I thought that was enough.

I had a pleasant call from Joe today, he is anxious to have a walk with you to the tower before we go away. I told him I thought you would undoubtedly be able to take it with him.

Susy said a sweet, lovely thing to me today. I took her to ride with me and we had a good time together. I have been a little worried at the much talking that there has been with Susy lately about mothers and daughters not agreeing. I think you will remember how many questions she asked Sue about Ida and her mother not getting on quite well together, she has been quite exercised on the subject and I have been afraid that she might begin to feel that it would be rather interesting not to get on quite well with me. Today as we rode she alluded again to mothers and daughters not getting on smoothly together, and I said "Susy I

hope we shall always agree," she said "Mamma we can never dis-
agree we think just alike about things, why Mamma we seem like
one person." I was happy![14]

NARRATOR: While Sam was away, Susy and Clara had a party, a
"reception." They invited their Hartford playmates and their
favorite adults, including Cable, who telegraphed regrets. Sam
wrote Cable.

SAM: The girls were mightily delighted with your telegram. I am
ever so glad you sent it. They had a royal time at their reception,
but I missed it through being at a social spree in Canada.[15]

NARRATOR: Everyone received a box of candy, as a favor, at the party.

SUSY: I thought it was very nice to have a place where candy was
kept and be able to go to it and get a piece of candy but to think
of having it crowded like this and an entire box for each of us.[16]

NARRATOR: The Day children, Katharine and Alice, daughters of
Livy's friend, Alice Hooker Day, were living in Hartford on Garden Street at this time.

KATHARINE DAY: Of the Clemens house I remember best at this
period the schoolroom where my sister and I played with the
children, their governess Miss Lily Foote, George, the impressive
colored butler, the greenhouse, the lovely conservatory opening
out of the library with its marble pebble walk around a marble
basin and three-tiered fountain, to us children's eyes the height
of elegance and luxury. At the top of this hierarchy of joys were
the fleeting glimpses of Mr. and Mrs. Clemens—vague, lovely
figures, deities, ordering all things well.

NARRATOR: Sam was much in demand at children's parties.

KATHARINE DAY: The first definite recollection of Mark Twain comes
when he stepped visually into our young circle through the kindness of his heart in coming with Susy and Clara to a children's
party at our house arranged by my mother, to tell his fear-com-
pelling story of the *Golden Arm!* After various other games, the
gas lights of the chandelier were lowered . . . we gathered in a
huddled circle, and he, a little outside of it, began the tale. The
piercing intensity of the question, "Whose got ma golden arm?"
repeated and gradually increasing to a high crescendo, and ending
with almost a shriek *"You"* and his outstretched arm pointing
toward the group in the dim light, produced a most dramatic
reaction. We all jumped terrified but delighted, and more fully
appreciated the return of the light and the coming of refresh-
ments.[17]

KATY: When Mr. Clemens told that story (he was always telling it at dinner parties) he would frighten everybody stiff. The company always said the shivers went straight down their spines—they felt like they was freezing to death![18]

NARRATOR: Sam and the children had had an active spring, but Livy had remained an invalid many weeks.

SAM: Mrs. Clemens is steadily improving, and probably weighs thirty or forty pounds now. We leave here for the summer a couple of weeks hence, and then I shall expect her to come right up and be her old self within thirty days.[19]

NARRATOR: They arrived at the farm in mid-July; an Elmira boy, who became a newspaperman, remembered Sam.

S. EDWARD ROSE: . . . a man in rumpled white clothes with a big cigar in his mouth. . . . His eyebrows were kind of bushy . . . and he had a droopy kind of mustache and when he took off his hat his hair wasn't combed. He talked kinda slow like and I wasn't afraid of him.[20]

SAM: Mrs. Clemens . . . is still proportioned like the tongs, but she is pulling up, now, and by and by will get some cushions on her, I reckon. I hope so, anyway—it's been like sleeping with a bed full of baskets. The children are booming, and my health is ridiculous, it's so robust, notwithstanding the newspaper misreports.

I haven't piled up MS so in years as I have done since we came here to the farm three weeks and a half ago.[21]

CLARA: The house in which my aunt lived was simple but very comfortable, with enough rooms to accommodate our family. Susy and I slept together, my younger sister, Jean, roomed with the nurse, and Father and Mother occupied a third room. Mrs. Crane often referred to her home as "Do as you Please Hall."[22]

SAM: Why, it's like old times, to step straight into the study, damp from the breakfast table, and sail right in and sail right on, the whole day long, without thought of running short of stuff or words. I wrote 4000 words to-day and I touch 3000 and upwards pretty often, and don't fall below 2600 on any working day. And when I get fagged out, I lie abed a couple of days and read and smoke, and then go at it again for 6 or 7 days. I have finished one small book, and am away along in a big one that I half-finished two or three years ago. I expect to complete it in a month or six weeks or two months more. And *I* shall *like* it, whether anybody else does or not. It's a kind of companion to Tom Sawyer. There's a raft episode from it in second or third chapter of Life on the Mississippi. . . .

We stay here till Sept. 10; then maybe a week at Indian Neck for sea air. Then home.[23]

NARRATOR: The Franklin Whitmores, Hartford friends, asked the Clemenses to go to the shore with them.

LIVY: Indeed I like the idea of going with you to Indian Neck in the Fall. I think it would hardly be best for us to stop there on our way back to Hartford, I should like better to run down there from Hartford, I think it would do the children good and would be exceedingly pleasant for us all.

We are having a delightful time here. Mr. Clemens is at work— and I never saw him in better working condition, or with more enthusiasm for his work. My principal occupations are reading aloud to the children, and cutting and basting dolls' clothes for them to make, we all enjoy it.

Mother seems very well and in good spirits this Summer, we spend a day in town with her occasionally.[24]

NARRATOR: Sam invented a history game.

SUSY: At the farm . . . he drove pegs into the ground all around the place representing each king's reign. . . . Then we used to play games running between these different pegs till finally we knew when each king or queen reigned, and in reference to the kings preceding them.[25]

SAM: Day before yesterday [July 19th], feeling not in condition for writing, I left the study, but I couldn't hold in—had to do something; so I spent eight hours in the sun with a yardstick, measuring off the reigns of the English kings on the roads in these grounds, from William the Conqueror to 1883, calculating to invent an open-air game which shall fill the children's heads with dates without study. I give each king's reign one foot of space to the year and drive one stake in the ground to mark the beginning of each reign, and I make the children call the stake by the king's name.[26]

CLARA: He made use of a large circular plot of ground in front of the house which was bounded by a road. Stakes were driven into the ground at varying intervals, suggesting the longer or shorter reigns of kings, and each stake bore the name of a king. Now the game consisted in racing past the stakes and calling out names and dates of the numerous kings and their reigns. The panting aspirant was pronounced victor according to the lack of mistakes his voice made while his feet led the pace. . . . Father's curly hair waved in the breeze, caused by the speed of his rapid feet.[27]

SAM: You can stand in the door and take a bird's-eye view of English monarchy, from the Conqueror to Edward IV.; then you can turn and follow the road up the hill to the study and beyond with an opera-glass, and bird's-eye view the rest of it to 1883.

You can mark the sharp difference in the *length* of reigns by the varying distances of the stakes apart. You can see Richard II., two feet; Oliver Cromwell, two feet; James II., three feet, and so on—and then big skips; pegs standing forty-five, forty-six, fifty, fifty-six, and sixty feet apart (Elizabeth, Victoria, Edward III., Henry III., and George III.). By the way, third's a lucky number for length of days, isn't it? Yes, sir; by my scheme you get a realizing notion of the *time* occupied by reigns.

The reason it took me eight hours was because, with little Jean's interrupting assistance, I had to measure from the Conquest to the end of Henry VI. three times over, and besides I had to whittle out all those pegs.[28]

JERVIS LANGDON: To us as little children Mr. Clemens as the uncle of the study at Quarry Farm . . . was a source of wonder and joy. To be sure there were hours when the six children [3 Clemenses, 3 Langdons] must keep away from the study, but there were other hours of wonderful games and stories. My uncle indulged in "making out," as we called it, stories from pictures that we would choose. We recall that the Vicar of Wakefield was the first favorite. Fancy the possibilities lying in scenes devised by sedate old Goldsmith and interpreted to small children by Mark Twain's fantasy. . .

Mr. Clemens was fond of some card games, though billiards were his chief delight. His comments while playing bezique made cards tolerable even to those who didn't like them. "We-ell, I've detained this dark lady long enough. Never did like her—can't see what that King of Spades sees in her—but land! he can have her. Let 'em have a Royal Marriage and see where they come out."[29]

NARRATOR: News came from Hartford of the illness of their beloved Dr. Taft. Sam wrote Mrs. Taft for himself and Livy.

SAM: I must not add a hair's-weight—not even the weight of a friendly and solicitous letter—to the sick man's burdens; so we come to you, Mrs. Clemens and I, to say we are troubled by these newspaper reports; we cannot *have* him helpless who has been everybody's help, we cannot have him "weak" who has been everybody's strength, we cannot have him tottering from mountain to sea, seeking health, who all these years has been health's own chosen messenger to waiting thousands. Rest?—*yes;* let him rest, for he has earned it, wasting his impaired forces in untimely night journeys to such as us, that we might live and be strong again: but let it stop with resting; do not tell us he shall not be himself again; nor that he must withdraw and clothe another in the semblance of his art and skill and send him in his place—for what is Sir Kay in Sir Launcelot's armor, but only Sir Kay, after all, and not Sir Launcelot?

To my poor mind, the first of holy callings is the physician's; and he should walk before Pope and Cardinal, and all the priestly tribe, for he heals hurts that are real, not imaginary; and his charity is above theirs, for he heals all that fall in his way, not merely the chance sufferer here and there who is willing to say, first, "Good Galilean, I subscribe to the conditions." And to my mind, first of all the good physician is *our* good physician; and to him I and mine send homage and greeting, and the highest best hopes and the broadest and deepest and warmest good wishes that can be spoken. And the same also to you, if we may.[30]

NARRATOR: As customary, they all went down to Elmira to celebrate Mrs. Langdon's birthday.

SAM: It was lovely in you to turn the tables on us all so happily, and make the season which was properly the season of love-offerings *to* you a festival of love-offerings *from* you.[31]

NARRATOR: At the Langdon house, the children always gravitated to the third floor where a curtained platform in an alcove was known as the St. Nicholas Theater. Julie Langdon and her friend Fanny Darby set up elaborate tea parties with Julie's doll, Hilda, sitting in the doll's rocker. Little Ida was somewhat bothersome to the older girls and Clara was "giggly," but Susy's arrival completely disrupted the tea party; she always wanted to play charades. She organized the little ones, turned the house upside down for costumes and proposed words that the others had never heard of, like "ingratiate." Even a game like "Duck on a Rock," where a small stone had to be knocked off a rock to "get in free," was "improved" by Susy to make it "more dramatic."[32]

Susy put up with younger children's activities, but they paled beside *The Adventures of Huckleberry Finn,* the story Sam had been working on, off and on, for almost seven years.

SAM: I've just finished writing a book; and modesty compels me to say it's a rattling good one, too—"Adventures of Huckleberry Finn." (Tom Sawyer's comrade.)[33]

SUSY: Ever since papa and mama were married papa has written his books and then taken them to mama in manuscript, and she has expergated them. Papa read *Huckleberry Finn* to us in manuscript, just before it came out, and then he would leave parts of it with Mama to expergate, while he went off to the study to work, and sometimes Clara and I would be sitting with mama while she was looking the manuscript over, and I remember so well, with what pangs of regret we used to see her turn down the leaves of the pages, which meant that some delightfully terrible part must be scratched out. And I remember one part pertickularly which was perfectly fascinating it was so terrible, that Clara and I used to delight in and oh, with what despair we saw mama turn down the leaf on which it was written, we thought the book would almost be ruined without it. But we gradually came to think as mama did.[34]

SAM: The children always helped their mother to edit my books in manuscript. She would sit on the porch at the farm and read aloud, with her pencil in her hand, and the children would keep an alert and suspicious eye upon her right along, for the belief was well grounded in them that whenever she came across a particularly satisfactory passage she would strike it out.[35]

I remember the special case mentioned by Susy, and can see the group yet—two-thirds of it pleading for the life of the culprit sentence that was so fascinatingly dreadful, and the other third of it patiently explaining why the court could not grant the prayer of the pleaders; but I do not remember what the condemned phrase was. It had much company, and they all went to the gallows; but it is possible that that especially dreadful one which gave those little people so much delight was cunningly devised and put into the book for just that function, and not with any hope or expectation that it would get by the "expergator" alive. It is possible, for I had that custom.[36]

For my own entertainment and to enjoy the protests of the children, I often abused my editor's innocent confidence. I often interlarded remarks of a studied and felicitously atrocious character purposely to achieve the children's brief delight and then see the remorseless pencil do its fatal work. I often joined my supplications to the children's for mercy and strung the argument out and pretended to be in earnest. They were deceived and so was their mother. It was three against one and most unfair. But it was very delightful and I could not resist the temptation. Now and then we gained the victory and there was much rejoicing. Then I privately struck the passage out myself. It had served its purpose. It had furnished three of us with good entertainment, and in being removed from the book by me it was only suffering the fate originally intended for it.[37]

NARRATOR: At home in Hartford, the children settled down to lessons; cats still played a large part in family life.

SAM: Susy said the other day when she saw Jean bringing a cat to me of her own motion, "Jean has found out already that mamma loves morals and papa loves cats."[38]

It is a pleasure to me to recall various incidents which reveal the delicacies of feeling which were so considerable a part of her budding character. Such a revelation came once in a way which, while creditable to her heart, was defective in another direction. . . . Her mother had been making the Christmas purchases and she allowed Susy to see the presents which were for Patrick's children. Among these was a handsome sled for Jimmy, on which a stag was painted; also in gilt capitals the word "DEER." Susy was excited and joyous over everything until she came to this sled. Then she became sober and silent—yet the sled was the choicest of all the gifts. Her mother was surprised and also disappointed, and said:

"Why, Susy, doesn't it please you? Isn't it fine?"

Susy hesitated and it was plain that she did not want to say the thing that was in her mind. However, being urged, she brought it haltingly out:

"Well, mamma, it *is* fine and of course it *did* cost a good deal—but—but—why should that be mentioned?"

Seeing that she was not understood, she reluctantly pointed to that word "DEER." It was her orthography that was at fault, not her heart. She had inherited both from her mother.[39]

CLARA: When Christmas Eve arrived at last, we children hung up our stockings in the schoolroom next to our nursery, and did it with great ceremony. Mother always recited the thrilling little

Sam and Livy Clemens and their daughters on the *ombra* of their Hartford House.

Sam and Livy about the time of their marriage

Livy's parents, Olivia and Jervis Langdon

Drawing room of the
Langdon house, where Sam and
Livy were married
February 2, 1870

The Jervis Langdon house, Elmira, New York

Olivia Susan (Susy) Clemens, b. 1872

Clara Langdon Clemens, b. 1874

Jane Lampton (Jean) Clemens, b. 1880

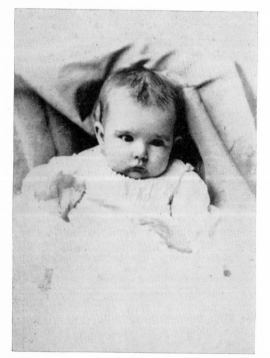

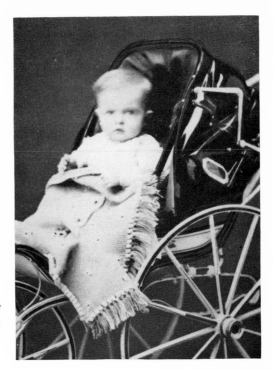

gdon Clemens, Sam and Livy's only
son, died in infancy (1870–1872).

Clara, Jean and Susy with their dog Hash in 1884

Dr. and Mrs. A. R. Jackson, friends from the *Quaker City* voyage, with the Clemenses at Hartford

The Clemens house in Nook Farm, Hartford

George and Lilly Warner were Nook Farm neighbors

Susan and Charles Dudley Warner, co-author with Mark Twain of *The Gilded Age*, lived next door to the Clemenses

Harriet Beecher Stowe

Mrs. Stowe's house in Nook Farm

Clara Spaulding, Susy, Livy, Sam and Dr. John Brown, author
of *Rab and His Friends*, in Edinburgh, 1873

John Lewis, tenant farmer at Quarry Farm, who stopped Mrs. Charles Langdon's runaway horse

Quarry Farm, home of Sue and Theo Crane, where the Clemenses spent their summers

Susan Langdon Crane, Livy's adopted sister, and her husband, Theodore Crane

Charles Jervis Langdon, Livy's brother, and his wife, Ida Clark Langdon

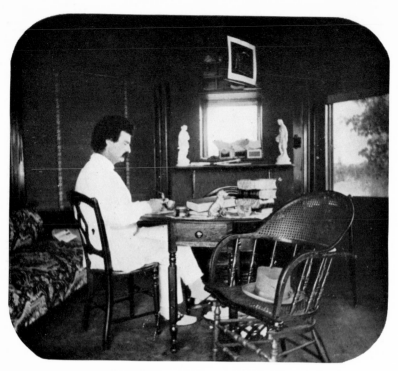

Sam in his study at Quarry Farm

Sam's study on the hill above the house was built for him by his sister-in-law, Sue Crane

Susy and Clara
in Munich
in 1878

Clara with her pet calf Jumbo in Hartford

Katy Leary, the Clemenses' devoted servant for twenty-nine years

Patrick McAleer, the Clemenses' long-time coachman

The Rev. Joseph Hopkins Twichell

The Rev. Thomas K. Beecher   William Dean Howells   Thomas Bailey Aldrich

Clara as Lady Jane Grey in the family production of *The Prince and the Pauper*

Elsie Leslie, celebrated child actress, as the Prince in Abby Sage Richardson's dramatization of *The Prince and the Pauper*

Daisy Warner as the Pauper, Susy as the Prince, in the family production

poem, " 'Twas the night before Christmas, when all through the house," etc. Father sometimes dressed up as Santa Claus and, after running about a dimly lighted room (we always turned the gas down low), trying to warm himself after the cold drive through the snow, he sat down and told some of his experiences on the way.

His little talk usually ended with words something like these: "As I often lose the letters I receive, or get them mixed up, I may have confused all your wishes, so that the stocking which should have bulged out with a donkey's head may be depressed by a hair-ribbon. Therefore, I should like to gather up your thanks now, as you may not feel like giving me any after Christmas. Anyway, I shall be gone then."

We all squealed, "Thank you, thank you, Santa Claus, for the things we hope to like," and then after a short game of tag Father ran away to remove his cotton beard and red coat.[40]

NARRATOR: George Washington Cable came to visit in January and was taken ill.

LILLY WARNER: We were over to see Mr. Cable last evening, but he was ill in bed—neuralgia or rheumatism—unable to go on to Philadelphia today as planned.[41]

NARRATOR: Cable dictated letters to his wife in New Orleans to Livy.

CABLE: I have every want gratified here and every freak of a sick man's mind, I have even the pleasure of knowing that I am not the same burden on the household here that I might be in less favored attitudes. Or in plainer words I have a regular trained nurse from the training school, who does everything with the greatest perfection.[42]

NARRATOR: When he was convalescent, Sam and the children entertained him.

CABLE: I have enjoyed Mr. Clemens' company today not a little. When I come home I will try and repeat to you some of the funny stories he tells the little Jean. Jean has a magnificent mental digestion. She must have a tiger in every story, and no tiger seems to her to be really worth the money unless he's in a jungle. . . .

I wish I could write long today, for I have enjoyed the day extremely. From the breakfast-table Clemens and I went into the drawing-room. He was complaining that he had overworked during the last few days and was tempted to take a half-holiday. We sat down together and fell a-chatting.[43]

SAM: Cable was at breakfast, and he and I have sat in the library and talked ever since—which is 4 hours. I believe this is my first idle day in 4 weeks. In that time I have written one 4-act play [dramatization of *Tom Sawyer*], and (3½) 2½ acts of another [*The Prince and the Pauper*]. But my head was so sore, this morning, and my body so sodden with fatigue, that I thought I would knock off till tomorrow [February 14th]. Cable's nurse went yesterday. She was a very good one; indeed all the trained modern ones are.[44]

CABLE: Time passed and we continued talking. He finished his pipe and [as] we went on each seemed to kindle the other's mind and so we kept up our converse. By and by we were both on our feet, he walking up and down the drawing-room and I back and forth across it. Our talk was generally earnest—about our great Century and the vast advantages of living in it—the glory and beauty of it, etc., etc.

Only when we were talking of publishers Mark got ferocious and funny.

"Oh!" he groaned with longing, in contemplation of discomfiting some fellows who he thinks have cheated him in copyright, "if it could be, I could lie in my grave with my martial cloak around me and kick my monument over and laugh and laugh!"

He went to the piano and sang a German song—one that Longfellow has translated—

> O, hemlock tree, O hemlock tree,
> How faithful are thy branches.

I sang a tenor part not trying to use the words. Then back to our talk and out into the library where Mark proposed a little literary scheme for him and me and three or four others; and when Mrs. Clemens came in at 1 P.M. we were still talking.

Part of the time—I forgot to say—was spent in consulting Audubon to identify a strange and beautiful bird that we had seen at breakfast-time from the window of the library.

Mrs. Clemens is reading aloud to Mark and the children Howard Pyle's beautiful new version of Robin Hood. Mark enjoys it hugely; they have come to the death of Robin and will soon be at the end.[45]

NARRATOR: Cable's visit had long-lasting effects.

KATY: That old blooming doctor never knew what was the matter with Mr. Cable. He was doctoring him all the time for a sore throat, but what he had was the mumps! And little Mr. Cable did a good job, too. He did it up brown. He give everybody in the house the mumps, and the children was really very sick[46]

SAM: Susy's turn: she has had 4 of the most hellfiredest days and nights, now, with the mumps—has suffered 13 times more than Cable did (whose pains lasted but 2 days), and yet has not made as much fuss in the 4 days as he used to make in 15 minutes; though she has shed whole barrels of noiseless tears. She staid in our room last night [March 4th]. None of us slept. I think she and her mother spent the night praying. But I didn't.[47]

SUSY'S THIRTEENTH YEAR

1884–1885

NARRATOR: At about this time, Susy attended the West Middle School on Asylum Avenue for a while. She had very fair hair and her eyes were eager behind her spectacles. Her cheeks were rosy pink; her outstanding feature was eagerness.

On Sundays the Clemenses walked to the Asylum Hill Congregational Church; Clara, with long black braids, was very striking in appearance. Everyone noticed the family.

ARTHUR THOMPSON: [Mark Twain] used to walk downtown from his home on Farmington Avenue just for the exercise. He never wore a hat and his hair, face and moustache caught everyone's eye. He and his family came regularly to the Asylum Hill Church. The Clemens' pew was on the left side of the center aisle, seven or eight rows from the front. In those days pews were sold at a public auction in the Church once a year. The reason Mark Twain came to our Church was not because he was religious (he was a skeptic) but because of his close friendship with Dr. Twichell.

We lived on Gillette Street. I . . . owned a boat which I kept on the river. My father once wrote Mark Twain for permission to me to moor my boat to some willows at the bend in the river just beneath his house. Twain gave permission for this.[1]

SAM: Yes, your son can chain his boat there, and if he will speak to my coachman, he will provide a place for his oars in our stable, if he would like that.[2]

NARRATOR: Sam and Livy went to Boston in April and received letters from home.

SUSY: Dear Papa and Mamma. Jean seems bright and well, and she has only cried once while you have been away; she has not been down stairs since she was down to say good-by to you, and I am not sure that she knows whether you are in Boston, or in Hartford, and I wonder what she will say when she comes down to supper tonight. She has been out too, and she wore her little blue sack, but I don't think it was any too warm for her, because by the time she went out there had come up some wind clouds, and so I think her little blue coat was just right.

I had a very delightful music lesson, because Miss Corey played to me quite a good deal in it, and I liked that very much.

Jean wants me to tell you that she is going to hied behind the chair tonight, and she wants me to send you her love, and with a great deal of love from me too, I am your loving Susy.[3]

NARRATOR: Clara's letter concerned Jumbo, her pet calf. Patrick, the coachman, had been urging Clara to curry the calf every morning; he told her it would turn into a pony.

CLARA: I must tell what Jumbo did. Patrick said that if I wanted too, I could take Jumbo down to the pasture for a little while; so I took him down there and I put up the railings so that she could not get out, and she went right to eating grass; and when I got half way to the house I turned around and Jumbo had her head out of the railings, and she tried to get out, then in a second she took back her head and dashed for an open place, she ran down the road and passed the little green house very near the pasture.

I ran after her but she went way out of sight and I could not tell where she had gone. There was a horse in the yard by the little green house, but I went up to the house and I knocked on the door, and as I was starting to go back, a woman came to the door, and she asked me if I had nocked, and I said "yes," and I asked her if she had seen a calf go by the house, and she said "yes," but that she did not know where it went to, so I went back, and got Patrick and there was a man that waved his hand to Patrick, and so we went up to the man, and there he had Jumbo tied in a shed with two or three other little calfs.

There were lots of dogs there, chained, and they all were wild to get near me, so I petted them, and the man took us where some other calfs were, and one of them put its little head in my neck and licked and licked, and it was almost the sweetest one, there.[4]

NARRATOR: Their Elmira friend, the Rev. Thomas K. Beecher, came to Hartford and stayed with the Clemenses.

LILLY WARNER: Livy asked me to dinner, just me, to meet Dr. Thomas Beecher, and then he preached for us this morning [May 11th].[5]

SAM: Mention was made of a certain young lady at breakfast; and Susy remarked that she was very pretty. Her mother said no, she had a good face, a face which answered to her exceptionally fine character, but she would hardly call it a pretty face. Susy said—

"But mama, I think that when a person has a good figure and a pleasant face that one likes to look at, she *is* pretty."

Rev. Thos. K. Beecher was present, and said it was a nice distinction, and that Susy's position was sound.[6]

BEECHER: You must know . . . that yours is one of the few *restful* homes in which intelligence, culture, luxury and company combine to the compounding of a pleasure which every visitor longs to taste again.[7]

NARRATOR: The girls were enjoying the lovely May weather.

LILLY WARNER: Daisy is off on a picnic today with the Clemens and some other children in the Woodland Street woods, and went off at 11 with her basket and a joyous heart.[8]

HELEN POST CHAPMAN: Back of our home on Woodland Street and of the Perkins' next door was a piece of land almost a peninsula bordered by the Meandering Swine [Park River]. The earliest wild flowers grew here, the fairy pencils, dog tooth violets, anemone, hepatica, with a background of good old skunk cabbage. The first note of spring would send us down there to our fairy dell where we would fall on our knees and kiss the ground.[9]

NARRATOR: It was soon time to leave for the farm.

CLARA: On a sunny day one could see the Chemung River sparkling far below as it wound it[s] way through the town of Elmira, nestled cozily between the hills surrounding it. At night the streets and houses, though at a great distance, seemed ablaze with artificial fire. It was a lovely sight.[10]

NARRATOR: The Gerhardts returned from Europe and came to Elmira. Sam wrote Howells about sculptural matters; the monument being erected in Cedar Hill Cemetery, Hartford, to J. P. Morgan, burned.

SAM: I suppose you heard how a marble monument for which [Augustus] St. Gaudens was precuniarily responsible, burned down in Hartford the other day, uninsured,—for who in the world would

ever think of insuring a marble shaft in a cemetery against fire?—
and left St. Gaudens out of pocket $15,000. It was a bad day for
artists. Gerhardt finished my bust that day, and the work was
pronounced admirable by all the kin and friends; but in putting
it in plaster (or rather in taking it *out,*) next day it got ruined.
It was four or five weeks' hard work gone to the dogs. The news
flew, and everybody on the farm flocked to the arbor and grouped
themselves about the wreck in a profound and moving silence—
the farm-help, the colored servants, the German nurse, the children,
everybody—a silence interrupted at wide intervals by absent-
minded ejaculations wrung from unconscious breasts as the whole
size of the disaster gradually worked its way home to the realization of one spirit after another. Some burst out with one thing,
some another; the German nurse put up her hands and said, "Oh
Schade! oh, schrecklich!" But Gerhardt said nothing; or almost that.
He couldn't word it, I suppose. But he went to work, and by dark
had everything thoroughly well under way for a fresh start in
the morning; and in three days' time had built a new bust which
was (as good as) a trifle better than the old one—and tomorrow
we shall put the finishing touches on it, and it will be about as
good a one as nearly anybody could make. . . .

If you run across anybody who wants a bust, be sure and
recommend Gerhardt on my say-so.[11]

NARRATOR: An engraving of the Gerhardt bust was used as the
frontispiece for *Huckleberry Finn*.

HARTFORD COURANT: The first requisite in this sort of work is the
likeness. The work may be a fair likeness and very bad art, but it
must first of all satisfy the desire for resemblance to the original.
This bust of Mr. Clemens does that completely. It is exceedingly
rare, even in the work of master artists, that this condition is so
completely complied with. And the resemblance is not the super-
ficial one of the photograph. We have seen occasional fat, smooth
busts which are not a grade above colored photographs as works
of art. This is not of that sort: it gives the character of the sitter,
his peculiarities, and we may say the nature and the temperament
of the man. But notice how this is effected. Not by petty and timid
details. The material is handled with perfect freedom and bold-
ness—this is as apparent in the modeling of the hair and moustache as of the face. Everything is given in broad masses, full of
strength and character—no prettiness here. . . . It is simple in all

its lines, but massive and solid in treatment, and it has a noble dignity and repose. . . . It is worth studying.[12]

NARRATOR: A local character was giving trouble in the neighborhood of Quarry Farm.

SAM: Old Clark, the low-down, the intemperate, used to go by the farm, last month, swearing. Susy's excuse for him (to Miss Foote) was, "he can't help it, he doesn't know any *nice intellectual naughty words.*" (From which the necessary inference is that she moves in a circle which does.)[13]

My whole interest, now, is centred in the task of hunting up, capturing, and sending to the penitentiary a drunken ruffian who has been a trouble to our neighboring farmers for a couple of years and who . . . drew a revolver on Susy and Clara last Wednesday when they were down the road a piece and without a protector.[14]

Mrs. Clemens has fallen sick, and our return home is frustrated, just as we were nearly ready to start. And that miscreant who drew the revolver escaped from the jailor and has got away into Pennsylvania. That is my share. Yet after all it was a sort of victory to make him show the white feather, since all the prudent advisers said it was a mistake to arrest the terror of the region— his tribe would burn us out, etc. He is gone, and his tribe are modest and quiet for the first time in their history.[15]

NARRATOR: Home, in Hartford, there were many congenial gatherings at the Clemens' house. Jervis Langdon and Mary Bushnell Cheney, daughter of Horace Bushnell, commented on the delightful evenings.

JERVIS LANGDON: One of the pleasantest neighborhood customs that grew up in the Hartford home was the gathering, of an evening, around the library fire while Mr. Clemens read aloud.[16]

MARY BUSHNELL CHENEY: When I took my seat first as a hearer in the library . . . I looked about the carved black oak panelling of the walls . . . and the books and little pictures which broke their dark surface, and perceived that the place was in itself a sort of revelation of poetic meanings. The fine, smooth outlines of the head of our hostess came out with wonderful clearness against the dark background, and seemed fitting and in perfect keeping with the flowers and filtered sunshine of the little conservatory.[17]

JERVIS LANGDON: He liked stirring poetry, which he read admirably, sometimes rousing his little audience to excitement and cheers. Shakespeare remained, by whichever name, the love of his heart, but he made his own unique programs, and once mischievously slipped between two of the deathless sonnets a particularly charming reading of a little set of verses accidentally come into his hands, that had been painstakingly written for a school periodical by one of the children.

The listeners invariably demanded at the end three favorites, "How they brought the Good News from Ghent to Aix," "Up at a Villa, Down in the City," and, for climax, "The Battle of Naseby," which he delivered with supreme eloquence and emotion.[18]

KATY: Then he used to sing to them, and oh! it was beautiful to hear him. He'd sing after dinner (he had a nice voice) and he'd sing nigger Spirituals and act them out, too, for the grown folks as well as the children. And then, sometimes, he'd play on the piano—try to anyway.[19]

CLARA: Father gave us performances of darky songs which he sang while he accompanied himself on the piano. He had a curious way of playing with his fingers stretched straight out over the keys, so that each time he played a chord it seemed as if a miracle had happened. He always cleared his throat many times before he began, and then sang quite loudly with his head thrown back and his eyes fixed on the ceiling. We thought he looked very "cute." He interrupted himself constantly to correct wrong chords, but usually in vain, for he could not find the right ones. Then, with some display of temper he would change to another song.[20]

KATY: He used to sing one song that was so lovely that I always used to sneak in and listen to it: "In the Days of Old When Knights was Bold." . . . Oh, the children would stand round just adoring him when they heard that![21]

CLARA: His two favorites were "Swing Low, Sweet Chariot," and "Go Chain the Lion Down," which he rendered in a truly impressive way, despite the fact that musically certain lacks were noticeable. When he sang "Rise and Shine and Give God the Glory, Glory," he gave out so much fervor of spirit that one could never forget it.[22]

KATY: They had a lovely, happy time. It used to strike me as heavenly. 'Twas a home just like you'd make for yourself—like a dream house, don't you know, that you would like more than anything else in the world. A happy, happy home—happiness budding all over—everybody always happy. Our life—it just rolled on like a smooth sea . . . not a bit of sadness of any kind.[23]

SAM: Our children and the neighbors' children played well; easily, comfortably, naturally and with high spirit. How was it that they were able to do this? It was because they had been in training all the time from their infancy. They grew up in our house, so to speak playing charades. We never made any preparation. We selected a word, whispered the parts of it to the little actors; then we retired to the hall where all sorts of costumery had been laid out ready for the evening. We dressed the parts in three minutes and each detachment marched into the library and performed its syllable, then retired, leaving the fathers and mothers to guess that syllable if they could. Sometimes they could. . . .

Those little chaps, Susy and Clara, invented charades themselves . . . and played them for the entertainment of their mother and me. They had one high merit—none but a high-grade intellect could guess them. Obscurity is a great thing in a charade. These babies invented one once which was a masterpiece in this regard. They came in and played the first syllable, which was a conversation in which the word *red* occurred with suggestive frequency. Then they retired—came again, continuing an angry dispute which they had begun outside, and in which several words like *just, fair, unfair, unjust,* and so on, kept occurring; but we noticed that the word *just* was in the majority—so we set that down along with the word *red* and discussed the probabilities while the children went out to recostume themselves. We had thus "red," "just." They soon appeared and began to do a very fashionable morning call, in which the one made many inquiries of the other concerning some lady whose name was persistently suppressed, and who was always referred to as "her," even when the grammar did not permit of that form of the pronoun. The children retired. We took an account of stock and, so far as we could see, we had three syllables, "red," "just," "her." But that was all. The combination did not seem to throw any real glare on the future completed word. The children arrived again, and stooped down and began to chat and quarrel and carry on, and fumble and fuss at the *register!* —(red—just—her). With the exception of myself, this family was never strong on spelling.[24]

Will Gillette . . . learned a part of his trade by acting in our charades.[25]

KATY: He was a great friend—came over every day when he was in Hartford.[26]

CLARA: . . . both men were funny, no one could ever be quite so ridiculous as Father was on one occasion. We were trying to enact the story of Hero and Leander. Mark Twain played the part of the impassioned lover obliged to swim across the Hellespont to snatch a kiss from his sweetheart on the other side of the foaming water. For this scene Father wore a bathing-suit, a straw hat tied under his chin with a big bow, and a hot-water bottle slung around his chest. William Gillette took part quite frequently in some of our theatrical nonsense, and always shed a bright light of humor and charm. We loved him dearly.

One stellar attraction in these gatherings was . . . Norman Hapgood [future dramatic critic and biographer]. He, too, visited in the neighborhood and gave us the great pleasure of his society. The brilliance of his mind and intellectual talents were evident at that early age when he was a freshman at Harvard College.[27]

NORMAN HAPGOOD: Mr. Clemens was in a way a natural actor. Indeed, my first association with him and his family involved a theatrical performance. Nook Farm, in Hartford, was a literary paradise not quite like anything I shall see again. . . . In such a setting I found myself during vacations of my college years, and it was on my first visit that Margaret Warner took me across to the Clemens house, where I was promptly cast for the rôle of the lover in a play written in scenario outline by Mark Twain and Charles Dudley Warner. Susy Clemens, the beautiful and poetic oldest daughter of the humorist, was the leading girl; the words in these plays were improvised by the actors; and my orders were to go upon the stage and make a violent declaration of love to Susy.

We had become friends at first sight, and more especially after a long walk in which the enthusiasm we both had for talking about English poetry, and quoting it, had full expression, and I was in truth not afraid of her, any more than a youth of that age is almost inevitably afraid of an especially lovely girl. The terror started only when I stepped out before the audience, of a dozen or so members of the group of families, under the sentence of making an open and continued declaration of consuming passion. My cheeks took fire, and not a single word would pass my lips. Susy, a seasoned actress, though several years my junior, did what trained artists on the professional stage do also in similar emergencies; she changed the direction of the plot immediately, and the girl it was who did the wooing. I stood and listened like a burning stick. When I stepped back from the Thespian boards at the end of that scene, it was to appear on any stage as an actor, alas, nevermore.[28]

NARRATOR: Sam had signed an agreement with James Pond as manager to lecture with Cable. They opened in New Haven on November 5th, and Livy went down for the opening.

KATY: Mr. Clemens and Cable was great friends, although they was very different and never could agree about anything. Mr. Cable was very prim and conventional. He hated to travel on Sundays, too, and of course that would make Mr. Clemens mad.[29]

NARRATOR: Howells attended Sam's performance in Boston.

HOWELLS: Three of us went to hear you read last night and I think I never enjoyed you more. You were as much yourself before those thousands as if you stood by my chimney-corner grinding away to the household your absence bereaves here. You *are* a great artist, and you do this public thing so wonderfully well that I don't see how you could ever bear to give it up.

—I thought that the bits from Huck Finn told the best—at least I enjoyed them the most. That is a mighty good book, and I should like to hear you read it all. But *everything* of yours is good for platform reading. You can't go amiss.[30]

SAM: Susy dear, I don't know how to sufficiently thank you and Ben for writing me such good letters and so faithfully. And I want to thank you both for making Jean say things to be sent to me, too. I called at Gen. Grant's the other morning, and when I saw all his swords, and medals, and collections of beautiful and rare things from Japan and China, I was so sorry I hadn't made Mamma go with me. And Mrs. Grant was sorry, too, and made me promise that I would bring Mamma there to luncheon, some time. Gen. Lew Wallace was there—he has an article in this month's Century about the great Victory of Fort Donelson—and when I told him Mamma was at the reading the other night and was sorry I didn't make her acquainted with the author of Ben Hur, he was very sorry I was so heedless himself. Mrs. Grant got up and stood between Gen Wallace and me, and said, "There, there's many a woman in this land that would like to be in my place and be able to tell her children that she had stood once elbow to elbow between two such great authors as Mark Twain and General Wallace." We all laughed and I said to Gen. Grant: "Don't look so cowed, General; you have written a book, too, and when it is published you can hold up your head and let on to be a person of consequence yourself."

Kiss 'em all for me, sweetheart—and I send love and kisses to you.[31]

NARRATOR: Sam had persuaded General Grant that Webster & Company should publish his memoirs. It was a great feather in Sam's cap.

HOWELLS: One of the highest satisfactions of Clemens's often supremely satisfactory life was his relation to Grant. It was his proud joy to tell how he found Grant about to sign a contract for his book on certainly very good terms, and said to him that he would himself publish the book and give him a percentage three times as large.[32]

NARRATOR: At Thanksgiving Cable and Sam were in New Jersey, where they stayed with Thomas Nast, the well-known cartoonist.

SAM: We dined and stayed all night with Tom Nast and family [Morristown, N.J.] and had a most noble good time. I occupied his eldest daughter's room—Miss Julia Nast, aged about 20— the most remarkable I was ever in—a curious and inexhaustible museum. Not an inch of the four walls could be seen—all hidden under pictures, photographs, etchings . . . Christmas cards, menus, fans, statuettes, trinkets and knick-knacks in all metals—little brackets everywhere, with all imaginable dainty and pretty things massed upon them and hanging from them—the most astounding variety of inexpensive and interesting trifles that was ever huddled together upon four walls in this world. It took me an hour to undress, and another hour to dress, because my eyes were so busy and the new surprises were so constant and so engaging. . . . I would like to see Susie's room decorated in that way. The thing is easy, and occupies years: whenever you get a hold of a new trifle, nail it to the wall with a pin. At a rough guess I should say there are 3,000 pretty trifles in Julia Nast's room. They didn't cost more than 3,000 dimes, perhaps, but they are worth twenty times the money to look at.

NARRATOR: Jean couldn't write; she made marks, Sam wrote to Livy.

SAM: Livy darling, I got your letter enclosing Jean's 4[s]—admirable child, cultivated child, how she is progressing!

Only one word, my darling, to say we have ridden the whole day [December 13th] in the train, and now I am in bed for an hour to rest me before going on the platform. You and the children have been in my mind all the day, and I have been very homesick and still am. I ate a lot of chestnuts that I found in my overcoat pockets, and that brought the children very near to me, for all three of them contributed to that stock.[33]

I love the platform, and I would like to live on it but I cannot be traveling about all the time.[34]

A DRAMA CRITIC: When Mark Twain walked on the stage, with his chin recently shaved and perceptibly powdered for the occasion, his unruly hair like a halo around his head, and his discouraged expression of countenance, he was welcomed with a prolonged clapping of hands. Without apparently recovering his spirits, he sauntered to the reading desk, felt for it with his right hand, and began.[35]

NARRATOR: He wrote a letter to Jean in German from Grand Rapids in December.

SAM: My dear—, I often think of you and your sisters. Whenever I see a sweet child in the trains or in the hotel, Jean comes before my eyes and I cannot see the other child for the tears. Your Mamma is inexpressibly dear, and right after your Mamma, Jean, Susy and Clara lie in the depths of my heart.

Last night a horrible monster came howling toward me and wanted to bite me; but I sprang through the window and escaped the danger. It was a dog almost 4 inches tall, with shining eyes and big wriggly ears and an altogether awful tail, and called a rat-terrier. I am leaving this city at once, because one can not stay here safely.

Last night I ate some of your chestnuts and while eating, thought of you, my dear. Papa.

Mr. Cable sends his love to you and your sisters.

P.S. Thanks for your good letters—Papa.[36]

NARRATOR: *The Adventures of Huckleberry Finn* was published in December. The Webster Company's first publishing venture was an immediate success.

ROBERT LOUIS STEVENSON: It is a book I have read four times, and am quite ready to begin again to-morrow.[37]

SUSY: Papa was away for many months reading with Mr. G. W. Cable . . . and while he was gone we composed the plan of surprising him when he came home by acting scenes from "Prince and Pauper."[38]

KATHY: They put *The Prince and the Pauper* on the stage (that was Mr. Clemens' play from his book). Mrs. Clemens did it herself, got it up all herself for the children.[39]

NARRATOR: Livy did the dramatization from Sam's book; Mrs. Gerhardt designed programs and tickets, and Gerhardt did the scenery. Everyone made costumes and planned sets.

SUSY: It took us a great while to commit all that was necessary but at last we were almost ready and we expected him to come home the next day on which evening we had planned to surprise him. But we received a telegram from him stating that he would reach Hartford "today at 2 o'clock". We were all dismayed for we were by no means prepared to receive him. The library was strune with costumes which were to be tried on for the last time and we had planned a dress rehearsal over at Mr. Warners for that afternoon.

But Mamma gathered the things up as quickly as possible and hustled them into the mahogany room. Soon we heard the carriage roll over the pavement in front of the house and we all rushed to the doors. After we had partially gotten over our surprise and delight at seeing papa we all went into the library. We all sat with papa a little while and then mamma dissapeared into the mahogany room. Clara and I sat with papa a while so as to prevent his being surprised of our seemingly uncalled disertion of him. But soon we too had to withdraw to the mahogany room so as to help mama sew on bucles onto slippers and pack costumes into a clothes basket. Papa was left all alone; except that one of us every once in a while would slipp in and stay with him a little while. Anyone but papa would have wondered at mammas unwonted absence but papa is to absence minded, he very seldom notices things as accurately as other people do, although I do not believe in this instance he could have been wholly without suspicion. (But I was. S.L.C.)

At last he went up to the billiard room and Jean went with him. Mamma as a special favor let Jean into this secret on condition that she would not breathe a whisper to any one on the subject especially to papa and Jean had promised.

But when alone up in papa's room, it was very hard for her not to tell papa the whole thing. As it was she was undecided whether to tell him or not. She did go so far as to begin with "It's a secret papa" and then dropping varius other hints about the secret and she went so far that papa said afterwards that if he had been anyone else he should have guessed it in a minute.

At ½ past three o'clock we all started for Mr. Warner's house there to have our rehearsal. Jean and the nurse went with us, so papa was left absolutely alone.

The next day the first information that papa got was that he was invited for the evening and he did not know that anything unusual was going to happen until he sat before the curtain.[40]

SAM: I was expecting to have a happy and restful season by a hickory fire in the library with the family, but was required to go at once to George Warner's house, a hundred and fifty yards away across the grounds. This was a heavy disappointment, and I tried to beg off, but did not succeed. I couldn't even find out why I must waste this precious evening in a visit to a friend's house when our own house offered so many and superior advantages. There was a mystery somewhere, but I was not able to get to the bottom of it. So we tramped across in the snow, and I found the Warner drawing-room crowded with seated people. There was a vacancy in the front row, for me—in front of a curtain. At once the curtain was drawn, and before me, properly costumed, was the little maid, Margaret Warner, clothed in Tom Canty's rags, and beyond an intercepting railing was Susy Clemens, arrayed in the silks and satins of the prince. Then followed with good action and spirit the rest of that first meeting between the prince and the pauper. It was a charming surprise, and to me, a moving one. . . . This lovely surprise was my wife's work. She had patched the scenes together from the book and had trained the six or eight young actors in their parts, and had also designed and furnished the costumes.[41]

JERVIS LANGDON: Susy as the Prince, the son of the irascible Henry the Eighth, in that first scene with the Pauper, the son of the brutal John Canty, was saying seriously: "Fathers be alike may-hap; mine hath not a doll's temper," when someone, I rather think Mr. Charles Dudley Warner, gave an irrepressible giggle, and the whole audience went off into appreciative shouts of laughter. The scene was interrupted, the children were indignant, but Mr. Clemens was highly pleased that the possibility of just such a connection had never struck Mrs. Clemens, who had coached the cast.[42]

KATY: Clara was Lady Jane Grey—and she was wonderful![43]

SAM: I can see little Clara doing her stately dignities and "distant politenesses" and hear her say, with fine disdain which was comical because it was so serious—

"My lord, since when must the Prince of Wales sue to common clay for leave to leave his room when he would?" A pause—with a gathering sense of injury. "You jest, my lord. And I—(with a toss of the head) I do not *like* it!"[44]

KATY: And the scenery was wonderful, real painted scenery that Carl Gerhardt did.[45]

SUSY: We got through the scenes quite successfully and had some delightful dancing afterward. . . . It was decided that we should have [the play] again in a few weeks.[46]

At the first Prince and the Pauper, there were about thirty people.[47]

NARRATOR: *The Prince and the Pauper* was produced again at the Clemens' house shortly after Christmas.

SUSY: At length the time was sett and we were nearly prepared, when Frank Warner who took the Miles Hendon part caught a severe cold and could not play it, so papa said he would take the part.[48]

SAM: I added a part for myself (Miles Hendon), also a part for Katy and a part for George.[49]

SUSY: Papa had only three days to learn the part in, but still we were all sure that he could do it. The scene that he acted in was the scene between Miles Hendon and the Prince, the "Prithee, pour the water" scene. I was the Prince and Papa and I rehearsed together two or three time a day for the three days before the appointed evening.[50]

SAM: These were great occasions in the household. Preparations were begun a week in advance of the performance; the ordinary home-traffic obstructed, interrupted, disordered, and sometimes even paralyzed for a while, for the play was the one important interest for the time being, and every other thing had to give way to it. With the actors part-studying went on constantly, and rehearsals were frequent; the non-actors were similarly busy, planning and perfecting the arrangements, overhauling and reno-vating the costumes, and so forth. The final day was particularly full. On that day the auditorium (the library and dining-room, which opened together, with folding doors) was stripped for action, cleaned, dusted and furnished with eighty-four chairs; the stage was brought from the stable and placed against the conservatory at the end of the library, and its equipment of scenery and curtains set up; the greenroom (mahogany room) was cleaned of superfluities and their places filled with costumes and matters connected with stage "business"; the piano in the drawing-room was tuned up for the marches and processions; then in the afternoon there was a dress rehearsal by the full strength of the company.

It was a day of consuming excitement and exhausting but willing and joyous labor, and not a member of the family nor any servant in house or stable had an idle moment. Susy and her troupe were in a happy heaven of excitement all the day, and all the busy household moved and toiled in an atmosphere that was electric with their enthusiasm.

We dined as we could—probably with a neighbor—and by quarter to eight in the evening the hickory fire in the hall was pouring a sheet of flame up the chimney, and the house was in a drench of gas-light from the ground floor up, the guests were arriving, and there was a babel of hearty greetings, with not a voice in it that was not old and familiar and affectionate; and when the curtain went up we looked out from the stage upon none but faces that were dear to us, none but faces that were lit up with welcome for us.[51]

KATY: Well, the play was done in the drawing-room [library] and the conservatory was the Palace garden, and it looked just like a real palace. Oh, it looked brilliant and lovely! . . . Mr. Clemens was in it, too, and he was so funny, just his walk was funny—the *way* he walked! He made out he was quite lame when he was walking out in the play. . . . Then he rang the bell for me to bring the pitcher of water in, and he poured it out the wrong way—by the handle and not by the nose—and of course that took down the house.[52]

SUSY: Papa acted his part beautifully, and he added to the scene, making it a good deal longer. He was inexpressibly funny, with his great slouch hat and gait—oh such a gait! Papa made the Miles Hendon scene a splendid success and every one was delighted with the scene, and papa too. We had great fun with our "Prince and Pauper," and I think we none of us shall forget how immensely funny papa was in it. He certainly could have been an actor as well as an author.[53]

KATY: They roared at him when it was over. Then he made a few remarks, telling how his wife got up this thing to surprise him, and it did surprise him, because it was the most wonderfully got up thing he'd ever seen. It couldn't have been got up better by a regular artist in the theater, he said—and that was so; and Mrs. Clemens was so happy, after all her hard work, just 'cause he was pleased.[54]

NARRATOR: One of the smallest actors was "Twichell's littlest cub."[55]

SAM: He was so small that people on the back seats could not see him without an opera-glass, but he held up Lady Jane's train very well. Jean was only something past three years old, therefore was too young to have a part, but she produced the whole piece every day independently, and played all the parts herself. For a one-actor piece it was not bad. In fact, it was very good—very entertaining. For she was in very deep earnest, and, besides, she used an English which none but herself could handle with effect.[56]

There were no dull places in the piece; it swept along, full charged with interest and animation, from the beginning to the end. Then came the grand climax—the "Coronation," with its impressivenesses, its waiting suspenses, its threatened defeats and miscarriages, its bursts of passion breaking the line here and there, its triumphant close, with martial music and processions.[57]

In the coronation scene Susy's throne fell over backwards into the conservatory with a crash, just as she was about to mount it. She was a timid creature and easily startled—but not when she was acting. When she was acting, she was full of her part, she was not herself, she was the person she was representing. When the throne fell the whole audience jumped, but she went on with her speech, undisturbed.[58]

As *we* played the piece it had several superiorities over the play as presented on the public stage in England and America, for we always had both the prince and the pauper on deck, whereas these parts were always doubled on the public stage.[59]

NARRATOR: Frances Johnson played the piano accompaniment at one of the preformances.

FRANCES JOHNSON: After the play there was informal dancing for the young people. Mrs. Clemens sat in the reception room. With her were Mr. and Mrs. Twichell and several of the neighbors. . . . [She wore a] purplish silk gown, flowing sleeves, a band around her hair. She seemed the ideal of exquisite refinement and innate gentleness.[60]

KATY: She wore brown a good deal, silks and velvets. She had one dinner dress that was a wonderful dress. Madame Fogarty (she was a great dressmaker in New York) made all her dresses, made her wedding dress and made her dresses. . . . Well, she had this wonderful brown dress of satin and velvet and the satin was all puffed out and made fringy, you know; and the skirt had panels to it. Oh, beautiful they was—they trailed on the ground. She always used to wear high collars too—never wore low neck.[61]

NARRATOR: Sam went on tour again with Cable, a tour which was to take him near enough Keokuk to visit his mother and Orion and Mollie. Livy wrote Mollie.

LIVY: I hope you will be able to have a quiet family together while "Sam" is with you. How I should like to be in it. I hope Ma will feel well and will not get too tired. Please give her my love and tell her to be careful—because it will not pay her if she should make herself sick.

The children have been all quite well this Winter except that they have had colds in the head. These colds have been very prevalent about here.

I don't know how I could get along with Mr. Clemens being away if the children should be sick. Of course it is hard enough anyway but I get along quite as well as I thought I should. I am very busy and that makes the time pass quickly. When I think that it is only the 11 of Jan. and that I must not expect to see him until the last of Feb. it seems long.[62]

NARRATOR: Sam wrote Livy on their wedding anniversary.

SAM: This is the great day, my darling; the day that gave you to me fifteen years ago. You were very precious to me, then, you are still more precious to me now. In having each other then, we were well off; but poor, compared to what we are now, with the children.

I kiss you my darling wife—and those dear rascals.[63]

NARRATOR: He reached Montreal.

SAM: I sent a toboggan for the children. They better not try to use it till I come.

I will send a pasteboard box, to-night which must remain closed till I come. It is for the children.[64]

CLARA: He returned with not only the gayest-colored toboggan costumes for my sisters and me, but a full-sized toboggan. At the same time he supplied us with three collies that we christened "I know," "You know," and "Don't know."

A toboggan slide had to be arranged behind the house, but this was not difficult, as our home stood on the top of a small hill that sloped gradually to a rather broad meadow bounded on the far side by a river. Father was as jubilant as any of us the first day we gathered on the crest of the hill to try the new toboggan. Viewed from the street at a distance of forty yards, we must have formed a bright picture on that sparkling winter's day—three small girls in their blue, yellow, and red costumes surrounded by three gamboling dogs, directed by a picturesque man dressed in a sealskin coat with a cap drawn down over his curly gray hair. The dogs barked so loudly, and the children laughed so much, that I doubt whether Father's explanations of the art of tobogganing were much appreciated.

In any case, either on that day or a few days later, we had a serious accident. Flying down the hill at full speed, the toboggan was hurled by some obstacle into a great oak tree. I was the only one hurt, but my damages were severe. One leg was bent around into the shape of a half-moon, and after the gardener and coachman had carried me into the house, my shoe had to be cut off the crooked foot.

During this period I slept in my parents' bedroom in a large Dutch [Venetian] bed that had an angel on each of the four posts ... my sisters and I had always adored this bed. The angels could be removed and we frequently took them down and washed them in a small bathtub.[65]

Susy: Clara sprained her ankle, a little while ago, by running into a tree, when coasting, and while she was unable to walk with it she played solotaire with cards a great deal. While Clara was sick and papa saw her play solotaire so much, he got very much interested in the game, and finally began to play it himself a little, then Jean took it up and, at last *mamma,* even played it occasionally; Jean's and papa's love for it rapidly increased, and now Jean brings the cards every night to the table and papa and mamma help her play, and before dinner is at an end, papa has gotten a separate pack of cards, and is playing alone, with great interest. Mamma and Clara next are made subject to the contagious solotair, and there are four solotaireans at the table; while you hear nothing but "Fill up the place" etc. It is dreadful!

After supper Clara goes into the library, and gets a little red mahogany table, and placing it under the gas fixture seats herself and begins to play again, then papa follows with another table of the same discription, and they play solatair till bedtime.[66]

NARRATOR: Coasting was a favorite sport in Hartford; Helen Chapman was a devotee.

HELEN CHAPMAN: Such coasting as there used to be! Starting at the very top of Prospect Hill the double ripper would carry us around the corner at Asylum and down that avenue almost to Woodland Street. Sometimes we had sleighs to carry us up the hill again, but if I remember rightly most of us spurned this evidence of luxury. Another favorite spot for coasting on a smaller scale was . . . on Woodland Street.

This is where Mr. Clemens often joined us when we were out with our sleds. One memorable day he appeared in a short seal-skin coat and cap, dragging a pig sticker and carrying a white bed pillow under his arm. There was a fine crust on the snow. He carefully placed the pillow on the sled, seated himself and with a gentle push was off. He had not reckoned that our weight was less than his so when he took the bump at the foot of the hill the sled broke through the crust and he and the pillow and the sled parted company, and went in opposite directions. Without saying a word he gathered up his belongings and went home.[67]

CLARA: Father also taught us to skate on the little river that flowed through the meadow behind the house, and often we glided back and forth on the white ice until the sun had set and the trees looked like giant specters. Then the stars came out and the lights of our "castle" beckoned us home, a home that was filled with cheer.

The expression of joy and light that emanated from Father and Mother mingled with the blazing fires on the hearth. Our hearts were filled with happiness.[68]

Not infrequently we awoke to find the many trees behind our house one mass of dazzling ice. Each branch and twig glistened with beauty and absorbed the attention of the entire family. Father would sit by the hour watching the bewildering miracles of little ice-pictures. And often I saw tears come to his eyes, for great beauty overwhelmed and moved him.[69]

SUSY'S FOURTEENTH YEAR

1885–1886

NARRATOR: Susy had been scribbling since the age of nine: poetry, plays, and now she began Sam's "Biography."

SAM: Susy, aged 13 . . . had begun to write my biography, solely of her own notion—a thing about which I feel proud and gratified. At breakfast this morning [March 23rd] I intimated that if I seemed to be talking on a pretty high key, in the way of style, it must be remembered that my biographer was present. Whereupon Susy struck upon the unique idea of having me sit up and purposely talk for the biography.[1]

She did this work in her bedroom at night, and kept her record hidden. After a little, the mother discovered it and filched it, and let me see it; then told Susy what she had done, and how pleased I was and how proud. . . . I had had compliments before, but none that touched me like this; none that could approach it for value in my eyes. . . . I have had no compliment, no praise, no tribute from any source, that was so precious to me as this one was.[2]

SUSY: We are a very happy family. We consist of Papa, Mamma, Jean, Clara and me. It is papa I am writing about, and I shall have no trouble in not knowing what to say about him, as he is a *very* striking character.[3]

Papa's appearance has been described many times, but very incorrectly. He has beautiful gray hair, not any too thick or any too long, but just right; a Roman nose, which greatly improves the beauty of his features; kind blue eyes and a small mustache.

He has a wonderfully shaped head and profile. He has a very good figure—in short, he is an extrodinarily fine looking man. All his features are perfect, exept that he hasn't extrodinary teeth. His complexion is very fair, and he doesn't ware a beard. He is a very good man and a very funny one. He *has* got a temper, but we all of us have in this family. He is the loveliest man I ever saw or ever hope to see—and oh, so absent-minded.[4]

Papa has a peculiar gait we like, it seems just to sute him, but most people do not; he always walks up and down the room while thinking and between each coarse at meals.[5]

SAM: The spelling is frequently desperate, but it was Susy's, and it shall stand. I love it and cannot profane it. To me it is gold. To correct it would alloy it, not refine it. It would spoil it. It would take from it its freedom and flexibility and make it stiff and formal. Even when it is most extravagant I am not shocked. It is Susy's spelling, and she was doing the best she could—and nothing could better it for me.

She learned languages easily; she learned history easily; she learned music easily; she learned all things easily, quickly, and thoroughly—except spelling.[6]

SUSY: Papa said the other day, "I am a mugwump and a mugwump is pure from the marrow out." (Papa knows that I am writing this biography of him, and he said this for it.) He doesn't like to go to church at all, why I never understood, until just now, he told us the other day that he coudn't bear to hear any one talk but himself, but that he could listen to himself talk for hours without getting tired, of course he said this in joke, but I've no dought it was founded on truth.[7]

Papa made arrangements to read at Vassar College the 1st of May, and I went with him. We went by way of New York City. Mamma went with us to New York and stayed two days to do some shopping. We started Tuesday, at ½ past two o'clock in the afternoon, and reached New York about ¼ past six. Papa went right up to General Grants from the station and mamma and I went to the Everett House. Aunt Clara came to supper with us up in our room.[8]

We and Aunt Clara were going to the theatre right after supper, and we expected papa to take us there and to come home as early as he could. But we got through dinner and he didn't come, and didn't come, and mamma got more perplexed and worried, but at last we thought we would have to go without him. So we put on our things and started down stairs but before we'd goten half down we met papa coming up with a great bunch of roses in his hand. He explained that the reason he was so late was that his watch stopped and he didn't notice and kept thinking it an hour earlier than it really was. The roses he carried were some Col. Fred Grant sent to mamma. We went to the theatre and enjoyed "Adonis" . . . acted very much. We reached home about ½ past eleven o'clock and went right to bed. Wednesday morning we got up rather late and had breakfast about ½ past nine o'clock. After breakfast mamma went on shopping and papa and I went to see papa's agent about some business matters. After papa had gotten through talking to Cousin Charlie (Webster), papa's agent, we went to get a friend of papa's, Major Pond, to go and see a Dog Show with us. Then we went to see the dogs with Major Pond and we had a delightful time seeing so many dogs together; when we got through seeing the dogs papa thought he would go and see General Grant and I went with him—this was April 29, 1885. Papa went up into General Grant's room and he took me with him, I felt greatly honored and delighted when papa took me into General Grant's room and let me see the General and Col. Grant, for General Grant is a man I shall be glad all my life that I have seen. Papa and General Grant had a long talk together and papa has written an account of his talk and visit with General Grant for me to put into this biography.

SAM: I called on General Grant and took Susy with me. The General was looking and feeling far better that he had looked or felt for some months. He had ventured to work again on his book that morning—the first time he had done any work for perhaps a month. This morning's work was his first attempt at dictating, and it was a thorough success, to his great delight. He had always said that it would be impossible for him to dictate anything, but I had said that he was noted for clearness of statement, and as a narrative was simply a statement of consecutive facts, he was consequently peculiarly qualified and equipped for dictation. . . . He received Susy very pleasantly, and then fell to talking about certain matters which he hoped to be able to dictate next day.[9]

SUSY: After papa and General Grant had had their talk, we went back to the hotel where mamma was, and papa told mamma all about his interview with General Grant. Mamma and I had a nice quiet afternoon together. . . .

Then papa went to read in public; there were a great many

authors that read, that Thursday afternoon, beside papa; I would
have liked to have gone and heard papa read, but papa said he
was going to read in Vassar just what he was planning to read in
New York, so I stayed at home with mamma.[10]

SAM: That pair of devoted comrades were *always* shutting themselves up together when there was opportunity to have what Susy
called "a cozy time." From Susy's nursery days . . . she and her
mother were close friends, intimate friends, passionate adorers
of each other. Susy's was a beautiful mind, and it made her an
interesting comrade. And with the fine mind she had a heart like
her mother's. Susy never had an interest or an occupation which
she was not glad to put aside for that something which was in all
cases more precious to her—a visit with her mother.[11]

SUSY: The next day mamma planned to take the four-o'clock car
back to Hartford. We rose quite early that morning and went to
the Vienna Bakery and took breakfast there. From there we went
to a German bookstore and bought some German books for
Clara's birthday.

Then mamma and I went to do some shopping and papa went
to see General Grant. After we had finished doing our shopping
we went home to the hotel together. When we entered our rooms
in the hotel we saw on the table a vase full of exquisett red roses.
Mamma who is very fond of flowers exclaimed "Oh I wonder
who could have sent them." We both looked at the card in the
midst of the roses and saw that it was written on in papa's handwriting, it was written in German. "Liebes Geshchenk on die
Mamma." [I am sure I didn't say "on"—that is Susy's spelling, not
mine.—S.L.C.] Mamma was delighted. Papa came home and
gave mamma her ticket; and after visiting a while with her went
to see Major Pond and mamma and I sat down to our lunch.
After lunch most of our time was taken up with packing, and at
about three o'clock we went to escort mamma to the train. We
got on board the train with her and stayed with her about five
minutes and then we said good-bye to her and the train started
for Hartford. It was the first time I had ever beene away from
home without mamma in my life, although I was 13 yrs. old. Papa
and I drove back to the hotel and got Major Pond and then went
to see the Brooklyn Bridge we went across it to Brooklyn on the
cars and then walked back across it from Brooklyn to New York.
We enjoyed looking at the beautiful scenery and we could see

the bridge moove under the intense heat of the sun. We had a perfectly delightful time, but were pretty tired when we got back to the hotel.

The next morning we rose early, took our breakfast and took an early train to Poughkeepsie. We had a very pleasant journey to Poughkeepsie. The Hudson was magnificent—shrouded with beautiful mist. When we arrived at Poughkeepsie it was raining quite hard; which fact greatly dissapointed me because I very much wanted to see the outside of the buildings of Vasser College and as it rained that would be impossible. It was quite a long drive from the station to Vasser College and papa and I had a nice long time to discuss and laugh over German profanity. One of the German phrases papa particularly enjoys is "O heilige maria Mutter Jesus!" Jean has a German nurse, and this was one of her phrases, there was a time when Jean exclaimed "Ach Gott!" to every trifle, but when mamma found it out she was shocked and instantly put a stop to it.

We at length reached Vasser College and she looked very finely, her buildings and her grounds being very beautiful. We went to the front doore and rang the bell. The young girl who came to the doore wished to know who we wanted to see. Evidently we were not expected. Papa told her who we wanted to see and she showed us to the parlor. We waited, no one came; and waited, no one came, still no one came. It was beginning to seem pretty awkward, "Oh well this is a pretty piece of business," papa exclaimed. At length we heard footsteps coming down the long corridor and Miss C, (the lady who had invited papa) came into the room. She greeted papa very pleasantly and they had a nice little chatt together. Soon the lady principal also entered and she was very pleasant and agreable. She showed us to our rooms and said she would send for us when dinner was ready. We went into our rooms, but we had nothing to do for half an hour exept to watch the rain drops as they fell upon the window panes.

SAM: We arrived at the college in that soaking rain, and Susy has described, with just a suggestion of dissatisfaction, the sort of reception we got. Susy had to sit in her damp clothes half an hour while we waited in the parlor; and then she was taken to a fireless room and left to wait there again, as she has stated.[12]

SUSY: At last we were called to dinner, and I went down without papa as he never eats anything in the middle of the day. I sat at the table with the lady principal and enjoyed very much seing all the young girls trooping into the dining-room. After dinner I went around the College with the young ladies and papa stayed in his room and smoked. When it was supper time papa went down and ate supper with us and we had a very delightful supper. After supper the young ladies went to their rooms to dress for the evening. Papa went to his room and I went with the lady principal. At length the guests began to arive, but papa still remained in his room until called for. Papa read in the chapell. It was the first time I had ever heard him read in my life—that is in public. When he came out on the stage I remember the people behind me exclaimed "Oh how queer he is! Isn't he funny!" I thought papa was very funny, although I did not think him queer. He read "A Trying Situation" and "The Golden Arm," a ghost story that he heard down South when he was a little boy. "The Golden Arm" papa had told me before, but he had startled me so that I did not much wish to hear it again. But I had resolved this time to be prepared and not to let myself be startled, but still papa did, and very very much; he startled the whole roomful of people and they jumped as one man. The other story was also very funny and interesting and I enjoyed the evening inexpressibly much. After papa had finished reading we all went down to the collation in the dining-room, and after that there was dancing and singing. Then the guests went away and papa and I went to bed. The next morning we rose early, took an early train for Hartford and reached Hartford at ½ past 2 o'clock. We were very glad to get back.[13]

NARRATOR: One morning in June, Sam heard Susy say thoughtfully: "How one happiness gets in the way of another, and one cannot have them both!"

"What is it now?" Sam asked.

"Well, I am to go to Cousin Susie Warner's in the morning, and now I have been to the kitchen and it turns out that we are to have Miss Corey [her piano teacher] and fishballs for breakfast."

"The collocation is the point," Sam commented, "if you don't perceive it yourself."[14]

Livy recorded Clara's birthday in a journal she kept that summer.

LIVY: The little maiden is eleven years old today and a precious little maiden she is. She had her school this morning only that it closed about half an hour earlier than usual. Then we had her table as has been our habit for several years on the Ombra. She had given to her a lawn tennis set, books—some little pieces of pottery, two little pins (brooches) one silver and one shell. Note paper, a pretty little Japanese pencil box—a work basket etc.

We had Susy, Julia and Harmony Twichell, Daisy Warner, Fanny Freese, Susy Corey and Miss Foote here for supper. A jolly time playing games, dancing, and so on. It is a great pleasure to see the children together they do have such a good time. There is much satisfaction in doing anything for Susy and Clara they are so grateful for every thing that is done for them, and express it so earnestly. It seems almost strange when they have always had so much done for them. When I came up to bed tonight they were both wide awake waiting to tell me what a good day they had had and how much they thanked me for it. They are blessed children and tremendous comforts.[15]

SAM: I am a fortunate person, who has been for thirteen years accustomed, daily and hourly, to the charming companionship of thoroughly well-behaved, well-trained, well-governed children. Never mind about taking my word; ask Mrs. Harriet Beecher Stowe, or Charles Dudley Warner, or any other neighbor of mine, if this is not the exact and unexaggerated truth.[16]

NARRATOR: Four days after Clara's birthday, it was examination time.

LIVY: Yesterday the children and I decorated the school room with wild flowers, grasses and ferns for today's examination. We made the room exceedingly pretty, the children enjoyed so much the process of doing it. This morning Mrs. Geo. Warner, Daisy, Miss Price and Miss Corey came to the examination. All the lessons went very nicely I thought. The children were both examined in Arithmetic. Next Susy was examined in Geography, then Clara in United States History.—then Susy in United States History, Susy's was a brief but very good synopsis of United S. H. from the earliest discoverers down to the Civil War—Clara's was giving more particulars of the Civil War.

Supper tonight on the Ombra. Billiard evening—Mr. Robinson, Mr. Bunce, Mr. Whitmore and Mr. Sam Dunham came for billiards.[17]

SUSY: Papa's favorite game is billiards, and when he is tired and wishes to rest himself he stays up all night and plays billiards, it seems to rest his head. He smokes a great deal almost incessantly.[18]

LIVY: This morning [June 13th] the last day of the children's examination, Clara passed a most excellent examination in her Geography. Susy told the story of Cupid and Psyche in Latin, Miss Foote asking her questions. Susy gave what I think without partiality was a brilliant recitation in Ancient History. She talked for fully an hour with an occasional question from Miss Foote, telling us in a most concise and felicitous way about what she had been going over in this last winter. Describing what History is —about the races of men, about Egypt, Assyria and Babylonia, Phoenicia etc. etc., etc. Going into the work of each in the world and upon Civilization. Occasionally she would, say well Miss Foote, the book says so and so, but it seems to me in this way, stating something quite different. It was surely wonderful to hear the child. . . .

After dinner which we ate on the Ombra we took a drive in the long carriage. First taking Jean a little way, then bringing her home as it was her bed time.

In the evening Mr. and Mrs. G. Warner and Miss Price came in, Lilly going home after a little—Miss Price and Mr. Warner staying for whist. After we had played four games Mr. and Mrs. Charles Warner came, he having just returned from a long trip away. A little later Dr. Smith and Miss Corey came, they having been down town playing eight hands. We had a jolly remainder of the evening, eating ice cream hearing and telling funny stories of which latter Mr. Clemens was full.[19]

NARRATOR: Livy and Sam went to "Armsmear," Mrs. Samuel Colt's house, for dinner on June 16th.

LIVY: Tomorrow if the children are well we start for Elmira. I have had a busy day—getting silver ready for the vault, packing and so on. This evening we dined at Mrs. Colts to meet some southern friends of hers. There were twelve of us at the table, a delightful time we had and the decorations were beautiful—Such superb masses of roses. About half past eight or nine other guests began to arrive and I should think there might have been two hundred there. A charming last evening in Hartford, seeing so many friends that I was glad to say good bye to. A band and fire works in the grounds as we sat about in the drawing room and on the porches. It has been an excessively hot day.[20]

On June 19th we arrived in Elmira, we went directly to Mother's spending a little more than a week with her. The six grandchildren had a delightful time together, and we elders all had a good visit. Yesterday morning [June 27th] we left Mother's and two loads of us drove up here [Quarry Farm]. . . . At once . . . the children all went out to see a new donkey that had been purchased in Kansas and sent to the farm for them. Jean's first exclamation was "dear old fellow" as she advanced toward the "creature" with a little embarrassed air. The children all had a ride on the donkey . . . and we began to get ourselves settled for our Summer's stay here. Susy said, "how good Aunt Sue is to let us come here and stay all Summer." I most heartily echo that sentiment. The great interest with the children during these two days since we came has been the donkey. She seems a docile beast, the children have caught her in the field, bridled her and mounted her alone, but when they would ride their father went with them. We hope the donkey has no bad tricks that will in any way frighten or inconvenience the children. They have named her Patience Cadichon, pronouncing it Kaditchin.

This morning Theodore, Sue, Susy and I went down to church, it was Anniversary Sunday, there was a very large number.[21]

On the 4th of July Charlie and Ida with the children came up to dinner and to have some fire works in the evening. Mother had been here since the day before. Charlie set off the fire works as soon as it was dark, quite a number from outside gathered to see them. They were exceedingly pretty. Two carriage loads drove down after the fire works—I felt a little anxious about Charlie's horses as they seemed quite restive as they started away, but they arrived at home safely.[22]

NARRATOR: A charming playhouse had its inception in a corner of Quarry Farm. Susy found a vine-covered nook, near the study, one day. She rushed to Aunt Sue.

SUSY: Can I have it? Can Clara and I have it all for our own?[23]

NARRATOR: Susy and Clara set up housekeeping in the nook and called it "Helen's Bower" (they were reading *Thaddeus of Warsaw*). They played so happily in the bower that Sue Crane conceived the idea of building a more substantial playhouse just beyond it.

SAM: She gave them land in the field beyond my study, and built them a little bit of a house on it and furnished it with a complete kitchen outfit, tables, chairs, utensils, stove and all. That was "Ellerslie"—Susy's name for it [from Grace Aguilar's *Days of Robert Bruce*]—and they spent a great deal of time there cooking dishes that were not in the cook-book and giving me a chance to suspend work and eat them.[24]

LIVY: Susy is reading aloud to me Schillers' "Yungfrau von Orleans" —She reads it very well, and it is delightful to read it with her. Tonight I was reading to Susy and Clara from a book "Life and her Children" a very interesting book on the lower forms of Animal Life. I came to something about Carbonic Acid—and as we spoke a little about it Clara said, I always like to talk aloud to myself when I am alone in the woods, because I like to give the trees Carbonic Acid. The blessed child it was so sweetly and innocently said.[25]

Susy was mourning today [July 12th] because the summer time goes so quickly. . . .

Susy is reading Scott's "Betrothed." Tonight she said to me Scott has a cool way of writing—even when the event is exciting he writes of it cooly. Today as we were reading in the Bible together I took Clara's Bible from her to look at something and a poor uneven little piece of paper fell out, written closely on both sides, I saw at a glance that it was of interest to me, that some of the child's thoughts were on it, she picked it up, and evidently did not want it seen—but I insisted until she gave it to me—Susy saying too, "Why Clara, it is real sweet I saw it in your Bible the other day." I read it and later when Clara stepped out of the room Susy said, "that little piece of paper made me know Clara better than I ever did before." This is what was on the paper exactly except that I cannot copy the dear little irregularities of the childish hand.

Be good to Susy, be not rude, overbearing, cross or pick her up. Be considerate of Eliza (the nurse), and put yourself in her place. Be as sweet and generous to Jean as Susy is and even more so, and be not selfish with the donkey but think how much you like to ride her and Jean enjoys it just about as much. Be sweet to Mamma and when you see that she is tired you ought to ask her as few questions as you can not to bother her. Be not cross and unmannerly to Julie even if you do think her queer, perhaps she thinks you queer. Be good always.[26]

SUSY: While we were in Elmira an article came out in the "Christian Union" by name "What ought he to have done" treating of the government of children, or rather giving an account of a fathers battle with his little baby boy, by the mother of the child and put in the form of a question as to whether the father disciplined the child corectly or not, different people wrote their opinions of the fathers behavior, and told what they thought he should have done.[27]

SAM: [It was] enough to make a body's blood boil.[28]

SUSY: Mamma had long known how to disciplin children, for in fact the bringing up of children had been one of her specialities for many years. She had a great many theories, but one of them was, that if a child was big enough to be nauty, it was big enough to be whipped and here we all agreed with her. . . .

When Clara and I had been very nauty or were being very nauty, the nurse would go and call Mamma and she would appear suddenly and look at us (she had a way of looking at us when she was displeased as if she could see right through us) till we were ready to sink through the floor from embarasment, and total absence of knowing what to say. This look was usually followed with "Clara" or "Susy what do you mean by this? do you want to come to the bath-room with me?" Then followed the climax for Clara and I both new only too well what going to the bath-room meant.

But mamma's first and foremost object was to make the child understand that he is being punished for *his* sake, and because the mother so loves him that she cannot allow him to do wrong; also that it is as hard for her to punish him as for him to be punished and even harder. Mamma never allowed herself to punish us when she was angry with us she never struck us because she was enoyed at us and felt like striking us if we had been nauty and had enoyed her . . . she always postponed the punishment until *she* was no more chafed by our behavior. . . .

Our very worst nautinesses were punished by being taken to the bath-room and being whipped by the paper cutter. But after the whipping was over, mamma did not allow us to leave her until we were perfectly happy, and perfectly understoood why we had been whipped. I never remember having felt the least bit bitterly toward mamma for punishing me . . . she showed no signs of further displeasure, but acted as if we had not displeased her in any way.

When the article "What ought he to have done?" came out Mamma read it, and was very much interested in it. And when papa heard that she had read it he went to work and secretly wrote his opinion of what the father ought to have done. He told Aunt Susy, Clara and I, about it but mamma was not to see it or hear any thing about it till it came out. He gave it to Aunt Susy to read, and after Clara and I had gone up to get ready for bed he brought it up for us to read. He told what he thought the father ought to have done by telling what mamma would have done. . . .

Clara and I had great fun the night that papa gave it to us to read and then hide, so mamma couldn't see it, for just as we were in the midst of reading it mamma appeared papa following anxiously and asked why we were not in bed? Then a scuffle ensued for we told her it was a secret and tried to hide it; but she chased us wherever we went, till she thought it was time for us to go to bed, then she surendered and left us to tuck it under Clara's matress.

The article was a beautiful tribute to mamma and every word in it true. But still in writing about mamma he partly forgot that the article was going to be published, I think, and expressed himself more fully than he would do the second time he wrote it; I think the article has done and will do a great deal of good, and I think it would have been perfect for the family and friend's enjoyment, but a little bit too private to have been published as it was. And Papa felt so too, because the very next day or a few days after, he went down to New York to see if he couldn't get it back before it was published but it was too late, and he had to return without it.[29]

When the *Christian Union* reached the farm and papa's article in it, all ready and waiting to be read to mama, papa hadn't the courage to show it to her (for he knew she wouldn't like it at all) at first, and he didn't, but he might have let it go and never let her see it; but finally he gave his consent to her seeing it, and told Clara and I we could take it to her, which we did with tardiness, and we all stood around mama while she read it, all wondering what she would say and think about it.[30]

NARRATOR: The concluding paragraphs of Sam's article were:

SAM: The mother of my children adores them—there is no milder term for it—and they worship her; they even worship anything which the touch of her hand has made sacred. They know her for the best and truest friend they have ever had, or ever shall have; they know her for one who never did them a wrong, and cannot do them a wrong; who never told them a lie, nor the shadow of one; who never deceived them by even an ambiguous gesture; who never gave them an unreasonable command, nor ever contented herself with anything short of a perfect obedience; who has always treated them as politely and considerately as she would the best and oldest in the land, and has always required of them gentle speech and courteous conduct toward all, of whatsoever degree with whom they chanced to come in contact; they know her for one whose promise, whether of reward or punishment, is gold, and always worth its face, to the uttermost farthing. In a word, they know her, and I know her, for the best and dearest mother that lives—and by a long, long way the wisest. . . .

In all my life I have never made a single reference to my wife in print before, as far as I can remember, except once in the dedication of a book; and so, after these fifteen years of silence, perhaps I may unseal my lips this one time without impropriety or indelicacy. I will institute one other novelty: I will send this manuscript to the press without her knowledge and without asking her to edit it. This will save it from getting edited into the stove.

SUSY: She was too much surprised (and pleased privately too) to say much at first; but, as we all expected, publicly (or rather when she remembered that this article was to be read by every one that took the *Christian Union*) she was rather shocked and a little displeased.[31]

A little while after the article was published letters began to come in to papa crittisizing it, there were some very pleasant ones but a few very disagreable. One of these, the very worst, mamma got hold of and read, to papa's great regret, it was full of the most disagreable things, and so very enoying to papa that he for a time felt he must do something to show the author of it his great displeasure at being so insulted. But he finally decided not to, because he felt the man had some cause for feeling enoyed at, for papa had spoken of him, (he was the baby's father,) rather slightingly in his Christian Union article.

After all this, papa and mamma both wished I think they might never hear or be spoken to on the subject of the Christian Union article, and whenever any has spoken to me and told me "How much they did enjoy my father's article in the Christian Union" I almost laughed in their faces when I remembered what a great variety of oppinions had been expressed upon the subject of the Christian Union article of papa's[32]

NARRATOR: Jean's birthday was celebrated. Susy describes some of the cats and lists the daily occupations of the family.

SUSY: It is Jean's birthday to day [July 26th]. She is 5 yrs. old. Papa is away today and he telegraphed Jean that he wished her 65 happy returns.[33]

Papa is very fond of animals particularly of cats, we had a dear little gray kitten once that he named "Lazy" (papa always wears gray to match his hair and eyes) and he would carry him around on his shoulder, it was a mighty pretty sight! The gray cat sound asleep against papa's gray coat and hair. The names that he has given our different cats, are realy remarkably funny, they are namely Stray Kit, Abner, Motley, Fraeulein, Lazy, Bufalo Bill, Soapy Sall, Cleveland, Sour Mash, and Pestilence and Famine.[34]

There are eleven cats at the farm here now. Papa's favorite is a little tortoise-shell kitten he has named "Sour Mash," and a little spotted one "Fannie." It is very pretty to see what papa calls the cat procession; it was formed in this way. Old Minnie-cat headed, (the mother of all cats) next to her came aunt Susie, then Clara on the donkey, accompanied by a pile of cats, then papa and Jean hand in hand and a pile of cats brought up in the rear, mama and I made up the audience.

Our varius occupations are as follows. Papa rises about ½ past 7 in the morning, breakfasts at eight, writes, plays tennis with Clara and me and tries to make the donkey go, in the morning; does varius things in P.M., and in the evening plays tennis with Clara and me and amuses Jean and the donkey.

Mama rises about ¼ to eight, breakfasts at eight, teaches Jean German reading from 9-10; reads German with me from 10-11. Then she reads studdies or visits with aunt Susie for a while, and then she reads to Clara and I till lunch time things connected with English history (for we hope to go to England next summer) while we sew. Then we have lunch. She studdies for about half an hour or visits with aunt Susie, then reads to us an hour or more, then studdies writes reads and rests till supper time. After supper she sits out on the porch and works till eight o'clock, from eight o'clock to bedtime she plays whist with papa and after she has retired she reads and studdies German for a while.

Clara and I do most everything from practicing to donkey riding and playing tag. While Jean's time is spent in asking mama what she can have to eat.[35]

NARRATOR: Jean also liked to tease Sam.

SUSY: The other day we were all sitting when papa told Clara and I that he would give us an arithmetic example; he began if A byes a horse for $100—"$200" Jean interrupted; the expression of mingled surprise and submission on papa's face, as he turned to Jean and said "Who is doing this example, Jean?" was inexpressibly funny. Jean laughed and papa continued, "If A byes a horse for $100"—"$200" Jean promptly interrupted; papa looked perplexed, and mamma went into convulsions of laughter. It was plain to us all that papa would have to change his sum to $200, so he accordingly began. "If A byes a horse for $200 and B byes a mule for $140 and they join in copartnership and trade their creatures for a piece of land for $480, how long will it take a lame man to borrow a silk umbrella?"[36]

NARRATOR: Sam and Livy went to Onteora in the Catskills to visit Candace Wheeler, mother of Dora Wheeler Keith, the artist.

SUSY: Mamma and papa have returned from Onteora and they have had a delightful visit. Mr. Frank Stockton was down in Virginia and could not reach Onteora in time, so they did not see him, and Mrs. Mary Mapes Dodge was ill and couldn't go to Onteora, but Mrs. General Custer was there, and mamma said that she was a very attractive, sweet appearing woman.[37]

NARRATOR: Grandma Langdon's 75th birthday was August 19th; they all went into town to celebrate, at the Langdon house.

IDA LANGDON: The big brown house . . . on the corner of Main and Church Streets . . . was a much loved home. The acreage around it, which included fully half the block, with the vine-covered stable standing on First Street, was planted with some rare and many fine native trees; supplied with greenhouses (one of them for plants and flowers, the other mainly for grapes, but sheltering also a mammoth night-blooming cereus given to prolific blooming at twilight), bright with formal flower beds; ornamented by a fairly complicated, low boxwood labyrinth, alluring yet terrifying to the very young and still short; adorned in summer with palms in green tubs (they were a trifle incongruous among the apple trees left from a former orchard, but all except the purists admired them); and dotted with fountains and canopied iron garden-seats. Hammocks and bird cages, their occupants only mildly disturbed by an occasional passing horse-car, hung on the front porch.[38]

LIVY: We all made our various gifts to her, Susy had worked an umbrella case, and she had also learned the second part of the Merry Wives of Windsor to play with Clara, as part of her contribution, Clara had learned her part before with her teacher, but Susy learned hers alone. It seemed almost useless to prepare any thing for Mother, for she does so much for us, it seems wrong for her to give us gifts on her birthday besides doing so on ours—but it is her pleasure so I suppose we must all be content. She gave Sue and Charlie and me each of us a check of $100. so it made fifty dollars for each of the children and children-in-law Theodore, Ida and Mr. Clemens were to share our one hundred dollar checks. Beside the checks she made us gifts. She gave me three pieces of Crown Derby Tea-pot, sugar bowl and cream pitcher.[39]

NARRATOR: Sam described a typical Sunday at the farm.

SAM: The city in the valley is purple with shade, as seen from up here at the study. The Cranes are reading and loafing in the canvas-curtained summer-house, fifty yards away, on a higher (the highest) point; the cats are loafing over at Ellerslie. . . . Livy is down at the house, but I shall now go and bring her up to the Cranes to help us occupy the lounges and hammocks, whence a great panorama of distant hills and valley and city is seeable. The children have gone on a lark through the neighboring hills and woods, Susy and Clara horseback and Jean is driving a buggy, with the coachman for comrade and assistant at need. It is a perfect day indeed.[40]

CLARA: Except for the birthday party at my grandmother's, very little social life was courted by any of the family. My sisters and I were not allowed to go to parties and our parents sought solitude and repose during the summer months on the lovely farm.[41]

IDA LANGDON: It was not more than two and a half miles from the Farm to the center of Elmira, but the road up East Hill had steep pitches and hard pulls for horses. . . . Callers came in carriages or in livery hacks, a few walked. (The Cranes and Mr. Clemens frequently walked up and down.) The Farm was never lonely, never monotonous, never dull, but it was utterly quiet and undisturbed.

It was a wonderful place for my uncle to work (according to him the best anywhere in the world). It was also to him a very beautiful place, a place, he said, in which to take a foretaste of Heaven.[42]

CLARA: There was plenty of companionship with animals, however. Of these were represented various species in the household, both wild and tame. Starting with dogs large enough to be harnessed and pull a little express-cart, we progressed to a couple of donkeys (called "Kadichan" and "Polichon") and, finally, graduated in patience and courage with a pair of ponies in our possession.[43]

SUSY: Mamma is teaching Jean a little natural history and is making a little collection of insects for her. But mamma does not allow Jean to kill any insects. She only collects those insects that are found dead. Mamma has told us all, perticularly Jean, to bring her all the little dead insects that she finds. The other day as we were all sitting at supper Jean broke into the room and ran triumfantly up to Mamma and presented her with a plate full of dead flies. Mamma thanked Jean very enthusiastically although she with difficulty concealed her amusement. Just then Sour Mash entered the room and Jean believing her hungry asked Mamma for permission to give her the flies. Mamma laughingly consented and the flies almost immediately dissapeared.[44]

SAM: Susy's Biography interests itself pretty exclusively with historical facts; where they happen is not a matter of much concern to her. When other historians refer to the Bunker Hill Monument they know it is not necessary to mention that this monument is in Boston. Susy recognizes that when she mentions Sour Mash it is not necessary to localize her. To Susy, Sour Mash is the Bunker Hill Monument of Quarry Farm.

Ordinary cats have some partiality for living flies, but none for dead ones; but Susy does not trouble herself to apologize for Sour Mash's eccentricities of taste. This Biography was for *us*, and Susy knew that nothing that Sour Mash might do could startle us or need explanation, we being aware that she was not an ordinary cat, but moving upon a plane far above the prejudices and superstitions which are law to common catdom.[45]

SUSY: Papa says if the collera comes here he will take Sour-Mash to the mountains. . . . Sour Mash is a constant source of anxiety, care, and pleasure to papa.

SAM: I did, in truth, think a great deal of that old tortoise-shell harlot; but I haven't a doubt that in order to impress Susy I was

pretending agonies of solicitudes which I didn't honestly feel.
Sour Mash never gave me any real anxiety; she was always able to
take care of herself, and she was ostentatiously vain of the fact;
vain of it to a degree which often made me ashamed of her, much
as I esteemed her.[46]

NARRATOR: Time to return to Hartford was nearing.

LIVY: This afternoon as I lay on the bed feeling rather depressed at
the thought of leaving Mother and Sue and the friends here and
a little tired from the packing etc. Susy came to my bedside bringing a little bag that she had filled with articles to amuse Jean
on the journey. It was delightful to see the arrangements that
she had made—there were paper dolls cut out ready for Jean to
make the faces on them, a piece of silk with a needle and pieces of
thread for her to sew—a crochet needle with worsted for her
to "heckel", buttons for her to sew on. A paper book which Susy
had made for her, cutting out pictures and pasting them in the
book, then writing stories about them—all this and more to amuse
Jean on the journey to New York tomorrow. While I lay on the
bed mourning she was doing something for the pleasure of some
one else. The blessed child. Probably the next time I write in this
book will be in Hartford, if we are spared to arrive there safely.[47]

We arrived home safely on the 18th of Sept. and the children
began their lessons on the 21st. They have been going on busily
now ever since, being also much occupied with their Christmas
work. Mr. Clemens has had to be much in New York seeing to
the publication of Genl. Grant's book reading proof of it etc.
Today [November 27th] we have had a quiet day having only Miss
Corey to dinner, and Jean also eating with us, but we had a merry
time this evening. I invited Miss Foote, Ward Foote, Hattie Foote,
Daisy, Fanny Freese, the Twichell children and two or three
other children—the grown people came with them and we had a
most merry time—dancing, we all danced the Virginia-Reel—Mr.
Twichell, Mr. Clemens, both Mr. Warners, and then charades in
which the gentlemen led and all together a very good wholesome
time for the children.[48]

GEORGE WARNER: The Clemens house was the only one I have ever
known where there was never any *pre*occupation in the evenings,
and where visitors were always welcome. Clemens was the best
kind of a host; his evenings after dinner were an unending flow of
stories.[49]

HOWELLS: Clemens was then hard upon fifty, and he had kept, as he did to the end, the slender figure of his youth, but the ashes of the burnt-out years were beginning to gray the fires of that splendid shock of red hair which he held to the height of a stature apparently greater than it was, and tilted from side to side in his undulating walk. He glimmered at you from the narrow slits of fine blue-greenish eyes, under branching brows, which with age grew more and more like a sort of plumage, and he was apt to smile into your face with a subtle but amiable perception, and yet with a sort of remote absence; you were all there for him, but he was not all there for you.[50]

LIVY: My birthday, forty years old today.[51]

SAM: We have reached another milestone, my darling, and a very very remote one from the place whence we started; but we look back over a pleasant landscape—valleys that are still green, plains that still bear flowers, hills that still sleep in the soft light of that far morning of blessed memory. And here we have company on the journey—ah, such precious company, such inspiring, such lovely, and gracious company! and how they lighten the march! Our faces are toward the sunset, now, but these are with us, to hold our hands, and stay our feet, and while they abide, and our old love grows and never diminishes, our march shall still be through flowers and green fields, and the evening light as pleasant as that old soft morning glow yonder behind. Your husband.[52]

LIVY: When I went down to breakfast I found a little table trimmed with smilax and with my gifts on it beside my place at the breakfast table. Mr. Clemens gave me a most beautiful copper vase, shaped much like the old etruscan vases; with beautiful design and motto on it. Mother gave me some money to buy some silver, (I think I shall buy soup spoons.) Susy gave me a blotter, with some work of hers in sepia on the cover, her first attempt at using water color it is very pretty. Clara gave me a little Japanese match box. Jean a little steel implement to use in keeping your sleeves down when you draw on a sack over them.

Tonight or rather this afternoon at four o'clock we had Mr. Joseph Jefferson to dinner, with some friends to meet him—we sat twelve in number at the table.[53]

KATY: He was a great actor—one of the very best, and he used to come and stay at the house a lot—sometimes stay three and four days. He used to come at the same time William Gillette did, and they used to play billiards together.

Joe Jefferson was a little mite of a man, and I remember once

it was awful cold when he come down there, and Mr. Clemens
made him put on his big fur coat. Everybody that come to Hartford had to put on that fur coat of Mr. Clemens if they was cold.
Joe Jefferson was kind of lost in it—it was so big for him. But he
could talk, I tell you, and crack jokes, too—and he used to tell
awful funny stories at dinner. He was a very good actor, they said,
about one of the greatest that America ever produced—although
I never seen him myself. He did one play all the time—*Rip Van
Winkle,* that was.[54]

SAM: I am sorry enough to ever miss any moment of Jefferson for
some day I am going to need his influence when he is an arch-
angel.[55]

NARRATOR: Sam's fiftieth birthday followed Livy's fortieth by three
days.

SUSY: Papa was fifty years old, and among his numerous presents,
The Critic sent him a delightful notice of his semi-centenial; con-
taining a poem to him by Dr. Holmes, a paragraph from Mr.
F. R. Stockton, one from Mr. C. D. Warner and one from Mr. C. J.
Harris (Uncle Remus).

Papa was very much pleased and so were we all.[56]

HOLMES:

TO MARK TWAIN
(On his fiftieth birthday)

Ah, Clemens, when I saw thee last,
    We both of us were younger;
How fondly mumbling o'er the past
    Is Memory's toothless hunger!

So fifty years have fled, they say,
    Since first you took to drinking;
I mean in Nature's milky way—
    Of course no ill I'm thinking.

But while on life's uneven road
    Your track you've been pursuing,
What fountains from your wit have flowed—
    What drinks you have been brewing!

I know whence all your magic came,
    Your secret I've discovered,
The source that fed your inward flame,
    The dreams that round you hovered.

Before you learned to bite or munch,
  Still kicking in your cradle,
The Muses mixed a bowl of punch
  And Hebe seized the ladle.

Dear babe, whose fiftieth year to-day
  Your ripe half-century rounded,
Your books the precious draught betray
  The laughing Nine compounded.

So mixed the sweet, the sharp, the strong,
  Each finds its faults amended,
The virtues that to each belong
  In happiest union blended.

And what the flavor can surpass
  Of sugar, spirit, lemons?
So while one health fills every glass—
  Mark Twain for Baby Clemens!

NARRATOR: Sam wrote Holmes:

SAM: I shall never be able to tell you the half of how proud you have made me. If I could you would say you were nearly paid for the trouble you took. And then the family: If I could convey the electrical surprise and gratitude and exaltation of the wife and the children last night, when they happened upon that *Critic* where I had, with artful artlessness, spread it open and retired out of view to see what would happen—well, it was great and fine and beautiful to see, and made me feel as the victor feels when the shouting hosts march by; and if you also could have seen it you would have said the account was squared. For I have brought them up in your company, as in the company of a warm and friendly and beneficent but far-distant sun; and so, for you to do this thing was for the sun to send down out of the skies the miracle of a special ray and transfigure me before their faces. I knew what that poem would be to them; I knew it would raise me up to remote and shining heights in their eyes, to very fellow-ship with the chambered Nautilus itself, and that from that fel-lowship they could never dissociate me while they should live; and so I made sure to be by when the surprise should come.[57]

NARRATOR: The end of the year was jubilant. Grant's *Memoirs* was a great commercial success.

SAM: I'm out of the woods. On the last day of the year I had paid out $182,000 on the Grant book and it was totally free from debt.[58]

I am frightened at the proportions of my prosperity. It seems to me that whatever I touch turns to gold.[59]

NARRATOR: The typesetter, however, was continuing its monthly toll on the finances. Sam was continuously optimistic. Paige told him it would cost $20,000 to $30,000 to complete the machine. Sam said he would put in up to $30,000, that was his limit.

They were about to put on *The Prince and the Pauper* again and invited Mr. and Mrs. Howells to come.

HOWELLS: I shall be delighted to come to the play, but Mrs. Howells doesn't foresee her way. Now, you and Mrs. Clemens have often asked me to bring Pilla [Mildred Howells]. This winter she's out of school, and I can bring her instead. If this is wholly desirable on your part, let me know. If not—and possibly Susy may be too much occupied for the visit—not. We are too old friends, I hope, to be mealy-mouthed.

SAM: Good—we claim you and Pilla, then, for Jan. 13, since we can't get Mrs. Howells too. Everything is now planned, and the several guests' beds appointed them, in Mrs. Clemens's methodical fashion. Now I wish it were good for you to come a day before; but we shall be busy rehearsing; so come *on* the 13th, and then remain afterward as long as you can.[60]

NARRATOR: Sam admired Livy's dramatization of *The Prince and the Pauper*, but he wanted to see Clara's part, the Lady Jane Grey, enlarged in her scene with the Pauper, played by Daisy Warner.

DAISY: Saturday forenoon (Jan. 9th, 1886) when we were rehersing for the next Wednesday's performance, Mr. Clemens went up to his billaird room and wrote this adition to our Lady Jane Grey scene which was so very short before, it being only that which is in the book. Then Mama [Lilly Gillette Warner] sat right down and coppied it off from Mr. Clemen's, when he brought it down stairs. Then I took it home, learned my part and went over in the evening and rehersed it.[61]

SUSY: At the third [*Prince and the Pauper* there were] about seventy [people].

CAST OF CHARACTERS

Pauper	Margaret Warner
Prince	Susy Clemens
Princes Elizabeth	H[armony] Twitchell

Lady Jane Grey	Clara Clemens
Miles Hendon	Mr. S. L. Clemens
Lord Hertford	Fannie Freese
St. Jhon	Susie Twitchell
Archbishop	Mr. G. H. Warner
Page and crown bearer	Burton T[wichell]
Guard	Mr. A. W. Foote
Court Gentleman	David Twichell

The Coronation March was played . . . the third time by Mrs.
C. D. Warner.[62]

HOWELLS: The play was very pretty, but the broken-down trains
didn't bring us till it was half done.[63]

NARRATOR: Susy listed the scenes.

SUSY:

  1. First Gate Scene.—
  2. The Interview.—
  3. Second Gate Scene.—
  4. Lady Jane Grey and Pauper.—
  5. At Guild Hall.—
  6. The Prince and Miles Hendon.—
  7. The Coronation.—[64]

We have just had our Prince and Pauper pictures taken; two
groups and some little single ones. The groups (the Interview and
Lady Jane Grey scene) were pretty good, the Lady Jane
scene was perfect, just as pretty as it could be, the Interview was
not so good; and two of the little single pictures were very good
indeed, but one was very bad. Yet on the whole we think they
were a success.[65]

NARRATOR: In February a new contract was drawn up for the completion of the typesetter; Hamersley had a tenth interest and, in
a frightening clause, Sam was required to complete the machine
and capitalize it commercially. His friend and business agent,
Franklin Gray Whitmore, did not approve; he told Sam that the
clause could bankrupt him.

Jean had now become Sam's principal audience for storytelling,
and Susy delighted in the stories that Sam told to Jean because,
she said, "Papa has practise in telling stories of variety as Jean is
a child of variety and original ideas, and papa is too. (I mean
such a man), so half of the story he devotes to his own fancy,

(if Jean allows) the other half to Jean's."⁶⁶ Susy recorded this story as Jean told it to her later, remarking that Jean always had to have animal stories.

THE DONKEY WHAT COULD TALK

Once there was a donkey and he went out walking. And he saw some children and he wondered why those children had books under their arms. And he thought he would go with them to see what they did. And he went into the school-house with them, and they showed him their books. But he couldn't understand the words in the books. So one evening moonshine, he thought he would go to the school-house, and eat some of the books. He went and ate, German books, and English books, and French books and all kinds of books, and had a great deal of stomach ache afterwards. And when the children came home they wondered where their books were, and they couldn't see where the books were, they couldn't see. Then the children said, "Why this donkey must have eaten our books. But the donkey said he hadn't touched [the] books. Then the school-teacher came home and the children said that this donkey could talk. And the school-teacher wanted to hear him. So the children called him, and he came and spoke to them, and as soon as the people saw, and heard this wonderful donkey talk they immediately asked him to belong to their church. So he did, and when the choir sang he sang with it, but he was not satisfied to sing in company with others, fearing his voice might not be distinctly enough heard. So he asked for permission to sing alone, in place of the choir. So his request was granted him, and he sang regularly after that, every Sunday. At last people got so much interested in him that he was elected to be a member of Congress which honor he also accepted; and he was the first donkey that ever was a member of Congress. And finally he ran for President and so he was the learnedest donkey that ever was.⁶⁷

The family was concerned about Sam's not writing.

SAM: Susy and I used to "promonade" daily up and down the library, with our arms about each other's waists, and deal in intimate communion concerning affairs of State, or the deep questions of human life, or our small personal affairs.⁶⁸

SUSY: Mamma and I have both been very much troubled of late because papa since he has been publishing Gen. Grant's book has seemed to forget his own books and work entirely, and the other evening as papa and I were promonading up and down the library he told me that he didn't expect to write but one more book, and then he was ready to give up work altogether, die, or do anything, he said that he had written more than he had ever expected to, and the only book [*Captain Stormfield's Visit to Heaven*] that he had been partickularly anxious to write was one locked up in the safe down stairs, not yet published.

But this intended future of course will never do, and although papa usually holds to his own opinions and intents with outsiders, when mamma realy desires anything and says that it must be, papa allways gives up his plans (at least so far) and does as she says is right (and she is usually right, if she dissagrees with him at all). It was because he knew his great tendency to being convinced by her, that he published without her knowledge that article in the "Christian Union" concerning the government of children. So judging by the proofs of past years, I think that we will be able to persuade papa to go back to work as before, and not leave off writing with the end of his next story. Mamma says that she sometimes feels, and I do too, that she would rather have papa depend on his writing for a living than to have him think of giving it up.[69]

NARRATOR: The book he expected to write was finally started.

SAM: I have begun a book whose scene is laid far back in the twilight of tradition; I have saturated myself with the atmosphere of the day and the subject and got myself into the swing of the work. If I peg away for some weeks without a break I am safe.[70]

SUSY: Yesterday evening [February 22nd] papa read to us the beginning of his new book, in manuscript, and we enjoyed it very much, it was founded on a New Englanders visit to England in the time of King Arthur and his Round Table [*A Connecticut Yankee in King Arthur's Court*].[71]

He has the mind of an author exactly, some of the simplest things he can't understand. Our burglar alarm is often out of order, and papa had been obliged to take the mahogany room off from the alarm altogether for a time, because the burglar alarm had been in the habit of ringing even when the mahogany-room window was closed. At length he thought that perhaps the burglar alarm might be in order, and he decided to try and see; accordingly he put it on and then went down and opened the window; consequently the alarm bell rang, it would even if the alarm had been in order. Papa went despairingly upstairs and said to mamma,

"Livy the mahogany room won't go on. I have just opened the window to see."

"Why, Youth," mamma replied. "If you've opened the window, why of course the alarm will ring!"

"That's what I've opened it for, why I just went down to see if it would ring!"

Mamma tried to explain to papa that when he wanted to go and see whether the alarm would ring while the window was closed he *mustn't* go and open the window—but in vain, papa couldn't understand, and got very impatient with mamma for trying to make him believe an impossible thing true.

SAM: This is a frank biographer and an honest one; she uses no sandpaper on me.[72]

That word "Youth" . . . was my wife's pet name for me. It was gently satirical but also affectionate. I had certain mental and material peculiarities and customs proper to a much younger person than I was.[73]

That burglar alarm which Susy mentions led a gay and careless life and had no principles. It was generally out of order at one point or another and there was plenty of opportunity, because all the windows and doors in the house, from the cellar up to the top floor, were connected with it.[74]

HOWELLS: He used to give me a royal chamber on the ground floor, and come in at night after I had gone to bed to take off the burglar alarm so that the family should not be roused if anybody tried to get in at my window. This would be after we had sat up late.[75]

SUSY'S FIFTEENTH YEAR

1886–1887

NARRATOR: Susy now joined the adults in many social affairs.

SAM: Susy is *fourteen* to-day! Land, but I do feel old![1]

SUSY: The other day was my birthday, and I had a little birthday party in the evening and papa acted some very funny charades with Mr. Gerhardt, Mr. Jesse Grant (who had come up from New York and was spending the evening with us) and Mr. Frank Warner. One of them was "on his knees" honys-sneeze. There were a good many other funny ones, all of which I don't remember. Mr. Grant was very pleasant, and began playing the charades in the most delightful way.

SAM: Susy's spelling defeated me, this time. I cannot make out what "honys-sneeze" stands for.

SUSY: Mamma and Papa have been in New York for two or three days, and Miss Corey has been staying with us. They are coming home to-day at two o'clock.

Papa has just begun to play chess, and he is very fond of it, so he has engaged to play Mrs. Charles Warner every morning from 10 to 12, he came down to supper last night, full of this pleasant prospect, but evidently with something on his mind. Finally he said to mamma in an appologetical tone, Susy Warner and I have a plan.

"Well" mamma said "what now, I wonder?"

Papa said that Susy Warner and he were going to name the chess men after some of the old bible heroes, and then play chess on Sunday.[2]

Papa can make exceedingly bright jokes, and he enjoys funny things, and when he is with people he jokes and laughs a great deal, but still he is more interested in earnest books and earnest subjects to talk upon, than in humorous ones.

When we are all alone at home, nine times out of ten, he talks about some very earnest subject, (with an occasional joke thrown in) and he a good deal more often talks upon such subjects than upon the other kind.

He is as much of a Pholosopher as anything I think. I think he could have done a great deal in this direction if he had studied while young, for he seems to enjoy reasoning out things, no matter what; in a great many such directions he has greater ability than in the gifts which have made him famous.

SAM: Thus at fourteen she had made up her mind about me, and in no timorous or uncertain terms had set down her reasons for her opinion. . . . Right or wrong, it was a brave position for that little analyzer to take. She never withdrew it afterward, nor modified it. She has spoken of herself as lacking physical courage, and has evinced her admiration of Clara's; but she had moral courage, which is the rarest of human qualities, and she kept it functionable by exercising it. I think that in questions of morals and politics she was usually on my side; but when she was not she had her reasons and maintained her ground.[3]

SUSY: Papa has written a new version of "There is a happy land" it is—

> There is a boarding-house
> Far, far away,
> Where they have ham and eggs,
> Three times a day,
> Oh don't those boarders yell
> When they hear the dinner-bell,
> They give that land-lord rats
> Three times a day.

SAM: Susy has made a small error. It was not I that wrote the song. I heard Billy Rice sing it in the negro minstrel show, and I brought it home and sang it—with great spirit—for the elevation of the household. The children admired it to the limit, and made me sing it with burdensome frequency. To their minds it was superior to the Battle Hymn of the Republic.[4]

SUSY: The other day mamma went into the library and found papa sitting there reading a book, and roaring with laughter over it;

She asked him what he was reading, he answered that he hadn't stopped to look at the title of the book, and went on reading. She glanced over his shoulder at the cover, and found it was one of his own books.[5]

SAM: That is another of Susy's unveilings of me. Still, she did not garble history but stated a fact.[6]

SUSY: Mr. W. D. Howells and his daughter Pilla have been here to visit us. And we have enjoyed them very much. . . . Sunday night at supper papa and Mr. Howells began to talk about the Jews.

NARRATOR: Howells had written about a Jew in *Silas Lapham* when it appeared in the *Century,* and had received derogatory letters from Jewish readers.

SUSY: Mr. Howells said he thought the Jews were a persecuted race, and a race already down. So he decided to take out the sentence when the story appeared in book form.

NARRATOR: According to Susy, Sam had an acquaintance named Wood who had a friend, "a rich Jew," who said that Sam was the only humorist who never poked fun at Jews. He asked Wood to find out why Sam never ridiculed Jews.

SUSY: Mr. Wood soon did see papa and spoke to him upon this subject. Papa at first did not know himself why it was he had never spoken unkindly of the Jews in any of his books, but after thinking awhile he decided that the Jews had always seemed to him a race much to be respected; also they had suffered much, and had been greatly persecuted, so to ridicule or make fun of them seemed to be like attacking a man that was already down. And of course that fact took away whatever there was funny in the ridicule of a Jew.

He said it seemed to him that Jews ought to be respected very much for two things partickularly. One was that they never begged, one never saw a Jew begging; another was that they always took care of their poor.[7]

Mamma and papa Clara and Daisy have gone to New York to see the "Mikado." They are coming home to-night [April 18th] at half past seven.[8]

Papa has contrived a new way for us to remember dates. We are to bring to breakfast every morning a date, without fail, and now they are to be dates from English Historie.[9]

CLARA: Father was always ready to make jokes at the breakfast table, and my impression is that his wit was not half appreciated at that hour of the morning. Everybody was present in the dining-room by eight o'clock, but I don't think anyone wished to be. I would say that my father was the only one at the table who found any real joy in life so early in the morning, and of course he didn't *find* it; he created it.[10]

NARRATOR: George also provided breakfast entertainment.

SAM: Every day, in the Hartford racing-season, he made large winnings; and while he waited at breakfast next morning he allowed the fact and the amount to escape him casually. Mainly for Susy's benefit, who had been made to believe that betting was immoral, and she was always trying to wean George from it, and was constantly being beguiled, by his arts, into thinking his reform was imminent, and likely to happen at any moment. Then he would fall—and report a "pile" at breakfast; reform again, and fall again before night; and so on, enjoying her irritations and reproaches, and her solemn warnings that disaster would overtake him yet. If he made a particularly rich haul, we knew it by the ostentatious profundity of his sadness and depressions as he served at breakfast next morning,—a trap set for Susy. She would notice his sadnesses, presently, and say, eagerly and hopefully, "It has happened, George, I told you it would, and you are served just right—how much did you lose?—I hope ever so much; nothing else can teach you." George's sigh would be ready, and also his confession, along with a properly repentant look—

"Yes, Miss Susy, I had hard luck—something was wrong. I can't make out what it was, but I hope and believe it will learn me. I only won eight hundred dollars."[11]

NARRATOR: Evening activities included blowing bubbles.

SUSY: The other evening Clara and I brought down our new soap bubble water and we all blew soap bubles. Papa blew his soap bubles and filled them with tobacco smoke and as the light shone on them they took very beautiful opaline colors. Papa would hold them and then let us catch them in our hand and they felt delightful to the touch the mixture of the smoke and water had a singularly pleasant effect.

SAM: It is human life. We are blown upon the world; we float buoyantly upon the summer air a little while, complacently showing off our grace of form and our dainty iridescent colors; then we vanish with a little puff, leaving nothing behind but a memory —and sometimes not even that.[12]

NARRATOR: Outdoors, the children found animal life absorbing; besides the horses, cows and ducks were kept in Hartford.

SUSY: Jean and Papa were walking out past the barn the other day when Jean saw some little newly born baby ducks, she exclaimed as she perceived them "I don't see why God gives us so much ducks when Patrick kills them so."

SAM: Susy is mistaken as to the origin of the ducks. They were not a gift, I bought them. I am not finding fault with her, for that would be most unfair. She is remarkably accurate in her statements as a historian, as a rule, and it would not be just to make much of this small slip of hers; besides I think it was a quite natural slip, for by heredity and habit ours was a religious household, and it was a common thing with us whenever anybody did a handsome thing, to give the credit of it to Providence, without examining into the matter. This may be called automatic religion—in fact that is what it is; it is so used to its work that it can do it without your help or even your privity. . . . No elaboration of this matter is necessary; it is sufficient to say *I* provided the ducks. . . .

Patrick, who was fertile in good ideas, had early conceived the idea of having home-made ducks for our table. Every morning he drove them from the stable down to the river, and the children were always there to see and admire the waddling white procession; they were there again at sunset to see Patrick conduct the procession back to its lodgings in the stable. But this was not always a gay and happy holiday show, with joy in it for the witnesses; no, too frequently there was a tragedy connected with it, and then there were tears and pain for the children. There was a stranded log or two in the river, and on these certain families of snapping-turtles used to congregate and drowse in the sun and give thanks, in their dumb way, to Providence for benevolence extended to them. It was but another instance of misplaced credit; it was the young ducks that those pious reptiles were so thankful for—whereas they were *my* ducks. I bought the ducks.

When a crop of young ducks, not yet quite old enough for the table but approaching that age, began to join the procession, and paddle around in the sluggish water, and give thanks—not to me —for that privilege, the snapping-turtles would suspend their songs of praise and slide off the logs and paddle along under the water and chew the feet of the young ducks. Presently Patrick would notice that two or three of those little creatures were not moving about, but were apparently at anchor, and were not looking as thankful as they had been looking a short time before.

He early found out what that sign meant—a submerged snapping-turtle was taking his breakfast, and silently singing his gratitude. Every day or two Patrick would rescue and fetch up a little duck with incomplete legs to stand upon—nothing left of their extremities but gnawed and bleeding stumps. Then the children said pitying things and wept—and at dinner we finished the tragedy which the turtles had begun. Thus, as will be seen—out of season, at least—it was really the turtles that gave us so much ducks. At my expense.[13]

NARRATOR: The science of mental health was much discussed in the neighborhood.

SUSY: Papa has been very much interested of late, in the "Mind Cure" theory. And in fact so have we all. A young lady in town has worked wonders, by using the "Mind Cure" upon people; she is constantly busy now curing peoples deseases in this way—and curing her own even, which to me seems the most remarkable of all.

A little while past, papa was delighted with the knowledge of what he thought the best way of curing a cold, which was by starving it. This starving did work beautifully, and freed him from a great many severe colds. Now he says it wasn't the starving that helped his colds, but the trust in the starving, the mind cure connected with the starving.

I shouldn't wonder if we finally became firm believers in Mind Cure. The next time papa has a cold, I haven't a doubt, he will send for Miss H.[olden] the young lady who is doctoring in the "Mind Cure" theory, to cure him of it.

Mamma was over at Mrs. George Warners to lunch the other day and Miss H.[olden] was there too. Mamma asked if anything as natural as near sightedness could be cured she said oh yes just as well as other deseases.

When mamma came home, she took me into her room, and told me that perhaps my near-sightedness could be cured by the "Mind Cure" and that she was going to have me try the treatment any way, there could be no harm in it, and there might be great good. If her plan succeeds there certainly will be a great deal in "Mind Cure" to my oppinion, for I am *very* near sighted and so is mamma, and I never expected there could be any more cure for it than for blindness, but now I don't know but what theres a cure for *that*.[14]

"Yes, the "mind cure" *does* seem to be working wonderfully.

Papa, who has been using glasses now for more than a year, has laid them off entirely. And my near-sightedness is really getting better. It seems marvelous.[15]

SAM: It was a disappointment; her near-sightedness remained with her to the end. She was born with it, no doubt.[16]

SUSY: When Jean has stomack-ache Clara and I have tried to divert her by telling her to lie on her side and try "mind cure." The novelty of it has made her willing to try it, and then Clara and I would exclaim about how wonderful it was she was getting better. And she would think it realy was finally, and stop crying, to our delight.

The other day mama went into the library and found her lying on the sofa with her back toward the door. She said, "Why, Jean, what's the matter? Don't you feel well?" Jean said that she had a little stomack-ache, and so thought she would lie down. Mama said, "Why don't you try 'mind cure'?" "I am," Jean answered.[17]

Papa has done a great deal in his life I think, that is good, and very remarkable, but I think if he had had the advantages with which he could have developed the gifts which he has made no use of in writing his books, or in any other way for other peoples pleasure and benefit outside of his own family and intimate friends, he could have done *more* than he has and a great deal more even. He is known to the public as a humorist, but he has much more in him that is earnest than that is humorous. He has a keen sense of the ludicrous, notices funny stories and incidents knows how to tell them, so to improve them, and does not forget them. He has been through a great many of the funny adventures related in "Tom Sawyer" and in "Huckleberry Finn," *himself* and he lived among just such boys, and in just such villages all the days of his early life. His "Prince and Pauper" is his most original, and best production; it shows the most of any of his books what kind of pictures are in his mind, usually. Not that the pictures of England in the 16th Century and the adventures of a little prince and pauper are the kind of things he mainly thinks about; but that *that* book, and those pictures represent the train of thought and imagination he would be likely to be thinking of to-day, to-morrow, or next day, more nearly than those given in "Tom Sawyer" or "Huckleberry Finn."[18]

NARRATOR: In June they went to Elmira; the donkey continued to be a source of constant entertainment at the farm.

SUSY: The other day papa thought he would see how he could manage Cadichon who had been acting badly so he got onto her but papa wanted to go one way and Cadichon another, and as papa wouldn't submit Cadichon threw him off into the high grass.

About a half an hour later Jean came down onto the porch in her nightgown and sat on Mamma's lap. I said "Jean what do you think! Cadichon threw papa off into the high grass!" She answered in a very calm way "I know it." I said how do you know it? She said "Oh I saw it from the window." She had been in the habit of standing at the window in her night gown and critisizing the shotts papa and I made while playing tennis and we wondered why she did not crittisize the way papa fell from Cadichon.[19]

CLARA: A DONKEY had gotten the best of our father! We giggled ourselves to sleep that night and Father was in good spirits, too. He said he was "more attracted to the donkey than before, because the power to accompany an act of vengeance with so much grace and serenity proved the animal to be superhuman."[20]

NARRATOR: Sam immortalized the donkey in a poem entitled "Kiditchin."

SAM: O du lieb' Kiditchin
Du bist ganz bewitchin,
    Waw———— - he!

In summer days Kiditchin
Thou'rt dear from nose to britchin
    Waw———— - he!

No dought thoult get a switchin
When for mischief thou'rt itchin'
    Waw———— - he!

But when you're good Kiditchin
You shall feast in James's kitchin
    Waw———— - he!

O now lift up thy song—
Thy noble note prolong—
Thou living Chinese gong!

    Waw— - he! waw— - he waw
    Sweetest donkey man ever saw.[21]

NARRATOR: Jean continued to demand stories; she asked Sam to construct one based "on a kind of business copartnership between a 'bawgun strictor and a burglar.'"[22] She was also absorbed in the cows on the farm.

SAM: She goes out to the barn with one of us every evening toward six o'clock, to look at the cows—which she adores—no weaker word can express her feeling for them. She sits rapt and contented while David milks the three, making a remark now and then—always about the cows. The time passes slowly and drearily for her attendant, but not for her. She could stand a week of it. When the milking is finished, and "Blanche," "Jean," and "the cross cow" are turned into the adjoining little cow-lot, we have to set Jean on a shed in that lot, and stay by her half an hour, till Eliza, the German nurse, comes to take her to bed. The cows merely stand there, and do nothing; yet the mere sight of them is all-sufficient for Jean. She requires nothing more. The other evening, after contemplating them a long time, as they stood in the muddy muck chewing the cud, she said, with deep and reverent appreciation, "Ain't this a sweet little garden?"

Yesterday evening our cows (after being inspected and worshipped by Jean from the shed for an hour) wandered off down into the pasture and left her bereft. I thought I was going to get back home, now, but that was an error. Jean knew of some more cows in a field somewhere, and took my hand and led me thitherward. When we turned the corner and took the right-hand road, I saw that we should presently be out of range of call and sight; so I began to argue against continuing the expedition, and Jean began to argue in favor of it, she using English for light skirmishing and German for "business." I kept up my end with vigor, and demolished her arguments in detail, one after the other, till I judged I had her about cornered. She hesitated a moment, then answered up, sharply:

"Wir werden nichts mehr darüber sprechen!" (We won't talk any more about it.)

It nearly took my breath away, though I thought I might possibly have misunderstood. I said:

"Why, you little rascal! Was hast du gesagt?"

But she said the same words over again, and in the same decided way. I suppose I ought to have been outraged, but I wasn't; I was charmed.[23]

NARRATOR: A major family expedition took off from Elmira for Keokuk, that summer of 1886, to visit Jane Clemens, who was living with Orion and Mollie.

ANNIE MOFFETT: She was a great beauty, a fine dancer, and very witty. She kept her beauty . . . as well as her love of color and dancing. . . . She was very straight and dignified. When she went back to Keokuk in her last years to live with Uncle Orion he said that when she went into the theater dressed in her black velvet with white lace, her lavender kid gloves and ostrich-tip bonnet, she always created a stir.[24]

SUSY: We are all of us on our way to see Grandma Clemens, who is very feeble and wants to see us and partickularly Jean who is her namesake. We are going by way of the lakes, as papa thought that would be the most comfortable way.[25]

NARRATOR: From Buffalo, they took a lake steamer to Duluth and, at St. Paul, a Mississippi steamboat to Keokuk. The children were delighted with the leadsman's long-drawn chant, "Mark Twain, Mark Twain." Clara came running down the deck to Sam: "Papa," she said, "I have hunted all over the boat for you. Don't you know they are calling for you?"[26]

SAM: On a lake or a river boat one is as thoroughly cut off from letters and papers and the tax collector as though he were amid sea. Moreover, one doesn't have the discomforts of seafaring. It is very unpleasant to look at sea sick people—at least so my friends said the last time I crossed. . . .

It is strange . . . how little has been written about the upper Missisippi. . . . Neither in this country nor in any other have I seen such interesting scenery. . . . One finds all that the Hudson affords —bluffs and wooded highlands—and a great deal in addition. Between St. Paul and the mouth of the Illinois river there are over four hundred islands—strung out in every possible shape. A river without islands is like a woman without hair. She may be good and pure, but one doesn't fall in love with her very often.[27]

NARRATOR: Fourth of July in Keokuk was compounded of brass bands, picnics, a reception in honor of Grandma Clemens and miserably hot weather. As Orion's house was small, the children and Rosa stayed nearby at the McElroys.

SAM: Keokuk weather was pretty hot; Jean and Clara sat up in bed at Mrs. McElroy's and cried about it, and so did I. . . . Well it did need cooling; I remember I burnt a hole in my shirt, there, with some ice-cream that fell on it.[28]

NARRATOR: Whether it was the weather, the round of activities or the difficulty of reporting family life under tension, the Keokuk visit marked the end of Susy's biography; it was cut off abruptly.

SUSY: We have arrived in Keokuk after a very pleasant—[29]

NARRATOR: They stopped off in Chicago on the way back to Elmira. Will Clemens, who claimed to be a distant relative, tells of a Chicago reporter's interview with Sam.

WILL CLEMENS: "We came in last night," said Mark, pulling at the left side of his mustache. "Mrs. Clemens is not very well, neither am I. I have been amusing the children. I have taken them to a panorama. I understand there are three others near here. I will take them there too. I want to satiate them with battles—it may amuse them." Three little girls composed of three red gowns, three red parasols and six blue stockings stood on the steps and laughed.

"Run up and tell mamma what a jolly time you've had and I'll think of something else to amuse you."

When the three little girls had disappeared Mr. Clemens sighed. "Did you every try to amuse three little girls at the same time?" he asked, after a pause; "it requires genius. I wonder whether they would like to bathe in the lake?" he continued, with sudden animation, hardly pausing five minutes between each word, "it might amuse them. . . .

"I have just returned from a visit to my mother in Keokuk, Iowa. We came from Buffalo to Duluth by a lake steamer and then from St. Paul down the river to Keokuk."[30]

NARRATOR: They were all happy to get back to the farm.

SAM: We are here on top of the always-cool hill, after four or five days and night of hell-sweltering weather in Keokuk.—but barring those few days, we had the pleasantest and completest pleasure trip a family ever took. We left here June 21 and got back day before yesterday—10th.[31]

Yes, it was pretty hot weather. Now here, when a person is going to die, he is always in a sweat about where he is going to; but in Keokuk of course they don't care, because they are fixed for everything. It has set me reflecting, it has taught me a lesson. By and by, when my health fails, I am going to put all my affairs in order, and bid good-bye to my friends here, and kill all the people I don't like, and go out to Keokuk and prepare for death.[32]

NARRATOR: Sam was in New York the end of July and, as usual, homesick for his family.

SAM: I thought of you people all along, to-day, naturally enough: "Now they're at supper"—"now they're out on the porch, and

Theodore sitting in the roadway" [because there was not enough room on the porch]—"now the children and the pony are at it"—"now Jean is kissing good-night"—"now the children are playing the piano for Theodore"—"now *they're* off for bed"—"and now Aunt Sue is taking advantage of the absence of their natural protector to set out the Mash family an hour ahead of time"—"and finally all hands are off for early bed, and Mamma and Jean are bunking together, and all is quiet, all is still but the dog."[33]

NARRATOR: They returned to Hartford in September, and the girls resumed lessons and classes: piano, violin, sewing and dancing. Susy went, for a year, to Riley's dancing class.

HELEN CHAPMAN: Dancing School . . . used to be eagerly anticipated. For many years Harbison's Hall at the corner of Main and Sheldon Streets was known as Riley's Dancing Academy. There we lined up every Saturday afternoon to present ourselves to P. Harvard Riley, than whom there was never a better teacher. We learned fancy dances, the Highland Fling, the Sailors' Hornpipe, the Cachuca and others. We learned the Quadrille and the Lanciers from printed cards so that we danced without prompting and we also had taught us every known variety of round dances, as they were called from the schottische and polka to the waltz.

The utmost decorum was observed. At a signal to take partners, the "Young Masters" as they were called would each stand in front of the young miss of his choice, bow solemnly and say, "May I have the pleasure of dancing with you?" She would curtsy, replying, "Yes, sir, with pleasure."[34]

NARRATOR: A playmate described another form of education.

JULIA GILMAN: There was the embroidery club which I belonged to with Susy and Clara Clemens. The club was started by Mrs. Bartholomew on Capitol Avenue. Mrs. Whiting was the teacher. She was a widow in reduced circumstances—a gentle woman, you understand—with two daughters, and she did beautiful work. . . . The Clemens girls, Ethel Cheney of Manchester, Daisy Bartholomew, Roberta Whiting were some of those who attended Mrs. Whiting's class. We sewed together in the living room of Mrs. Bartholomew's house. After the class was over, we young girls would go up to the play room on the third floor.

One day Susy Clemens, who was the oldest girl in the class, suggested a game for us to play. One person was to wrap herself in a sheet and declaim lines from Shakespeare while another girl was to stand behind her and, thrusting her arms through the sheet make the appropriate gestures to accompany the speech. Well, Susy began it herself. She started quoting a long scene from Shakespeare—she knew it all by heart. I was only eleven or twelve and knew no Shakespeare at all then. . . . It was my job to make the gestures, and since I didn't understand what Susy was saying anyway, I conceived it *my* duty to attend strictly to the gestures and to pay no attention to Susy's words. Well, I began making various grand gestures with my arms stuck through the sheet from behind. The other girls shrieked with laughter, so out of keeping with Susy's words, were the awkward movements of my arms. Susy, herself, suddenly, could stand it no longer. She buried her face in her hands, dissolved with laughter.

Oh, I wish I could convey . . . the expression in those lovely eyes of Susy Clemens'! She had the most remarkable eyes. . . . They were large, lustrous, animated, expectant, alert. They would have seemed unusual in any intelligent adult, but in a fourteen-year-old girl they were striking.[35]

NARRATOR: The atmosphere of their house activated imaginations. Clara said that the guest room next to the billiard room on the third floor was "so spooky that my sisters and I decided it was a suitable home for the insane wife of Rochester in *Jane Eyre.*"[36] Dramatics flourished in the schoolroom when lessons were done.

SAM: Susy and her nearest neighbor, Margaret Warner, often devised tragedies and played them in the school-room, with little Jean's help—with closed doors—no admission to anybody. The chief characters were always a couple of queens, with a quarrel in stock —historical when possible, but a quarrel anyway, even if it had to be a work of imagination. Jean always had one function—only one. She sat at a little table about a foot high and drafted death warrants for these queens to sign. In the course of time they completely wore out Elizabeth and Mary, Queen of Scots—also all of Mrs. Clemen's gowns that they could get hold of—for nothing charmed these monarchs like having four or five feet of gown dragging on the floor behind. Mrs. Clemens and I spied upon them more than once, which was treacherous conduct—but I don't think we very seriously minded that. It was grand to see the queens stride back and forth and reproach each other in three- or four-syllable words dripping with blood; and it was pretty to see how tranquil Jean was through it all. Familiarity with daily death and carnage had hardened her to crime and suffering in all their forms, and they were no longer able to hasten her pulse by a beat. Sometimes when there was a long interval between death warrants she even leaned her head on her table and went to sleep. It was then a curious spectacle of innocent repose and crimson and volcanic tragedy.[37]

NARRATOR: Sam had a new diversion.

CLARA: He formed a Browning Club . . . which met at our house once in two weeks during the winter.[38]

SAM: Think of it!—I've been elected Reader to a Browning class—I who have never of my own inclination, read a poem in my life. It consists of Livy, and Susie Warner and Lilly Warner, and a New Haven lady and a Farmington lady, and meets in my billiard room every Wednesday morning. It is very enjoyable work: only it takes three days to prepare an hour's reading. It takes me much longer to learn how to read a page of Browning than a page of Shakespeare. And mind you, I'm on the ABC only—his *easy* poems. The other day I took a glance at one of his mature pieces, to see how I am likely to fare when I get along over there. It was absolutely opaque.

I am pretty proud of my Browning class. It meets in my billiard room every Wednesday morning, and one lady comes 9 miles and another 36 to attend it. I study and prepare 30 or 40 pages of new matter for each sitting—along with a modest small lecture, usually —and then re-read poems called for by the class. I suppose I have read Rabbi Ben Ezra and Up in the Villa a couple of dozen times, and Abt Vogler, Caliban upon Setebos, and some others nearly as often. Ben Ezra and Abt Vogler are called for oftenest—yes, and Up in a Villa. We should read Easter Day just as often, but for its length. Folk ask permission to come,—as if it were a privilege. When you consider that these folk, and the class, are women who are away above the intellectual average, it is no nickel-plated compliment for the poet.[39]

NARRATOR: Sam was also much in demand by the young ladies' literary group, the Saturday Morning Club, which he had helped to found.

HELEN POST CHAPMAN: Mr. Clemens was our patron saint and once a year we always met at his house. On one of these occasions he presented each one of us with a beautiful pin. Our flower was the lily of the valley. These pins were designed by Tiffany, a bunch of lilies embossed and enameled in the centers, a ribbon band making an oval setting in gold on which was inscribed in blue enamel

"Saturday Morning Club of Hartford." On the back was engraved the name of the owner.[40]

CLARA: The only poetry Father wholly enjoyed was that of Robert Browning, whereas Susy loved Tennyson, Swinburne, Shelley, and Rossetti, as well. She quoted these poets constantly when not more than twelve or thirteen. Whatever she did was done with her entire passionate nature. If she read poetry, she lived with it day after day, week after week. She could not give her attention with cool thought to anything. Whatever she took into her mind was gluttonously received, as if she were suffering from unappeased appetite of the brain. To me this power to feel ardently with the intellect is one of the real marks of genius. Most of the quoting that she did from the lighter poets like Tennyson was directed to Mother and me. She felt intuitively that Father found little pleasure in the charm of mere rhythm when unaccompanied by profound thought such as Browning offered. Father gave a great deal of time to the study of Browning's poems, even the longest of them.[41]

NARRATOR: The children were fascinated with visitors from England.

CLARA: Sir Henry Stanley and his wife, Dorothy Tenant (who was well known as an artist in England) and her mother, stayed several days in our home. They were the first English people I had ever seen, and their pronounced inflections fascinated me and helped me to remember remarks they made. For instance, Lady Stanley turned effusively to Father once and said in her lovely voice that had a sincere ring in it, "I did not know whether I should enjoy visiting you, Mr. Clemens, because Americans have customs and habits so different from ours. I feared I might not feel at home in the house of an American, particularly so distinguished a one, but I must confess I find you an easy host to get along with. Stanley agrees with me. Don't you, Stanley?" She always called her husband by his last name. She was a woman of genial charm and made an interesting contrast to her husband, who possessed the personality necessary for the discoverer of Livingstone.[42]

SAM: I have entertained him [Stanley] here rather elaborately, and have also gone to Boston to introduce him—a thing which was more or less cool, considering that Boston has no real need to send out of the city for capable and illustrious introducers.[43]

NARRATOR: The Hartford *Courant* reported on Sam's introduction.

SAM: Now Columbus started out to discover America. Well, he didn't do anything at all but sit in the cabin of his ship and hold his grip and sail straight on, and America would discover itself. (Laughter) Here it was barring his passage the whole length and breadth of the South American continent, and he couldn't get by it. (Laughter) He'd got to discover it; he couldn't help it. Neither did he have to find any particular part of America, and when he found any portion of it his contract was fulfilled. But Mr. Stanley started out to find Dr. Livingstone, who was hidden away some- where, scattered abroad, as you may say, over the length and breadth of a vast slab of Africa as big as the United States.[44]

NARRATOR: The children were growing up; family relationships were changing. Susy had written about her father for two years. Cer- tainly Susy, in her candidness, appeared unafraid of Sam, yet one can understand that the three children learned to avoid his more irascible moments.

KATY: When Mr. Clemens is very jolly and happy his eyes are *blue* to me; but when he gets angry or upset at anything, like losing his wonderful manuscript, his eyes are very fierce and *black*.[45]

SAM: Yesterday [December 12th] a thunder-stroke fell upon me out of the most unsuspected of skies which for a moment ranged me breast to breast and comraded me as an equal, with all men who have suffered sudden and awful disaster: I found that all their lives my children have been afraid of me! have stood all their days in uneasy dread of my sharp tongue and uncertain temper. The accusing instances stretch back to their babyhood, and are burnt into their memories: and I never suspected, and the fact was never guessed by *anybody* until yesterday. Well, all the concentrated griefs of fifty years seemed colorless by the side of that pathetic revelation.[46]

NARRATOR: After the holidays, there were delightful visitors and a month of portrait painting. Dora Wheeler Keith, portrait painter, and her mother, Candace Wheeler, came to stay with the Clemenses.

HARTFORD COURANT: Harper and Brothers commissioned Mrs. Keith to make a series of portraits of famous . . authors in this country and England.[47]

NARRATOR: Livy and Sam had met Mrs. Wheeler and her family at Onteora, where, with other artistic friends, she had established a delightful vacation colony. She was a partner in The Associated

Artists with Tiffany, Coleman and De Forest, and had founded the Woman's Exchanges; she had advised Livy on interior decoration in 1882.

MRS. WHEELER: Their house was very charming, one of a cluster in a little parklike border of Hartford. It had been but recently built, and, having all of what we call "modern conveniences," drew from Mr. Clemens the characteristic remark, "When it was done I had three hundred dollars in the bank which the plumber didn't know anything about." . . .

Of the three children in the Clemens family . . . "Little Jean," as she was always tenderly called, was the youngest and her father's darling; Susy had both beauty and talent; and Clara was a pretty girl with remarkable musical ability. . . .

As I have said, "Little Jean" was the darling of her father's heart. One morning at breakfast I noticed that she was not at the table, and, asking about her, was told that she was suffering from an earache. Up jumped her father and vanished up the stairs. It was some time before he returned, and when he sat down at the table he told in a half-broken voice of his hearing Jean upbraiding God for not paying more attention to her.

"O God!" she said, "I asked you to stop my earache, and you didn't, and I asked you to get me a goat, and you didn't, and I don't believe you care anything about me any more."[48]

KATY: Everything she wanted she would pray to God for nights. . . . She used to sleep in the nursery. Her bed was right near the fireplace and I think she used to talk up the fireplace—it sounded like it anyway.[49]

MRS. WHEELER: Her father had gone in and comforted the child as best he could, and finished telling us of it by saying, "Livy, if there is a goat in Hartford that prayer is going to be answered."

There was a suggestion from the gentle "Livy" that Jean would receive a false impression from this vicarious proceeding, but Mr. Clemens insisted that that had nothing to do with the matter; if Jean prayed for a goat she wanted it, and if she wanted it— especially when she was suffering—she must have it, and in a day or two the goat was forthcoming.

Susy and Clara were their father's constant companions in his afternoon walks, and, in fact, the three children, the father, and the dog had beautiful outings together, no matter what was the weather.[50]

NARRATOR: Dora Keith had trouble starting Sam's portrait.

HARTFORD COURANT: She was at that time a young woman in her early thirties, and by her own say-so, a very determined young woman. So when Clemens produced one of those "outbursts of temperament" which it often secretly amused him to stage, Dora Wheeler promptly ruffled up her own feathers.

Clemens decided that he did not want to be painted, but if he was going to be painted, it would be on the balcony off the billiard room, or not at all. Mrs. Keith hated to paint out of doors, and so far as she was concerned it would have been "not at all." But there was the Harper commission, so she tried to be patient and conceded.[51]

CLARA: There was a large balcony off the billiard-room, extending right into the tops of the trees. Sometimes Father hid there when he thought he heard some one coming. "Nothing can surpass the power of delicate leaves," he used to say, "to protect one against the evil decrees of a colored butler."[52]

HARTFORD COURANT: Then Clemens decided that he must sit in a red chair. More annoyance on the part of Mrs. Keith, more fussing and fuming all around—just as animated as if both artist and author were really serious about the thing—but you will see that Mark Twain sits in a red chair when you see the portrait. And has a corncob pipe in his hand, as he insisted—and a book.

It was the book that came near seriously upsetting Mrs. Keith's nerves. It was bad enough that Clemens insisted upon reading aloud to her as she painted, but that the work should be Browning's poems, was just about the last straw for the young painter. She heartily disliked Browning and heartily said so. Mark Twain heartily liked him. . . .

Mrs. Keith had no option but to "listen and like it."[53]

NARRATOR: Dora learned to love Browning and Sam had a good time, as he wrote Howells, who was next on her list after Hartford.

SAM: Don't you fret about Miss Wheeler; you will not find it irksome to sit to her; you will enjoy it. You can read, and talk, and have a good time. I am almost sorry my portrait was successful; I sh'd like to sit again.[54]

NARRATOR: Nook Farm neighbors wanted Dora to paint Mrs. Stowe.

MRS. WHEELER: They were all anxious that Dora should make a portrait of her, and Mr. Clemens proposed it.

"No," said Mrs. Stowe. "Why should I sit for a portrait? You know I do not like to meet strangers—new, outside people."

"But," urged Mr. Clemens, "this girl is one of the inside people. You will like her. She is just one of us and we all want her to paint you."

"No," said Mrs. Stowe, "I will not be painted, but if you like you may bring her to see me."

When Mr. Clemens returned we were all eager to know the result of his proposal.

"No, Dora," said he, "she will not sit for you, but I am going to take you around tomorrow morning to see her. You will lose your painting-hours, but I guess it will be worth while."

The next morning, when they "dropped in," as if for a casual morning call, they found the frail old lady waiting for them; then, after a greeting, Mr. Clemens went out "to see the dogs." . . .

"Are you the girl that Samuel wants to have paint a likeness of me?"

"Yes, Mrs. Stowe," and then Dora, as told me afterward: "I thought I should cry; she went on looking so quietly and steadily at me; until at last she said:

"Go home, dear, and get your things. I will wait for you."

In describing the sitting to me afterward, Dora said she had never had such a sense of disembodied soul, because Mrs. Stowe seemed entirely unconscious of her body, as much so as if it no longer existed. She talked freely and sweetly of her mental experiences, both former and present, and while the artist was working rapidly on a pastel portrait the subject seemed to be entirely unaware of it, talking of things spiritual as if *they* were being portrayed. There was a glimpse of very human satisfaction, however, in her showing Dora a cabinet of published translations of *Uncle Tom's Cabin* in almost every written language.

At the end of two mornings' sittings the portrait was finished. It was a picture of sweet old age in a delicate human envelope, a quiet and tranquil face, but, as Mr. Twichell used to say, "with something going on inside."

NARRATOR: Mrs. Wheeler recorded that Dora did a large oil sketch of Livy and Jean, and she painted Charles Dudley Warner for the Authors Series. She said that "The mutual comments of the subjects were always amusing."

"Yes, Dora," drawled Mr. Clemens, looking at Mr. Warner's picture, "you've got that old fish eye of hisn."[55]

SUSY'S SIXTEENTH YEAR

1887–1888

NARRATOR: Daisy Warner wrote her father about Susy's birthday party.

DAISY: Susy Clemens was fifteen years old yesterday and she had a lovely party. The two Twichell girls, Mary and Hattie Foote, Cousin Lilly, Ward Foote, Hattie Whitmore, and Fannie Freese, and Lucy Drake, and I were all there to supper. Mrs. Clemens had her beautiful big, round dinner table, and at each place was a *lovely* bunch of *beautiful* roses. Three or four at each place, and we all put them on. And, also, at each place was a lovely little glass dish of candy, tied around with pretty ribbons, and a little Japanese card with our name on it, on the top of the dish. In the middle of the table, was a kind of pyramid of nasturtiums and then there were other vases, of roses. And those tall silver candles were on the table too, and the whole thing was SO LOVELY. I wish that you could have seen it. We had soup, then turkey, and with it some little potato-cakes and jelly—Then salad, and then straw-berries and ice-cream, and cakes (lady-fingers etc.) and then the big birthdaycake was brought on, with fifteen lighted candles. It was VERY pretty. Of course we all had some of it; and then we had fruit and candy. After supper we danced and had charades. and Mr. Clemens read some "Uncle Remus" to us, and Mama and Frank, and Aunt Lottie, came in after supper. And altogether we had a DELIGHTFUL time.[1]

HOWELLS: No one could read *Uncle Remus* like him; his voice echoed the voices of the negro nurses who told in his childhood the wonderful tales.[2]

NARRATOR: Several years before, Joel Chandler Harris had stayed with the Clemenses.

SAM: He visited us in our home in Hartford and was reverently devoured by the big eyes of Susy and Clara, for I made a deep and awful impression upon the little creatures—who knew his book by heart through my nightly declamation of its tales to them—by revealing to them privately that he was the real Uncle Remus whitewashed so that he could come into people's houses the front way.

He was the bashfulest grown person I have ever met. When there were people about he stayed silent and seemed to suffer until they were gone. But he was lovely nevertheless, for the sweetness and benignity of the immortal Remus looked out from his eyes and the graces and sincerities of his character shone in his face.[3]

NARRATOR: Dancing usually took place in the drawing room.

CLARA: The drawing room was furnished with settees of celestial blue velvet, and straight back chairs of the same color with gilded rods. . . . The light-colored carpet was covered with a long oriental rug. A baby grand piano stood near the wall not far from the folding doors leading into the dining room. The curtains were a pale blue. . . . The ceiling was colored in a quiet gold design. . . . The whole room presented an impression of hospitable *light*—or a suggestively divine quality.[4]

NARRATOR: Harriet Foote Taylor, Lilly Foote's sister, said she would always remember Mr. Clemens at the grand piano, playing "Golden Stairs," with Susy sitting beside him.

There were other visitors in the spring. The Baroness Alexandra von Gripenberg "was immediately impressed by Mark Twain's tanned and weather-beaten appearance and by the dense clouds of tobacco smoke which enveloped him. His facial features were sharp and fine . . . Twain's face was that of a typical prospector, full of countless small and large wrinkles and furrows. His hair was thick, curly, grayish; his penetrating eyes were deep-set; his gestures were abrupt but at the same time slow. His clothes fitted him indifferently as though they knew that their wearer did not care how they looked on him. A brilliant red silk kerchief dangled round his neck in a peculiar manner."[5]

NARRATOR: Nook Farm paid honor to Mrs. Stowe.

CHARLES W. BURPEE: Harriet Beecher Stowe, seated in her home on Forest Street, Hartford, knew that the ten thousandth presentation of "Uncle Tom's Cabin" had been given. This event was celebrated in the neighborhood by a handshake and the conventional cup of tea. Mr. Clemens said on that occasion, "Mrs. Stowe, you have made a book, and you have given to the stage a drama which will live as long as the English tongue shall live."[6]

NARRATOR: Mrs. Stowe returned the compliment.

SAM: Day before yesterday I encountered Mrs. Harriet Beecher Stowe on the sidewalk. She took both my hands and said with strong fervency that surprised the moisture into my eyes—"I am reading your Prince and Pauper for the fourth time, and I *know* it is the best book for young folks ever written."[7]

NARRATOR: Grace King came to visit the Warners. She was from New Orleans and had been discovered by Richard Watson Gilder and Charles Dudley Warner.

GRACE KING: I have never forgotten that first glimpse of the Warner home. It remains with me, not only serenely beautiful, but filled with sentiment ready to break into emotion.

NARRATOR: Susan and Charles Warner had bought the house designed by Edward Tuckerman Potter from the George Warners. It, too, had a charming Stowe conservatory.

GRACE KING: The next morning while I was sitting with Mrs. Warner I heard a voice saying, "I have come to see Grace King!"

My heart stopped beating. I doubted my ears. . . . Mrs. Warner introduced informally, "Mrs. Clemens, the wife of Mark Twain." Did I hear aright? Could my ears be correct? She was rather small; no taller than I. I could not help noticing her dress—a long, silk negligée, red in color, with white at the neck and wrists. After that I saw only her eyes; great, luminous dark eyes set in a broad, satiny white forehead. Her smile was as gleaming as her eyes; her lips lifting over pretty, small white teeth.[8]

KATY: Mrs. Clemens always wore her hair parted—combed down very smooth and nice, and twisted in a kind of figure eight in the back, and sometimes, in the early days, she wore her hair on the top of her head in a great big braid—right on the top of her head, just like a coronet.[9]

GRACE KING: She carried a great bunch of beautiful roses that she gave me. The Clemenses were near neighbors of the Warners, and I was given to understand that a guest in one house was a guest in the other. She left after inviting me to dinner that day.

She had hardly gone when again I heard, "I have come to see Grace King!"

This was Mr. Clemens, Mark Twain . . . boyish-looking in figure, his thick hair, almost white then, hanging about his face turbulently.

He was dressed in white flannels and was smoking his morning pipe. With him my shyness vanished and my hesitating tongue found words.[10]

NARRATOR: At the farm for the summer, there was a change in the staff; Livy, who had never wholly approved of Jean's nurse, viewed the change with mixed feelings.

LIVY: Elize leaves us now in about a week. She gave me notice that she wanted to go before we left Hartford, but decided to stay until we reached Elmira and I could find another nurse. I have found one that has only been about six weeks from Germany, and the German minister says she is better educated than Elize, so I may find it an improvement, although I dread making the change. Jean does not know it yet, I expect she will be broken hearted when she does. It is well that there are dogs and cows and horses to amuse her in that emergency.[11]

SAM: It is not all holiday here with Susy and Clara this time. They have to put in some little time every day on their studies. Jean thinks she is studying too, but I don't know what it is unless it is the horses; she spends the day under their heels in the stables— and that is but a continuation of her Hartford system of culture.[12]

SUSY: We study, read, write, and ride, and keep house at "Ellerslie" and are busy all day long.[13]

NARRATOR: Quarry Farm was a fine vantage point on the Fourth of July.

CLARA: Downtown here it was very noisy, but up here it was quiet at least pretty [quiet]. Jean had torpedoes so it wasn't perfectly [quiet]. We had fireworks in the evening, and it was beautiful to see them in the town.

They had 6 fires in the town from firecrackers. I wish they had been in the evening and all at once, and it would have made a fine show.[14]

NARRATOR: The cats had a gay time, too; Sour Mash had a night out.

SAM: That cat of ours went down to town—3 miles, through the woods, in the night,—and attended a colored-people's church-festival where she didn't even know the deacons—was gone 48 hours, and marched home again this morning. Now think of that! That cat is not for sale. Talented cat. Religious cat. And no color prejudice either.[15]

SUSY: Our insects [cats] . . . come into our rooms at night, and jump upon the beds, or else upon the chairs, and laugh.—But as they are papa's own pets, and have been baptised by him. a great difference of opinion prevails concerning them, and while I am crazy to banish them . . . Clara will interfere, and go to sleep cuddling one in her arms. . . .

Papa's love for them and Clara's has made them *so* bold, that there is no such thing as being free of them at night.—

And at breakfast, every morning there is a discussion, concerning their night-visits, and the way of preventing them.[16]

SAM: Jean will be 7 years old day after tomorrow, and will celebrate the anniversary here at the farm—mainly on the Ellerslie part of it; but I shall be in New York, and can't take a hand, except by telegraph. Jean has got a good level head, but she is as dull at learning as I was—and am. She can spell—that is, as well as her mother or her aunt Sue—but children are *born* that far along.[17]

NARRATOR: Sam recalled an early encounter with the sisters' spelling during his engagement.

SAM: The daily letter that came for me generally brought me news from the front—by which expression I refer to the internecine war that was always going on in a friendly way between these two orthographists about the spelling of words. One of these words was scissors. They never seemed to consult a dictionary; they always wanted something or somebody that was more reliable. Between them, they had spelled scissors in seven different ways, a feat which I am certain no person now living, educated or uneducated, can match. I have forgotten how I was required to say which of the seven ways was the right one. I couldn't do it. If there had been fourteen ways, none of them would have been right. I remember only one of the instances offered. . . . That one was "sicisiors." That way of spelling it looked so reasonable—so plausible, to the discoverer of it, that I was hardly believed when I decided against it.[18]

She [Jean] reads German at 7 as well as the other children did at 5, but has had no chance at English yet, to speak of. Tolerably good at arithmetic. Her mother has taught her, every day since she was weaned; but she will pass largely into the governess's hands in the fall. Jean is an expert on animals, at any rate—she has Clara's gift and interest in that line.[19]

CLARA: We have a new dog here a Scotch Collie, and he is the most excitable dog that I have really ever seen he races around everywhere chases the cats, and drives the cows up from the pasture.

They are very intelligent dogs so it will be a very easy matter to stop him from running after the cats. He has only been here a day and we have almost taught him now.[20]

SAM: We have put in this whole Sunday forenoon teaching the new dog to let the cats alone, and it has been uncommonly lively for those 5 cats. They have spent the most of the time in the trees, swearing. He is the alertest dog that ever was; nothing escapes his observation; and as to movement, he makes a white streak through the air 30 yards long when he is getting started; after that he is invisible.[21]

CLARA: He will be very useful in the way of driving up the cows only that he goes too far, so far that they try and hook him but they don't succeed.[22]

NARRATOR: In the fall Sam went to Washington; Livy gave him some final instructions.

SAM: When I was leaving Hartford for Washington . . . she said: "I have written a small warning and put it in a pocket of your dress vest. When you are dressing to go to the Author's Reception at the White House you will naturally put your fingers in your vest pockets, according to your custom, and you will find that little note there. Read it carefully and do as it tells you. I cannot be with you, and so I delegate my sentry duties to this little note. If I should give you the warning by word of mouth, now, it would pass from your head and be forgotten in a few minutes."

It was President Cleveland's first term. I had never seen his wife—the young, the beautiful, the good-hearted, the sympathetic, the fascinating. Sure enough, just as I had finished dressing to go to the White House I found that little note, which I had long ago forgotten. It was a grave little note, a serious little note, like its writer, but it made me laugh. Livy's gentle gravities often produced that effect upon me, where the expert humorist's best joke would have failed, for I do not laugh easily.

When we reached the White House and I was shaking hands

with the President, he started to say something, but I interrupted him and said, "If Your Excellency will excuse me, I will come back in a moment; but now I have a very important matter to attend to, and it must be attended to at once." I turned to Mrs. Cleveland, the young, the beautiful, the fascinating, and gave her my card, on which I had written *"He did not"*—and asked her to sign her name below those words.

She said: "He did not? He did not what?"

"Oh," I said, "never mind. We cannot stop to discuss that now. This is urgent. Won't you please sign your name?" (I handed her a fountain pen.)

"Why," she said, "I cannot commit myself in that way. Who is it that didn't?—and what is it that he didn't?"

"Oh," I said, "time is flying, flying, flying! Won't you take me out of my distress and sign your name to it? It's all right. I give you my word it's all right."

She looked nonplused, but hesitatingly and mechanically she took the pen and said: "I will sign it. I will take the risk. But you must tell me all about it, right afterward, so that you can be arrested before you get out of the house in case there should be anything criminal about this."

Then she signed; and I handed her Mrs. Clemens's note, which was very brief, very simple, and to the point. It said, *"Don't wear your arctics in the White House."* It made her shout; and at my request she summoned a messenger and we sent that card at once to the mail on its way to Mrs. Clemens in Hartford.[23]

NARRATOR: At home, when dinner parties were given, Livy and the girls concentrated on Sam's behavior.

SAM: *Always*, always without fail, as soon as the guests were out of the house, I saw that I had been miscarrying again. Mrs. Clemens explained to me the various things which I had been doing and which should have been left undone. The children had a name for this performance. They called it "dusting off papa."[24]

Susy took up the phrase and was always seeing to it that Mamma did it before functions. "Mamma don't forget to dust him," and "Did you dust Papa off?"

She was *intense*. That was her marked characteristic.[25]

At last I had an inspiration. It is astonishing that it had not occurred to me earlier. I said: "Why, Livy, you know that dusting me off *after* these dinners is not the wise way. You could dust me off after every dinner for a year and I should always be just as competent to do the forbidden thing at each succeeding dinner as if you had not said a word, because in the meantime I have forgotten all those instructions. I think the correct way is for you to dust me off immediately before the guests arrive, and then I can keep some of it in my head and things will go better."

She recognized that that was wisdom and that it was a very good idea. Then we set to work to arrange a system of signals to be delivered by her to me during dinner; signals which would indicate definitely which particular crime I was now engaged in, so that I could change to another. The children got a screen arranged so that they could be behind it during the dinner and listen for the signals and entertain themselves with them. The system of signals was very simple, but it was very effective. If Mrs. Clemens happened to be so busy, at any time, talking with her elbow neighbor that she overlooked something that I was doing, she was sure to get a low-voiced hint from behind that screen in these words:

"Blue card, mamma"; or, "Red card, mamma"—"Green card, mamma"—so that I was under double and triple guard. What the mother didn't notice the children detected for her.

As I say, the signals were quite simple, but very effective. At a hint from behind the screen, Livy would look down the table and say, in a voice full of interest, if not of counterfeited apprehension, "What did you do with the blue card that was on the dressing table—"

That was enough. I knew what was happening—that I was talking the lady on the right to death and never paying any attention to the one on my left. The blue card meant "Let the lady on your right have a reprieve; destroy the one on your left"; so I would at once go to talking vigorously to the lady on my left. It wouldn't be long till there would be another hint, followed by a remark from Mrs. Clemens which had in it an apparently casual reference to a red card, which meant, "Oh, are you going to sit there all the evening and never say anything? Do wake up and talk." So I woke up and drowned the table with talk. We had a number of cards, of different colors, each meaning a definite thing, each calling attention to some crime or other in my common list; and that system was exceedingly useful. It was entirely successful. It was like Buck Fanshaw's riot. It broke up the riot before it got a chance to begin. It headed off crime after crime all through the dinner, and I always came out at the end successful, triumphant, with large praises owing to me, and I got them on the spot.[26]

NARRATOR: There were business problems: The Webster Company had not realized its expectations with the publication of a *Life of Pope Leo XIII*, and Charley Webster retired, his health broken. Fred G. Hall took his place. Christmas was not going to be lavish, as Sam wrote his sister, Pamela.

SAM: Will you take this $15 and buy some candy or other trifle for yourself and Sam and his wife to remind you that we remember you?

If we weren't a little crowded this year by the type-setter I'd send a check large enough to buy a family Bible or some other useful thing like that. However, we go on and on, but the type-setter goes on forever—at $3,000 a month which is much more satisfactory than was the case the first 17 months, when the bill only averaged $2,000, and promised to take a thousand years. We'll be through now in 3 or 4 months, I reckon, and then the strain will let up and we can breathe freely once more, whether success ensues or failure.

Even with a type-setter on hand we ought not to be in the least scrimped—but it would take a long letter to explain why and who is to blame.[27]

KATY: Paige was all the time thinking up something new that he would invent before it would be perfect, and Mr. Clemens had to give him money all the time. . . . Of course, Paige was always promising and expecting it would be all ready next month, and then poor Mr. Clemens, he'd to send more money, and the next month it wasn't ready and that's the way it went.[28]

NARRATOR: Rarely could Sam persuade Livy to leave the children, but he managed to do just that in March. He was going to New York on the tenth to attend a dinner given by Charles A. Dana in honor of Henry Irving. Livy would join him and, later in the week, they would both go to Washington to visit their Hartford friends General (now Senator) Hawley and his wife, Harriet Foote Hawley. It began to snow in Hartford Sunday, March 11th.

HARTFORD COURANT: The storm began early Sunday night with the temperature about 40°. After a few inches of snow had fallen there was a lull about midnight. But soon after two o'clock it began with violence, the snow coming in blinding sheets and the wind blowing with fury which increased during the day. Had the air been still the snow would have covered the ground to a level of two or three feet, but the wind piled it in great drifts . . . very many being from four to six feet in height, while here and there in favorable localities the piles of snow were eight, ten and twelve feet high.[29]

NARRATOR: All communications, rail, phone, telegraph, came to a halt. Livy couldn't go anywhere. On Tuesday a stalwart soul from the suburbs tried to go downtown.

HARTFORD COURANT: A dweller out west, who made his way in yesterday afternoon after several hours struggle, reports that beyond Mark Twain's house some people are getting out of their second story windows with ladders.[30]

NARRATOR: Sam, holed up in the Murray Hill Hotel, finally wrote Livy on Friday, March 16th.

SAM: Livy darling, I have only just this moment given you up. All these years since the blizzard ceased I have expected you "next day," and next day, and next day—until now. I give it up. I no longer expect you. It is perfectly manifest that that road will not be open for one or two—or possibly 30 days yet. So I will go along to Washington this afternoon in the special car with the rest of the menagerie, and be rested-up and fresh for Mrs. Hawley's dinner tomorrow night.

I was going to wait here for you till Monday—I have had no other plan recently—but after declining, a half hour ago, to go with the menagerie to-day, it suddenly occurred to me that you would regard it as simply criminal for both of us to be absent from the dinner when one of us could be present. To be present, one must go *to-day*—for only an ass attends a dinner party after 6 hours' railway travel.

And so, after all my labor and persuasion to get you to at last promise to take a week's holiday and go off with me on a lark, this is what Providence has gone and done about it. It does seem to me the oddest thing—the way Providence manages. A mere simple *request* to you to stay at home would have been entirely sufficient: but no, that is not big enough, picturesque enough—a blizzard's the idea: pour down all the snow in stock, turn loose all the winds, bring a whole continent to a stand-still:

that is Providence's idea of the correct way to trump a person's trick. Dear me, if I had known it was going to make all this trouble and cost all these millions, I never would have said anything *about* your going to Washington. Now in the light of this revelation of the methods of Providence, consider Noah's flood— I wish I knew the *real* reason for playing that cataclysm on the public: like enough, somebody that liked dry weather wanted to take a walk. That is probably the whole thing—and nothing more *to* it.

Blast that blasted dinner party at Dana's! But for that, I—ah! well, I'm tired: tired calling myself names. Why, I could have been at home all this time. Whereas, here I have been, Crusoing on a desert hotel—out of wife, out of children, out of linen, and out of cigars, out of every blamed thing in the world that I've any use for. Great Scott!

However, I will pack, now, and then go down town and make one more attempt to get a word to you—by long-distance telephone or somehow: though of course it will be the same old story and I shan't succeed.

But I love you my darling, and I am sharply disappointed. Blast the blasted reading, I wish it were in Jericho. Please to kiss those unmatchable jewels for me, and assert that I love them. I kiss you again, sweetheart.[31]

NARRATOR: The children had a glorious time, and they were fascinated with the efforts by the city to get the horsecars going.

HARTFORD COURANT: Several eight-horse teams were employed yesterday [Tuesday, March 13th] to clear the horse railroad tracks with snow-plows. It was a tremendous job and the great teams of strong horses struggled with it with more or less success, according to the depth of the drifts and the compactness of the snow. It was a fine and picturesque sight to see the teams in line, the leaders ridden by their drivers, and several men on the plough, rushing at an obstinate mass of snow higher than the horses' heads, plunging and struggling through the drift and sweeping out triumphant, or, as often happened, stalled in the thickest of the snow. One horse at least went almost out of sight and had to have a free space dug around him before he could be got up and another attempt made.[32]

SUSY'S SEVENTEENTH YEAR

1888–1889

NARRATOR: In April Paige said the machine would be done in September.

SAM: Livy [is] getting steadily along and regaining her health by sure degrees. She has no disease now—that is all gone, quinzy and all, several days ago. Dr. Kellogg requires her to eat something every two hours, and she faithfully obeys. Consequently, although she is necessarily pretty weak, she is by no means as weak as previous attacks of similar violence made her. Her strength was husbanded and taken care of from the start, and is now being carefully and constantly built up. She now sits up an hour at a time in her room, at regular intervals—and this she has been doing for the past three days. Livy has been at sea and unsatisfied and unrestful, as to physicians, from the day that Dr. Taft died until now. But that is all past. She is thoroughly satisfied with Dr. Kellogg and will want no substitute for him, nor accept of any. . . .

I go to Montreal tonight, [April 19th] and get back again in 48 hours.[1]

NARRATOR: Summer at Quarry Farm passed quickly and pleasantly.

SAM: I had a sort of half-way notion that I might possibly finish the Yankee at King Arthur's Court this summer, but I began too late, and so I don't suppose I shall finish it till next summer. We go home to Hartford a week hence [September 24th]; and if at that time I find I am two-thirds done, I mean to try to persuade myself to do that other third before spring.[2]

NARRATOR: Grace King sent Sam a carrot of the celebrated perique

[251]

tobacco of Louisiana which her brother had obtained from a plantation in Natchitoches. She had accepted an invitation to visit the Clemenses again in October. Sam wrote Grace.

SAM: The handless forearm of the mummy has arrived! [This was in fact the shape and color of a carrot of tobacco.] If the whole mummy was as good as this fragment, he must have been the most principal Pharaoh of the very most principal dynasty, and worth the ransacking of the great pyramid to fetch the rest of him! I thank you, and also your brother, and also his friend, and do hold myself under special obligation to all of you.

There is power in that tobacco; it makes the article which I usually smoke seem mighty characterless. . . . Of course I could modify its enthusiasm by mixing it with the baser sort, but that would be to modify champagne with beer; and no righteous person would do that. All of us are glad you are coming with the other splendours of October; and together, you'll make a team, I tell you.[3]

NARRATOR: The machine was not done in September, but a speech that Sam planned to make in Chicago was set up on it.

SAM: To-day [October 30th] I pay Pratt & Whitney $10,000. This squares back indebtedness and everything to date. They began about May or April or March 1886—along there somewhere, and have always kept from a dozen to two dozen master-hands on the machine.

That outgo is done; 4 men for a month or two will close up that leak and caulk it.[4]

NARRATOR: There were so many interruptions at home in October that Sam went over to Twichell's house to work; it wasn't much better there.

SAM: I am here in Twichell's house at work, with the noise of the children and an army of carpenters to help. Of course they don't help, but neither do they hinder. It's like a boiler factory for racket, and in nailing a wooden ceiling on to the room under me the hammering tickles my feet amazingly sometimes and jars my table a good deal, but I never am conscious of the racket at all, and I move my feet into positions of relief without knowing when I do it. I began here Monday morning [October 1st], and have done eighty pages since. I was so tired last night that I thought I would lie abed and rest to-day; but I couldn't resist. I mean to try to knock off to-morrow, but it's doubtful if I do. I want to finish the day the machine finishes, and a week ago the closest calculations for that indicated Oct. 22—but experience teaches me that the calculations will miss fire as usual.

The other day the children were projecting a purchase, Livy and I to furnish the money—a dollar and a half. Jean discouraged the idea. She said, "We haven't got any money. Children, if you would think, you would remember the machine isn't done." . . .

I got it all wrong. It wasn't the children, it was Marie. She wanted a box of blacking for the children's shoes. Jean reproved her and said, "Why, Marie, you mustn't *ask* for things now. The machine isn't done."[5]

NARRATOR: The entire household comforted itself with saying, "When the machine is finished everything will be all right again."[6] In October Grace King arrived for her promised visit.

GRACE KING: Life with them followed the simplest and most natural lines. Worldly deviations and social complications were ignored. The two daughters, Susy and Clara, were just growing into their young ladyhood. More entrancing characters I have never met in my life. They were both beautiful in an original way. Susy was imaginative, *tête montée*, as it is prettily expressed in French; wonderfully gifted in languages, and an ardent lover of the stage and its world. Her mimicry of Sarah Bernhardt was perfect, and her imitation of Ada Rehan was fine and delicately discriminating. She had a true feeling for acting.

Clara was a musician. . . . Young as she was, her playing was full of power and brilliancy. She improvised for Susy's recitations.[7]

SAM: I am glad Clara is banging away on the piano—work is the darlingest recreation in this world and whomsoever Nature has fitted to love it, is armed against care and sorrow.[8]

GRACE KING: The two [girls] were equipped for full bellehood in society, as we know it in New Orleans, and they craved its glamorous intoxication of music and dancing and the brilliant gayety of the ballroom. They loved to hear me tell of our balls and belles at home. . . . They sighed ruefully that they would "never have a chance to enjoy that" and wear low-necked dresses to balls. In fact, in Hartford such toilettes were not *de rigueur*, for balls. In Hartford, in truth, balls were not given. . . .

Little Jean, the third daughter, black haired and black eyed, was in face and mind the replica of her father, who adored her. . . . One of her delights—in which he shared—was, when on a drive, to descend from the great family carriage and ride in the street car, leaving Patrick to drive the empty carriage home. . . .

Our dinner-table talk was free and unconventional, with much laughter, Susy and Clara taking the lead in their bright, girlish way, expressing themselves boldly, without fear of criticism or correction.[9]

NARRATOR: Grace describes an episode when Susy, in place of Livy who was unwell, accompanied her to a reception in Hartford.

GRACE KING: We sallied forth in state, taking our seats in the handsome carriage that the prancing black horses drew up at the porte-cochère. We drove along happily until we came to a railroad bridge over which a long train of cars was passing. . . . The spirited horses took fright . . . and Patrick, the coachman, seemed to have more than he could do to control them. . . . We were apparently on the point of being crushed, carriage and all, against a pillar, when Susy in a panic pulled open the door of the carriage and jumped out. I, not to desert her, jumped out on my side at the moment when Patrick, with the reins gathered up in his hands, gave the horses a lashing that sped them through the bridge and sent them galloping down the street.

Susy and I, left alone, stood irresolute, and then decided to walk home.[10]

NARRATOR: After Grace left, Susy and Theodore Crane came for a long visit; Theodore had been very ill. Sam wrote "Mother" Fairbanks.

SAM: We are hermits, now, and must doubtless remain so the rest of the winter. Theodore Crane has been here a month or two in a precarious state, because of a stroke of paralysis. Sometimes he picks up a little, and then for a day or two it is a cheerful home; after that, he drops back again, and the gloom and the apprehension return. It is pulling Susie Crane down a good deal, and Livy also, of course. These two women will get sick if this continues; they ought to get away and have a month's rest, but of course neither of them will do it. And so, inasmuch as your plans and your time-table do not allow you to come to us, you do not lose anything, anyway. I wish we were back at Endor a little while, for a change. With the pilgrims, too—some of them.

NARRATOR: In *The Innocents Abroad*, Sam had described Endor: "Dirt, degradation, and savagery are Endor's specialty."[11]

Livy's birthday preceded Thanksgiving by two days.

LIVY: I had a very pleasant birthday the children fixed me a very pretty table with flowers and their gifts and we had an exceedingly good time.[12]

SAM: Livy, Darling, I am grateful—gratefuler than ever before—that you were born, and that your love is mine and our two lives woven and welded together![13]

LIVY: We had an unusually good and gay Thanksgiving. . . . Theodore laughed so heartily that I really felt afraid he would overdo himself—but he feels no worse this morning and says he wishes he could have just such a gay time every evening.[14]

NARRATOR: Sam wrote Orion, who was thinking of buying a new house.

SAM: The machine is apparently almost done—*but,* I take no privileges on that account. It must *be* done before I will spend a cent that can be avoided. I have kept this family on very short commons for 2 years, and they must go on scrimping until the machine is finished, no matter how long it may be. I refrained from saying "Buy that house," just as I would have said it if Livy had been the person proposing to make a purchase.[15]

NARRATOR: Livy scrimped on Christmas.

SAM: She is scouring around all the time, after economical Christmas presents—presents unobtrusively capable and clever in the expression of love and a low financial condition—and I judge she has collared what there were in stock.[16]

NARRATOR: They went to New York for a family spree right after Christmas. Jean was rich with a $5 gold piece from her grandmother.

JEAN: I had but 5 cents and wanted more because we were just going to new york it was 2 days before we went to new york and I could not buy very much with 5 cts. and as you see I wanted some money very much indeed.[17]

NARRATOR: By the end of the year nothing could satisfy the typesetter; Livy's income, the income from Sam's books and from the publishing company—everything was being swallowed up. Livy received a printed message on New Year's Eve.

SAM: To Mrs. S. L. Clemens—Happy New Year!

The machine is finished and this is the first work done on it. S. L. Clemens Hartford, Dec. 31, 1888.

EUREKA! *Saturday, January 5, 1889—12.20 P.M.* At this moment I have seen a line of movable type *spaced and justified by machinery!* This is the first time in the history of the world that this amazing thing has ever been done. Present:

> J. W. Paige, the inventor;
> Charles Davis ⎫ Mathematical assistants
> Earll   ⎬ and mechanical
> Graham ⎭ experts
> Bates,   foreman, and
> S. L. Clemens

This record is made immediately after the prodigious event.[18]

LIVY: How strange it will seem to have unlimited means to be able to do whatever you want to do, to give whatever you want to give without counting the cost.

SAM: *Monday, January 7—4.45* P.M. The first proper name ever set by this new keyboard was William Shakspeare. I set it at the above hour; and I perceive, now that I see the name written, that I either mis-spelled it then or I've mis-spelled it now.

The space-bar did its duty by the electric connections and steam and separated the two words preparatory to the reception of the space.[19]

All the other wonderful inventions of the human brain sink pretty nearly into commonplaces contrasted with this awful mechanical miracle. Telephones, telegraphs, locomotives, cotton-gins, sewing-machines, Babbage calculators, Jacquard looms, perfecting presses, all mere toys, simplicities! The Paige Compositor marches alone and far in the land of human inventions.[20]

We need only one more thing, a phonograph on the distributor to yell, "Where in H——— is the printer's devil, I want more type."[21]

NARRATOR: Shortly, it was found that the machine was breaking type; the monthly expense of $3,000 or $4,000 was resumed.

SAM: Paige and I always meet on effusively affectionate terms, and yet he knows perfectly well that if I had him in a steel trap I would shut out all human succor and watch that trap till he died.[22]

NARRATOR: The Monday Evening Club met at the Clemenses, and Susy attended a discussion of "Eloquence."

HOWELL CHENEY: Another minor question has been the practice of the Club as to the attendance of ladies. It was the early rule that the wife of the host invited two or three of her intimates to sit with her. . . . At rare times the hostess engaged in the conversation

as did Mary Bushnell Cheney and Mrs. Charles Dudley Warner.[23]
NARRATOR: The essayist of the evening contended that the only form of eloquence was verbal. In the debate which followed the reading, Sam said that there were many kinds of eloquence: sunsets, music, the dumb appeal in frightened animals' eyes, and even the army marching into the jaws of death.

Shortly after this evening, Susy, inspired by her father's contentions, wrote a poem.

SUSY: PERFECTION

Dedicated to, and inspired by, my dear Pater

"Anything *perfect* stirs one to tears"—S. L. CLEMENS

> In *any* form Perfection
> Should force our tears to flow;
> When men attain to this, love,
> Humanity may grow
>
> Unto the highest height, love,
> Of goodness, greatness, strength,
> Until it know the Truth, love,
> The breadth, and depth and length
>
> For what is Good is Perfect;
> And when a man can see
> And comprehend Perfection
> Whatever it may be,
>
> So that his eyes fill up, love,
> With reverential tears,
> He's very near to Heaven!
> It is his Soul that hears
>
> Its first song! sung Divinely
> From a far distant sphere,
> By other, purer, voices
> Than those that sing down here,
>
> Then is the true uplifting
> Toward heaven, of the soul,
> The unearthbound steps higher,
> Nearer the highest goal.[24]

SUSY'S EIGHTEENTH YEAR

1889–1890

NARRATOR: Livy worried about the children's schooling; Susy wanted to go to college.

LIVY: It is a wonderful day [March 24th]. . . . Clara and I have been to church. Susy staid at home, she has not been feeling quite well, having had quite a sore throat. . . .

Of course the children are full of their lessons and very busy with their studying. I feel very unsettled about what I shall do with them, nothing in the way of a school seems to be exactly what I want.

I think Susy and Clara are both doing very well with their music this year.[1]

NARRATOR: Theodore Crane had returned to Quarry Farm; he was dying now. Sam wrote him about all the family anecdotes.

SAM: You know how absent-minded Twichell . . . is and how desolate his face when he is in that frame. At such times he passes the word with a friend on the street and is not aware of the meeting at all. Twice in a week our Clara . . . had this latter experience with him within the past month. But the second instance was too much for her and she woke him up, in his tracks, with a reproach—she said—

"Uncle Joe, *why* do you always look as if you were just going down into the grave, when you meet a person on the street?"

And then went on to reveal to him the funereal spectacle which he presented on such occasion. Well, she has met Twichell three times since then, and would swim the Connecticut River to avoid meeting him the fourth. As soon as he sights her, no matter how publicly placed, nor how far off she is, he makes a bound into the air, hurls arms and legs into all sorts of frantic gestures of delight, and so comes prancing, skipping and pirouetting for her like a drunken Indian entering heaven. She feels as embarrassed as the Almighty.[2]

It tickled Susy—Jo[e] Twichell's war-whooping, when he would meet Clara on the street.[3]

NARRATOR: Daniel Frohman was planning to produce *The Prince and the Pauper*, and Will Gillette was eager that a child actress, Elsie Leslie Lyde, known professionally as Elsie Leslie, play the parts of the Prince and of the Pauper.

SAM: Jean neglected my books. . . . Will Gillette invited her and the rest of us to a dinner at the Murray Hill Hotel in New York, in order that we might get acquainted with Mrs. Leslie and her daughter. Elsie Leslie was nine years old, and was a great celebrity on the stage. Jean was astonished and awed to see that little slip of a thing sit up at table and take part in the conversation of the grown people, capably and with ease and tranquility. Poor Jean was obliged to keep still, for the subjects discussed never happened to hit her level, but at last the talk fell within her limit and she had her chance to contribute to it. *Tom Sawyer* was mentioned. Jean spoke gratefully up and said,

"I know who wrote that book—Harriet Beecher Stowe!"[4]

NARRATOR: Sam and Gillette were enchanted with Elsie and, as rehearsals progressed, undertook an unprecedented labor of love for her. Sam wrote her.

SAM: Gillette and I pooled intellects on this proposition: to get up a pleasant surprise of some kind for you against your next visit—the surprise to take the form of a tasteful and beautiful testimonial of some sort or other, which should express somewhat of the love we felt for you. Together we hit upon just the right thing—a pair of slippers. Either one of us could have thought of a single slipper, but it took both of us to think of two slippers. In fact, one of us did think of one slipper, and then, quick as a flash, the other thought of the other one. It shows how wonderful the human mind is. It is really paleontological; you give one mind a bone, and the other one instantly divines the rest of the animal.

Gillette embroidered his slipper with astonishing facility and splendor, but I have been a long time pulling through with mine.

You see, it was my very first attempt at art, and I couldn't rightly get the hang of it along at first.[5]

KATY: Mr. Clemens and Mr. Gillette thought they'd give her a present—something they made themselves (as a joke, I guess). So they embroidered her a pair of slippers. Each one had a slipper to embroider all himself. Oh, my! You should have seen the awful mess they made of it! Mr. Clemens was always carrying his around with him and had a great big needle and embroidery silk, working on that slipper, and my land! them slippers was big enough for a giant and the funniest-looking things you ever saw.[6]

NARRATOR: Gillette's design and execution were masterly: a brilliant yellow Connecticut River wound the length of the slipper, and a green frog and a baby in a basket were superimposed in high relief. Sam made a slow start.

SAM: I began with that first red bar, and without ulterior design, or plan of any sort—just as I would begin a Prince and Pauper, or any other tale. And mind you it is the easiest and surest way; because if you invent two or three people and turn them loose in your manuscript, something is bound to happen to them,—you can't help it; and then it will take you the rest of the book to get them out of the natural consequences of that occurrence, and so, first thing you know, there's your book all finished up and never cost you an idea. Well, the red stripe, with a bias stitch, naturally suggested a blue one with a perpendicular stitch, and I slammed it in, though when it came daylight I saw it was green—which didn't make any difference, because green and blue are much the same anyway, and in fact from a purely moral point of view are regarded by the best authorities as identical. Well, if you will notice, a blue perpendicular stitch always suggests a ropy red involved stitch, like a family of angle-worms trying to climb in under each other to keep warm—it would suggest that, every time, without the author of the slipper ever having to think about it at all.[7]

NARRATOR: The annual departure for Elmira interrupted the embroidering. Their arrival there was tempered with sadness because of Theodore Crane's illness and death; it was a moving experience for the children.

SAM: Theodore Crane departed this life July 3d, after ten months of longing to go; for he was smitten with paralysis of one side Sept. 6, '88, and from that day forth was a half wreck, physically, and suffered a good deal of pain of a bodily sort, together with a mental depression and hopelessness that made him yearn for death every day, and break into impatience every time the sun went down on his unsatisfied desire. Sue bears up under her calamity with a great and fine fortitude which I would call brave and heroic but that those words have lost the (honorable place) noble place that once was theirs, through the degradation of over-use and application to trivial instances. We were all here, on the hill, when the end came; had come early, from Hartford, expecting it; so Sue was not solitary on the mountain-top. It was a solace and a happiness to Theodore, who lived largely in the children. Jean's grief was good to see. The earned heartbreak of a little child must be high and honorable testimony for a parting spirit to carry before the Throne.[8]

I came on from Elmira a day or two ago, where I left a house of mourning. . . . Mrs. Crane and Mrs. Clemens and the children were in a gloom which brought back to me the days of nineteen years ago, when Mr. Langdon died. . . .

I shall be here [in Hartford] ten days yet, and all alone; nobody in the house but the servants.[9]

It is lovely and cool and nice and twilighty and still, here in the home after breakfast.[10]

CLARA: The charm of the situation of our house was that, although within easy reach of the town, we still had all the atmosphere of the country—lovely woods, a river, and silence.[11]

SAM: I can see the dog-house down the slope, and past its roof a burnished square yard or two of river with rich foliage-reflections in it; and this way a little, by the dog-house, is a grassy swale, the half of which is deeply shaded and the other half glares with sun; and at my right—among some ferns to the right of the tree that has Sue's old squirrel-boot nailed to it—is the peaceful picture of Satan and her child, blinking up devout and drowsy, praising God for the weather.[12]

The black lady-cat was named Satan, her kitten was not a neutral, yet was named Sin. And it was well enough, for the children took no heed of sexes anyway, but mixed them up frankly in speech. Answering an inquiry as to Satan's whereabouts, one day, Jean said—

"She was fooling around the green house not doing anything, and I made him go down cellar and feed his kitten."[13]

NARRATOR: Before he returned to Elmira Sam dined with the Charles Dudley Warners and he wrote Clara, whose ambition was to become a concert pianist.

SAM: I asked Cousin Susy Warner to play the Seventh Symphony for me, and she done it. Also she played that other deep, rich, noble Beethoven piece—the one where, all along and all along, half a dozen of the bass notes keep rolling back down-stairs a little way—only to the first landing; and then get up again and roll down again, and are the darling of the piece and the charm of it.[14]

NARRATOR: It may have been on the train back to Elmira that Sam tried to resume work on Elsie Leslie's slipper.

SAM: They wouldn't let me embroider on the cars; they said it made the other passengers afraid. They didn't like the light that flared into my eye when I had an inspiration. And even the most fair-minded people doubted me when I explained what it was I was making—especially brakemen. Brakemen always swore at it, and carried on, the way ignorant people do, about art. They wouldn't take my word that it was a slipper; they said they believed it was a snow-shoe that had some kind of a disease.[15]

NARRATOR: *A Connecticut Yankee in King Arthur's Court* was finished; the proofs were expected from New York. Sam wanted Howells to read it.

SAM: If Mrs. Clemens could have sat down and read the book herself, I could have got you off, maybe, but she has not had an hour's use of her eyes for reading since she had the pink-eye six months ago. So she is afraid I have left coarsenesses which ought to be rooted out, and blasts of opinion which are so strongly worded as to repel instead of persuade. I hardly think so. I dug out many darlings of these sorts, and throttled them, with grief.

HOWELLS: You know it will be purely a pleasure to me to read your proofs. So far as the service I may be is concerned, that I gladly owe you for many generous acts; and if I didn't want to read the book for its own sake or your sake, I should still want to do it for Mrs. Clemens's.[16]

NARRATOR: Sam had a visitor in Elmira who intrigued Susy.

KATY: Mr. Kipling came to America from India, and was looking for Mr. Clemens. He wanted to see him so much 'cause he had heard a great deal about him. Of course nobody knew who

Kipling was or what he had written—or his name, hardly. He warn't famous then. Mr. Clemens hadn't even heard of him.

Well, Kipling went up to Hartford to find Mr. Clemens, but the Clemens family never stayed there summers, you know, so when he got to Hartford, Mr. Clemens was in Elmira, and Kipling, he hurried up to Elmira.[17]

NARRATOR: Kipling was not impressed with his first glimpse of Elmira; he arrived at "the door of the frowsy hotel at midnight."

KIPLING: Morning revealed Elmira, whose streets were desolated by railway tracks, and whose suburbs were given up to the manufacture of door-sashes and window-frames. It was surrounded by pleasant, flat, little hills, rimmed with timber and topped with cultivation. The Chemung River flowed generally up and down the town, and had just finished flooding a few of the main streets.[18]

SAM: [He] made a tedious and blistering journey up to Quarry Farm in quest of me. He ought to have telephoned the farm first; then he would have learned that I was at the Langdon homestead, hardly a quarter of a mile from his hotel. But he was only a lad of twenty-four and properly impulsive and he set out without inquiring on that dusty and roasting journey up the hill.[19]

KIPLING: Then the chase began . . . in a hired hack, up an awful hill, where the sunflowers blossomed by the roadside, and crops waved, and Harper's Magazine cows stood in eligible and commanding attitudes knee-deep in clover, all ready to be transferred to photogravure. The great man must have been persecuted by outsiders aforetime, and fled up the hill for refuge.[20]

SAM: He found Susy Crane and my little Susy there and they came as near making him comfortable as the weather and circumstances would permit.

The group sat on the veranda and while Kipling rested and refreshed himself he refreshed the others with his talk, talk of a quality which was well above what they were accustomed to, talk which might be likened to footprints, so strong and definite was the impression which it left behind.[21]

NARRATOR: The trip down the hill was frightening to Kipling, with the driver "skidding the wheel and swearing audibly."[22]

SAM: Kipling came down that afternoon and spent a couple of hours with me, and at the end of that time I had surprised him as much as he had surprised me, and the honors were easy.[23]

KIPLING: A big, darkened drawing-room; a huge chair; a man with eyes, a mane of grizzled hair, a brown mustache covering a mouth as delicate as a woman's, a strong, square hand shaking mine, and the slowest, calmest, levelest voice in all the world saying:

"Well, you think you owe me something, and you've come to tell me so. That's what I call squaring a debt handsomely."

"Piff!" from a cob-pipe (I always said that a Missouri meerschaum was the best smoking in the world), and behold! Mark Twain had curled himself up in the big arm-chair, and I was smoking reverently, as befits one in the presence of his superior.

The thing that struck me first was that he was an elderly man; yet, after a minute's thought, I perceived that it was otherwise, and in five minutes, the eyes looking at me, I saw that the gray hair was an accident of the most trivial. He was quite young. I was shaking his hand. I was smoking his cigar, and I was hearing him talk—this man I had learned to love and admire fourteen thousand miles away.

Reading his books, I had striven to get an idea of his personality, and all my preconceived notions were wrong and beneath the reality. Blessed is the man who finds no disillusion when he is brought face to face with a revered writer.[24]

SAM: I believed that he knew more than any person I had met before, and I knew that he knew I knew less than any person he had met before—though he did not say it and I was not expecting that he would.[25]

KIPLING: You are a contemptible lot over yonder. Some of you are Commissioners and some are Lieutenant-Governors, and some have the V.C., and a few are privileged to walk about the Mall arm in arm with the Viceroy; but I have seen Mark Twain this golden morning, have shaken his hand and smoked a cigar—no, two cigars—with him, and talked with him for more than two hours![26]

Once . . . he put his hand on my shoulder. It was an Investiture of the Star of India, blue silk, trumpets, and diamond-studded jewel, all complete. If hereafter, in the changes and chances of this mortal life, I fall to cureless ruin, I will tell the superintendent of the workhouse that Mark Twain once put his hand on my shoulder; and he shall give me a room to myself and a double allowance of pauper's tobacco.[27]

To my mind he was the largest man of his time, both in the direct outcome of his work, and, more important still, as an indirect force in an age of iron Philistinism.[28]

SAM: When he was gone, Mrs. Langdon wanted to know about my visitor. I said, "He is a stranger to me but he is a most remarkable man—and I am the other one. Between us, we cover all knowledge; he knows all that can be known and I know the rest."[29]

He was a stranger to me and to all the world, and remained so for twelve months, then he became suddenly known, and universally known.[30]

They [Sue and Susy] often spoke wonderingly of Kipling's talk afterward and they recognized that they had been in contact with an extraordinary man, but it is more than likely that they were the only persons who had perceived that he was extraordinary. It is not likely that they perceived his full magnitude, it is most likely that they were Eric Ericsons who had discovered a continent but did not suspect the horizonless extent of it. His was an unknown name and was to remain unknown for a year yet, but Susy kept his card and treasured it as an interesting possession. Its address was Allahabad.

No doubt India had been to her an imaginary land up to this time, a fairyland, a dreamland, a land made out of poetry and moonlight for the Arabian Nights to do their gorgeous miracles in; and doubtless Kipling's flesh and blood and modern clothes realized it to her for the first time and solidified it. I think so because she more than once remarked upon its incredible remoteness from the world that we were living in, and computed that remoteness and pronounced the result with a sort of awe, fourteen thousand miles, or sixteen thousand, which ever it was. Kipling had written upon the card a compliment to me. This gave the card an additional value in Susy's eyes, since as a distinction it was the next thing to being recognized by a denizen of the moon.[31]

KATY: Susy always kept that little visiting card of Kipling's, as a kind of momento of his visit. She thought then that he must be somebody that would turn out wonderful, so she kept that card 'cause he had written something on it—his address in India—and she liked that.[32]

NARRATOR: At home in Hartford, work recommenced on the slipper.

SAM: Young Dr. Root came in, and of course he was interested in the slipper right away, because he has always had a passion for art himself, but has never had a chance to try, because his folks are opposed to it and superstitious about it, and have done all they could to keep him back; and so he was eager to take a hand and see what he could do. And it was beautiful to see him sit there and tell Mrs. Clemens what had been happening while we were off on summer vacation, and hold the slipper up toward the end of his nose, and forget the sordid world, and imagine the canvas was a "subject" with a scalp wound, and nimbly whirl in that lovely surgical stitch which you see there—and never hesitating a moment in his talk except to say "Ouch" when he stuck himself, and then going right on again as smooth and easy as nothing. Yes, it was a charming spectacle. And it was real art, too,—realistic; just native untaught genius; you can see the very scalp itself, showing through between the stitches.

Well, next I threw in that sheaf of green rods which the lictors used to carry before the Roman Consuls to lick them with when they didn't behave—they turned blue in the morning, but that is the way green always acts.

The next week, after a good rest, I snowed in that sea of frothy waves, and set that yellow thing afloat in it and those two things that are skewered through it. It isn't a home-plate, and it isn't a papal tiara with the keys of St. Peter; no, it is a heart—my heart—with two arrows stuck through it—arrows that go in blue and come out crimson—crimson with the best drops in that heart, and gladly shed for love of you, dear.

Now, then, as you strike to the south'ard and drift along down the starboard side, abaft the main-to'-gallant scuppers, you come to that blue quarter-deck which runs the rest of the way aft to the jumping-off place. In the midst of that blue you will see some big red letters—M.T.; and west'ard, over on the port side, you will see some more red letters—TO E.L. Aggregated, these several groups of letters signify, Mark Twain to Elsie Leslie. And you will notice that you have a gift for art yourself, for the southern half of the L, embroidered by yourself, is as good as anything I can do, after all my experience.

There, now you understand the whole work. From a professional point of view I consider the Heart and Arrows by all odds the greatest triumph of the whole thing; in fact, one of the ablest examples of civil-engineering in a beginner I ever saw—for it was all inspiration, just the lightning-like inspiration of the moment. I couldn't do it again in a hundred years,—even if I recover this time and get just as well and strong as I was before. You notice what fire there is in it—what rapture, enthusiasm, frenzy—what blinding explosions of color. It is just a "Turner"— that is what it is. It is just like his "Slave Ship," that immortal work. What you see in the "Slave Ship" is a terrific explosion of radiating rags and fragments of flaming crimson flying from a common center of intense yellow which is in violent commotion —insomuch that a Boston reporter said it reminded him of a yellow cat dying in a platter of tomatoes.[33]

NARRATOR: The slippers were finally finished and sent off with explanations and messages.

SAM: I have pulled through, and within twenty-four hours of the time I told you I would—day before yesterday. There ought to be a key to the designs, but I haven't had time to get one up.[34]

Take the slippers and wear them next your heart, Elsie dear; for every stitch in them is a testimony of the affection which two of your loyalest friends bear you. Every single stitch cost us blood. I've got twice as many pores in me now as I used to have; and you would never believe how many places you can stick a needle into yourself until you go into the embroidery line and devote yourself to art.

Do not wear these slippers in public, dear; it would only excite envy; and, as like as not, somebody would try to shoot you.

Merely use them to assist you in remembering that among the many, many people who think all the world of you is your friend, MARK TWAIN.[35]

NARRATOR: Sam then added another note.

SAM: Dear Elsie: I forgot the presentation-speech I made, and I find that the letter I have written in place of it to put in here, won't go in—wouldn't go in a canal boat, let alone a slipper— examine it yourself, and you will see. Will you please explain that I embroidered this slipper all by myself, without *any* instruction in Art, and all for love of you? Mark Twain. Oct. 5, 1889.[36]

ELSIE LESLIE: My dear Mr. Clemens: The slipper the long letter and all the rest came this afternoon [October 9th], I think they are splendid and shall have them framed and keep them among my very most prechus things. I have had a great many nice things given to me and people often say very pleasant things but I am not quite shure they always mean it or that they are as trustable as you and "Leo" and I am very shure they would not spend their prechus time and shed their blood for me so you see that is one reason why I will think so much of it and then it was all so funny to think of two great big men like you and "little Willie" (that is what "Leo" calls himself to me) imbroidering a pair of slippers for a little girl like me of corse you have a great many large words in your letter that I do not quite understand. One word comencing with P. has fifteen letters in it and I do not know what you mean by pooled unless you mean you and Leo put your two minds together to make the slippers which was very nice of you both I think you are just right about the angle worms they did look like that this summer when I used to dig them for bate to fish with please tell Dr. Root I will think of him when I look at the part he did the Surgicle Stich I mean I hope you will be quite well and strong by the time you get this letter as you were before you made my slipper it would make me very sad if you were to be ill. Give my love to Mrs. Clemens Susy Clara Gene [Jean] I-know and you-know and Vix and all of my Hartford friends tell Gene I wish I was with her and we would have a nice jump in the hay loft. When you come to New York you must call and see me then we will see about those big words my address is up in the top left corner of this letter. To my loyal friend Mark Twain From his little friend ELSIE LESLIE LYDE.

(Not Little Lord Fauntleroy now but Tom Canty of Offal Court and Little Prince Edward of Wales.)[37]

NARRATOR: Elsie's visits to Hartford were thrilling to the girls.

KATY: And then we had Elsie Leslie, too. She was a child actress, you know. She stayed with us all the time she acted in Mr. Clemens' play, *The Prince and The Pauper,* when it played in Hartford. . . . It was a terrible exciting time when the rehearsing was going on, because the Clemens children was just crazy about it—the theater. . . .

Elsie Leslie was a little mite of a thing when she acted in Hartford that time, why, she used to play with Clara and Susy up in the hay loft and sometimes she didn't want to go to the theater at all to do her part—she just wanted to stay and play with the children, and then Mr. Clemens, he'd have to coax her and tell her stories and take her there himself sometimes, because she was an awful stubborn little rat—but then, you couldn't blame her none because she was nothing but a child.[38]

SAM: The children have settled down to their studies, the household life has settled down into the old grooves and goes smoothly; and my sister Mrs. Moffett is this evening finishing up a week's visit and starts west tomorrow.[39]

KATY: Susy wrote a little play of her own at that time and they put it on one Thanksgiving night and Clara and Jean and Margaret Warner was in it, too.[40]

SAM: Livy and the children have spent the most of this evening upstairs rehearsing a variegated program of Susy's devising for Thanksgiving. Jean plays a part in it. As I was not inserted, I suppose I shall have to get up a shindy of my own and invent it for myself.[41]

CLARA: My elder sister, Susy, . . . was altogether the genius among the children. She had marked talent for writing and composed a charming little play. . . . We performed it . . . Thanksgiving night for a large company of invited friends.[42]

SAM: ["The Love Chase"] was drawn upon Greek lines and reflected the spirit of its inspiration, being sweet and simple and light-hearted and pure. The costumes were Grecian. Susy was "Music;" Clara was "Art;" Daisy Warner was "Literature;" Fanny Freese was the "Shepherd Boy;" and Jean was "Cupid."

[The play ended with] "Music" wreathed and draped in fresh roses, holding the curtains apart, and singing her final song with the glow of youth in her face and eyes, and all her heart in her voice, the response of the house was a moving thing to see and hear.

This was perhaps the happiest night that Susy ever knew.[43]

In my own house

It was. Within, was light and cheer; without,
A blustering winter's night. There was a play.
It was her own; for she had wrought it out
Unhelped, from her own head—and she
But turned sixteen! A pretty play,
All graced with cunning fantasies
And happy songs, and peopled all with fays,
And silvan gods and goddesses,
And shepherds, too, that piped and danced,
And wore the guileless hours away

In care-free romps and games.
Her girlhood mates played in the piece,
And she as well; a goddess she—and looked it, as it seemed to me.
'Twas fairyland restored—so beautiful it was,
And innocent. It made us cry, we elder ones,
To live our lost youth o'er again
With these its happy heirs.

Slowly, at last, the curtain drooped;
Before us there she stood, all wreathed and draped
In roses pearled with dew: so sweet, so glad,
So radiant!—and flung us kisses through the storm
Of praise that crowned her triumph.[44]

NARRATOR: A Hartford neighbor, Eleanor Johnson, loved the Clemens' dramatic evenings.

ELEANOR: There was always such a sense of expectancy when one entered the doors of the Clemens house for a party or a play. Something was bound to happen! There was magic in the air!

I can remember . . . a play where, among the big green branches, making a very acceptable forest background, Margaret Warner was Literature, dressed in russet color, Clara as Art and Susy in pink and silver, and laurel leaves in her hair, with a lyre in her hand, was Music. They gave a most lovely plastic play and Jean Clemens was Cupid shooting darts. . . .

After it was over two or three of us gathered together, crestfallen and awed, wondering why the Clemens plays were always so much better than our own. We scarcely realized . . . that we were within the portals of genius. What glorious times they were![45]

KATY: Oh, it was lovely! And Mr. Clemens was just wild over it and he had them do that play two or three times, he liked it so much. He was telling everybody how proud he was of Susy— for writing that play—and how talented she was.[46]

CLARA: When that was over, Father joined us in playing charades, even adding as guest star William Gillette, who was visiting his relatives, the George Warners, neighbors of ours. How the audience rocked and roared with laughter at those two men![47]

SAM: George Warner came over the next morning and had a long talk with Susy. The result of it was this verdict:

"She is the most interesting person I have ever known, of either sex."[48]

LILLY WARNER: Dearest Livy: . . . George put this note in a letter to me—*not* to give you, but to let me see what he had thought. He is apt to think what he does isn't worth while, but I generally believe in impulses. Anyhow I think this will please you a little.[49]

GEORGE: Dear Mrs. Clemens: Instead of merely thanking you for the pleasure of the Thanksgiving evening I ought to have told you what I was thinking about it; and what you said as we were walking over to your house on Sunday [December 1st]—that Susy was pleased by what I said to her—reminded me. As I sat there it seemed to me that this was a *new* drama and a *good* one and, of course, that as there are so many fine and noble things to say and do, why do the coarse and ignoble ones at all. And then this expression came into my mind—this is the "consummate flower" of civilization—and to have girls do naturally and of their own accord so fine a thing.

When I get rich I shall found a school for girls with this as the Prospectus. Teach all the noble thoughts of antiquity to be played upon by the emotions of the present.[50]

NARRATOR: Mrs. Frank W. Cheney, daughter of Horace Bushnell, was also in the audience Thanksgiving night.

MARY BUSHNELL CHENEY: It is so odious to even seem a flatterer that I often am silent when praise is on my tongue. Therefore I said little or nothing the other night about Susy's play; and now it really must out. It seemed to me something so rare and ideal that ordinary praise was almost a profanation. That Susy should have imagined it and known how to give it beautiful form, and then should have been able also to act it with such impassioned feeling and *sing* it, and fill it all with her own radiant beauty— why it is something unique, unheard of! Clara also contributed much with her quiet humor and pretty dancing, and the delicious naïveté of her demeanor, and Margaret by her sweet sincerity and Fanny with her grace and her voice, and dear little Jean with her wonderful look and her conscientious dancing, so much too good for cupid; but after all your Susy was the soul of it, and never shall I cease to think of it as the ideal work of her fresh, romantic, unsullied maidenhood, something too rare and poetic for this humdrum world. But we need not call it, (the world), humdrum or prosaic as long as ardent youth and sentiment are coming into bloom about us! Thank God for youth—the youth of our children!

This needs no answer, it is just my tribute to your motherhood.[51]

CLARA: One remarkable characteristic of both Mother and Father was that they never showed partiality to any child . . . they must always have loved and admired my elder sister, Susy, by far the most, which made it all the more wonderful that they could so completely disguise the fact.[52]

NARRATOR: Sam and Livy had seen Mrs. Langdon and Sue Crane in New York in November.

SAM: We had a most darling visit with you and Sue, and I do not think we could have improved it in any way except by staying longer. Livy would have written you long ago, for she has had otherwise little or nothing to do that fourteen people and a horse couldn't do, but every time she got an idle couple of days some hindrance or other always shoved itself in the way and prevented her from writing. And now at last just as she has got everything cleared away and nothing in the world to do but sit around and buy Christmas gifts for 4,000 people and lie awake nights wondering if they'll be "satisfied with theirs," along comes this malignant and despotic cold in the head, and *that* just knocks any lingering and belated notion of getting a letter penned to you galley-*west*, you see. Such is Providence, who orders all things for the best.

I have been laid up with a cold myself ever since I saw you, and only got out on the street yesterday. Of course I missed my West Point engagement, and it stands postponed for three weeks. All the children are well, and hard at work with their lessons—so busy in fact, and absent such long intervals from view are they, that the memory of them grows dim and I often mistake them for the children of strangers and am embarrassed in their presence.[53]

We are in the full rush of the holidays now, and an awful rush it is, too.[54]

Livy is banging away with all her might on her Xmas preparations.[55]

NARRATOR: Mrs. Langdon sent her usual, lavish Christmas check.

LIVY: We had an exceedingly pleasant time, many beautiful gifts, among them yours I assure you stood very high.

With your check I bought the gold beads for Clara that I told you I should buy. I bought a very dainty little gold comb for Susy's hair. It was almost a pin, yet it was a little too broad for that. A pair of skates for Jean which was precisely her hearts desire, for myself the lions share, I bought myself a narrow gold comb wider than Susy's but less than half the width of the other one that you gave me. Katy declared it to be just what I needed because it fills a little bare spot on the top of my head. I intend to wear it every afternoon and I shall take great pleasure in it. I also bought myself, but for all the family to enjoy, a small silver jardiniere for ferns, it is lovely for the center of the dining room table. . . .

"Samuel" will send you his thanks for his books.[56]

CLARA: We had a very Merry Xmas and a mighty warm one. . . . It is a beautiful day today [December 29th] and if it had not been so desperately muddy I should have ridden.

I hope I can ride tomorrow before breakfast, but no doubt it will rain.

We are greatly satisfied with Papa's book [*Connecticut Yankee*], but I should think he would almost fear England. . . .

We are going to New York Saturday to see Ada Rehan in "As You Like It," and I don't know yet what else.[57]

NARRATOR: Livy wrote her mother on February 2nd.

LIVY: Until I wrote the date . . . I had not remembered that this is my wedding day. Mr. Clemens is in New York for the day, he went yesterday and will I think return tomorrow. . . . Susy has gone to church Clara is in New York with Miss Foote attending to her teeth, Jean is upstairs reading.

It is a grey Sunday and looks like snow.

NARRATOR: They all went to the opening night of *The Prince and the Pauper*, with Elsie Leslie starring, at the Broadway Theater on January 20th. Sam made a speech.

LIVY: We took Jean with us to see it, it was her first theater experience and she enjoyed it very much. Mr. George Warner who sat across the house from us said it was one of the funny things to see Jean. We sat in a box and she clapped every time anyone did, even her father when he made his speech.[58]

NARRATOR: They made some tentative summer plans early in March.

LIVY: We have a great hope that we may be able to go to Europe the first part of June for the Summer months. We are not entirely certain just whether we can go or not, it will depend somewhat upon Mr. Clemens' business. It may be that it will be necessary for him to go to England on account of the machine. . . . Then we want to have the children settle in France for a little while on account of their French. If Susy enters Bryn Mawr next year she must get more French during the Summer and this seems the best way to do it.[59]

SUSY'S NINETEENTH YEAR

1890–1891

Narrator: The day before her eighteenth birthday, Susy wrote a letter to her aunt, Sue Crane.

Susy: Some day when I have learned to sacrifice myself and do my duty faithfully I may attain the self-mastery, and self-possession which I so much admire in you. I see now that the causes of my many savage moods were lack of earnestness in living with a definite purpose placed before all other things, and a lack of sense of eternity or any of the great things which ought to subordinate the small in one's mind.

I awakened suddenly to the consciousness that by emotionalizing and fussing and fuming over the trivial things of not even temporal importance, simply for the sake of indulging myself in sensations, I was gradually eliminating my soul. For as Mr. [Horace] Bushnell deplored the "extirpation of religion through disuse," so might I have to deplore the extirpation of my soul some day.

Certainly if anything can eliminate the soul, I believe it is thinking of the trifling things of a rather full and a very pleasant life, which can not demand any use of the immortal part of one in any way. The soul deals not with narrow, trammelling matters. I should like to realize that it is not only my duty but my privilege to suffer all and do all that I can for others in this world. But, oh! One's horrible earthly weaknesses! There's the trouble. It is so hard to control them. While one can have a good sized piece of sky in one's sight, though, one must possess some

[275]

consciousness of Eternity—even if it be an unconscious consciousness.

Tomorrow I am eighteen! Eighteen! I dread to have to say I am so old! And nothing done and such unsettled notions of things. Why, I should be a well-poised woman instead of a rattle-brained girl. I should have been entirely settled and in mechanical running order for two years! I am ashamed I am not a more reliable, serene character, one to be depended upon. I know so well what a girl of eighteen should be![1]

NARRATOR: She wrote a thank-you letter to her Grandmother Langdon.

SUSY: Dearest, dearest Grandma, I have written you a letter of deepest gratitude and love every day since the 19th of March, with my heart, but alas! not with my hand till now.

How I thank you for your beautiful birthday gifts! and how Clara and I both enjoyed your letter! but Grandma you have given me too much! And yet your gifts have given great, great pleasure.

I have added the money to some other money which I received from you at other times and in Europe I shall get something beautiful with it, a reminder of Europe and you. I must say again and yet again that I thank you Grandma dear and that I love you. This is written in school hours, when I realy should be studying; so I must stop for now. With Endless Affection Your Grandaughter Susan.

P.S. The spoon is perfectly beautiful! the pattern on it is so exquisite! just think how rich I am in beautiful silver from you! My lover (if I ever have one, and I *hope* I will!) will be pleased with these lovely spoons to go to housekeeping with, I know. And I,—of course shall be delighted! They make "housekeeping!" When I go to housekeeping! How sure it sounds! So charmingly taken for granted! Yes I am not to be an old maid! the spoons will save me! Lovingly S.C.[2]

NARRATOR: Susy, Clara and their parents went to a Nook Farm wedding; Miss Mary Robinson was married to Louis R. Cheney on April 16th.

LIVY: Wednesday evening last Miss Molly Robinson was married and all the family except Jean went to the wedding. . . . It was a pink wedding. The house was decorated in smilax and Mermet roses. All about the top of the room was festooned smilax and where the festoons were caught up there were sprays of five or seven exquisite Mermet roses. Back of where the bride stood was a solid canopy of evergreen (perhaps ground pine) dotted all over with mermet roses. The bride wore white tulle and carried an immense bunch of white lilacs. The bridesmaids were dressed in pink tulle and carried very large bunches of Mermet roses. . . . The gifts were also very fine; the bride wore a diamond necklace, the front of it composed of five large stars made of diamonds, the gift of her sister Miss Lizzie Robinson.

We have been rather gay for us this week on Friday evening we went to South Manchester; again all the family going but Jean. It being *Friday* evening and a number of young people that are not yet in society being among the invited guests I let Susy and Clara go.

There were four or five cars full of invited guests, all the nice people pretty much of Hartford were of the party. We were invited for theatricals we had first a most charming play "A Box of Monkeys." I think I never saw a better play or one better given. The actors and actresses were all Cheneys, one Mrs. Cheney, two Misses Cheney and two Mr. Cheneys. They were all truly accomplished actresses and actors. After the play a beautiful supper and then a dance for the young people.[3]

NARRATOR: The gay social life did not alleviate Sam's troubles. Nothing was going well: neither the typesetter, the publishing firm nor the business of writing. He and Livy both had rheumatism; his was in his right arm and shoulder, which made writing painful. They gave up the trip to Europe.

LIVY: Youth don't let the thought of Europe worry you *one bit* because we will give that all up. I want to see you happy *much* more than I want any thing else even the childrens lessons. Oh darling it goes to my very heart to see you worried.[4]

NARRATOR: In an atmosphere full of tension, Susy took Bryn Mawr entrance examinations in six subjects: arithmetic, algebra, English, physical geography, German grammar and translation and Latin grammar and composition, and Vergil—prose sight passage and prose authors. Clara wrote to her grandmother that they couldn't make definite plans for the summer until Susy heard whether she had been accepted at Bryn Mawr. Clara wrote that she was not optimistic, but when the news came, it was good, although Susy would have to study all summer and take examinations in French grammar and translation and plane geometry in the fall.

GEORGE WARNER: Susy Clemens is in and happy, the dear girl.[5]

NARRATOR: Summer plans were finally made. Responding to

Candace Wheeler's years of urging, they decided to take a cottage at the Onteora Club near Tannersville, New York.

BRANDER MATTHEWS: In the summer of 1890 Mark took a cottage at Onteora Park . . . then a newly founded settlement of artists with pen and pencil.[6]

MRS. WHEELER: It was generally our particular friends who came in to stay for longer or shorter periods at the Inn—those who had visited us in our cabin and eaten our roasted corn between rocks, or sat in the moonlight on my brother's broad piazza, listening to wonderful music played upon the piano which toiling oxen had brought along the steep zigzag heights of the old Catskill road. Friends who had spent the days with us in the open, playing with our tamed fox cubs or climbing mountains by day and sleeping away at night the tire of tramping days in our little bedrooms.

The Clemenses . . . came to the Inn for the season—the father and mother, and Clara, Susy, and "Little Jean." They took "Balsam," a bit of cottage across the road from the Inn, and it became a sort of jewel-box for the summer—a thing that held values untold.[7]

ROBERT UNDERWOOD JOHNSON: At first the houses were chiefly log cabins and an inn built for warm weather. Of the latter Mark said that "the partitions were so thin that one could hear a lady in the next room changing her mind."[8]

NARRATOR: Carroll Beckwith painted Sam's portrait.

MRS. WHEELER: Mr. Carroll Beckwith was the first of our painter residents, and his house was built on a projecting ledge of the Onteora Mountain. . . . Here in the face of this delectable sky and mountain picture dwelt the kindly, courtly man and skillful draftsman and painter through the summer of many years, painting the portraits of many Onteorians, receiving pupils in the great studio which stood at the back of his house, and charming the audiences which met for his instructive morning lecture.[9]

ROBERT UNDERWOOD JOHNSON: Mark was the centre of attraction for the Onteora colony and for none more than the children, between whom and him there was an ideal relation of mutual devotion.[10]

NARRATOR: Susy studied long hours; a "Mademoiselle" was employed to drill her in French.

SUSY: I have been very busy and am still, studying for the Bryn Mawr french examination in the fall. . . .

The days pass by quickly and pleasantly with us; *charmingly* for Onteora days but still they are not Elmira days (the *happiest* ones of all our years!). . . .

There is no driving or riding for me but walking and reading and nice people to meet. The sky is large and blue here and there has been very little rain; altogether it is pleasant here.

I am reading "Daniel Deronda" and enjoying it, endlessly; much more than I did Adam Bede.[11]

NARRATOR: Susy and Clara took part with the grownups in charades and theatrical entertainments. Clara impersonated Modjeska, whom she admired tremendously, and did Ophelia, with Susy playing Hamlet. Modjeska had visited the Warners in Hartford and the girls adored her and treasured the photographs she gave them. Jean gravitated, as usual, toward the animals.

JEAN: It is a very hot day and I expect to go barefooted this afternoon. There are now 8 donkeys here 1 is a new one and his neck on both sides is all biten.[12]

NARRATOR: There were interruptions to the holiday for Sam and Livy; he had to go away on business and both visited their mothers, who were in failing health.

LIVY: I found the children all in good health and they seemed very glad to get me back and . . . it seemed very good to get back to them. Everyone here . . . was so nice and cordial to me that it was very delightful and seemed quite like getting home.

We find the weather very very cold here and we have some trouble to keep warm.

We keep a good roaring fire in the fire place and our little parlor is very cozy and pretty. . . .

Mr. Clemens left us or rather we left him to go to Washington. A telegram rec'd from him today [August 24th] says he shall remain there several days.[13]

NARRATOR: They prepared to go home about the middle of September.

LIVY: We begin to feel that our time here is very short as we expect to leave a week from tomorrow [September 16th]. We have enjoyed our summer exceedingly. . . . Tomorrow morning quite a number of them are going. Mademoiselle leaves us and Susy is through with her work for the present.[14]

NARRATOR: A few days after their return to Hartford, George Warner came in and reminded Sam and Susy of the summer of '89.

SAM: [He] asked me if I had ever heard of Rudyard Kipling. I said "No."

He said I would hear of him very soon, and that the noise he made would be loud and continuous. . . . A day or two later he brought a copy of the London *World* which had a sketch of Kipling in it, and a mention of the fact that he had traveled in the United States. According to the sketch he had passed through Elmira. This remark, with the additional fact that he hailed from India, attracted my attention—also Susy's. She went to her room and brought his card from its place in the frame of her mirror, and the Quarry Farm visitor stood identified.[15]

NARRATOR: Susy's little blue room opened off the second-floor alcove, known as Livy's private sitting room. Ever since Sam had described the delightful clutter of Tom Nast's daughter's room, Susy had decorated shelves, walls and frames with her treasures: invitations, souvenirs and a great many seashells entwined with seaweed. Now in early fall, piles of books stood on chairs and on the floor preparatory to being packed off to Bryn Mawr.

The tension was high; everyone in the household, family, Miss Foote, Katy, George and the other servants, were all concentrated on Miss Susy's great adventure. It was an emotional setting for an experience which was almost certainly doomed to failure. Susy had rarely been separated from the family and Sam continuously added tinder to the smoldering fires of impending separation. Susy and Sam and Livy left for Bryn Mawr a few days early and stopped for a week at the Murray Hill Hotel in New York; Susy wrote to Clara.

SUSY: Dearest, dear Clara; I am sitting in a bright sunny room just now, and would realy be perfectly happy for the time being if only you were here. . . .

This room is exactly the kind that would suit you, bright and warm and with the mirrors all in the correct light. (you know, Clara). I have been rushing around till now with Mamma; and she has gotten me a *lot* of beautiful undressed kid gloves.

The new dresses *are* stunning! You would hardly recognize your unstylish sister in them. They fit perfectly without a

wrinkle and are so narrow in the back that I have to stand up
straight. . . .

Tonight when I come back from the theater it will seem *so*
doleful not to be able to talk it over with you, Clara. I would
give anything if you were only here! I shall be so glad when we
can be together again and I can hear you play the dear old
familiar things. Because even tho' I have been cross and horrid
a great deal you know I have loved and admired you all the time.
This you must never forget!

Remember there is no one in the world I have as good times
with, as with you, remember . . . there is no one I love to be
with as much as with you. We have always had good good times
together, and I have depended on you so, when we were together
that I don't know what I shall do without you.

I hope you will tell Mamma when you don't feel well, and
get strong and perfectly happy.

A hand organ has just been playing. It didn't play particularly
well, tho'.

Think of me when you play the Onteora and Elmira music
and write me very soon, Your ever loving Susy.[16]

NARRATOR: At Bryn Mawr Susy and Sam and Livy stayed at the
Summit Grove Inn. Rooms had not been assigned to all students
as a new dormitory was still unfinished. Several of them were
staying at the Inn, and it was close to two weeks before Susy
was assigned a room. Among the girls at the Inn were Evangeline
and Ethel Walker, the former a sophomore and the latter a
classmate of Susy's.

EVANGELINE: In the dining room at the same table with my sister
and me were Mr. and Mrs. Clemens of Hartford (Mark Twain)
and their daughter—Susy to them, and to us always Olivia—a
frail, attractive, charming young girl. As Mr. and Mrs. Clemens
were not willing to leave Olivia alone in a hotel, even though
there were chaperones, we had the pleasure of their company
for several weeks and found them delightful.

The long tables in the dining room seated I think about a dozen
or more people, and our service was that of colored waiters who
had been employed by the hotel for their summer and early
autumn season. Seated opposite us was a Norwegian woman by
the name of Wergeland. . . . Miss Wergeland, as a Fellow in
History, had come to study with Professor Charles M. Andrews,

then the very young head of the History Department of Bryn Mawr. . . . However, she spoke no English, and when Mr. Clemens discovered that she was having difficulty in ordering her meals, he very quietly removed himself from our group to the other side of the table, introduced himself to her, and speaking German fluently as he did, helped her order her meals. This he did . . . three times a day for at least two weeks. His friendliness and gayety were delightful, and evidently he and Miss Wergeland found much of interest to talk about. Later she told Mrs. Clemens how grateful she was to him. "Just like him," commented Mrs. Clemens.

Finally, Mr. Clemens convinced the College authorities that, much as he would like to spend her Freshman year with Olivia at Bryn Mawr College, he was obliged to get back to work, but added that he would not leave her in a hotel. So, suddenly, Olivia was given a room in Radnor Hall and, owing to Mr. Clemens' good offices, the two Walker sisters found themselves happily settled in a suite in Merion Hall, for which they had applied long before and in which I had spent my Freshman year. How we blessed Mr. Clemens!

During these weeks we had come to know Mr. and Mrs. Clemens and Olivia very well and all of us were sorry to part; but they promised to come down to see us during the winter and commended Olivia to our care.[17]

SAM: The last time I saw her was a week ago on the platform at Bryn Mawr. Our train was moving away, and she was drifting college-ward afoot, her figure blurred and dim in the rain and fog, and she was crying.[18]

EVANGELINE WALKER: At the time, it seemed to us very natural that Olivia like ourselves should be coming to college, but later I realized how strong was the tie between her and her father, how much they minded being separated, and also how eager Mrs. Clemens was that Olivia should be happy in a new environment, leading an independent life of her own as a college student among girls of her own age, free from the limiting influences of home.[19]

NARRATOR: Sam was the despondent one.

SAM: It's about the longest week the almanac has ever furnished to this fambly. Livy's general health is rather shabby, and she is being put under a course of toning up by the doctor, who says good results will show by spring. Clara and Jean are in fine health. Clara decides to stay out of college and devote herself to music.

Goes to New York twice a month and takes a lesson from an old and brilliant pupil of Liszt and Clara Schumann, who says she will pan out to admiration on the piano. She practices 3 hours a day. We haven't forecast Jean's future yet, but think she is going to be a horse jockey and live in the stable.[20]

NARRATOR: Susy signed up for three courses in Latin: prose, Sallust and Livy, and Horace. She was taking French and the required physical education.

SUSY: I am glad of course that I am in Bryn Mawr as I was working all last year to get in and now that I am here there is a great deal that I enjoy most thoroughly. The work is delightful and the people are lovely and altogether Bryn Mawr is an ideal place, but oh! it *does* not, *can* not compare with home![21]

EVANGELINE WALKER: She was emotional, high-strung, temperamental, and all of us—Mrs. Clemens, too—were afraid she might be homesick at first.[22]

NARRATOR: Sam couldn't bear Susy's homesickness; he went back to Bryn Mawr.

LIVY: Jean and I went to church this morning [October 26th] it was grey and chilly. We are alone in the house, Mr. Clemens and Clara having gone down to Bryn Mawr to spend Saturday and Sunday with Susy.[23]

SAM: Reached B.M. 8:15; walked to the College—no Susy there— gone to a dance, some girls said. But in a moment Susy burst in— she had heard of our arrival. She was for going straight and hospitably to her room and giving up the dance; but I wouldn't allow that. Clara didn't seem tired, and I wasn't, and had been free from rheumatism all day and was feeling like a bird; so I joined the crowd.

To my joy it turned out the dance was *here* [at the Summit Grove Inn]—right at home. I danced two Virginia reels and another dance, and looked on and talked the rest of the time. It was very jolly and pleasant, and everybody asked after you and was disappointed when I said you hadn't come.[24]

NARRATOR: The weekend visit did not improve Susy's state of mind.

LIVY: We get rather homesick letters from Susy still. I am afraid when she goes back after being at home for Thanksgiving that she will be still more homesick.[25]

NARRATOR: A few days later the picture was brighter.

LIVY: Susy seems by her letters to be well and the last one was not as homesick as the other ones have been.[26]

NARRATOR: Both Sam's and Livy's mothers died in the fall and Jean became seriously ill.

Sam wrote Howells in November, after his mother's death.

SAM: Your words of sympathy are most kind and consoling, and were needed; needed in a double way; for I have rushed here [Hartford] by rail from Elmira to get at the truth as to Jean's condition, for she has been very ill while her mother and I have been watching since last Friday by what is to be the death-bed of Mrs. Clemens's mother.

All day yesterday the telegrams read alike, without change: "Mother is steadily failing." To-day the news is: "Mother is very low."

I ought to be there to [be] a support to Mrs. Clemens in this unspeakable trouble, and so ought Susy and Clara; but Jean pleads to be not wholly forsaken; so, when the death-telegram falls, I think I shall stay with Jean and send Susy and Clara to their mother.

NARRATOR: Jean's illness had strange symptoms and was never accurately diagnosed. The family noticed a "sudden and unaccountable change" in her personality.

SAM: I have fed so full on sorrows, these last weeks that I seem to have become hardened to them—benumbed.[27]

KATY: He'd joke about anything. He'd joke even at a funeral! I remember when Mrs. Clemens' mother was dying. She was sick a long time, and Mrs. Clemens was in Elmira and kept telegraphing Mr. Clemens every morning to come that day. Finally he said he'd go, but the children all began to cry and hung on to him and begged him not to, so he hadn't the heart to leave 'em and he got terrible upset. So he went over to Mr. Warner and says: "Warner, I've written a letter to everybody who has a single drop of my blood in their veins and whose funeral I may ever have to go to, and I have asked them *all* to come and settle right down here within a radius of two blocks and just *stay* until they all die, so I won't ever have to go out of town to attend their funeral!" Yes, he'd joke about anything.[28]

NARRATOR: There was no joking about the typesetter; the "monster" kept on eating money.

LIVY: I wish there was some way to change our manner of living but that seems next to impossible unless we sell our house.[29]

NARRATOR: Sam tried to raise money all over the country. He seemed to be mesmerized by Paige.

SAM: I will remark here that James W. Paige, the little bright-eyed, alert, smartly dressed inventor of the machine is a most extraordinary compound of business thrift and commercial insanity; of cold calculations and jejune sentimentality; of veracity and falsehood; of fidelity and treachery; of nobility and baseness; of pluck and cowardice; of wasteful liberality and pitiful stinginess; of solid sense and weltering moonshine; of towering genius and trivial ambitions; of merciful bowels and a petrified heart; of colossal vanity and—But there the opposites stop. His vanity stands alone, sky-piercing, as sharp of outline as an Egyptian monolith. It is the only unpleasant feature in him that is not modified, softened, compensated by some converse characteristic. There is another point or two worth mentioning. He can persuade anybody, he can convince nobody. He has a crystal-clear mind as regards the grasping and concreting of an idea which has been lost and smothered under a chaos of baffling legal language; and yet it can always be depended upon to take the simplest half dozen facts and draw from them a conclusion that will astonish the idiots in the asylum. It is because he is a dreamer, a visionary. His imagination runs utterly away with him. He is a poet, a most great and genuine poet, whose sublime creations are written in steel. He is the Shakespeare of mechanical invention. In all the ages he has no peer. Indeed, there is none that even approaches him. Whoever is qualified to fully comprehend his marvelous machine will grant that its place is upon the loftiest summit of human invention, with no kindred between it and the far foothills below.[30]

NARRATOR: Sam ended a letter to Hall at the publishing company:

SAM: Merry Christmas to you, and I wish to God I could have one myself before I die.[31]

NARRATOR: Christmas vacation came and then Susy returned to Bryn Mawr.

EVANGELINE WALKER: Mrs. Clemens would come down occasionally for a short stay, I think in order to keep Mr. Clemens from coming, because she told me that he would make anything an excuse, even to bringing down Olivia's laundry.

NARRATOR: Susy's voice and dramatic talent were discovered by the college community.

EVANGELINE WALKER: She had an exquisite soprano voice, was very musical, and liked to sing and act, so having a prima donna among us, we almost immediately decided to give the opera "Iolanthe," with lovely Olivia for Phyllis. She was a natural for the part, and soon, everywhere—in Hall and on the campus, wherever one happened to be—one would hear individuals and groups singing the choruses and practicing their parts for the opera. Olivia was in her element, and all of us were enchanted with our Phyllis.

NARRATOR: The opera was to be given early in February.

EVANGELINE WALKER: To our great joy and as time came near for the production of the opera, Mrs. Clemens was established in the then empty infirmary on the top floor of Merion Hall, where she helped us cut out and fit our innumerable fairy costumes, told us stories of her travels and won our hearts. She was a charming person and all of us adored her. She stayed for the opera, which was very successful; but . . . men were not invited to our student productions, so Mr. Clemens was not with us![32]

NARRATOR: *The Lantern,* a college publication, commented on the success of the show: "The Glee Club . . . has thus just completed its second year of self-management. A club consisting of some forty students out of one hundred and forty, especially in a college which offers no department of music, can hardly be expected to boast voices of very superior quality or even mediocre training: yet it seems to have pleased its audience in this its first ambitious attempt, and certainly so far as concerns performing the office for which it exists—namely, that of giving pleasure and profit to its members—it must be pronounced a most unqualified success.[33]

SAM: Mrs. Clemens has been in Philadelphia a week . . . with Susy (who, to my private regret is beginning to love Bryn Mawr) and I've had to stay here [Hartford] alone. But this is the last time this brace of old fools, old indispensables-to-each-other, are going to separate themselves in this foolish fashion.[34]

NARRATOR: It was inevitable that Sam would be asked to give a reading at Bryn Mawr.

EVANGELINE WALKER: It occurred to us that it would be very interesting to have Mr. Clemens come down and give us one of his Readings in the Chapel. Olivia was delighted with this plan even though . . . her mother was not particularly enthusiastic about it, for I think she felt the nervous strain would be too great for Olivia. And she was quite right, for from the moment he accepted the invitation and the date was set, Olivia became very restless and nervous and it seemed to our committee that it was going to be impossible for her and her father to agree upon a program. Letters were written back and forth and details were discussed. Apparently there were some of his stories—especially the "Ghost Story"—that she did not like and felt were not suitable for what she called "the sophisticated group at Bryn Mawr College." "No," she said, she was "not going to allow him to tell *that story!*" Finally, the two of them settled upon a program satisfactory to both and the day arrived when he was to come and give his lecture. Olivia asked me if I would go to the station with her to meet him because, she said, he would like to walk from the station to the College, a matter of not more than ten minutes. Of course I was delighted to be asked and to see her father again, for all of us had lost our hearts to him when we were at the Bryn Mawr Hotel together. The moment we met him at the station and had exchanged greetings Olivia clung to his hand saying repeatedly as we walked from the Bryn Mawr Station to the College: "Father, *promise* me that you will not tell the 'Ghost Story!'" He laughed and patting her hand said: "I have written you that I would not tell the 'Ghost Story.' Let's forget about it."

Needless to say, the entire College turned out for his lecture in the late afternoon, and he kept his audience laughing. I was sitting with Olivia on the main aisle about the middle of the room holding her damp hand in mine, while she was shaking like a leaf. I tried to encourage her because everyone was enjoying Mr. Clemens thoroughly, and I hoped his success was reassuring her. There were no printed programs, and after each "number" he would walk back and forth on the platform, his fine head thrown back, and when the applause ceased, he would announce the next title and continue. Finally we came to the end of the program, and as the room grew darker he walked up and down the platform apparently deliberating—now a familiar and amusing stunt.

Olivia was whispering in my ear: "He's going to tell the 'Ghost Story'—I *know* he's going to tell the 'Ghost Story.' And he's going to say 'Boo' at the end and make them all jump."

"Now don't worry," I said. "You know he *always* walks up and down and *pretends* to be thinking what he is going to say. In any case the audience adores him!"

His audience was so entirely with him I was not worried. However I must say I got a bit nervous as time went on and he said nothing, and the audience began to grow a little restless. Where-upon, with no announcement, he began the "Ghost Story." By this time the room was quite dark, and Olivia quietly fled up the aisle, I following. Once out of the room we crossed the hall to a large classroom, the door of which was open. In she went and there flung herself down and with her head on a desk wept aloud! She was heartbroken! There was nothing to do or to say, no comfort that I could give her, except to reiterate that she must *know* the audience was simply delighted with her father and that the performance was completely successful! The applause was thunderous and people began to pour out of the Chapel. Finally, Mr. Clemens appeared and seeing Olivia in the classroom, he rushed in, and in a moment he had her in his arms trying to comfort her. "But Father," she moaned, "you promised, you promised!" "Oh my Dear," he wailed, "I tried to think of something else and my mind refused to focus. All I could hear was your voice saying 'Please don't tell the *Ghost Story*, Father—*Promise not* to tell the 'Ghost Story'—and I could think of *nothing* else. Oh, my Dear, my Dear, how could I!"

I closed the big doors quickly and fled leaving them to comfort each other.[35]

SUSY'S TWENTIETH YEAR

1891–1892

NARRATOR: Livy brought Susy home the first week in April; it was a dreary spring. Sam and Livy were suffering from rheumatism and Livy had symptoms of heart trouble. The financial situation was such that they could no longer afford to run the expensive house.

SAM: Bryn Mawr began it. It was there that her [Susy's] health was undermined.[1]

For her health's sake Mrs. Clemens *must* try some baths somewhere, and this it is that has determined us to go to Europe. The water required seems to be provided at a little obscure and little-visited nook up in the hills back of the Rhine somewhere and you get to it by Rhine traffic-boat and country stage-coach.[2]

I have not had the use of my right arm for some time, and so I have been obliged to do the little writing absolutely necessary to be done through the medium of dictation!—a vehicle so awkward for me and so irritating that I not only curse and swear all the time I am dictating, but am impatient and dissatisfied because God has given me only one tongue (with which) to curse and swear with. I could give employment to a hundred and fifty if I had them, these days.[3]

CLARA: It happened at this time that Father found himself in serious financial difficulties. . . . Owing to bad business years, bad investments and mismanagement . . . the publishing house was rapidly losing ground.[4]

NARRATOR: Sue Crane recalled that she went to Hartford in April to support Livy when she broke the news to the household that the family was going to Europe to live for a year or two.

SUE CRANE: She [Livy] wished to make it as cheerful, and hopeful of return as possible, although she had grave doubts of their returning as a whole family.

With all her desire to have it otherwise the occasion was like a funeral of several days. The adverse report of the Council of physicians in Mrs. Clemens' case at that time contributed largely to the depression.[5]

SAM: We are going to Europe in June, for an indefinite stay. We shall sell the horses and shut up the house. We wish to provide a place for our coachman, who has been with us 21 years, and is sober, active, diligent, and unusually bright and capable.[6]

KATY: They found a place for Patrick, the coachman, and George, too. He went to the Players Club in New York later on. I was the only one of the servants that went with them. First they thought they'd just take that German nurse for the children, but Mrs. Clemens really thought I could pack and do things better than this German girl, so finally it was settled I should go. I was glad of it. Mrs. Clemens said, "Katy, you'd like to go to Europe, wouldn't you?" I said, "Yes, I'd be delighted." Then she says: "We was talking it over last night, Mr. Clemens and I, and decided it would be best to take you. You would be a great help to the children and me and tend to the packing and everything." You see there was twenty-five trunks to pack and remember what was in every one of them. That was no small job, I'll tell you.[7]

SAM: I don't know how long we shall be in Europe—I have a vote, but I don't cast it. I'm going to do whatever the others desire, with leave to change their mind, without prejudice, whenever they want to. Travel has no longer any charm for me. I have seen all the foreign countries I want to see except heaven and hell, and I have only a vague curiosity as concerns one of those.[8]

We are working and packing night and day, now—part of the trunks and two of the children go to New York tomorrow [June 4th] and the rest of us follow Friday. We sail at 5 A.M. Saturday in La Gascoigne for Havre, and shall remain three days in Paris making plans.[9]

We are leaving for Europe in a few days, to remain there until we shall get tired—a point which I shall reach in thirty-days, Jean in sixty, Clara in ninety, Susy in a hundred, and Livy in six months.

Thirty and 60 are 90, and 90 are 180, and a 100 are 280. So that it is 280 days and six months that we are to be away, if my figures are right. I am dismayed at the result of this calculation, and wish I hadn't made it. I was supposing up till this moment, that we were to be gone only six or eight months.[10]

KATY: They closed the house, but they didn't know then it was forever. It was a sad time.[11]

CLARA: Pulling up anchor and sailing away from our beloved Hartford was a sorrowful episode. We adored our home and friends. We had to leave so much treasured beauty behind that we could not look forward with any pleasure to life abroad. We all regarded this break . . . as something resembling a tragedy. We had showered love on the home itself—the library; the conservatory sweet with the perfume of flowers; the bright bedrooms; and, outside, the trees, the tender eyebrights, the river reflecting clouds and sky. These were our friends. They belonged to us; and we to them. How could we part? . . .

We passed from room to room with leaden hearts, looked back and lingered—lingered. An inner voice whispered we should never return. . . .

We scanned the faces of friends, servants, pets. We spoke that heart-breaking word "Good-by," and, tear-blinded, passed, for the last time, through the front door.[12]

KATY: So we all went to Europe, Jean, Susy, Clara, Mr. and Mrs. Clemens, and Mrs. Crane, Mrs. Clemens' sister. She wanted her to go, too.[13]

SUE CRANE: Mr. Langdon took me to N. Y. and we all met at the Murray Hill Hotel. . . .

We sailed at six A.M. having remained on the steamer all night.[14]

SAM: One deck steward to 200,000 passengers. Began at nine to hunt for him and pray to him—got the order to him at 10:15, at 10:30 he has not appeared, and I have retreated from the sight of the starving family. . . .

Divans all around a great square salon, occupied by silent folk in the squeamish stage. A piano in there—hated by the above.[15]

NARRATOR: They stayed in Paris for a week and then went to Geneva, where they left Susy and Clara with a French family. Sam, Livy, Jean, Sue Crane and Katy went to Aix-les-Bains, which Sam called a "Paradise of Rheumatics."

SAM: Aix is handsome, and is handsomely situated, too, on its hill slope, with its stately prospect of mountain range and plain spread out before it and about it. The streets are mainly narrow, and steep and crooked and interesting, and offer considerable variety in the way of names; on the corner of one of them you read this: "Rue du Puits d'Enfer" ("Pit of Hell Street"). Some of the sidewalks are only eighteen inches wide; they are for the cats, probably. There is a pleasant park, and there are spacious and beautiful grounds connected with the two great pleasure resorts, the Cercle and the Villa des Fleurs. The town consists of big hotels, little hotels, and *pensions*.[16]

The doctor said I was a grand proof of what these baths could do; said I had come here as innocent of disease as a grindstone, and inside of three weeks these baths had sluiced out of me every important ailment known to medical science, along with considerable more that were entirely new and patentable.[17]

Now, we are living at a most comfortable and satisfactory *pension*, with a garden of shade trees and flowers and shrubs, and a convincing air of quiet and repose. But just across the narrow street is the little market square, and at the corner of that is the church that is neighbor to the Roman arch, and that narrow street, and that billiard table of a market place, and that church are able, on a bet, to turn out more noise to a cubic yard at the wrong time than any other similar combination in the earth or out of it.[18]

Dear Children—I love you both, and when I shall have finished learning to write with my left hand, I will communicate with you more frequently.

C'est mon premier leçon et je ne suis pas encore maitre de l'art. Je la trouve un peu plus difficile qu'a ecrire de la main droit. (Ah, grace à Dieu, ces dernieres mots sont fait à merveille!)

Adieu, mignonnes.[19]

But what I came here for five weeks ago was the baths. My right arm was disabled with rheumatism. To sit at home in America and guess out the European bath best fitted for a particular ailment or combination of ailments, it is not possible, and it would not be a good idea to experiment in that way, anyhow. . . . So it is necessary to let your physician name a bath for you. . . . I had the rheumatism and was advised to go to Aix, not so much because I had that disease as because I had the promise of certain others.[20]

My first baths developed plenty of pain, but the subsequent

ones removed almost all of it. I have got back the use of my arm these last few days, and I am going away now.[21]

KATY: We went back to Geneva where the girls was studying French in some French family—and then we all started for Bayreuth and the Wagner Opera. It was all the rage then. We bought our tickets in America a year before (and our dinners too!). . . . That's the way the thing was managed. . . . Bayreuth was just a little place —a little German village way up in the Barbarian Mountains. . . .

But it was kind of a "shrine," as they called it, over there, for them Wagner operas. The opera house was way up in the mountains and was beautiful.[22]

We stayed there ten days and we seen everything, I think, and heard all them operas. . . .

The family was just crazy about the opera.[23]

NARRATOR: They went next to Marienbad, another "health factory," as Sam called it. They stayed there six weeks.

CLARA: We all fell in love with Marienbad, which, as a watering-place, can hardly be surpassed. The great pine woods offered poetic walks without number, and there was plenty of entertainment provided by people of many types that congregated from all lands to heal their maladies. Fortunately, there were many young people present, and in the early morning, when files of travelers strolled along the promenade which led to the health-giving spring, numerous bright uniforms were visible. These uniforms filled our hearts with satisfaction; naturally I refer to my sisters' hearts and mine. What a world of romance lay in those braided coats and plumed helmets! . . .

Among the foreigners who called on Father was an old Russian lady. She was very fat, self-assured, and penetrating. . . . She could get into a room where no one else managed to set foot . . . an overwhelming woman . . . who draws from under her cloak a large package of songs with the clear intention of singing them all to my helpless father. As soon as he gathers the drift of her outpouring and voluble announcement, he hastens to explain that he knows nothing of music. . . .

But Father might just as well have been in another city. . . . On she rattled. . . . Then she opened the door . . . and pulled in a young girl . . . whom she hastily pushed onto the piano-stool. . . . Standing near the piano, she commanded the girl to start, and then let loose such a blast herself that Father instinctively pushed back his chair several feet. . . .

Father moved restlessly in his chair and shifted his eyes to and from her glance. One had to think of a serpent and a bird. My sisters and I sat in a row on the sofa, consumed with giggles. It was a new experience to see Father's positive temperament yielding to all this vulgar vanity. . . . She looked as strong as a German hussar. She kept on singing and fixing Father with her coquettish eyes until he grew pale and left the room.[24]

SAM: It is a mistake that there is no bath that will cure people's manners. Bet drowning would help.[25]

NARRATOR: Everyone in the family took the mud baths.

KATY: 'Twas a kind of a ceremony, the way you took 'em. All the people would go to that mud-bath house very serious and march in a regular procession every morning . . . then they'd have kind of a little cake or biscuit that they'd eat, and then they'd march up to a fountain where they'd drink the water, and eat that tough old cake, and then march along to the mud-bath place . . . there was a nice band there that used to play for them. . . . Then after drinking the water and eating the cake, they'd march up to the bathroom and jump right into the mud! There was three baths in the room. The first one was solid mud. They'd set in that for a while, then pull themselves out, dripping all over, and step into another one that warn't quite so thick. Then the last one was pure water.[26]

LIVY: We stopped two days in our old rooms in Heidelberg, and enjoyed it tremendously.[27]

KATY: The morning we were starting for Geneva, she said to Mr. Clemens: "Youth, dear, I want to take Katy to Heidelberg along with the children on this trip. You know, she's always talking about that picture of Heidelberg in my room being so wonderful, and I promised her some day to let her see the real thing. So I want to take her up there to see that lovely Castle and to see the great barrel there that's so big wagons can turn around on it, and to see them pretty gardens and the river."

And Mr. Clemens says, "Oh, yes, we must do that, Livy." So we went and they took me up to the Castle and then we stopped at that wonderful Schloss Hotel, and the first thing Mr. Clemens did he took me out to the front of the hotel ('twas built way up on a hill, you know). "Because," he says, "Katy, I want to show you a string of diamonds—the most beautiful string of diamonds in the whole world," he says. And so he took me out there to the open, and looking down there was rows and rows of these pretty little gas lights—all down that hill—two rows of them—glittering and sparkling and flashing in the night. And, oh! it did look just like a string of diamonds. It was a great sight, and Mr. Clemens he loved that.[28]

NARRATOR: In late summer they settled down in a charming cottage on the grounds of the Hôtel Beau Rivage at Ouchy, near Lausanne.

LIVY: We have taken the usual trip through Switzerland . . . to Lucerne, and over the Brunig to Interlaken, then on here. My sister and the children were happy in it all as it seems to me every one must be. I was particularly desirous that my sister should have it this year, because if any thing happens that makes her feel as if she must return before we do, she will at least have seen the most marvelous natural beauty of Europe. . . .

We enjoy it extremely here at Ouchy, when the weather is pleasant the boating is perfect.

Jean has learned to row since we came and I hope Susy and Clara will before we go away. . . .

Clara is now doing a little practicing getting ready to be tried by her teacher when we reach Berlin.[29]

CLARA: During the latter part of our stay in that charming town, Mother went to Berlin to look for rooms and took my elder sister with her. Father, Jean and our good maid, Katy, [and Clara] were left behind.[30]

NARRATOR: Sue Crane went with Livy and Susy, and they found a flat at Number 7, Kornerstrasse, on the ground floor, as Livy could not climb stairs.

LIVY: We are going to keep house there in a flat. I found it would be much the most economical way. We have secured what we think is a very pleasant sunny flat and we hope to take up our abode there between the 5th and 10th of October. We expect to remain there six months at least and perhaps seven. . . .

Mr. Clemens arm is somewhat better but still very far from well. He is not able to get on his coat alone and he has a great deal of pain in it. Just now [September 23rd] he is taking a trip down the Rhône having left us here in Ouchy. . . .

How I wish we might hear something good about it [the machine]. . . .

As the Autumn comes and the time is here when we usually make preparations to go home, it has given me waves of home-sickness. I think much of friends and much of the roses which John would so soon have ready for us.[31]

NARRATOR: John O'Neil, the gardener, and his wife, Ellen, had been left as caretakers of the Hartford house.

KATY: Well, after Switzerland, the family went to Berlin for the winter, and I came back to America—the first time I ever left them. They didn't want me to come home but I felt they could get along without me and it would save money. Mrs. Clemens thought maybe the girls were getting so big they could pack for themselves, and as they didn't have much money then, I thought they could get along without me. They were going to live in one place all winter and I told Mrs. Clemens I'd come back any time they wanted me. Mrs. Clemens thought it would be a good thing if the girls took care of themselves—get used to packing twenty-five trunks! We had to have lots of trunks because we carried all our bed linen and table linen, too. You didn't rent that there on the other side, then; you had to take your own in them days.[32]

CLARA: As Father's financial affairs were still in a bad condition we were obliged to economize, so Mother had selected a cheap apartment in a disagreeable quarter of the city. . . .

Father's presence was now needed in America to look after the Webster Publishing Company and the Paige typesetting machine, which seemed irrevocably lost. . . . Should we ever become accustomed to this dismal apartment? And think of it as home?

We did not have to remain there very long, however. After we had endured it two or three months, Father cabled that he could afford to send us to a better abode. We moved with gay hearts to a comfortable, if simple, hotel on Unter den Linden. . . .

Father soon rejoined us and was occupied much of the time in attending all sorts of social functions with Mother. My sisters and I were not permitted to take any part in the gayeties, with the exception of one or two parties at the American Embassy, which made us open our eyes very wide. Such people, clothes, uniforms![33]

NARRATOR: The confining customs of European Victorianism were difficult for Susy, who, in America, had been considered almost an adult.

SUSY: I was dreadfully restless and discontented . . . most of the time, in spite of the Opera and the gayety.[34]

CLARA: The combination of Susy's striving for high moral development with her inclination to live the life of a feverish, impassioned
artist of various talents, which by nature she was, is something to
wonder at.[35]

NARRATOR: She was not at ease, socially. William Walter Phelps was
American Ambassador to Berlin, and he delighted in teasing the
girls by trying to make them appear younger than they were.

SUSY: When I saw Mr. Phelps I put out my hand enthusiastically
and said, "Oh, Mr. Phelps, good evening," whereat he drew back
and said, so all could hear, "What, you here! why, you're too
young. Do you think you know how to behave?" As there were
two or three young gentlemen near by to whom I hadn't been
introduced I wasn't exactly overjoyed at this greeting.[36]

NARRATOR: Captain Bingham, attaché at the Embassy, was a favorite
of Susy's.

SUSY: He never left me sitting alone, nor in an awkward situation of
any kind, but always came cordially to the rescue. My gratitude
toward him was absolutely limitless.[37]

CLARA: A great fuss was made over Father, and Susy and I felt proud
to be his daughters. In fact, with satisfied vanity we enjoyed
watching people point out our family when we entered a dining-
room. At first we pretended to be indifferent to the visible attention we attracted, but at last my sister and I confessed to each
other that it must be queer to belong to a family in which no one
was distinguished or famous.

Father himself seemed utterly unconscious of the sensation he
always created. . . . And I often wondered how the news of his
identity could possibly spread around so rapidly. It was also surprising that his popularity should be international. . . . Sometimes
groups of people would stand a couple of yards away from our
table to watch every mouthful Father took. . . . Occasionally Susy
or I would exclaim: "Look at those people, Father! They are
getting a fine view of your appetite." He would laugh a little then,
but did not seem to be embarrassed by the fact that he was an
object of scrutiny.[38]

NARRATOR: One day, he was mistaken for an eminent German historian and archaeologist, the Secretary of the Berlin Royal Academy of Sciences. He noted: "Been taken for Mommsen twice.
We have the same hair, but on examination it was found the brains
were different."[39]

CLARA: Now and then arrangements were made for private meals.

NARRATOR: A young German waiter named Ernest Koppe was assigned by the hotel to serve them in their apartment. Ernest spoke English and French; he was particularly helpful to Sue Crane, who spoke no German, as an interpreter. The whole family became very attached to Ernest, and Sue told him that if he ever decided to come to America, he should come to Elmira, to Quarry Farm, to work for her.

CLARA: Susy and I greatly preferred the public dining-room where we could examine interesting types.

On one such occasion, we fell in love with a most distinguished-looking man. We exclaimed so much . . . that Father decided to do what he had never done before and certainly did not do again. He addressed the man (an Englishman) and introduced himself . . . the gentleman refused to believe the self-introducer was Mark Twain, and, as Father did not care to prove his identity, the matter was dropped right there. After that, my sister and I kept very quiet about our ideals.[40]

I personally was perfectly happy because I could stand at the window and watch the German Emperor drive by. He was a most romantic and brilliant figure and we never tired of hearing stories about him.[41]

SAM: One morning at breakfast a vast card arrived—an invitation. To be precise, it was a command from the Emperor of Germany to come to dinner. During several months I had encountered socially, on the Continent, men bearing lofty titles; and all this while Jean was becoming more and more impressed, and awed, and subdued, by these imposing events, for she had not been abroad before, and they were new to her—wonders out of dreamland turned into realities. The imperial card was passed from hand to hand, around the table and examined with interest; when it reached Jean she exhibited excitement and emotion, but for a time was quite speechless; then she said,

"Why, papa, if it keeps on going like this, pretty soon there won't be anybody left for you to get acquainted with but God."

It was not complimentary to think I was not acquainted in that quarter, but she was young, and the young jump to conclusions without reflection.[42]

NARRATOR: Christmas was a simple affair.

SAM: I am glad, for one reason, that financial losses have struck us!

Your mother will have to give up that infernal Christmas-suicide.[43]

NARRATOR: In January Sam had a long bout with a cold which settled in his lungs.

SAM: I am 2 weeks in bed with congestion of the lungs, but am mending. [44]

NARRATOR: When he was well enough, he and Livy went to Mentone with Joseph Verey, their favorite courier, leaving the family in Berlin.

SUSY'S TWENTY-FIRST YEAR

1892–1893

NARRATOR: Sam and Livy had a quiet time in Mentone sight-seeing. The girls were busy with their lessons in Berlin, and Susy was spending more and more time writing.

SAM: Livy and I are here alone—to get some healing weather. We left all the others at school in Berlin. We have been here 3 weeks. The courier will take us to Pisa next Wednesday and then we shall go on to Rome while he goes to Berlin and fetches the tribe.

I am getting strong again, and Livy is doing pretty well; So I suppose we should be content. But I am not content; for I cannot touch a pen without disabling my right shoulder. . . .

Susy reached 20 day before yesterday.[1]

Susy dear: Send your M.S. to the Editor of Century Magazine with stamps enough to pay the return of the M.S. in case it is not accepted. And don't be grieved or humiliated if it comes back. Don't be discouraged, but go on writing. There's literary success in you, and you will bring it out if you keep trying. I feel sure of that.[2]

I have been delighted to note your easy facility with your pen and proud to note also your literary superiorities of one kind and another—clearness of statement, directness, felicity of expression, photographic ability in setting forth an incident—style—good style—no barnacles on it in the way of unnecessary, retarding words (the shipman scrapes off the barnacles when he wants his racer to go her best gait and straight to the buoy.) You should write a letter every day, long or short—and so ought I, but I don't.[3]

NARRATOR: In April Joseph Verey, the courier, was sent back to Berlin to fetch the girls to Rome. From there they went to Florence, where they decided to lease a villa, the Villa Viviani, near Settignano, for the next winter.

They went on to Venice, where they met congenial friends from home, Sarah Orne Jewett, Mrs. James T. Fields, the Robert Underwood Johnsons and William Gedney Bunce, their friend in Paris in '79. Sam was in high feather and gave an evening of readings from Browning at the Hotel Danieli for his friends. Johnson recalls delightful hours sitting in St. Mark's Square, Sam telling stories. Susy refused to join the group. She stayed "in the hotel fuming and worrying."[4]

JOHNSON: The great humorist did most of the talking, the others only putting in a few words now and then by way of keeping him going. At this time he was deeply interested in occult things, dreams, second-sight, etc., and I remember that he told a remarkable story of a trip on the Mississippi River, when he was working as a pilot, including a circumstantial dream which he had, foreshadowing his brother's death, and how, when he reached his home, the details of this dream were found to be exact.[5]

NARRATOR: Sam had told the story of the tragic accident in which his brother, Henry, died, in *Life on the Mississippi*, but he waited years to write about the dream as he didn't want his mother to read the story. Sam was steersman on the *Pennsylvania*, a New Orleans and St. Louis packet, and he found Henry a job as a "mud" clerk. When the steamboat was in port in St. Louis, Sam slept at the Moffetts' house, but Henry's duties required him to sleep on board.

SAM: The dream begins when Henry had been mud clerk about three months. . . . On the night of the dream he started away at eleven, shaking hands with the family, and said good-by according to custom. . . . These good-bys were always executed in the family sitting room on the second floor, and Henry went from that room and downstairs without further ceremony. But this time my mother went with him to the head of the stairs and said good-by again. As I remember it, she was moved to this by something in Henry's manner, and she remained at the head of the stairs while he descended. When he reached the door he hesitated, and climbed the stairs and shook hands good-by again. In the morning, when I awoke, I had been dreaming, and the dream was so vivid, so like reality, that it deceived me, and I thought it *was* real. In the dream

I had seen Henry a corpse. He lay in a metallic burial case. He was dressed in a suit of my clothing, and on his breast lay a great bouquet of flowers, mainly white roses, with a red rose in the center. The casket stood upon a couple of chairs.[6]

NARRATOR: On the next trip Sam had a fight with the pilot and was left ashore at New Orleans. On the trip north the *Pennsylvania's* boilers exploded at Ship Island below Memphis. Henry was badly scalded but was expected to recover. He died from an overdose of morphine, and when Sam saw his body, his dream had come true.

SAM: The coffins provided for the dead were of unpainted white pine, but in this instance some of the ladies of Memphis had made up a fund of sixty dollars and bought a metallic case, and when I came back and entered the dead-room Henry lay in that open case, and he was dressed in a suit of my clothing. I recognized instantly that my dream of several weeks before was here exactly repro- duced, so far as these details went—and I think I missed one detail, but that one was immediately supplied, for just then an elderly lady entered the place with a large bouquet consisting mainly of white roses, and in the center of it was a red rose, and she laid it on his breast.[7]

NARRATOR: From Venice they headed north to Berlin and on to Bad-Nauheim, where Sam left Livy and the girls while he made another business trip back to the United States.

CLARA: Great effort was spent in seeking health for my mother, who suffered from heart disease [and goiter]. Among other places we tried Bad Nauheim, which Father rechristened "Bath No-Harm." Certainly, not much benefit was evident from this cure, and the spot was none too cheerful, except when the sun shone brilliantly. There was nothing to do but walk through the valley.[8]

NARRATOR: In America the Webster Company's liabilities were in- creasing and Paige had, he claimed, lined up Chicago capital and would start manufacturing in that city. Sam accomplished nothing material in the two weeks he was in the United States. He wrote an entertaining article, "All Sorts and Conditions of Ships," on the voyage back.

SAM: Livy is getting along pretty well, and the doctor thinks another summer here will cure her.

The Twichells have been here [Bad-Nauheim] four days and we have had good times with them. Joe and I ran over to Homburg, the great pleasure resort, Saturday, to dine with some friends, and in the morning I went walking in the promenade and met the

British Ambassador to the Court of Berlin, and he introduced me to the Prince of Wales, and I found him a most unusually comfortable and unembarrassing Englishman to talk with—quick to see the obscurest point, and equipped with a laugh which is spontaneous and catching.[9]

NARRATOR: Chauncey Depew was also in Homburg.

DEPEW: Brother Twain and I were walking on the concourse, where all Homburg meets to take the cure. He had the general appearance of a tramp. His trousers were too short, because they had been worn too long . . . and the sleeves of his coat had the same appearance; his linen was clean, but his hat was an old-timer. The Prince of Wales, the most companionable and tactful of all royalties, came along about that time and wanted to know who this apparition was. When informed it was Mark Twain he expressed a wish for an introduction. . . .

I was present at a dinner given by the Prince that evening, and his Royal Highness remarked, "I would have invited Mark Twain if I thought he had any clothes." I said Mark Twain had clothes, and he said, "Bring him down; I would be pleased to have him for dinner."[10]

SAM: Am invited by a near friend of his to meet him at dinner day after tomorrow, and there *could* be a good time, but the brass band will smash the talk and spoil everything.[11]

DEPEW: Many of the notables and all the wits of the place were present. . . . There was general expectation that Mark would give us original stories, which had not yet been published, and the raciest things in his repertoire. He, however, contributed nothing in the line which was expected until the end of the evening. Then he started out on a story which was a phenomenal success and received more laughter and applause than any he had ever told.[12]

SAM: We are expecting to move to Florence ten or twelve days hence, but if this hot weather continues we shall wait for cooler.[13]

We are in the clouds because the bath physicians say positively that Livy has no heart disease but has only weakness of the heart muscles and will soon be well again. That was worth going to Europe to find out.[14]

NARRATOR: Charley Langdon was planning to be in Europe and hoped to see the Clemenses, but Sam thought seeing him would upset Livy, who had gone to pieces when Sue Crane had returned to America.

SAM: I've seen the effects of the parting with Sue, and *that* has entirely decided *me*. It has set her back weeks. . . . It was not possible for a logy person like me to foresee what a disaster the parting with Sue was going to be. . . . Livy is going to pull through and come out sound and well, and these last few days have swung the family into line, and they are buckling to *help*, now, instead of standing apart and doubting their mother's wisdom and making her plans by that much harder to carry out.

We set out to oppose her going to Florence, and after giving her infinite trouble and worry and distress, found we had nothing to offer in the place of Florence that was even half-way rational; but are done, now, and have taken a back seat—that is, the children have; I am humbler, and have gone up in the gallery with the niggers. She will try Florence thirty days, and then if she wants to try the Polar Circle there is not going to be any opposition.[15]

NARRATOR: They left Nauheim the 10th of September.

SAM: We are breaking camp and leaving for Frankfort today, and expect to leave there for Florence next Tuesday. Our villa is equipped and the servants are in it—all except coachman and horses.[16]

NARRATOR: The weather continued warm so they stopped over in Lucerne at the Hotel des Balances.

SAM: We are two days out from Frankfort, now; and after a rest of two or three days here, we shall make another start if Mrs. Clemens is fit to travel. She is tortured with headaches which never cease, therefore railroading comes mighty hard.[17]

The children are all right. They paddle around a little, and drive—so do we all. Lucerne seems to be pretty full of tourists.[18]

We remained in Nauheim a little too long. If we had left four or five days earlier we should have made Florence in three days. Hard trip because it was one of those trains that gets tired every 7 minutes and stops to rest three-quarters of an hour. It took us 3½ hours to get there instead of the regulation 2 hours. We shall pull through to Milan to-morrow if possible. Next day we shall start at 10 A.M. and try to make Bologna, 5 hours. Next day, Florence, D.V. Next year we will walk.[19]

CLARA: Father [had] selected a villa about three miles from town, formerly occupied by the poet, d'Annunzio.[20]

SAM: It is a plain, square building, like a box, and is painted light yellow and has green window-shutters. It stands in a commanding position on the artificial terrace of liberal dimensions, which is walled around with masonry. From the walls the vineyards and olive orchards of the estate slant away toward the valley. There are several tall trees, stately stone-pines, also fig-trees and trees of breeds not familiar to me. Roses overflow the retaining-walls, and the battered and mossy stone urn on the gate-posts, in pink and yellow cataracts exactly as they do on the drop-curtains in the theaters. The house is a very fortress for strength. The main walls—all brick covered with plaster—are about 3 feet thick. I have several times tried to count the rooms of the house, but the irregularities baffle me. There seem to be 28. There are plenty of windows and worlds of sunlight. The floors are sleek and shiny and full of reflections, for each is a mirror in its way, softly imaging all objects after the subdued fashion of forest lakes. The curious feature of the house is the salon. This is a spacious and lofty vacuum which occupies the center of the house. All the rest of the house is built around it; it extends up through both stories and its roof projects some feet above the rest of the building. The sense of its vastness strikes you the moment you step into it and cast your eyes around it and aloft. There are 5 divans distributed along its walls. They make little or no show, though their aggregate length is 57 feet. A piano in it is a lost object. We have tried to reduce the sense of desert space and emptiness with tables and things, but they have a defeated look, and do not do any good. Whatever stands or moves under that soaring painted vault is belittled.[21]

We have been in the house several days, and certainly it is a beautiful place,—particularly at this moment, when the skies are a deep leaden color, the domes of Florence dim in the drizzling rain, and occasional perpendicular coils of lightning quivering intensely in the black sky about Galilee's [Galileo's] Tower. It is a charming panorama, and the most conspicuous towers and domes down in the city look to-day just as they looked when Boccaccio and Dante used to contemplate them from this hillock five and six hundred years ago. . . .

With the furniture in and the curtains up the house is very pretty, and not unhomelike. At mid-night last night we heard screams upstairs—Susy had set the lofty window curtains afire with a candle. This sounds kind of frightful, whereas when you come to think of it, a burning curtain or pile of furniture hasn't any element of danger about it in this fortress. There isn't any conceivable way to burn this house down, or enable a conflagration on one floor to climb to the next.

Mrs. Ross laid in our wood, wine and servants for us, and they are excellent.

NARRATOR: Mrs. Janet Ross lived in the Villa Castagnola and was their nearest neighbor. She was a writer and the daughter of Lady Duff Gordon, a noted Englishwoman of the early Victorian period.

SAM: She is a wonderful woman, and we don't quite see how or when we should have gotten under way without her.[22]

She had the house scoured from cellar to roof, the curtains washed and put up, all beds pulled to pieces, beaten, washed and put together again, and beguiled the Marchese [the owner] into putting a big porcelain stove in the vast central hall.[23]

That house had a room in it which was forty feet square and forty feet high, and at first we couldn't endure it. We called it the Mammoth Cave; we called it the skating-rink; we called it the Great Sahara; we called it all sorts of names intended to convey our disrespect. We had to pass through it to get from one end of the house to the other, but we passed straight through and did not loiter—and yet before long, and without our knowing how it happened, we found ourselves infesting that vast place day and night, and preferring it to any other part of the house.[24]

CLARA: The whole house was so large that a lot of time was wasted looking for different members of the family. Finally Father made the law that we should all assemble in the skating-rink every hour or two, if only for a moment.[25]

SAM: Even with the work and fuss of settling the house Livy has improved—and the best is yet to come. There is going to be absolute seclusion here—a hermit life, in fact. We (the rest of us) shall run over to the Ross's frequently and they will come here now and then and see Livy—that is all. Mr. [Willard] Fiske is away—nobody knows where—and the work on his house has been stopped and his servants discharged. Therefore we shall merely go Rossing —as far as society is concerned—shan't circulate in Florence until Livy shall be well enough to take a share in it.

This present house is modern. It is not much more than two centuries old; but parts of it, and also its foundations are of high antiquity. The fine beautiful family portraits—the great carved ones in the large ovals over the doors of the big hall—carry one well back into the past. One of them is dated 1305—he could have known Dante, you see. Another is dated 1343—he could have known Boccaccio and spent his afternoons in Fiesole listening to the Decameron tales. Another is dated 1463—he could have met Columbus. . . .

One person is satisfied with the villa, anyway. Jean prefers it to all Europe, save Venice. Jean is eager to get at the Italian tongue again, now, and I see that she has forgotten little or nothing of what she learned of it in Rome and Venice last spring.[26]

Thus far Jean is our only glib French scholar.[27]

I am the head French duffer of the family. Most of the talk goes over my head at the table. I catch only words, not phrases. When Italian comes to be substituted I shall be even worse off than I am now, I suppose.

This reminds me that this evening the German girl said to Livy, "Man hat mir gesagt dass Sie una candella verlaught habe"—unconsciously dropping in a couple of Italian words, you see. So *she* is going to join the polyglots, too, it appears. They say it is good entertainment to hear her and the butler talk together in their respective tongues, piecing out and patching up with the universal sign-language as they go along. Five languages in use in the house (including the sign-language—hardest-worked of them all) and yet with all this opulence of resource we do seem to have an uncommonly tough time making ourselves understood.

What we lack is a cat. If we only had Germania! That was the most satisfactory all-round cat I have seen yet. Totally ungermanic in the raciness of his character and in the sparkle of his mind and the spontaneity of his movements. We shall not look upon his like again.[28]

NARRATOR: The lack was soon remedied.

SAM: Il ghatto (the cat) has been running away and returning until he knows how, now. . . . He is a mighty small ghatto and very reserved and bony. His name is Michelangelo Buonarotti Botticelli, but he doesn't answer to it when he doesn't want to, and he never wants to.[29]

I take Clara to Berlin for the winter—music, mainly, with German and French added.[30]

NARRATOR: Clara was entered as a boarder in Mrs. Mary B. Willard's American School for Girls, 21 Nettelbeckstrasse, which the girls had attended as day students the previous winter. Mrs. Willard was a sister-in-law of the temperance advocate, Frances Willard.

CLARA: A bad storm broke over our heads the night of my departure for Berlin.[31]

SAM: The storm thundered away until night, and the rain came down in floods. For awhile there was a partial break, which furnished about such a sunset as will be exhibited when the Last Day comes and the universe tumbles together in wreck and ruin. I have never seen anything more spectacular and impressive.[32]

CLARA: [The storm] was the second dark incident of the day. That morning I was sitting in one of the bedrooms with Susy, when I heard her give a little stifled cry. Turning to look, I observed that she had blushed to the roots of her hair and way down her neck. Following the direction of her eyes, I saw Father standing in the door with his head clipped like a billiard ball. His wonderful hair all gone! No wonder Susy blushed. He looked more like a gatepost than himself . . . he must have consented to all this shorn beauty for the fun of seeing horror expressed not only in our faces, but also in the face of the artist who was painting his portrait at the time.[33]

SAM: Got my head shaved. This was a mistake.[34]

I seem able to forget everything except that I have had my head shaved. No matter how closely I shut myself away from draughts it seems to be always breezy up there. But the main difficulty is the flies. They like it up there better than anywhere else; on account of the view, I suppose. It seems to me that I have never seen any flies before that were shod like these. These appear to have talons. Wherever they put their foot down they grab. They walk over my head all the time and cause me infinite torture. It is their park, their club, their summer resort. They have garden parties there, and conventions, and all sorts of dissipation. And they fear nothing. All flies are daring, but these are more daring than those of other nationalities. These cannot be scared away by any device. They are more diligent, too, than the other kinds; they come before daylight and stay till after dark.[35]

NARRATOR: This was not the first time that Sam had tormented a portrait painter in such a way. He was very proud of his hair; Katy used to massage his head every day and he took great care of it, "thoroughly scouring it with soap and water every morning, then rinsing it well; then lathering it heavily, and rubbing off the lather with a coarse towel, a process which leaves a slight coating of oil upon each hair."[36]

Sam took Clara to Berlin and returned to his lonely family.

LIVY: The house is empty, *empty,* EMPTY and it is very hard for Susy and me to settle ourselves to doing anything. We want to sit down and cry all the time. . . . When I think that for eight or nine months I am not to hear your dear voice say "of course" or "that's the point" it seems as if I could *not live* so long without you. Yet it is right and I am glad to have you go where you can pursue your music as you desire to.[37]

SUSY: I have missed you *terribly* and it was dreadfully hard to see you go, but still *for your sake* I am very very glad that you could. I am sure you will have a lovely profitable winter. I do hope you will write soon and tell all about your trip. . . .

Your photographs have come and they are simply *stunning!* We have put them up on the piano.[38]

SAM: We are getting wonted. The open fires have driven away the cold and the doubt, and now a cheery spirit pervades the place. Livy and the Kings and Mademoiselle have been taking their tea a number of times, lately, on the open terrace with the city and the hills and the sunset for company.[39]

SUSY: Grace [King] has arrived and she is her old fascinating self.[40]

GRACE KING: Mr. Clemens was waiting for us at the station in Florence grumbling at the delay of the train "always late, except when you counted upon it to be late." His house, the Villa Viviani, lay on the road to Settignano, beyond the walls of Florence. The road was long and the evening dark. But there was a blaze of light awaiting us when the carriage stopped, and a warm welcome. The household was assembled in the doorway, Livy, Susy, and Jean. . . .

There was no time to look around, dinner was served immediately. We talked as fast as we could, but dinner came to an end while we were still at the beginning of our experiences, so much more interesting when related to friends than we had found them in fact.[41]

SUSY: We enjoy her immensely. I never heard so brilliant a woman talker.[42]

GRACE KING: Susy Clemens was at this time exquisitely pretty, but frail-looking. Her health was always an anxiety to her mother and father.[43]

[She] was now twenty, in the full bloom of her delicate blonde beauty and her delicately fine intellect. We took great delight in her company and in her fresh, outspoken, naïve thoughts. On account of her delicacy, her mother would not send her away from home as she had done with the hardy, practical Clara. She was, in truth, to use a frequently misused term, a rare soul, ethereal and unworldly, and perfectly unconscious of self. She was ever seeking something, craving something, she could not find; and meeting only disappointment. She panted for music which was divine, and her heart, in its thirst, was a dying flower. She dwelt apart from us, and joined us for the drive into Florence but seldom. She had a pretty soprano voice, and took singing lessons in the city; and she studied French with a remarkable teacher, Mademoiselle Lanson.[44]

SUSY: She [Grace] looks a good deal older to me and she has lost a great deal of her hair, so that she can't arrange it nearly as effectively, as she did. It's too bad! She has been very nice to me and we have had one nice long talk. She took a tremendous fancy to the way I arrange *my* hair and can't say enough in praise of it, which you can imagine was a great surprise to me, poor me with my hair which usually dissatisfies all parties![45]

GRACE KING: In Berlin, where her father and mother were received by the Kaiser, she was taken to a court ball, a most brilliant function. She showed the pretty silk dress that she had worn, made by a great modiste, but she had not enjoyed the function. It had bored her, in fact. She loathed the memory of it and hated her pretty dress. She had received no attention save as the daughter of Mark Twain.

"How I hate that name! I should like never to hear it again! My father should not be satisfied with it! He should not be known by it! He should show himself the great writer that he is, not merely a funny man. Funny! That's all the people see in him—a maker of funny speeches!"

Thus she walked in the clouds, like a goddess.

At the time, Mr. Clemens was writing his *Joan of Arc*, and he too complained, as Susy did, that he could not be taken as a serious writer, and he shuddered at the idea that his Joan might be considered funny, when it was meant to be serious history. And he would not sign his name to it—vain precaution![46]

NARRATOR: While pacing the floor one day, Sam said to Livy, "I shall never be accepted seriously over my own signature. People always want to laugh over what I write and are disappointed if they don't find a joke in it. This is to be a serious book. It means more to me than anything I have undertaken. I shall write it anonymously."[47]

GRACE KING: He read aloud several chapters from his manuscript one night after dinner, watching our faces anxiously. But in spite of our assurances to the contrary, he wrote as Mark Twain, not as Michelet. Mrs. Clemens did not share his doubts nor Susy's criticisms. Her great eyes shone with emotion and admiration as he read. . . .

Some evenings were given over to pure fun, when Susy, an inimical mimic, would parody scenes from Wagner's operas and Mr. Clemens would give an imitation of a ballet dancer, posturing, throwing kisses, and making grimaces, while Susy played a waltz on the piano.[48]

NARRATOR: Grace and her sister, Nannie, did not wear well with Susy.

SUSY: . . . they . . . the very saints in *heaven* couldn't get on with them! I don't know whether I wrote . . . how aggravating and cantankerous they were the last part of their visit. They were always sure we had treated them "impolitely" in some way or other.[49]

NARRATOR: Everyone was cheered by the sight of Sam's hair growing.

SAM: My hair is showing up again. It is about as long as a door-mat's, now, and just booming—very thick and tough, and never a hair comes out. But last summer it used to come out by the hatful.

I'm a worker, these days! I wrote 6,000 words on my new novel in 13 hours, yesterday [December 1st]; and I consider 2,000 an honest day's work. The family say yesterday's chapters are the best I've turned out yet.[50]

I stop work, a few minutes, as a rule, when the sun gets down to the hilltops west of Florence, and join the tea-group to wonder and exclaim. There is always some new miracle in the view, a new and exquisite variation in the show, a variation which occurs every 15 minutes between dawn and night. Once early in the morning, a multitude of white villas not before perceived, revealed themselves on the far hills; then we recognized that all those great hills are snowed *thick* with them, clear to the summit.

The variety of lovely effects, the infinitude of change, is something not to be believed by any who has not seen it. No view that I am acquainted with in the world is at all comparable to this

for delicacy, charm, exquisiteness, dainty coloring, and bewildering rapidity of change. It keeps a person drunk with pleasure all
the time. Sometimes Florence ceases to be substantial, and becomes just a faint soft dream, with domes and towers of air, and
one is persuaded that he might blow it away with a puff of his
breath.

Livy is progressing admirably. This is just the place for her.[51]

LIVY: Susy is taking singing lessons and her father and I feel that
she is making good progress.[52]

SUSY: I have just been in to my first singing lesson. Oh, but I have
dreaded it! I finally decided to take of *Vanuccini* after all, for
he seems to stand so far above all the rest here, and Teety said he
was one of the great teachers of the world with a world-wide
reputation. Don't let Moszkowski [Clara's teacher] know I didn't
follow his recommendation. Vanuccini is a fat genial kindly old
gentleman that I liked very much. He seemed pleased with my
voice, said it was very sweet, very high, and very true, and that I
would sing "tres agreablement." This verdict is certainly all I
expected and more. So I am out of suspense for the present and am
to take a lesson a week from now on. . . .

I am interested in reading and writing but I *am* blue a good
deal, I must confess, and lonely and anxious for a taste of "the
rage of *living*." Reading all day *can* get tiresome. As for writing I
never think of that nowadays. I should love to, but I can't now
anyway, and I don't ever expect to be able to.[53]

LIVY: I find that a great deal of my time is taken up visiting with
Susy. She sits down in my room and we talk and talk and so the
hours fly. She has three or four pleasant young girl acquaintances
but of course no close friends so I have to try to make up to her
as well as I can for that. She is pretty well this winter although
she is not quite as strong as I could wish, she gets easily tired.[54]

NARRATOR: Susy wrote to Clara.

SUSY: Your last letter was immensely interesting as all your others
have been. . . .

Oh that Berlin life is perfection! ! ! . . .

I am glad glad Blackie that you are in beloved Berlin and I
hope you are *happy*. I wouldn't have you back here for anything
much as I miss you because I am sure you are better off where you
are.[55]

SAM: The first month is finished. We are wonted now. This carefree life at a Florentine villa is an ideal existence. The weather is divine, the outside aspects lovely, the days and nights tranquil and re- poseful, the seclusion from the world and its worries as satisfactory as a dream. Late in the afternoon friends come out from the city and drink tea in the open air and tell what is happening in the world; and when the great sun sinks down upon Florence and the daily miracle begins they hold their breath and look. It is not a time for talk.[56]

NARRATOR: From little-girl adoration, Susy and Clara had moved to finding life with father difficult.

SUSY: I have to go down to breakfast now and I don't enjoy this one bit, altho Papa hasn't *stormed* yet. Still I feel constrained and he pierces me thru with his eyes as if he were determined to see whether I am embarrassed or not. Ah well, I will keep sewing and reading and trying to make the best of everything but I must say it's a good deal of an effort.[57]

CLARA: He was a constant surprise in his varied moods, which dropped unheralded upon him, creating day or night for those about him by his twinkling eyes or his clouded brows. How he would be affected by this or that no one could ever foresee.[58]

NARRATOR: Clara's delight in Berlin and its gaiety was almost de- pressing to Livy; it seemed to her as if Clara were gone for good. Susy undertook to modify Clara's epistolary exuberance.

SUSY: I have just one little suggestion to make to you and you mustn't mind it will you? Enthuse just as much as you *want* to about Berlin in your letters to *me* but not *quite* so much in your letters to *Mamma*. Your last letter to her where you speak of having such a perfect time and wanting to stay till July etc. made her cry her eyes out nearly. She thought you didn't care any more for her or any of us or—"Why did you want to stay away?" Now you know Blackie *I* understand how you feel *perfectly* and your love for music and how it makes you want to stay in Berlin *forever* as long as you know we're all well. But *she* doesn't, she can't. She never has had any great artistic interest and she can't understand why it should make you *want* to stay away from her. So after this write *me* all the questions about plans and so on and don't dwell on wanting to stay away in your letters to her.[59]

NARRATOR: Susy's own musical interests were not always as fully satisfied as Clara's.

SAM: Poor Susy, she can't go to the Mascagni Opening night at the Opera this evening [November 10th]—for two reasons: no places to be had, and the 6-franc boxes are put up to 120 francs. I am thinking of writing an Opera myself—just an opening-night 120-franc Opera, you know, not one of the staying kind. I can't write the staying kind, but I am capable of the other sort.[60]

NARRATOR: Sam wrote a poem to Livy on her birthday.

THE EARTH INVOKETH THE SUN

(To Livy, November 27, 1892)

If that rich source were not,
    My robes were stript from me!
    My fields would naked lie,
    My flowers fade and die.
All bare my world would be,
If that rich source were not.

If that warm ray grew cold,
    My saps would cease in me,
    My dews turn sleet and snow,
    And chill the winds would blow.
Full drear my world would be
If that sweet sun grew cold.

If that dear light should pale,
    My skies were lost to me!—
    My summits drown'd in night,
    My valleys hid from sight.
All dark my world would be
If that sweet light should fail.[61]

SUSY: We went to "La Traviata" last night and enjoyed it immensely. It was really most beautiful.

NARRATOR: Susy solved one problem: she had breakfast in her room.

SUSY: I am getting on very peacefully here, *unberufen!* I have been reserved because I was superstitious and afraid if I *said* anything matters might change. . . .

I don't ever go downstairs to breakfast and things go on very peacefully (unberufen!)

NARRATOR: Susy may have been leading a quiet life, compared to Clara's experiences as related in her ecstatic letters, but she soon became interested in various activities.

Susy: My old religious feeling has suddenly come back to me and I
find going to church and reading the Bible the greatest comfort.
I am lonely often but I don't seem to have those strange moods
any more. (unberufen!) I can feel I am not so queer or so nervous
and that mental difficulty has left me. The English Episcopal
Church is the one we go to and the service is perfectly beautiful,
and the minister *very* fine. Now that I am reading the New Testa-
ment again after so long a time of not reading it, it seems to me like
a new impression, a *revelation,* as beautiful, beautiful and *wonderful* beyond words. I read one Chapter in the morning and two at
night. Betty has a big roaring fire made when I come up to bed so
it isn't lonely at all but cosy and cunning up here, and when I put
out the lights the firelight dances over the ceiling as it used to
Xmas eves at home. . . .

   Today we have perfect weather and Lina Duff Gordon is coming
to lunch. She and I have joined a very amusing dancing class which
we go to twice a week on Tuesdays and Thursdays. The teacher
is a ballet dancer and we are learning the Tarantella and a lot
of fancy things with tambourines. The music is good and we dance
common dances to last twenty minutes, so it's great fun and I
enjoy it very much. . . .

   Mlle. and I went to Mrs. Fahnstock's on last Sunday. It was the
only interesting tea I have been to. There were many young
people present and music, two singers and some piano playing by
Miss Fahnstock, sister in law of the hostess. The singing was
excellent and the piano playing correct, but utterly without passion or any sort of *abandon.* I disliked Miss Fahnstock extremely.
She was all dressed up in a pale blue evening rig and posed, and
flourished about with many airs and graces. But she received
very little attention to my great satisfaction. . . . Well we came
away having had a very delightful afternoon with no dragging
minutes.

Narrator: In the back of their minds there was always the question: "When will we go home?"

Susy: I can't see that there's the least prospect of our going to
America next year, so you [Clara] will most likely return to the
Willards next winter anyway.[62]

Livy: I wish I could say that we are going home next Fall but I do
not know I fear it may be an other year yet. There are reasons

why I should be glad to stay but more reasons why I should be most happy to turn my face homeward.[63]

SAM: [We] shall hope to have visits in our house when we get back—which will be by and by, we don't know when, yet.[64]

LIVY: She [Susy] does not feel that her voice amounts to anything.[65]

SUSY: I am very busy and making real progress in my French I think. —Regarding my singing,—I practise regularly and *get* the lessons and the songs so that Vanuccini seems satisfied, but I don't see much change in that strange little voice of mine![66]

NARRATOR: Christmas came.

SUSY: This Xmas week is very crowded even for us living out here "Up at a villa". We have been in town all the morning doing shopping, Mlle. Jean and I. . . .

I like Mlle. *immensely* much better than I did when the Kings were here. She is very easy to get on with. . . .

I have Mamma's presents at *last* and feel so relieved tho' I am not at all sure they are what she will like—a jar to hold her plant in the centre of the great hall, and "Cosmopolis" by Paul Bourget, prettily illustrated. . . .

Florence didn't look especially gay this morning [December 22nd], but the photograph shops are pretty.[67]

NARRATOR: Clara reported elegant holiday festivities in Berlin.

SUSY: Your description of Thanksgiving was perfectly fascinating and evidently Xmas is going to be just as delightful there at 21 Nettelbeck which seems to be a most lovely place.[68]

I suppose Berlin is simply *rachant,* and *exciting* and wintry! I can just imagine the Berlin streets and the crowds and the life!!!

We are going to celebrate here on Christmas *eve* so as to make it as unlike home as possible. I think people are more in the mood, more sort of *thawed* out at night anyway.[69]

SAM: Great times here last night. Jean had a tree and it was a very nice one indeed. The servants all came in and smiled; and that and the candles made the place almost uncomfortably bright.[70]

The Mademoiselle is a great help to Livy in the housekeeping, and is a cheery and cheerful presence in the house. The butler is equipped with a little French, and it is this fact that enables the house to go—but it won't go *well* until the family get some sort of facility with the Italian tongue, for the cook, the woman-of-all-work and the coachman understand only that. It is a stubborn and devilish language to learn, but Jean and the others will master it. Livy's German Nauheim girl is the worst off of anybody, as there is no market for her tongue at all among the help.[71]

NARRATOR: Jean was unwell in December; Sam blamed her trouble on her love for horses.

SAM: Jean's got some kind of a horse-complaint. I don't know what it is, but I think it's the Horse-Kiss-Hives. It comes out on the mouth, and is not becoming.[72]

NARRATOR: Sam's Christmas present from the family was a set of cuff links.

SAM: I have some new sleeve-buttons . . . beautiful anticussers. You can put them in and take them out without change of temper. They are scarabei—that is to say, tumble-bugs of cornelian, set in gold, and very handsome, with patent antiblasphemers attached on the under side.[73]

NARRATOR: Clara sent him handkerchiefs.

SAM: Dear old Ben: I thank you ever so much for the elegant handkerchiefs, although it does give me a little pang of pain every time I think of your taking time to work at them when you are entitled to use that time for a holiday, you who are so crowded with work. I love you for it, but you mustn't rob yourself that way any more.

I am going to get up a scheme whereby I may get the use of the handkerchiefs sometimes. Jean wears out all my handkerchiefs, and I seldom can find anything in my box but a square hole with a rag border around it.[74]

LIVY: Clara is absolutely happy and content in Berlin with her music. I judge from what Moszkowsky says to her that he is well content with the progress that she is making.[75]

SAM: It may take Clara another year to finish her musical studies in Berlin. She has made great progress and wants to continue. She . . . is having a marvelously good time.

Which I'm afraid Susy isn't, for she is . . . away out here on the hills overlooking Florence, which is three miles away—by measurement, but forty in fact, as I realize when I have to drive down there twice a month—though it's the coming back which is the long way, being up hill and always after dark. Susy goes to the theatre and the opera, and that helps to ease the dulness of eternal study. To me this serene and noiseless life out here, with the unimaginable beauty of the view—which is never twice the same, for God persistently neglects the rest of His universe to play with the sun and get up "effects" and show off what He can do here—is heaven, and I want to stay in this one when I die, on account of doubts about being a pet in the other one, there's so many people gone there who know about me and will talk, of course. I can work here every day in the month; there is no feeling of dulness or laziness or lack of interest—so I have ground out mighty stacks of manuscript in these 3½ months, and some day I mean to publish some of it. But not the book I am in the middle of now—that is private and not for print, it's written for love and not for lucre, and to entertain the family with, around the lamp by the fire (the day's chapter of the tale, the day's product of "work" as this sort of literary dreaming has been miscalled).[76]

Every book, from Huck Finn and Prince and Pauper on, was read to the household critics chapter by chapter nightly as it was written. Joan was thus read: the first half at the Villa Viviana [Viviani] winter of '92-3.[77]

SUSY: Papa is progressing finely with his "Joan of Arc" which promises to be his loveliest book. Perhaps even more sweet and beautiful than "The Prince and the Pauper." The character of Joan is pure and perfect to a miraculous degree. Hearing the M.S. read aloud is an uplifting and revealing hour to us all. Many of Joan's words and sayings are historically correct and Papa cries when he reads them. In fact he almost always fills up when reading any speech of hers. Mademoiselle has decided that he loves two women—Mamma in the present, and Joan retrospectively. Father is very happy here. He is devoted to the villa and the quiet and his writing. All things considered the villa seems the best living arrangement we have found, since leaving our beloved home in America.[78]

NARRATOR: Jean's aptitude for languages was remarkable.

SAM: Jean is a big girl, now, though still a child—12½. She is a colt for play and out-door activities, and a fanatic for indoor study. When she talks German, it is a German talking—manner and all; when she talks French she is French—gestures, shrugs and all, and she is entirely at home in both tongues. She is getting a good start in Italian and will make it her property presently.[79]

NARRATOR: The winter before, in Berlin, the Clemenses had seen a good deal of General Von Versen and his wife; Frau Von Versen was a distant relative, a Clemens from St. Louis, and her husband was attached to the Emperor's Court. They gave brilliant parties and Clara attended a ball at their house during the Christmas holidays. Her description of the gay party shocked Livy and Sam. He wrote her, mincing no words.

SAM: Clara dear, your letter brought strong delight in your pleasure, but at the same time a deep sense of regret. From the outspoken frankness with which you tell about excluding yourself with forty officers, one is compelled to believe that you did not know any better—if that is much of a palliation. The average intelligent American girl who had never crossed the ocean would know better than to do that in America. It would be an offence against propriety there—then what name shall it be called by when done in Berlin—I mean, of course, by an American girl, for what European girl would dream of doing it? Are not the ways of American girls in Europe matter of common talk over here? Is it possible that you have heard none of it? Of the forty officers was there one, old or young, who would have allowed his daughter or sister to stay in your place a minute? Was there occasion to add yourself to the list of American girls who bring their country into disrepute? Didn't it occur to you that there was but one course for you to pursue—leave that room the moment you found yourself the only representative of your sex in it? I wish to impress upon you one thing so that it will stay: that an American girl in Europe cannot offend in the least degree against the proprieties of these countries and not get herself talked about. The obscurest girl cannot escape—then what is to be the result with the conspicuous—that is to say, with the relative of a full General of the German army and my daughter? There is not an American girl in Berlin who cannot better afford to make her conduct a matter of criticism than you. Your privilege in this regard is the narrowest of them all. If you would not have yourself and us talked about, there is but one course for you—to make yourself acquainted at the earliest moment, with the nicest shades of what is allowable by German custom and keep strictly within the boundaries of it for the future. Do not expose the fact again that you do not know what the canons of the country are. I heard the free ways of "Willard girls" at concerts criticised more than once at our table over a year ago. I think it should have made an impression on you.

Are you going to other balls?—and to operas and concerts?

Then post yourself, right away—and not surfacely, but thoroughly. It is worth the trouble.

We love you, and are proud of your talents, and we want you to be a lady—a lady above reproach—a lady always, modest and never loud, never hoydenish—a lady recognizable as such at a glance, everywhere, indoors and out. If you have any friends who are short of this pattern you cannot afford their society—for one's intimacies either refine or corrupt—this is a commonplace.

Watch yourself at Miss Phelps's ball—be conspicuous for not being conspicuous; let no canon of perfect breeding suffer by you.

With worlds of love—and sorrow, too, for feeling obliged to afflict you.

Papa.

NARRATOR: Susy wrote, too, for the tenderhearted Livy, who did not feel well enough to write.

SUSY: Blackie dear; I am writing this for Mamma as an explanation of Papa's letter to you, which I suppose has reached you by this time. You mustn't misunderstand Papa's letter or think he's *severe* or *angry* or anything of the sort, for he was delighted that you had a good time at the Von Versen ball, and the only trouble is, he *cannot* make out *how* you happened to take your dinner *alone* with forty officers! Mamma wants you to write me or her some explanation of it, and of how it came about, and then as she feels sure that it was entirely improper and will be talked about all over Berlin she thinks perhaps you had better take papa's letter to Frau Von Versen and let her read it and say to her "Frau Von Versen, *did* I do anything out of the way at your house, *was* it not comme il faut? etc.," so that she can see that *you* were innocent and meant no harm, and also that papa and mamma have brought you up in the right way. Mamma says that the minute you saw there were only officers in the room you should have gotten up and asked your partner to take you to the rest of the ladies. Don't be cross at me, Blackie, I am not preaching. I'm only writing all this for Mamma.

I think you must have had a beautiful time and all that, but you know that even in *Carmen* when she is drinking healths with the officers in the second act she has her aunts there present as chaperones. I am perplexed as Mamma and Papa. I cannot understand how you got into such a position!!! Mamma says that if you dined alone with forty officers that *eighty* knew it before the end of the evening and all Berlin the next day! She is afraid you have injured your reputation.[80] She wants all the particulars you can give her. I am very sorry to write you this troublesome letter after your sweet enthusiastic ones, but it seems to be necessary. Do not forget a minute that we are all sympathetic and are glad to hear of your good times.

NARRATOR: In their worried state over Clara's behavior, Sam suggested sending Susy to spend the rest of the winter with Clara; this proposal appealed to neither girl.

SUSY: Papa wanted me to go to Berlin and be with you because he thought I would have more gayety.[81]

NARRATOR: Susy did not want to go to Berlin; she was beginning to enjoy herself in Florence.

SUSY: A good many things have happened here lately in a social way and I have been quite gay, but don't feel any more excited than I did before. . . . I have been to two balls and once or twice to the theater.

NARRATOR: She met a Count de Calry at a tea; sometimes he was most attentive.

SUSY: He *is* a fascinating man altogether the most fascinating person I have met in Europe.[82]

De Calry is a married man! My goodness yes, married to the homeliest woman in existence, a rich American. I am afraid he does not love her, poor thing, but she worships him.[83]

NARRATOR: But de Calry was not always attentive.

SUSY: At the balls, in both cases I had very *pleasant* times, nothing more or less. I danced plenty and two young fellows seemed attracted by me, but as they were most unattractive to me, this bored and repelled me rather than anything else. My great disappointment which spoiled everything for me, and which I can't get over was that at the Corsini ball the Count de Calry with whom I am really smitten never came near me or asked me to dance with him *once*. It was a marked discourtesy, for he knew I was to be there and had talked to me about wanting to dance with me at teas and lunches where I had met him two or three times before. He expects to have a dance soon, and I don't know whether to accept it or not, now. . . . I cannot understand his performances. Not long ago he didn't visit our box at the Opera when he should and when I met him next I was so cold and distant *(actually!)* that he finally made a most meek and humble apology and was all attention for the rest of the time.

NARRATOR: Lina Duff Gordon admired de Calry, too.

SUSY: He has sent admiring messages through Lina Duff Gordon to me, and then through me to Lina. I can't make him out yet. Lina and I are mystified about him, and are anxious to meet him together, once. . . .

Florence is certainly attractive. The weather is charming. I have grown fond of it here.

NARRATOR: Even a remote romantic interest was therapeutic.

SUSY: I am very busy and for the most part peaceful and contented, unberufen. I have come to the sure conclusion that to get on at all in this world one must be as nearly right *oneself* as possible. Asking one's family to make allowances for one, because one is nervous or unhappy isn't the proper idea. People won't make allowances so one must not act either nervous or unhappy. I believe it is useless *perfectly* useless to expect help or sympathy from others. One must be *sufficient unto oneself*. This is what I am trying to learn, what I expect to learn in time. Now when I have a quarrel with anyone, I don't waste time thinking how unjust *they* were, I just realize that if I had been reasonable and not a *fool* I could have escaped the difference. I don't build any more castles in the air or wish that things might be different. In fact I cannot feel really that things *will* ever be much different. As for a great change, marriage or sudden real happiness—*those* things have grown to seem far far out of reach and quite *impossible*. So I don't think about them any more, or *very* rarely and then not at all as I used to.[84]

NARRATOR: Since Christmas, Clara had lost her enthusiasm for Berlin; she talked of coming back to Florence where life sounded very pleasant.

SUSY: I know so well what that feeling is of being tired of people and I think it generally comes because we are tired ourselves, and we seem to have nothing to give people.

Do think well before you plan to exchange the life of the Villa Viviani for the life of that great Berlin!! Much as I should enjoy having you here I cannot but feel that you do not realize what you are doing when you plan to come. You know I have grown to be contented here and become less lonely gradually, *gradually*, slowly, *very* slowly and even yet I have dreadfully lonely times altho' I have of course grown so used to the place in these six months. But *you!* Why my dear Blackie, I assure you you would be *wretched* here coming straight from Berlin or any other large city for that matter. I really cannot bear to have you make the experiment for I feel *sure* you would be so *unhappy*. Of course I can only judge from *my* experience. I am contented here much of the time and satisfied but with me it is different for entre nous I have rather given up expecting much real happiness constructed as I am and all. But you have your music, your work, your talent and your natural good luck; so why should you come here when you might as well stay in a gayer freer place? Clara, my *dear* Clara, be careful what you do! You know how you will be fretted here by the family discipline, after the freedom of the Willard school. You seem to *forget* the life of the Villa Viviani. What *are* you thinking of? . . .

I am absolutely mystified and in the dark. But I feel perfectly sure, perfectly certain that if you come to the Villa Viviani any sooner than you positively *have* to, you make a big, big, big mistake!!!!!!

NARRATOR: Clara stayed in Berlin; happiness for Susy depended largely on whether she saw de Calry. As was customary in Florentine society, the Clemens ladies had a day "at home" each week. The rest of the afternoons Livy and Susy went to their friends' "at homes."

SUSY: I haven't seen de Calry. . . . No one came out on Wednesday. We sat up in state dressed in our best the whole afternoon waiting and no one appeared! I have been to the usual number of teas this week, and as usual was almost always the only young person present. Florence society consists of *old* people's teas. It's too funny! No dances, no lunches, no dinners—just teas! Papa is invited to an occasional dinner but I am almost never included. . . . So it is still read read read! and sew, sew, sew![85]

NARRATOR: Out in the carriage one day, Livy and the girls had a scare.

SAM: Driving from Prato this afternoon [March 4th], a child darted across the road under the noses of the horses, was knocked down, and disappeared. Vitorio pulled the horses to a dead standstill, suddenly, and men ran out to gather up the remains. The child was actually not hurt. The men pulled it out from under the carriage and stood it on its feet. A singular escape. The family were well frightened.[86]

SUSY: Florence grows more and more attractive. Today is like a day in May. The carnival time is here and the people crowd the

sunny streets in holiday costume wearing masks. . . . You know
I've grown awfully fond of Florence in a way, in a certain way
fonder than I was of Berlin. . . . The truth is I have had more
real peace here than I ever had in Berlin. . . . I think the people
here are more interesting than they were in Berlin. But next
summer I can compare Florence and Berlin more easily.[87]

I have been to two balls lately. They were pleasant, both of
them. The palace was interesting and beautiful, the guests
brilliantly dressed and the Princess was charming, simple and
sweet. The young Duke of Aosta was present and looked like
a gay, good-natured boy much bored with all the forms and
ceremonies. At the ball before this one he became so tired of
the slow, sedate quadrille that he proposed the dancers should
dance through the last three or four figures on ONE foot. Since
this was his request it had to be carried out, although he and
his partner were the only young people in the set, all the rest being
ladies and gentlemen between sixty and seventy. Nevertheless
they managed to hop through the dance on one foot. The Duke
was afterwards severely reproved by the King for requiring such
an unheard-of thing and his conduct at the ball last night was
very dignified in consequence. You can imagine, Clara, how tickled
Papa was over the Duke's jest. My! how he did laugh![88]

NARRATOR: Sam went out in society very little; he was writing
steadily and *Joan of Arc* commanded an enormous amount of
research.

SAM: I could not get the Quicherat and some of the other books in
English and I had to dig them out of the French.[89]

SUSY: Today is our reception day (Wednesday) and we expect a
good many people out because it is tolerably fair weather and it
usually rains on Wed. There is the rarest possibility that The
Count de Calry may appear, which fact puts me in a state of
discomfort and trepidation for I really don't know how to treat
the man after his rudeness at the Corsini ball. Lina and I have as
yet received no invitation from him to a dance. . . .

Wed. is over and de Calry didn't come. Now I am wondering
when and where I shall meet him next. When he first met me
here he seemed taken with me and I thought it would last but
might have known better for no one ever stays fascinated with
me . . . he is quite different entirely unlike the people who have
generally charmed us. His is not the cold mysterious Stanchfield

style altho' he has plenty of reserve of course. He talks much and with an immense chic and cachée. . . . His hands are beautiful and he uses them constantly in quick magnetic gestures. He looks at you with a strange sort of distant caressingness and often gets very near you. Then suddenly he stops short and is quite silent and at such times he is apt to droop and quiver his eyelids a little.

NARRATOR: Livy was also fascinated with de Calry.

SUSY: When he calls she seems quite engrossed with him. Last time she said, "Count de Calry I hope you will come out here Wednesdays whenever you feel inclined," at which he bowed and said "Thank you for the privilege". . . . When you expect him to say much he says little and when you expect him to say little he says much. He is always unexpected. He talks philanthropy and republicanism. He is proud of being very fond of America. When he is going to pass some little criticism on America he usually says—"Pray do not misunderstand me, Miss Clemens, I say this in all good faith for after the kindness I met with in America, I certainly cannot criticise it seriously *in any way shape or form!*"[90]

SUSY'S TWENTY-SECOND YEAR

1893-1894

NARRATOR: Sam wrote his sister-in-law, Sue Crane, in Elmira, March 19th.

SAM: This is Susy's birthday and she is 21—facts which will be drifting through your mind as you sit at your breakfast three hours from now—and there will be pictures drifting with the facts, —and ghosts. Well-a-day!

I dreamed I was born, and grew up, and was a pilot on the Mississippi, and a miner, and journalist in Nevada, and a pilgrim in the Quaker City, and had a wife and children and went on to live in a Villa out of Florence—and this dream goes on and on and on, and sometimes seems so real that I almost believe it *is* real. I wonder if it is? But there is no way to tell; for if one applied tests, *they* would be part of the dream too, and so would simply aid the deceit. I wish I knew whether it is a dream or real.

Betty [Livy's maid] the perfect-tempered, left last night for Bad-Nauheim—her mother is dying. It is only a dream, probably, and doubtless there is no Betty and no mother; but it all has the effect of reality. Jean cried a good deal.[1]

SUSY: I don't enjoy being twenty one at all. I have ignored my birthday as much as possible in my own mind. Mamma gave me the most exquisite little pearl necklace with a clasp of sapphire set in diamonds.

NARRATOR: She wrote Clara.

SUSY: I am so glad, you dear little thing, so very glad that you didn't take anything from your cramped allowance to get me a birthday present with. I am most happy to take the will for the deed and greatly prefer to in this case. It was sweet of you to send me a letter on my birthday and I *did* enjoy it so much, *every, single solitary* word of it!

Your life sounds so absolutely profitable and wholesome and ideal. You are really to be envied in it. I don't doubt you're an eloquent little orator by this time. I assure you I couldn't utter a syllable on the silver question or any other such complicated and profound subject. I am filled with awe at your Willard school table-talk. . . .

I live as busily and profitably as possible tho' my life isn't as finely systematized as yours. I still do my translating from the French and this with my reading and sewing and studying keeps me occupied. I haven't been very well this winter having had queer times of feeling faint, but I am so much better off in my *mind* that I am endlessly grateful. I can see now that up to this time I have been pretty much the same as *crazy*. I think I am much changed now. (unberufen!) . . .

You make me smile with your explanation of de Calry's conduct.

Oh mercy, I have given you an entirely false impression of the whole situation! There never was the slightest *approach* to *love* in his relation toward me! Oh goodness, no never! Not at first even when he was most attentive. He was merely gallant and pleasant and full of gentlemanly admiration. But he's too much of an egotist to fall in love with *anyone*. He's not that kind. He may flirt a little with young women in general. But there is nothing serious in his attitude *ever*. Besides I have seen him with his wife and he apparently loves her. Oh no, my dear sister, your explanation is miles out of the way as you would see if you were here. Mamma thinks as I do that he is a rather ill bred spoiled capricious man who doesn't take the trouble of being polite except when he wants to.

Mlle. L[anson]. and I are going in to a tea at the Countess Riccardi's today and he *may* be there. It is perfect weather now, the sky is that delicate fragile blue, just the right day to go into Florence.[2]

NARRATOR: The family made plans to leave Florence for a while; Livy and the girls were going to Venice.

SAM: I am busy getting ready to sail the 22d, in the Kaiser Wilhelm II.[3]

SUSY: The time for our departure to Venice is drawing near. . . . I feel quite in the mood of going now but didn't as much at first. Here, it is warm, sunny, *heavenly!* the garden is simply a little paradise. I have been out strolling between the green hedges and picking the flowers. I have a great gorgeous pink camelia lying by me on the table. When we come back everything will be out and summer will be at our doors. Isn't it *wonderful?* . . . The birds have been singing all the morning.

NARRATOR: Count de Calry did attend the Riccardi tea.

SUSY: He was about as usual not specially rude but *certainly* not specially polite. When he came in and shook hands with me *coldly,* I being tired and nervous and not very well, changed *color!!!* I could have *committed suicide* afterward. I kept out of his way and finally he past me between the dining room and parlor and stopped me to ask some questions about papa's departure. I answered them quickly and coldly, and then without another word turned my back on him, and went to the sofa, leaving him standing alone in the middle of the room. I fancy he was surprised at this. When he was going he came over to me (which was quite unnecessary at a *tea*) and bade me his characteristic caressing goodby. . . . I cannot make him out at all.

NARRATOR: Livy went out very little in society; Mademoiselle Lanson acted as duenna.

SUSY: On Monday next [March 27th] I am to give a little farewell luncheon to try and pay off some of my social debts. Mamma will not be present. Only Mlle. L. I have really grown to be quite an adept at social intercourse now, having been out so much by myself this winter.

NARRATOR: Livy, Susy, Jean, the Mademoiselle and Livy's maid went to Venice the first week in April.

SUSY: We shall arrive in Venice just as we did last year by moonlight about eleven o'clock at night. Antonio is to meet us at the station with the gondola. The only thing I dread is the cannon! oh dear, I wish it could be dispensed with! I am going to make more of Venice this time and be out of doors—not in the hotel fuming and worrying as I was last time. Just think I shall walk about those fascinating back streets past the dear little shops and through the piazza San Marco.[4]

NARRATOR: She did get out and see Venice this time.

SUSY: The life here is gay and pleasant. This morning I saw the house of my beloved Othello and his statue.[5]

Yesterday we went up the Campanile and the view from there was superb, all of Venice and the Lido with the Alps and the blue Adriatic in the distance. I have also been over the Rialto which I didn't do last year. I am grown so fond of the piazza and of the dear winged lion of Venice and of all the strange fanciful decorations which belong to this place. St. Marks towards evening when the light is no longer too strong and dazzling to the eyes, is brilliant and beautiful to a degree that I never realized last Spring.[6]

NARRATOR: Afternoons were spent calling on Livy's friends and going to the Lido; they entertained occasionally at the Royal Hotel Danieli. Her romantic life was derived from books; she also did some French translations, as she wrote Clara.

SUSY: I am conscientiously translating a little life of Mme. de Sevigné and pretending that I am performing a very useful and necessary work, neither of which things it is. This takes my time when I am not reading. I have been reading the most precious, the most delightful book! At least I have found it so. It has made me feel somehow the way I used to feel when I read and enjoyed a book in the school room or the nursery a long time ago. Oh I have enjoyed it and loved it and lived in it these last days! Committed passages to repeat for my special delectation after I am in bed, and dreamed of the hero in my sleep. I don't know that the story is anything remarkable in fact it's quite commonplace but it's the *style* of thing you and I like to know. Then I haven't read a novel all winter and am just in the mood for one now and here in these hotel rooms it has seemed a delight somehow or other! It resembles "Jane Eyre" a good deal and is a little old fashioned and it isn't grand and stunning like "Wages" but sort of old timey and nice. By this time you *will* be wondering what the name of the thing is. It's "Barbara's History" by Amelia B. Edwards. Now do read it and write me what you think of it!

NARRATOR: Clara, in Berlin, was restless and longing to see the family, but Susy discouraged her coming.

SUSY: But aren't you as fond of Berlin as you were? You somehow don't sound quite so enthusiastic. Venice is perfectly charming and I enjoy it more each day, but it certainly can't compare with your useful industrious Berlin life for interest. If I could spend two absorbing hours a day playing the piano with other instruments I should certainly want to stay in Berlin and do it! but then

we are never satisfied with what we have in this life. I think
Venice is just the place for idle, useless people to go to, but let
a useful, busy "musical artist" like Miss Clara Clemens stay in
Berlin with her art and be grateful she can! So there! this is my
opinion on our respective positions!

NARRATOR: But she longed to have Clara come for she was with-
drawing again after her brief excursion into Florentine society.

SUSY: Ah but I do *wish* you were here with me nevertheless! There
is no one in the world I care much about seeing now but you. We
do understand each other so excellently well without the bore of
having to *explain* all our emotions.[7]

NARRATOR: The news from Sam was not unhopeful; he still believed
that he could salvage the publishing company, and Paige persuaded him that the manufacturing of the machine was going
ahead in Chicago, where Sam went to see for himself.

SAM: Paige shed even more tears than usual. What a talker he is!
He could persuade a fish to come out and take a walk with him.
When he is present I always believe him; I can't help it.[8]

NARRATOR: He saw Twichell, who then wrote Livy.

TWICHELL: "When are the Clemenses coming home?" is a question
raised hereabouts with a frequency, a tone and an accent, which,
could they be statistically and phonographically reported to you,
would leave you in no doubt of the welcome that awaits your
reappearance among us. Indeed, Livy, you *are* missed very sorely
by ever as many people whose hunger for you I am sure you would
—though humbly—own to be a tribute to your worth.[9]

NARRATOR: News from home depressed Susy. She began to dread
seeing old friends from America who turned up in Europe, and
even news of the Hartford neighbors depressed her. A Bryn Mawr
classmate, Louise Brownell, received a European fellowship and
planned to come abroad in the fall.

SUSY: I am scared to find that the news gives me the blue shivers!
I don't want to see her yet at all! I dread the thought of a meeting
like poison! . . .

I find that I dread more and more the thought of meeting old
friends. I have an undescribable shrinking from it. In fact I have
a great horror nowadays of being "stirred up" and an intense
desire to keep cool. The little agitations and excitements that
friends bring, don't seem worth while to me, any more. I can
imagine now only being satisfied with the emotional excitement

that a lasting life long love would bring but the other sorts of agitation seem so childish somehow.[10]

One of the great reasons why I have been glad to stay here and not return to my beloved Florence is that I find the place has somehow become associated in my mind with de Calry's abominable rudeness. It leaves a bad taste in my mouth and I can't help it. *Oh, if I could wipe it out!*[11]

NARRATOR: Soon after Livy and the girls returned to Florence and the Villa Viviani, they received a letter from Sam saying that within a year the royalty returns from the machine would be pouring in.

LIVY: Youth darling: Your letters rec'd this morning made me just about wild with pleasurable excitement. It does not seem credible that we are really again to have money to *spend*. . . .

Well I tell you I think I will jump around and spend money just for fun, and give a little away if we really get some. . . .

I do love you so my darling! what should we do and how should we feel if we had no bright prospects before us and yet how many people are situated in that way? . . .

It is astonishing to think that perhaps there is not yet a very long time for us to keep up this economy. I find already that it does not seem to me so important whether the house bills are 350 or 375 francs a week.[12]

SUSY: It is atrociously hot weather and there is a great deal of wind— there always is here. We seldom go out at all before five o'clock. Up to that time *read, sew, read, sew, read sew* till my patience is quite gone! . . .

I don't think I should ever care to spend another winter in Italy. I think one gets more profit and interest and health out of a northern city. I should so like something a little interesting to happen today. I wish I had "Castle Blair" and "Alice Thro' the Looking Glass" to read.

NARRATOR: She ran into de Calry one day.

SUSY: I wonder I didn't jump and say "Oh!" I was so scared and surprised. I merely said "Oh, how do you do Count de Calry?" and passed on out to the carriage. He looked silly and cold and cross as usual, but Mlle. said my manner was quite natural. I was mad at running across him so. I hoped not to see him again.— the sight of him agitates me always.[13]

NARRATOR: Sam returned to the villa in the middle of May.

SAM: I was ill in bed eleven days in Chicago, a week in Elmira and 3 months in New York (seemingly) and accomplished nothing that I went home to do.[14]

LIVY: It is so good to have Mr. Clemens back and he seems very well now, the voyage having taken away the last of his cough.

I was very much frightened about him while he was gone. Grip is such a terrible disease that one does not like to have it get hold of those that are dear to one. . . .

We have no definite plan as yet about our return, but Mr. C. is much more desirous of going back than he was before this last trip—however I think we must stay away a little longer.[15]

SUSY: I have been bored to death by this place during the past week. I have decided that Florence is the most uninteresting tiresome city on the face of the earth! Whenever Mlle. and I expect a little pleasure at one of the everlasting teas, the person we went to talk to doesn't come near us, or isn't there, or something of the sort. . . . Never any young people present, the conversation carried on in low tones of voice, no gaity, no laughter, no pretty costumes! We would like never to go to any more teas while we are here. We have entirely given up anticipating anything. We say, "Oh n'esperons rien! rien! pas meme que le soleil se levera demain!"

NARRATOR: Everything went wrong, even a performance of *Carmen*.

SUSY: Well the performance was given on the silver wedding of the king and queen of Italy and the placards said "gala night;" so of course we dressed in evening dresses supposing that there would be a little elegance. But in the first place the theater didn't begin to be full, and the audience was all in black!

NARRATOR: The orchestra was excellent and the scenery beautiful; Susy thought it compared favorably with the *Carmen* scenery in Berlin but Carmen, herself, "spoiled everything."

SUSY: Such a horror I never saw! *homely, hideous,* awkward! . . . Her acting was so dreadful and coarse and without the first particle of talent, that we simply couldn't stay and left the theater after the second act! So there is Florence again! In no other city in the world would they have put such a Carmen on the stage.[16]

NARRATOR: She was not the only unhappy member of the family; news from America was bad, the panic of '93 was setting in. Sam walked the floor nights and sent word to sell his royalties, but there were no buyers.

SAM: I am terribly tired of business. I am by nature and disposition unfit for it, and I want to get out of it.[17]

NARRATOR: They closed Viviani in June; Livy and Jean and Sam went to Munich. Susy went to Paris, where she sang for a well-known teacher, Madame Blanche Marchesi.

MARCHESI: Mark Twain was a delightful man to meet, and he paid me the compliment of sending his eldest daughter, Miss Olive [Olivia] Clemens, to me. . . . The girl was intelligent and sympathetic. She looked delicate, and at the voice trial I detected a formidable *tremolo,* which did not only come from forcing the high notes, but which seemed to have its source in a physical weakness.[18]

NARRATOR: Marchesi suggested a treatment of baths in Austria and Bavaria.

SAM: I think Mrs. Clemens is improving distinctly under the hands of her physician here [Munich]. In a week or ten days he will send her to a mountain resort two hours from here and we shall all spend the summer there. I brought Clara from Berlin day before yesterday [July 1st]; Susy will return from Paris in a fortnight.[19]

NARRATOR: The mountain resort was Franzenbad.

SUSY: Franzenbad is more natural now and my homesickness is somewhat consoled. . . . The music is very good and there is some every day and often two or three times a day. I do so like to take sewing to the park in the afternoon and listen to the orchestra. It's an ideal way to spend the time.

NARRATOR: Her outlook on life had grown more cheerful since seeing Marchesi.

SUSY: I am very proud of something I accomplished the other day. Frau Von Lentner . . . sings a good deal but doesn't know how to treat her voice. She asked me to show her something of the Marchesi method and I gave her a singing lesson. You should have seen her voice change within the hour! She is to sing in some theatricals soon and is going to bring over her songs to try with me. So you see if we go bankrupt perhaps I can give instructions in singing.[20]

NARRATOR: Sam, growing more and more worried, decided to sail again to New York. He had planned to leave the family in Paris, but there was a report of cholera in several European cities so they stayed on in Franzenbad.

SAM: I do not feel very *very* cheerful this morning [August 28th], leaving you homeless and no home selected or possible of selection until the cholera shall have exhibited its plans. It would be a crime to leave some women as you are being left; but with your grit and intelligence and unapproachable good sense *you* are better off than if you had two or three husbands to help you and confuse you and make your efforts abortive.[21]

NARRATOR: Sam sailed on August 29th and Clara went with him.

CLARA: As I had been troubled many months with a cough it was decided I should accompany him for the benefit of the ocean trip. We were rather a careless pair to let loose on a voyage alone.

NARRATOR: Almost left behind at a train stop on the way to Hamburg, Sam exclaimed, "God! I wish we had a couple of nurses with us."[22] In New York, he cabled Livy. Susy wrote to Clara.

SUSY: Well Blackie dear: And so you are in America! the telegram came to us last evening. It seems impossible. I think you will have a beautiful time but I would not have the courage to be in your place. All those friends, the looks, the questions, the scrutiny— oh no—I would die outright of fright! And pretty soon you will be taking the four o'clock train to Hartford and perhaps today you take the nine o'clock to Elmira! It is all too strange and "weirn"! to think that you are no longer in Europe but in America! —Oh how, *how* will it seem to you? *I* wish you were back here! I think I depend on you now more than anyone else in the world! because I love you so much and you are so sweet and then you *understand* and seem to like me as I *am*, without critising. Oh yes, I have a comfort and rest and pleasure in *you* that I find in no one else.

I can't explain the unspeakable *cowardice* that has taken possession of me lately about every conceivable person and thing. I would rather be locked up in a box *alone* for the rest of my life than gather up courage to go out into the world and enjoy myself. And so you see as I admire you and love you and am infinitely interested in you without being afraid of you—you're just everything in the world to me! Oh I *have* such a shuddering horror of being found fault with and criticised and yet I manage to do more things that merit criticism in a week than others do in a year. This is a horrid letter but you see there is positively *nothing* to tell. We shall soon be through with Franzenbad and then may go into Switzerland to Geneva, Interlaken or Montreux. If you were only to be here to go with us! Come back as soon as you can.[23]

NARRATOR: After a few days in New York, Clara went to Elmira and most of her relatives were charmed by her.

SAM: They speak ever so fondly of Clara; that witch has witched her way into their and the other folks's admiration and affection and is having a good time.[24]

NARRATOR: Clara and Susy apparently felt an intense sense of rivalry with their cousin, Julie Langdon, who in turn may have been jealous of the glamorous cousin from Europe. There were plans for Clara to give an informal concert in Elmira.

SUSY: I was *so* afraid that you would go back from Europe and let Julie run over you, and snub you just as she did of old, and I am so glad that she has found her match *at last!* You keep up this same beautiful independence and never let her lord it over you. . . . I never can help being ill at ease with her, but this is just why I want *you* to be equal to her which I don't doubt you are, you sweet dignified, effective Black Spider! . . . I only hope that when you give that concert in the Church play room, you will make the house come down around your ears,—and she'll be—*nowhere!* Ah me! revenge is sweet! . . . I'd like to draw you through Elmira in a car of triumph with six prancing steeds in front![25]

LIVY: Isn't she a wicked girl to write so . . . when I have just written you to be patient and get on with her as well as you can on account of the *fambly*.[26]

NARRATOR: Sam's business affairs were complicated by one of the greatest financial panics in the history of the United States. It had its roots in the growth of the great monopolies and the resulting organization of labor to fight them. He managed to arrange for publication of recent work, the major portion of the money to be sent to Livy in installments.

SAM: I've sold the Esquimaux Girl's Romance to the Cosmopolitan, for eight hundred dollars (which I will keep to live on here), and Pudd'nhead Wilson to the Century for six thousand five hundred, which will go to you by and by—first payment after Nov. 1—for it is even hard for the Century to get money.[27]

NARRATOR: One person at least was doing well, George, their former butler.

SAM: George called at the hotel, faultlessly dressed, as was his wont, and we walked up town together, talking about "the Madame" and the children, and incidentally about his own affairs. He had been serving as a waiter for a couple of years, at the Union League Club, and acting as banker for the other waiters, forty in number of his own race. . . .

Also he was lending money to white men outside; and on no kinds of security but two—gold watches and diamonds. . . . The times were desperate, failure and ruin were everywhere. . . . But George's ark floated serenely upon the troubled waters, his white teeth shone through his pleasant smile in the old way, he was a prosperous and happy person, and about the only one thus conditioned I met in New York.[28]

NARRATOR: Clara wrote Livy suggesting that it might be less expensive for her to stay in America.

LIVY: No it would not be cheaper for me to leave you in America, there would be too much expense of longing for you to make it profitable. Come when Papa comes and I hope he will not have to be gone a great while longer. How I wish he could have been saved all this perplexity and anxiety. I love you two precious people away off there in America and long to see you.

NARRATOR: They were proposing to settle down in Paris; Clara thought a small town would be better as there was not enough money to live well in Paris.

LIVY: Yes, my dear child I understand . . . and I feel just *exactly* as you do. I like to do a thing or else not do it. I hate going to Paris with no money to spend. To feel that we cannot go to the Opera or theater or do any of the things that we should like to do, yet on account of Susy's lessons I feel that we must go if we can possibly afford it. She feels that she has lost so much time, in fact all her time in Europe. I feel sorry for her in this respect. If she had had good advantages all the time that we have been here I should feel that if we could settle down in some inexpensive French town it would be just as well and better for the present, but I think on the whole we better try Paris, and if we find it too expensive we must go elsewhere.

I believe . . . that it is not best for us to settle outside of the city, at any rate I shall not do that at present. I am told that rents are much cheaper in Paris this winter because so many Americans have gone home on account of the terrible times. . . .

I feel my dear that you ought to pay Aunt Sue some board as

you stay there so long; and also pay the board of your friends that visit there. Particularly the board of your friends *should be paid*. I am so glad Miss Willard could visit you, and I am truly sorry that she feels poor. I am glad you paid her expenses. Poverty is hard![29]

NARRATOR: Katharine Willard was the daughter of the headmistress of Clara's Berlin school. Sam and Clara spent a few days visiting in Hartford and then Clara sailed back to Europe with Miss Willard. Sam went to live at the Players Club and, through his friend, Dr. Clarence Rice, became reacquainted with Henry Huddleston Rogers, Standard Oil magnate.

SAM: The best new acquaintance I've ever seen has helped us over Monday's bridge. I got acquainted with him on a yacht two years ago.[30]

I have got the best and wisest man in the whole Standard Oil group of multi-millionaires a good deal interested in looking into the type-setter (this is private, don't mention it.) He has been searching into that thing for three weeks, and yesterday he said to me, "I find the machine to be all you represented it— I have here exhaustive reports from my own experts, and I know every detail of its capacity, its immense value, its construction, cost, history, and all about its inventor's character. I know that the New York Co. and the Chicago Co. are *both* stupid, and that they are unbusinesslike people, destitute of money and in a hopeless boggle."

Then he told me the scheme he had planned, then said: "If I can arrange with these people on this basis . . . then the thing will move right along and your royalties will cease to be waste paper. I will post you the minute my scheme fails or succeeds. In the meantime, *you stop walking the floor.* Go off to the country and try to be gay. You may have to go to walking again, but don't begin till I tell you my scheme has failed." . . .

If I should even divulge the fact that the Standard Oil is merely *talking* remotely about going into the type-setter, it would send my royalties up.[31]

NARRATOR: Clara returned to Mrs. Willard's.

SUSY: The thought that you are sojourning in Berlin on this side of the water after this long separation out of our reach irritates me past expression. Truly that Katharine Willard should possess you *now* is hard! I am righteously jealous. Here we sit knowing that you are on this side and no more able to get hold of you than if you were still in America! You cannot picture our unhappiness and impatience. Now please do make as short a visit as you can and come to us soon, soon! How I long to see you and what numberless things I have to talk over with you and ask you! And you cannot think how much happier I shall be when you are here. And then of course you want to start your winter's work.[32]

SAM: Mamma is troubled about how you are to get company from Berlin to Paris. Be sure you secure an escort that will be satisfactory to her.[33]

NARRATOR: Livy, Susy and Jean finally settled down in some dreary rooms in Paris. Susy started voice lessons with Marchesi and her daughter, Madame Caccamesi.

SUSY: I am having a great disappointment just now. When I got here Caccamesi said my voice was *"immense"* and I thought I should go right ahead.[34]

SAM: Madame Marchesi said she had a grand-opera voice—"Marvelous voice" was one of her expressions. Madame Blanche said her voice was competent for the part of Elsa and Elizabeth in Lohengrin and Tannhäuser; and later she added Isolde to this list—which was the equivalent of saying it was competent for any soprano part.[35]

Livy's health is improving and the doctors think they can cure her in another year over there. The children are hard at work on music and the languages, and they make perfectly satisfactory progress.[36]

NARRATOR: Susy was not making progress, as she wrote Clara, but Sam was only told cheerful news.

SUSY: But suddenly after the second lesson what she call[s] my "general anemia" took hold of my breathing power and ever since, my breath has been so short and weak that all my volume of voice has gone. She says that the voice is all right but the breath being so short makes it impossible for me to do anything with it. . . . I am frightened to death for fear this will last, in fact I am entirely broken-hearted. Cold douches, eating, walking, sleeping, *nothing* helps. I am also frightened at the thought of what you may have said of my voice at home and nobody knows what will become of it now. If my breath doesn't return to me it will be a wasted winter. Isn't it dreadful?

I oughtn't to bore you with this but I wanted to prepare you before you should hear me sing. There seems to be no limit to the misfortunes that can befall us.

Please come as soon as you possibly can. We are still uncomfortable and unsettled and expect to move soon to some hotel in town.[37]

MARCHESI: Cross-examining her, I found that she slept very little and ate next to nothing, and her education, as is frequently the case in America, seemed to have been taken in hand by the girl herself, the question of food being thrown aside as very uninteresting. Here was a case of voluntary self-starvation, and she laughingly confessed to have lived chiefly on mixed pickles, ice-cream, candies and similar foods. I warned her most severely, and as her voice was so pretty and her personality very marked, I accepted her as a pupil, on condition that she would take the meals prescribed by me regularly, so as to build up health and strength, without which my teaching would be of no avail.[38]

NARRATOR: Susy's tensions were not relieved by a letter from Sam.

SAM: I will drop a line to the dearest of all the dear Susies to say, bear up mamma's hands and help her to endure our long separation as patiently as she can, for I absolutely must not budge one step from this place *until we are safe from the poorhouse.*

That I shall succeed, I have not the slightest doubt—if I don't go rushing across the ocean again too soon. If I budge too soon, I shall fail.

I believe I could run over to France now, for a couple of weeks, but I am not absolutely sure; therefore I am going to wait until I am sure.

We are millionaires if we hold the royalties 12 months. And we shall hold them if I stand by until they are safe from getting into trouble through Webster & Co's debts. And that I mean to do.

I have wasted not a moment in America: I am wasting no moments now. I have four irons in the fire and I take vigilant care of *all* of them.

I will see to it that we have twelve or fifteen thousand dollars to live on for the next ten or twelve months; and if more should be necessary I will turn out and earn it. Make Mamma believe these things. She will believe me anyway, but you *help.* It is necessary to her health that she be kept free from money-anxieties. We must all look sharp to that. We must never let her be low-spirited for one moment if we can help it. She is my only anxiety; I have no other. When I get that out of my mind I am buoyant, and destitute of forebodings.

My new book [*Tom Sawyer, Detective*] that I am writing makes me jolly. I live in it. But when I think of Joan of Arc, how I long to get at that again! I should be fixed just right if I could have both books to work on month-about. . . .

Be good to Mamma, child! Love her and pet her and make her just as happy as you know how.

I kiss you, dear heart.[39]

NARRATOR: Livy found a school for Jean.

LIVY: Jean the beloved is off this morning for school. It is her first day. She and I went yesterday afternoon to see about it and the teacher said she could begin this morning. It is a school recommended by Miss Goodridge who knows a good deal about schools here in Paris.

Jean goes at nine in the morning and stays until five or six at night. Most of the girls remain until six but the teacher said as Jean took no music perhaps she could come out at five.

She takes her luncheon there with the girls and takes an afternoon walk with them. I hope it will be a pleasure to her and give her the young life that she needs. It may prove to be too confining as she has never been used to such long hours. Of course I shall keep watch and try to see that she does not droop. She is so very well now, unberufen. She is the dearest, sweetest, helpfullest child in the world.

There is an Irish Countess here in the house who has been writing articles about the abuse of the cab horses here and sending them to the Herald. Jean has become very much interested and goes down into the reading room every day to see if there is anything new in the papers about the horses. Of course we have entered the ranks and every time before we get into a cab we tell the driver not to whip his horse, naturally we take some pretty long, slow drives in consequence.

Yesterday I was slightly appalled by Jean's saying to me as we were driving out alone together, "Mama I think it would really be better and we would do more good, if we were always to choose the worst looking old horses when we go out, because you know the good horses are well taken care of any way and their masters do not beat them. In that way we could protect the old bony horses." So I expect to be driving around Paris with the worst horse that we can find by carefully searching. She is as cheerful and sunny as the day is long and an increasing comfort. Susy is again not at all well.[40]

NARRATOR: Susy missed Clara dreadfully and worried over Clara's doubts about Marchesi as a teacher.

SUSY: I cannot be resigned to having you so near and yet so far! it is *dreadful.* Do hurry and come to us. I think Paris will be very nice when we really get settled here tho I think Berlin will always remain the darling of our hearts. How you must enjoy being there! and what a lot of the "rage of living" you have had since we parted in Franzenbad. I cannot say how I am *dying* to see you but you can imagine for yourself. I shall be infinitely happier when you are here. So far I have been at times rather lonely even in Paris. We lead the same tranquil existence here you know. I fancy that you with your more eventful fate may help *me* to adventures more or less by your mere presence. . . .

I am not going to try to answer the letter which I am expecting from you about Marchesi until I see you. I cannot easily talk of those rather elaborate things by letter. I hope you have no really strong objection to her as I have already begun my lessons, and cannot think of stopping them now, especially as they are the object of our stay in Paris. Of course I haven't heard yet what you have heard against her but every singing teacher has her enemies, and Marchesi has so many monuments to her good teaching in her famous pupils, but—we will see. We can talk this all over. I care greatly for your opinion in musical matters always and should be dreadfully upset if you did not approve of what I was doing with my singing, but then on the other hand, my voice never was *anything* before I came to Marchesi. I am anxious to visit with you about this beside everything else.

Tonight we are going to spend the night in a hotel which we hope to move into if it's *quiet.* I think you will like it if we do. The rooms are pleasant and look out on the Rue de Rivoli and the Tuileries.[41]

NARRATOR: They moved into those rooms, in the Hotel Brighton. Life in Paris became more cheerful.

SUSY: John Howells called here in the afternoon and we liked him very well, Mamma extremely, and I tolerably. He is living with two other young fellows, Art students, over on the other side of the river and I suppose they may call here later, so there's a wee opening into "young" society![42]

KATY: He was a great friend . . . of all the family, and he was always at the house for all the jollifications. Everybody liked him—I did myself. He was a very nice young man. He and his sister was always great friends of the girls.[43]

SUSY: Then the Parquez often give dances I think and we will be invited to them. Altogether Paris would look delightful to me if it wasn't for my continued bad sleeping and my consequent loss of voice. Night before last I slept as I used to one good long night and yesterday the voice was in fine condition, as good as it was in Franzenbad or Homburg but then that's the only really good night I've had for a month, and today the voice is quite gone as I slept none last night. Isn't it trying? . . .

Caccamesi . . . said last time that if I get back my sleep and my breath and the power of voice I had when I got here, there was no hall whatever too large for me to fill, that the voice would carry anywhere provided I grew really strong. But for the present I am stopping all the hard exercises, and everything, and may have to stop the lessons even if I don't get to sleeping again. I'm dreadfully discouraged. I'm paying now for my past sins. There's a poor pupil of Marchesi's who *lost seven months* last year because the climate here didn't agree with her.[44]

NARRATOR: Clara, sensing that Susy couldn't stand the rigors of Marchesi's training, wrote suggesting that she give up lessons for a while or perhaps try another teacher.

SUSY: Thank you many times for your good letter. But I am crazy to see *you*! ! this is too awkward your being stuck there in Berlin without any means of getting to us! And we here are all ready to receive you and so pleasantly situated at last that I think you will really be enchanted with our quarters. They remind me somehow of old times in beloved Berlin. Our two little rooms are next each other as they were there and are much the same long narrow shape. When you come Paris will seem just twice as delightful to me. Mamma has written you this morning and I hope you will be able to find some way to get to us *soon.*

Now you will forgive me when I say that I cannot believe one single word of what you have heard against Marchesi and *nothing* and *nobody* would induce me to stop my lessons with her. One of her great powers is that she makes you trust her *absolutely*. Daisy

Warner with all her ignorance could have persuaded me to give up Frau Von Asten or Vannuccini but not even *you* whom I admire so much musically can even make me *think* of leaving Marchesi. I only hope this doesn't irritate you. I will give you my reasons which are good when I see you and I hope I *feel* that you will agree with me. But even if you do not don't be angry with me for not taking your advice and don't lose your interest in my singing will you?[45]

NARRATOR: Livy's birthday brought a letter from Sam.

SAM: I am desperately disappointed because my photograph is not ready for your birthday. I was going to send it to Susy and have her put it with the other tokens of love and remembrance Nov. 27th. But I see I can't manage it now. I went there and sat 7 times and got one or two very good negatives. Sarony should have had the pictures here two days ago but he has failed me.[46]

NARRATOR: Livy wrote Clara.

LIVY: It is my birthday and I wish that you were here. Anniversaries are rather sad things when one has lost those who used to make much of them. I hope I may get a letter from you today. I rec'd two cablegrams from Papa this morning. . . .

I hope this will be the last letter that I shall write you, that you will soon come to me. We *long* so to have you here and we do need your dear presence. I wish you were going to be with us on Thanksgiving, but we shall think as little about the old Thanksgiving days as possible. Four years this coming Thanksgiving that Susy first gave her play. Three years since Grandmamma lay so low.

Last night John Howells called. We enjoyed his call very much. I think he is a sweet fellow. As soon as you get here I shall invite him to dinner.

Hurry and come, your room is waiting for you. I told the Landlord he could use it for two or three days if he needed it, but after that I should use it, that is for my darling Black Spider. I think it is a pretty little room (it is quite small,) it opens into the salon and the window, only one, looks out on to the rue de Rivoli. I feel sure if no misfortune comes to us that we shall have a happy winter here. Do *hurry,* we do want you with us. Susy needs you and I need you. She does not sleep well and is consequently very much discouraged. I feel so very sorry for her, it seems as if it was too trying just at this time when she has never needed to sleep as much as she needs it now. She is not going to her lesson this morning on account of a bad night.[47]

NARRATOR: Livy had never received the much-needed first payment for *Pudd'nhead Wilson* from the Century Company.

SAM: The Century people misunderstood me about the money; but they will send part of it to you Dec. 1st. They feel the hard times like the rest. And bless your life they're *bitter* hard times! You have never seen anything to remotely compare with them.

I love you deeply, my Livy, and I wish I could be with you on your birthday, but it cannot be and I am sorry for that. But I hope you will be light-hearted and happy, and that you will have all the children around to bless you.[48]

LIVY: We have just had a visit from our new doctor. He has examined Susy most thoroughly, he says there is some extension of the cells of the lungs, he thinks it comes from enemia and will not long resist treatment. I like him exceedingly. He says that one great trouble with her is that she is not sufficiently developed, particularly her chest he is going to have her take gymnastics for developing that, and also massage. I hope now she will soon be on the road to health. It has been very pitiful to see her look so miserable. And sometimes it has been hard to keep cheerful with her so down hearted.

NARRATOR: Clara finally arrived, and Livy told Sam how she cheered them up.

LIVY: You should have been here today [December 17th] to see Clara imitate you telling them stories and eating at the same time, it was just as funny as it could be. She bit a piece of bread exactly as you bite it. She said "I don't know what it is but Papa always seems to be having a quarrel with his piece of bread to make it let go."

NARRATOR: Sam suggested finding a Christian Scientist for Susy. He had been to a "mind curist" on George Warner's recommendation to cure his cough.

SAM: Then to Dr. Whipple's arriving on time, and took half an hour's treatment. He sits silent in the corner with his face to the wall, and I walk the floor and smoke. . . . Mr. Rogers has been buying homeopathic powders and feeding them to me ever since. They kept the cough down and moderated it, but didn't remove it. I tried the mind-cure out of curiosity. That was yesterday. I have coughed only two or three times since. Maybe it was the mind-cure, maybe it was the powders.

Whipple cured the (Perkins) boy, and now he is a prominent athlete at Yale and plays in the football team. . . . These things are mighty interesting.

He could tell me of no mind-curist in Europe; said they would be jailed promptly if they attempted to practice in France.[49]

NARRATOR: Sam and Rogers arrived back from Chicago for Christmas; Sue and Sam sent a cable off to Livy: "Merry Xmas! Promising progress made in Chicago." Sam was very gay at this time; he was called the "Belle of New York."

SAM: By half past 4 I had danced all those people down—and yet was not tired; merely breathless. I was in bed at 5, and asleep in ten minutes. Up at 9 and presently at work.[50]

NARRATOR: He went to Hartford to see a play, *A Masque of Culture* by their old friend, Annie Eliot Trumbull, put on by members of the Saturday Morning Club. He stayed with the Twichells.

SAM: I was proud to be the father and sole male member of a club that could write and play plays like that.[51]

Joe and Harmony want Susy to come and live with them many months—they say the young Hartford life will set her up mentally and physically, and Hartford is full of delightful girls of her age. *That* part of it is sound (but privately the table would not nourish Susy).

Joe is just as darling and delicious as ever.[52]

NARRATOR: Mrs. William Dean Howells suggested to Sam that Susy try hypnotism.

SAM: She convinced *me*, before she got through, that she and William James are right—hypnotism and mind-cure are the same thing; no difference between them. Very well; the very source, the very *centre* of hypnotism is *Paris*. Dr. Charcot's pupils and disciples are right there and ready to your hand without fetching poor dear old Susy across the stormy sea. Let Mrs. Mackay . . . tell you whom to go to to learn all you need to learn and how to proceed. *Do*, do it, honey. Don't lose a minute.[53]

NARRATOR: There was another heart-breaking flurry of optimism early in the new year. Livy received a cable: "Ship in sight. Bearing down under a cloud of canvas."

CLARA: My! but the streets of Paris glittered in gold that day! We saw ourselves rich with theater tickets, and drives in the Bois de Boulogne; with flowers in all the bedrooms and bonbons at every plate. But Mother was cooler: "Children, take care. The cable said that the ship was in sight; nothing more."

I, being the most greedy of the three, asked permission to cable a question to Father, "When does she unload?" Back came the answer, "Wind uncertain." Heavens! all the candy, flowers, tickets, spilled before they ever reached us. We must wait again. The ship will probably be becalmed once more.

Father wrote from New York:

"Darling Livy: You say in your letter 'but do not come until it is right to do so.' That sentence gave me a splendid uplift! All day I am tortured by a conscience which howls and tugs and pulls and upbraids and reproaches—an infernal conscience which is twins—the one twin pulling one of my arms and saying 'come, sail!' and the other tugging at the other arm and saying 'stay where you are and settle your business matters!' I hardly know which one of these devils causes me the most trouble. However, I've got to stay here a while longer. Things look very promising but still they drag to the complete conclusion."[54]

SUSY'S TWENTY-THIRD YEAR

1894–1895

NARRATOR: Sam was in Paris for Susy's birthday. On April 1st Livy
wrote her friend, Alice Day, who was in Stuttgart with her
family.

LIVY: It is pleasant to know that you expect to come to Paris this
Spring, because unless something happens to change our plans
we expect to remain here until the last of June.

Unhappily for us Mr. Clemens is obliged to return to America
he goes back on Saturday of this week. However this time he
expects to be away only five weeks. At first—we thought we would
break up and go with him, but we were compelled to give that up
because I am in the hands of an electrician and he said if I
stopped my treatment now I would lose all that I had gained. . . .

Susy is now for a few days in Tours with friends. She is much
better there than she was here. She sleeps much better and so
naturally her days are better.[1]

NARRATOR: Shortly after Sam's arrival in America, the Charles L.
Webster Company went into bankruptcy. Rogers handled the
creditors.

HENRY ROGERS: They were bent on devouring every pound of flesh
in sight and picking the bones afterwards, as Clemens and his
wife were perfectly willing they should do. I was getting a little
warm all the time at the high-handed way in which these few men
were conducting the thing, and presently I got on my feet and
said, "Gentlemen, you are not going to have this thing all your
way. I have something to say about Mr. Clemens's affairs. Mrs.

Clemens is the chief creditor of this firm. Out of her own personal fortune she has lent it more than sixty thousand dollars. She will be a preferred creditor, and those copyrights will be assigned to her until her claim is paid in full. As for the home in Hartford, it is hers already."[2]

SAM: Nobody finds the slightest fault with my paying you with all my property. . . .

It was confoundedly difficult at first for me to be always saying "Mrs. Clemens's books," "Mrs. Clemens's copyrights," "Mrs. Clemens's type-setter stock," and so on; but it was necessary to do this, and I got the hang of it presently. I was even able to say with gravity, "My wife has two unfinished books, but I am not able to say when they will be completed or where she will elect to publish them when they are done."[3]

NARRATOR: Sam returned to France in the middle of May; he and Livy were, if anything, even closer, and she sustained him, as usual, in his despair.

SAM: She was always cheerful; and she was always able to communicate her cheerfulness to others. During the nine years we spent in poverty and debt she always was able to reason me out of my despairs and find a bright side to the clouds and make me see it. In all that time I never knew her to utter a word of regret concerning our altered circumstances, nor did I ever know her children to do the like. For she had taught them, and they drew their fortitude from her. The love which she bestowed upon those whom she loved took the form of worship, and in that form it was returned—returned by relatives, friends, and servants of her household.[4]

NARRATOR: To her sister, Sue Crane, Livy wrote her true feelings.

LIVY: The hideous news of Webster & Co.'s failure reached me by cable on Thursday, and Friday morning *Galignani's Messenger* had a squib about it. Of course I knew it was likely to come, but I had great hope that it would be in some way averted. Mr. Rogers was so sure there was no way out but failure that I suppose it was true. But I have a perfect *horror* and heart-sickness over it. I cannot get away from the feeling that business failure means disgrace. I suppose it always will mean that to me. We have put a great deal of money into the concern, and perhaps there would have been nothing but to keep putting it in and losing it. We certainly now have not much to lose. We might have mortgaged the house; that was the only thing I could think of to do. Mr. Clemens felt that there would never be any end, and perhaps he was right. At any rate, I know that he was convinced that it was the only thing, because when he went back he promised me that if it was possible to save the thing he would do so if only on account of my sentiment in the matter.

Sue, if you were to see me you would see that I have grown old very fast during this last year. I have wrinkled.

Most of the time I want to lie down and cry. Everything seems to me so impossible. I do not make things go very well, and I feel that my life is an absolute and irretrievable failure. Perhaps I am thankless, but I so often feel that I should like to give it up and die. However, I presume that if I could have the opportunity I should at once desire to live.[5]

NARRATOR: In June they left Paris; Clara went to Fluelen in Canton Uri, Switzerland to study voice with Mrs. Hopekirk Wilson. The rest of the family went to La Bourboule-les-Bains, a village in the south of France, in search of treatment for Livy and Susy. As usual, Livy and Sam worried about Clara's deportment.

LIVY: To think you are in that lovely spot! I cannot but wish that we were with you . . . I do most sincerely hope that you are comfortably and pleasantly situated. I am sure all that region about there is one that you cannot go about alone in, because there are so many tourists about. So do not try it my dear for I should be anxious if you did.[6]

SAM: Clara dear, yours was a fluent and delightful letter, and we are all glad you are so happy. Continue to be happy, but beware! for we are a little troubled about your isolated situation. We had not contemplated that shape of the matter, and naturally we are disturbed by it. We had thought only of a pleasant home for you—a private house, not a public hotel. Why, even in America a public hotel would be rather objectionable. Mamma prefers that if you are not perfectly private on that balcony and not under fire of curious eyes, you had better take all your meals in your room. I think you had better take this suggestion as a require-ment—and so keep on the safe side and out of range of foreign criticism and remark.

Mamma is in perfect sympathy with your joyful spirits and your happy sense of emancipation—she says she knows just how you feel, and is glad you are having this let-up and this life-giving spiritual refreshment. And that is my feeling about it, too.[7]

LIVY: We have had some trouble to get ourselves adjusted here, but I cannot but believe in the end it will do Susy good, the air here is surely superb. Papa says he thinks he has never been in any air that seemed to him so invigorating. We are twice as high as the farm and the air is most delightful. Poor Susy has not been able to enjoy it much for she has been shut up for four or five days with sore throat and fever and a stiff neck and a little cough. I have been a little anxious about her (in fact I may say more than a little). She has looked so very miserable, but now she is better and we thought of taking her for a drive today, but we have decided to wait one more day.

Before she was taken ill she was so extremely discontented and unhappy (and I did not wonder that she was) that I felt as if we must give it up and go somewhere else, though I did not know where. But Papa was very greatly opposed to our doing that, he argued that we did not know where else to go, that the doctor had sent us here thinking it would be a benefit to Susy, now we had made that long and very wearisome journey and he thought we ought to stay long enough to see whether Susy would be benefited or not. I knew he was right but Susy felt so unhappy that it was hard to decide to remain. I think one reason that it was so difficult for her to make up her mind to it was, that this sickness was coming on, consequently she was very wretched. She took one douche before she was taken ill and felt no bad effects from it. She said she did not feel in the least weaker than before she took it. Poor dear little girl how I wish she might get well! . . .

Susy is sweet and dear and I do *long* that this experience shall do her good.[8]

NARRATOR: Susy was unwell in La Bourboule, and her condition was aggravated by a riot that threatened in the hotel following the assassination of Carnot, President of the French Republic, by an Italian.

SAM: When we were about to go to bed we heard a good deal of noise about a hundred yards away—shoutings of a great crowd . . . and at last the shouts became furious howlings. We have Italian waiters in the house, and I became uneasy, but I tried to make the family believe it was only a mob of drunken merrymakers. However, that assertion soon lost force. The noise approached, and took the form of the Marseillaise. Then stones began to fly. . . .

I was afraid they would fire the house. But they didn't. They kept everybody up to the small hours with their threats and howlings and cries of "A bas les Italiens!"[9]

NARRATOR: Sam, who was to leave for New York the next day, postponed his trip.

SAM: Susy . . . is up and around again, though pale and not blithe. If she makes the most of the advantages offered by these waters and baths and this wholesome air I am sure she will reap a good profit accordingly and for a lasting period.

The riot here consequent upon the assassination stopped us from leaving a week ago. I am glad I stayed; for if I had gone I believe the rest would have cleared out in a day or two. They had not become wonted to the place and were feeling homeless and dismal; but everything has a cheerier look, now, and I hope and believe they will now abide here long enough to get good effects from the waters.

I start again tomorrow, [July 5th] and shall expect to sail from Southampton in the Paris Saturday noon, 7th.[10]

NARRATOR: Livy, Susy and Jean returned to Paris and invited some friends to watch Carnot's funeral procession; the windows of their rooms in the Brighton afforded an excellent view. Among the American friends were the Calvin Days from Hartford and their daughters, Alice and Katharine.

KATHARINE DAY: Carnot was greatly respected, and had given a most successful administration, so that unusual horror and grief were felt, and the procession carrying his body to the Pantheon for burial was extremely impressive, with great numbers of infantry, cavalry and especially engineers, (for Carnot was trained in that branch), and the superb mounted cuirassiers in their plumed helmets and shining breastplates.

NARRATOR: Alice and Katharine were about the same age as Susy and Clara.

KATHARINE DAY: Susy was especially charming, a beautiful slender girl, fair, with light golden-brown hair and dark eyes full of intelligence and an alert eager manner. She was devoted to music and was cultivating her voice, already considered exceptional . . . and Jean was a charming serious girl of fourteen. . . .

Mrs. Clemens talked longingly with mother of the Hartford house and of her desire to return to it.

NARRATOR: Livy and Alice Hooker Day, having been lifelong friends, had a joyful reunion, but Susy, although she was amused at being called a "child of talent," had little in common with the Day girls.

KATHARINE DAY: Having been presented at the English Court the preceding year, in addition to the two years residence in England, my sister and I were young and impressionable enough to have acquired fine British accents in speech, and a great fondness for things English including Court dressmakers.[11]

NARRATOR: The Days planned to spend some time at Étretat, a Normandy watering place. Livy thought it sounded like the simple, charming type of place they would like, but they made no plans as they felt that Susy should return to La Bourboule and finish the cure. Sam wrote from the ship.

SAM: Livy darling, we shall arrive [in New York] early tomorrow [July 14th] morning—Saturday. . . .

I have worked every day, but have accomplished nothing; what I have written is not satisfactory and must be thrown away. However my time was put in most pleasantly; without the work I should have been worrying about you and Susy all the time; with it I have worried only a part of the time.

Part of my work was not lost, for I have revised Joan of Arc and made some good corrections and reductions. . . .

Mrs. P. T. Barnum is on board. She was an invalid 8 years, with nervous and other troubles, and spent most of her time in hospitals. She said her case was apparently hopeless, but she fell into Dr. Playfair's hands in London and in 5 months he has made a well woman of her. She thinks Susy ought to go to him.[12]

NARRATOR: On paper, Sam and Clara were making plans which would never materialize.

SAM: You dear old Black Spider! how glad I was to get your letter an hour or two ago. I was able to *read* it, too—which is a marvel.

Bless your dear heart, I am in the most thorough sympathy with your scheme, and proud of you for inventing it. I want you to go right ahead with it. Between us we will lay such a siege to Mamma that she will be obliged to yield. I will fetch the rest of the tribe over here in October for a few months if I can persuade them to come, and you can remain there if the Wilsons can find a room. I've a project to board and lodge them at George Warner's.

I hope to reach Étretat before the end of this month—can't tell just when.

I am glad you are where you are and having those wholesome and delightful times. You are laying in a stock of health and vigor that you can draw upon for many a year to come. I do wish we had put Susy through a course like that instead of sending her to that deadly college.

I saw Mrs. Susy Warner in Hartford yesterday. I have never heard her praise any one so fervently as she praised Mrs. Wilson's character and her abilities as teacher and composer. She was enthusiastically glad your lines have fallen so fortunately. I wish you would give my love to the Wilsons and tell them how grateful I am for the countless kindnesses they have heaped upon my dear old blatherskite of a Black Spider.[13]

NARRATOR: Susy finished the cure at La Bourboule.

SUSY: Somehow at La Bourboule life wasn't worth describing.

NARRATOR: They traveled slowly back to Paris, stopping at Fontainebleau.

SUSY: Our trip . . . was adorable, our stay in Fontainebleau especially delightful.[14]

LIVY: We did hate to leave that lovely spot. It was simply charming there. Susy enjoyed it very much. She has rather dreaded having our travels end, and so have I, for that matter still I believe I shall be glad to get settled in Étretat.

NARRATOR: They rented a house at Étretat called Chalet des Abris. Livy laid her plans carefully; Susy was apt to take a dislike to any place that the family talked up.

LIVY: We went out this afternoon [July 31st] to get our cup of tea and while we were taking it Miss Dater came into the Café where we were. She had just returned from Etretat, and she told Susy it was perfectly lovely down there. I have been careful not to say one single encouraging thing about the place, but have put forward everything that could strike one unpleasantly. The loneliness of the situation of the cottage etc. Thinking it better to let all that was agreeable be unexpected to her.[15]

NARRATOR: Livy's worries were groundless; Susy wrote Clara.

SUSY: I suppose Mamma has written what a nice place this Etretat is and how beautifully we are situated, good food, good air, good beds, lovely walks, charming rooms etc. etc. We are in clover and I had dreaded this place so.[16]

LIVY: No, we have not seen anyone as yet, not one soul outside of the house. And we *delight* in the fact. I am surprised that Susy does, but she does. She said the other day, "Well the first person that enters the gate I shall say, 'Well you old fool, what have you come for? We don't want to see anybody.'" So you see what is her state of mind. I am afraid to express it or I would tell you that she is better.

Clara darling we shall be so glad when you come and you will like it, it is perfect here and the servants are so nice and do the work so well. The cooking is perfect and we eat enormously.[17]

NARRATOR: Life again made one of its sudden changes for Susy; she was on the upswing. The horrors of sleeplessness and agonizing voice lessons were forgotten for the time being.

SAM: Through all her seasons of unhappiness there were outbursts of happiness—exaltations of it.

I cannot remember when she first began to carry around a vast Shakespeare. She was never without it. It was a trouble in traveling, but she had to have it. She was fond of Browning.

To us she was a prodigy. I mean, in speech she was that. We of the family believed . . . that she had no equal among girls of her own age in this regard. Even the friends thought highly of her gift, though they could never see her at her best, which was in the unembarrassing limits of the family circle.[18]

SUSY: I am in quite a new mood for me and I hope it will last. I have become *hopeful* and *industrious,* and am interested in life. It is long since I have been so contented as I have been the past month *(unberufen)* It seems to me now that the *only* thing in life is work and that I must never again let myself fall back into my old idle habits. But who knows, perhaps this is only a spirt. I hope not with all my heart.[19]

SAM: She was not industrious, except in the things in which she was gifted; she was indolent; she lived mainly in the clouds; hard, persistent work went against the grain with her. As a rule, I mean. She mastered the French and German and Latin grammars, and of course that does mean hard, persistent work. Still, as I say, she had a distaste for toilsome work—a trait which she got from me.[20]

NARRATOR: There were young people in Étretat: the Day girls and John and Pilla Howells. John was attracted to Susy, but she, increasingly shy with young men, couldn't respond; her failure made her miserable.

SUSY: Johnny and Pilla and I went to a little operetta of Offenbach's last night. It was very lovely but it is as impossible a book as ever! Pilla is *lovely* and we get on swimmingly now. . . .

I have written out a program of occupations for the future as follows: 1. singing, 2. acting, 3. singing teaching 4. study of the languages 5. guitar playing 6. (possibly) writing. . . .

I have been writing again as an experiment, and I am interested in this new undertaking in quite a serious absorbed way. I have written quite a little package of Mss. which Mamma seems to like very much. It is only the beginning of what must be a long story. I do not think I am at all equal to really doing the whole thing now, but I pray it will work out before our next century. At any rate it keeps me busy and the time passes quickly and I do translating and such things between times. I have been called to meals long before I dreamed it was time lately, just as I used to be in the busy days at home. This has been an unspeakable pleasure to me, the being so taken out of myself. Of course I feel *very, perfectly* uncertain whether I shall ever write after all but I'm going to try thoroughly once any way. And if writing doesn't go then, it must be the singing or something else, something, *anything* to keep one busy and useful and prevent one's being a fearful . . . society gal!!!!! Them's my sentiments at the present moment!

The world looks so attractive when one has something to *do!*[21]

NARRATOR: There is a paragraph from the end of a story she wrote.

SUSY: And now at last when they lie at rest they must go hence. It is always so. Completion, perfection, satisfaction attained—a human life has fulfilled its earthly destiny. Poor human life! It may not pause and rest, for it must hasten on to other realms and greater consummations.[22]

NARRATOR: By the end of August, the whole family was reunited at Étretat, Sam had made arrangements for *Joan* to be published by Harper and he must now finish the book.

SAM: I find Madam ever so much better in health and strength. The air is superb and soothing and wholesome, and the Chalet is remote from noise and people, and just the place to write in. . . .

Mrs. Clemens is in great spirits on account of the benefit which she has received from the electrical treatment in Paris and is bound to take it up again and continue it all the winter, and of course I am perfectly willing. She requires me to drop the lecture platform out of my mind and go straight ahead with Joan until the book is finished.[23]

KATHARINE DAY: At Étretat . . . the Clemenses were living in a retired villa where Mark Twain worked intensely on *Joan of Arc;* both Mr. and Mrs. Clemens were feeling the strain of the failure and were seeing fewer people than usual, so that it was principally at the bathing beach that we saw the girls. It was a joy to mother to be again with Mrs. Clemens.[24]

NARRATOR: Susy and Sam discussed *Joan.*

SAM: She liked "l'Arbre fée de Bourlemont," and said it was poetry, which greatly pleased me. She was fond of Joan's transitions from playful girl to official activities: "Messenger from the King!" And La Hire's speech when he backed up Joan's war methods.[25]

   She was a poet—a poet whose song died unsung.

   Every now and then in her vivacious talk she threw out phrases of such admirable grace and force, such precision of form, that they thrilled through one's consciousness like the passage of the electric spark.[26]

NARRATOR: When they left Étretat, they went to Rouen; Sam wanted to saturate himself with the atmosphere of the place where Joan had been imprisoned. Susy, the happy routine of Étretat broken, was taken ill, so that they had to stay on in Rouen several weeks. While there, Sam received a letter from Rogers with typesetter news which raised all their hopes once more.

SAM: I can hardly keep from sending a hurrah by cable. I would certainly do it if I wasn't superstitious.[27]

NARRATOR: When Susy was better, they went on to Paris.

SAM: I am on my back the past 5 days with a formidable attack of gout in my off hind leg—ankle joint. In an hour from now [November 16th] I am to get up and be carted in a closed carriage to the above address [69 rue de l'Université]—our quarters for the winter. It is not a flat, but a small house by itself, and it seems a comfortable and home like place.[28]

CLARA: Here Mother started housekeeping and made Father feel more at home, although the servants were French and the Paris skies dull with heavy mists. Rarely did the sun shine in those winter months and we longed for sparkling American days.[29]

SAM: . . . a charming mansion in the rue de l'Université, on the other side of the Seine, which, by good luck, we had gotten hold of through another man's ill luck. This was Pomeroy, the artist.

Illness in his family had made it necessary for him to go to the Riviera. He was paying thirty-six hundred dollars a year for the house, but allowed us to have it at twenty-six hundred. . . . The studio was coziness itself. We used it as drawing-room, sitting-room, dancing-room—we used it for everything. We couldn't get enough of it. It is odd that it should have been so cozy, for it was forty feet long, forty feet high, and thirty feet wide, with a vast fireplace on each side in the middle, and a musicians' gallery at one end. But we had, before this, found out that under the proper conditions spaciousness and coziness do go together most affectionately and congruously.[30]

NARRATOR: The winter season started well; Susy was better and singing again.

SAM: Susy is driving out every day, now.[31]

She had no care about money, no notion of its value. She spent it, wasted it, lost it. Lost her opera glasses, her gloves, her parasol, her purse. It was always wise to examine a cab when she left it. In one day in Paris she left things in three different cabs. She was such a flutter-mill; always in the air; always singing, dancing, making her tongue fly.

She was full of little loving ways with her mother, whom she ennobled with pet names and enriched with ceaseless caresses. She would pet my hair, and fuss at it, sometimes—which always made me wish she would go on.[32]

LIVY: She was so well that last winter in Paris and so full of pleasure and interest.[33]

NARRATOR: There were congenial friends and Livy was able to entertain informally. Clara and Susy, too, enjoyed the social life.

CLARA: Oh, them were times never to be forgotten.[34]

. . . that red room glinting with sunshine, and the studio opposite, your [Susy's] voice coming from it, the delicious blue hall and all . . . The little Boulevard, the green-sloped front door with a pale light creeping through its glass late at night . . . The Saturday nights too, when Julienne would go for a voiture fermée and usher us into it (you with your green plush Sara cloak and I with my pink one) calling to the driver "Avenue Wagram vingt-cinq et aussi vite que possible," then the bridge, the river crowned with different colored lights, the dark Avenue Marceau and finally the distant notes of a favorite waltz as we climbed the stairs anticipating the histrionics of the evening.[35]

We gave no large parties, as we were still obliged to live simply, but many a laughing voice . . . rings in my ears from that bright *salon* by the Seine. Young architects came from the Beaux Arts to pay their respects; English authors on flying trips to Paris discussed the sins of nations by Father's fireside, always disclosing the fact that they preferred their own sins to any other nation's. The famous Whistler crossed our threshold and left the imprint of his individual personality behind.[36]

NARRATOR: Clara and Jean, incensed by the treatment given Parisian horses, joined the Society for the Prevention of Cruelty to Animals. They were very proud of their blue membership cards, which entitled them to remonstrate with cruel drivers.

CLARA: But Father, although theoretically in sympathy with our new profession, found it extremely inconvenient at times.

NARRATOR: One time, driving to a reception with Sam, Clara stopped the carriage and got out to admonish a man who was standing up in a wagon beating his horse. Her blue card did no good so she turned to a policeman who was standing near unconcernedly.

CLARA: Very unwillingly conceding me my rights, he returned with me to the savage driver . . . when I returned to the cab Father was almost as rabid against me as the driver had been against the horse, partly because he did not enjoy seeing me in the center of a large crowd. . . .

Later Father said to Mother: "Do you know, Livy, that Clara holds up the entire Paris traffic with that blue card? Do you approve of that?" And mother answered: "Youth dear, you would do the same thing if the blue card were yours."[37]

NARRATOR: This pleasant life was a lull before the storm; in December word came from Mr. Rogers of the final and irrevocable demise of the typesetter. The last hope, the Chicago *Times-Herald*, had lost interest.

CLARA: The typesetting machine, though a wonderful invention, proved to be too delicately constructed for practical use. It was constantly in need of repair. The doors had to be shut against hope for success in that quarter.[38]

SAM: I *seemed* to be entirely expecting your letter, and also prepared and resigned; but Lord, it shows how little we know ourselves and how easily we can deceive ourselves. It hit me like a thunder-clap. It knocked every rag of sense out of my head, and I went flying here and there and yonder, not knowing what I was doing, and only one clearly defined thought standing up visible and substantial out of the crazy storm-drift—that my dream of ten years was in desperate peril and out of the 60,000 or 70,000 projects for its rescue that came flocking through my skull not one would hold still long enough for me to examine it and size it up.

NARRATOR: He was going to sail the next day, to reconstruct the machine, but Livy calmed him down and he wrote Rogers a few days later.

SAM: It is six days or seven days ago that I lived through that despairing day, and then through a night without sleep; then settled down next day into my right mind (or thereabouts)... . I put in the rest of that day till 7 P.M. plenty comfortably enough writing a long chapter of my book; then went to a masked ball blacked up as Uncle Remus, taking Clara along, and we had a good time.[39]

NARRATOR: Rogers took care of the final settlements.

SAM: Well, whatever I get out of the wreckage will be due to good luck—the good luck of getting you into the scheme—for, but for that there wouldn't *be* any wreckage; it would be total loss.[40]

We shall try to find a tenant for our Hartford house; not an easy matter, for it costs heavily to live in. We can never live in it again; though it would break the family's hearts if they could believe it.[41]

NARRATOR: He wrote Franklin Whitmore, who was looking after the house.

SAM: I have got to pay the creditors of C L Webster & Co a heavy sum before this year closes. Therefore I am going to cut expenses down to the bone.

I want *repairs* on the house reduced at once to $15 a month, even if the roof fall in. ...

We've *got* to rent that house.[42]

NARRATOR: The Calvin Day family had returned to Hartford in November.

KATHARINE DAY: Our own home having been rented for these past seven years, my father and mother did not wish to disturb our excellent tenants (the Lorenz family) until it was definitely decided whether we were to continue to live in Hartford or elsewhere. ... Therefore, we took temporary refuge in the Allyn House, Hartford's ... best hotel. As a refuge it was not so bad, but as a home it left much to be desired! It was of good country style with no taint of metropolitan elegance. ... The Legislature was sitting and the hotel was full of legislators and smoke. We stood this somewhat unaccustomed atmosphere for a while, and then would have fled to other climes had not my mother had the happy idea of writing to Mrs. Clemens asking her as a great favor to consider renting their beloved house to us. A period of suspense followed; I still remember the anxiety with which the letter bearing the French postmark was opened and mother's pleasure in reading its contents, wherein Mrs. Clemens granted her request, saying that only for her dear Alice would she have considered it, as they had closed the house in '91 expecting to return before long themselves, and practically nothing but the silver had been put away; everything else was in place.[43]

NARRATOR: With one problem solved, Sam settled down to finish *Joan* and it went well. He read the closing chapters aloud to the family as he finished each one. The tragedy in the book was drawing to a close; they were all in tears.

SUSY: Wait, wait till I get a handkerchief.[44]

SAM: I finished my book last night [February 8th] at 7 P.M.,— 170,000 words. I have been at it off and on for more than two years, and have written two other books in the meantime.[45]

With the long strain gone, I am in a sort of physical collapse today, but it will be gone tomorrow.[46]

Do you know that shock? I mean, when you come, at your regular hour, into the sick room where you have watched for months, and find the medicine bottles all gone, the night table removed, the bed stripped, the furniture set stiffly to rights, the windows up, the room cold, stark, vacant—and you catch your breath. Do you know that shock?

The man who has written a long book has that experience the morning after he has revised it for the last time, seen the bearers convey it from the house, and sent it away to the printer. He steps into his study at the hour established by the habit of months—and he gets that little shock. All the litter and the confusion are gone. The piles of dusty reference books are gone from the chairs, the maps from the floor; the chaos of letters, manuscripts, notebooks, paper knives, pipes, matches, photographs, tobacco jars, and cigar boxes is gone from the writing table. The furniture is back where it used to be in the long ago. The housemaid, forbidden the place for five months, has been there, and tidied it up, and scoured it clean, and made it repellent and awful.

I stand here this morning, contemplating this desolation, and I realize that if I would bring back the spirit that made this hospital homelike and pleasant to me, I must restore the aids to lingering dissolution to their wonted places, and nurse another patient through and send it forth for the last rites, with many or few to assist there, as may happen; and that I will do.[47]

SUSY: To-night Joan of Arc was burned at the stake.[48]

SAM: Sometimes in those days of swift development in Paris her speech was rocket-like; I seem to see it go up and up and up, a soaring, streaming, climbing, stem of fire, and finally burst in the zenith and rain colored sparks all around. And I felt like saying "You marvelous child!"[49]

Dull as I was I always knew enough to be proud when she commended me or my work—as proud as if Livy had done it herself—and I took it as the accolade from the hand of genius.[50]

I judged that this end of the book would be hard work, and it turned out so. I have never done any work before that cost so much thinking and weighing and measuring and planning and cramming, or so much cautious and painstaking execution. . . .

Possibly the book may not sell, but that is nothing—it was written for love.[51]

We can't have this little house after May 1; and so it may be that the family will go home for the summer—and they may not. An undecided question, as yet.

I shall run over myself toward the end of this month—and return in the same ship.[52]

NARRATOR: He went the end of February to tend to publishing matters.

SUSY'S TWENTY-FOURTH YEAR

1895–1896

NARRATOR: At about the time of Susy's birthday, Sam went up to Hartford. The house had been opened and put in order by Katy and John and Ellen O'Neil. Sam dined with the Days the night they moved in.

SAM: Livy darling, when I arrived in town I did not want to go near the house, and I didn't want to go anywhere or see anybody. I said to myself, "If I may be spared it I will never live in Hartford again."

But as soon as I entered this front door I was seized with a furious desire to have us all in this house again and right away, and never go outside the grounds any more forever—certainly never again to Europe.

How ugly, tasteless, repulsive, are all the domestic interiors I have ever seen in Europe compared with the perfect taste of this ground floor, with its delicious dream of harmonious color, and its all-pervading spirit of peace and serenity and deep contentment. You did it all, and it speaks of you and praises you eloquently and unceasingly. It is the loveliest home that ever was. I had no faintest idea of what it was like. I *supposed* I had, for I have seen it in wraps and disguises several times in the past three years; but it was a mistake; I had wholly forgotten its olden aspect. And so, when I stepped in at the front door and was suddenly confronted by all its richness and beauty minus wraps and concealments, it almost took my breath away. Katy had every rug and picture and ornament and chair exactly where they had always belonged, the place was bewitchingly bright and splendid and homelike and natural, and it seemed as if I had burst awake out of a hellish dream, and had never been away, and that you would come drifting down out of those dainty upper regions with the little children tagging after you.

Your rocking chair (formerly Mother's) was in its place, and Mrs. Alice [Day] tried to say something about it but broke down. . . .

I was to dine there at 6:30—and did. It was their first day, and their first meal. I was there first, and received them. Then John [O'Neil] sent the roses and your card, which touched Mrs. Alice to the depths.[1]

KATHARINE DAY: The house was opened and we began living there about March, 1895. It was a charming, delightful, artistic house to live in; there was still the glory of the western sunsets over the meadow, trees and Little River, although already the neighborhood was far less rural than twenty years before when the house was built. The furnishings were delightful.

Friends and neighbors came often to us, and to my sister and me it was a curious combination of Nook Farm and Europe, with the Garden Street associations all changed—our house occupied by others, my dear Day grandparents and Seymour relatives dead, and the houses closed. Nook Farm, too, was changed, the chief difference being the absence of the Clemenses themselves, but Uncle Stowe, Aunt Mary and others were gone. What afflicted our young lives most was the lack of opportunity for exercise—no girls walked, there were no country clubs—, and no one but ourselves had afternoon tea with its pleasant relaxation and talk.[2]

SAM: Hartford is resounding with a thundering roar of welcome for you and the children—for I have spread it around that you are coming to America in May. Words cannot describe how worshipfully and enthusiastically you are loved in this town; and the wash of the wave reaches even to me, because I belong to you; it would wash to your dog, if you had a dog. I avoid everybody. I traveled from Joe's to Main Street in the electric car with Sam Dunham and never let on that I saw him. Some hours later I returned over the whole distance with him and never let on. He and a lady and I were the last ones left in the car, and as I was following them out he turned and recognized me. Why, his touching and flooding outpouring of welcome and delight was the most moving thing I ever saw. And his beaming face—and his caressing great hands—well, you should have seen it, if you like being overcome.

I have made up my mind to one thing: if we go around the world we will move into our house when we get back; if we don't go around the world we will move in when the Days' time is up.

I can't describe to you how poor and empty and offensive (Europe) France is, compared to America—in my eyes. The minute I strike America I seem to wake out of an odious dream.

The Twichells are lovely—but you knew that. They claim Susy and Clara for a limitless visit; they even want them to go to the Adirondacks with them. The Days require a visit, too. I say *you* can't visit anybody, but they may have the elder girls. You will stay in New York till that doctor leaves in July. He has got to cure you.

Good-bye my darling, I shall leave for New York now [March 21]. This is nearly the last letter I'll write you—possibly the last —don't know. . . .

The Twichells send worlds of love; Mrs. Whitmore also. Our Katy is the same old Katy. She won't stay with the Days, because with "the family" not here she would be so homesick she couldn't stand it.[3]

NARRATOR: Sam was back in Paris after a trip of a little more than a month and he was full of plans. He had talked with Major Pond and had decided to go on a world lecture tour. He wanted to make a lot of money fast.

CLARA: There were still creditors connected with the failure of Webster's Publishing Company who had to be paid off. There was but one way to do it. Mark Twain must go on a lecture tour. A very long tour—around the world, in fact. Much excitement and heartache went into the preparation for this trip. Father came to Paris to gather up the family and return to America. My sisters and I had become attached to life abroad after a long period of homesickness, and were now aghast at the prospect of leaving our newly beloved home.[4]

LIVY: It is, in a way, hard to go home and feel that we are not able to open our house. But it is an immense delight to me to think of seeing our friends.[5]

SAM: According to Mrs. Clemens's present plans—subject to modification of course—we sail in May; stay one day, or two days in New York, spend June, July and August in Elmira and prepare my lectures; then lecture in San Francisco and thereabouts during

September and sail for Australia before the middle of October and open the show there about the middle of November. We don't take the girls along; it would be too expensive and they are quite willing to remain behind anyway.

Mrs. C. is feeling so well that she is not going to try the New York doctor till we have gone around the world and robbed it and made the finances a little easier.

NARRATOR: They moved from the Pomeroy house to a hotel the end of April.

SAM: I have hidden an hour or two, reading proof of Joan and now I think I am a lost child. I can't find anybody on the place. The baggage has all disappeared, including the family. I reckon that in the hurry and bustle of moving to the hotel they forgot me. But it is no matter. It is peacefuller now than I have known it for days and days and days.

In these Joan proofs which I have been reading for the September Harper[s] I find a couple of tip-top platform readings—and I mean to read them on our trip. If the authorship is known by then; and if it isn't, I will reveal it. The fact is, there is more good platform-stuff in Joan than in any previous book of mine, by a long sight.

Yes, every danged member of the tribe has gone to the hotel and left me lost. I wonder how they can be so careless with property. I have got to try to get there by myself now.

All the trunks are going over as luggage; then I've got to find somebody on the dock who will agree to ship 6 of them to the Hartford Customhouse. If it is difficult I will dump them into the river. It is very careless of Mrs. Clemens to trust trunks and things to me.[6]

NARRATOR: They arrived at Quarry Farm the middle of May. The house was lovelier than ever; it was vine-covered now, and the gardens and a little greenhouse were tended by Ernest Koppe, the young German waiter, who had followed Sue Crane's suggestion and had come to the United States in October, 1892. He quickly became a Quarry Farm fixture, could grow anything and took the greatest pride in Sue's fine horses. Sue lived alone at the farm with Ossmann, a big Saint Bernard, as her constant companion.

As plans for the trip progressed, Sam and Livy considered taking the girls with them.

KATY: I was with them while they was making all their plans to go around the world, and it was then that Susy decided not to go with them.[7]

SAM: We wanted her to go around the world, but she dreaded the sea and elected not to go.[8]

CLARA: It was decided that I was to be taken along as sort of maid, secretary-nurse, being somewhat less unhealthy and unpractical than my sisters, though not very much so; even if all my shortcomings had not been discovered before my ticket was bought for Australia, they were discovered as soon as we were under way. My sisters were to remain in Elmira with Aunt Sue—and I think they preferred the comforts of home to uncertain joys in India and Africa.[9]

SAM: Two members of my family elected to go with me. Also a carbuncle. The dictionary says a carbuncle is a kind of jewel. Humor is out of place in a dictionary.[10]

LIVY: I wish we might have a sight of our beloved Hartford friends before we start off on this long trip, but I very much fear we are not going to be able to do so. Mr Clemens is confined to the sofa yet with his carbuncle and I very much fear it will be yet ten days or two weeks before he is able to get about much—then his time will be so short in which to get ready for his readings, that I am very nearly persuaded that we shall not be able to do any visiting.

I have great hope that by a year from this coming Fall we shall be able to settle down in our own home and live there.[11]

NARRATOR: Sam and his manager, Major James B. Pond, worked out details of the tour.

SAM: If you've got to have a circular for this brief campaign, the chief feature, when speaking of me, should be, that he (M. T.) *is on his way to Australia and thence around the globe on a reading and talking tour to last twelve months.* You get the idea? Traveling *around the world* is nothing—everybody does it. But what I am traveling *for* is unusual—everybody doesn't do that.[12]

NARRATOR: It was hoped that the climate at the farm would make Susy strong and healthy. Her teachers in Paris had told Sam that she could "Then . . . go back to Paris and prepare for the stage (opera)."[13]

KATY: Madame Marchesi, the great singing teacher in Paris, had told her she could be a fine singer if she would only get a little stronger. She advised her to go on a farm for a year and drink lots of milk, live outdoors and everything like that, to get her chest stronger, because if she could do that, she'd have more volume to sing with. Of course Susy took in everything old Marchesi said and believed every word, so she wanted to live on a farm while the family was going round the world. So they had to give up Susy. Then when Susy backed out, Mr. and Mrs. Clemens said they'd let Jean stay in America, too. She was going to a preparatory school in Elmira. So I was to live with them and take care of Susy and Jean. I had a little horse and wagon and used to drive down to the college to get Jean every night.[14]

LIVY: Mr. and Mrs. Day desire to keep it [the Hartford house] until the first of December. Then we will put John and Mrs. O'Neil back in it.[15]

CLARA: The sad moment of farewells came at last when we steamed slowly out of the Elmira station, leaving dear faces on the platform. It seemed all wrong that Susy should have no part in this new experience, Jean was still but a child and expected to work hard in school during our absence.[16]

SAM: When we started westward upon our long trip at half past ten at night, July 14, 1895, at Elmira, Susy stood on the platform in the blaze of the electric light waving her good-byes to us as the train glided away, her mother throwing back kisses and watching her through her tears.[17]

NARRATOR: Sam opened his tour in Cleveland and lectured his way across the country.

SAM: It has been reported that I sacrificed for the benefit of the creditors the property of the publishing firm whose financial backer I was and that I am now lecturing for my own benefit. This is an error. I intend the lectures as well as the property for the creditors. The law recognizes no mortgage on a man's brain, and a merchant who has given up all he has may take advantage of the laws of insolvency and start free again for himself. But I am not a business man, and honor is a harder master than the law. It cannot compromise for less than a 100 cents on the dollar and its debts never outlaw. From my reception thus far on my lecturing tour I am confident that if I live I can pay off the last debt within four years, after which, at the age of sixty-four, I can make a fresh and unencumbered start in life. I am going to Australia, India, and South Africa, and next year I hope to make a tour of the great cities of the United States. I meant, when I began, to give my creditors all the benefit of this, but I am beginning to feel that I am gaining something from it, too, and that my dividends, if not available for banking purposes, may be even more satisfactory than theirs.[18]

NARRATOR: Letters and photographs streamed back to the farm, Clara calling Susy all the pet names: "Pea," "Sweet Pea" and, often, "Porc Pigg."

SUSY: Your letters are a perfect delight. . . . What great adventures you are having! I sometimes wish I were with you with all my heart. . . . Oh dear, much of it must be *immense.* And the photographs Mamma sent are wonderful. My how natural you and Mamma *do* look in your veils and your travelling hats! I feel as if I must be with you and as if these were pictures of our wanderings in Europe.[19]

CLARA: At the Farm one could never be haunted by Europe, for your life there is another individual one. Out here in a hotel where nothing appeals to your senses in any way you naturally turn to the memory of the most sympathetic year you ever spent, everything considered.[20]

SUSY: Things go on here just as they did, pleasantly evenly and absolutely uneventfully. The other night was a great exception for we all drove down to the old base-ball grounds for a band-concert and some fire-works. Oh, and I forgot the other night also, a day or so previous there was a ball at the Reynolds where I did my usual duty as wall-flower. Since then I have been two or three times at the Coreys and have established an interesting and, for me, advantageous relationship with Susy [Corey]. Mrs. Corey is interesting and will prove a friend in need this winter, I believe.

And so it goes. England looms before me in the future, beautiful and golden and alluring. When the time comes to start toward her, I will throw *up up* my hat![21]

CLARA: My! When we meet in England won't it be nuts?! . . . Think of us now and then and remember that we love you. . . . Do have a nice winter and get your health in perfect condition. . . . I am glad you impressed that old crow with your voice, and probably you didn't act as nervous in her presence as you think. At any rate she knows you're a sensitive pea, even out of her awful presence.[22]

NARRATOR: Major Pond and his wife accompanied the Clemenses to the West Coast.

CLARA: It was surely a triumphal march across the continent of America. Each city turned out to welcome my father in great numbers and with such vehemently expressed cordiality that he soon got into the spirit of his task and found much enjoyment mingled with the hardship of returning to the platform.[23]

SUSY: Dear old Pond! He is a manager after my own heart. "Have 'em in *convulsions* in fifteen minutes!" Poor little modest Mamma! I suppose she is learning to put up with much splurge.[24]

Will you tell me dearest Spider whether you feel that this trip is going to be a benefit to Mamma or not?[25]

CLARA: You want to know how the travelling affects Mamma. It is good for her I think. She rests a lot and looks chipper and bright. Change is always good for her and she has plenty of it. She has borne this hard travelling so *excellently* that I am not afraid of the future. . . . She won't have to be on the go like this in Australia, where she will get a maid and have nothing to do but rest and read and enjoy herself.

Well au revoir ducky . . . don't worry at all about us for Providence will see us safely through all our journeys I am sure, and I shall look out for Mamma and see that she does not get overtired. This year will be quickly gone I hope.[26]

NARRATOR: Sam was in fine form.

SAM: Lecturing is gymnastics, chest-expander, medicine, mind-healer, blues-destroyer, all in one. I am twice as well as I was when I started out. I have gained nine pounds in twenty-eight days, and expect to weigh 600 before January. I haven't had a blue day in all the twenty-eight. My wife and daughter are accumulating health and strength and flesh nearly as fast as I am. When we reach home, two years hence, we think we can exhibit as freaks.[27]

TACOMA MORNING UNION: The thing that Mark Twain looks like least is a funny man. He looks more like Hamlet, the melancholy Dane. . . . his hair . . . dressed . . . like Ophelia's . . . after she loses her mental reckoning.[28]

CLARA: Think of our having actually reached the boundary line of mail-carriers, and now we must jump off this jumping-off place and go without letters for *three weeks*. . . . You know Pigg it's the queerest thing, lately Paris is always on my mind and those good old times. Europe seems to stand up a homesick reality, as a result of travelling I imagine. . . .

But we have said *good-bye* to that place where we passed so

many sympathetic months. We are sympathetic aren't we Pigg? . . .
It's nice that sisters can be so congenial.[29]

SUSY: Well, dear little Spider; I will try to get one little word to you
before you sail so far away out of reach. Oh dear, dear, the thought
makes me ill! We have had so many good times together and
it seems all wrong that we should be separated in this way.[30] Keep
well and happy and safe for us, all of you! Try, try to do this.
Your sailing away seems like another terrible parting and goodbye
almost worst than the first, for we shall be such an eternity without
news of you, and that will be hard. I hope you *will* telegraph occasionally.

NARRATOR: Susy was practicing.

SUSY: I have been singing a little new English ballad (it cost almost
nothing), the words are by Charles Kingsley. The song is beautiful
and unspeakably pathetic. The closing lines are

> Airly Beacon, Airly Beacon!
> Oh the weary haunt for me
> All alone on Airly Beacon
> With his baby on my knee.

NARRATOR: But she was not happy; she wrote Clara.

SUSY: I keep thinking of that nice talk we had together one of those
last nights and the things you said are such a comfort even altho
it is hard to believe they are true. I don't really know how I would
have gotten thro the year without them, for I am often deeply cast
down with the thought of how I have failed to be what I should
have been to you all. This realization takes possession of me and
horrifies me often in the middle of the night. But perhaps I shall
have a chance to try again. In any case, you *know* I love you all and
could not have *wanted* more to be a "nice child". The only difficulty is that our duty doesn't end with wanting.[31]

NARRATOR: Clara wrote of going to a palmist.

SUSY: I was intensely interested and excited by your fortune-telling
letter and on the whole am satisfied with the predictions of the
lady. Most of all, I *am* glad and my heart is set at rest at last,
in the assurance that you are to have an "artistic" life and a
career, for I can't help feeling that those things must bring you
something more than a "kind of consolation." It seems to me that
you leading a congenial life will be happy! and oh, I *am* so glad
that all the artistic part of it is settled at last, for I feel that

it is. Ah, and what a "genre" your fate has! Many adventures, affairs and much travel! Don't you think that on the whole it sounds *well* and promising? I would like so much to have that lady see my hand, for perhaps she might enable *me* to prevent some mishaps, but I suppose I shall never see her. . . .

I hope that lady saw no great disaster in your hand that cannot be warded off. And I hope that she saw no danger to either Mamma or Papa on this trip. I think your life will be very fine.[32]

NARRATOR: Perhaps it was just as well that Susy did not see the palmist, for she took all fortunetelling very seriously as Sam recalled.

SAM: She was sensitive to everything. The palmist (lady at a party) told her she would have an unhappy life and that with all her gifts she would fall just short of success. She would be a failure. It distressed her for days.[33]

NARRATOR: Of her own volition, Susy now decided to turn to some form of mind cure as Sam had been urging her to do for years.

SUSY: Today I have been in town lunching with Mrs. Corey to have a talk with Miss Brush upon "physical culture" and "suggestion", a modified form of mind cure, I think I don't particularly care for Miss Brush but was interested in much that she said. I have become determined to get hold of a philosophy that will if possible straighten me out morally, mentally, and physically and make me less of a burden to myself and others. I am tired *tired* of all my *sins,* and all myself! this hitch, this discord, this restlessness making every undertaking impossible, and spoiling and frittering away my life—*why* should it not be trampled under foot and annihilated? I have also written Miss Foote a questioning letter about mind-cure, and hope that she is going to help me to live anew.[34]

NARRATOR: Lilly Foote, her former governess, had taken up mind cure.

The Ponds returned from the West Coast and came to Elmira after seeing Sam and Livy and Clara off on the *R.M.S. Warramoo* for Australia.

SUSY: Major Pond and his wife arrived last night [September 15th] and we have enjoyed them so immensely much. They do bring you near again. They are both very nice, aren't they? The Major showed us the last photographs taken of you [Clara] standing on board the Warramoo, above the sign "all stowaways etc." These last are certainly the best of all the wonderful collection. Ah me, was I not a fool to stay here instead of going with you? How happy and adventurous and chic you do look in these pictures! Major Pond seems to be so proud of your relations with Mrs. Pond and keeps reiterating that he and Mamma always called you "the girls". You must have had a wonderul, wonderful trip. He enthuses and enthuses and gushes and gushes until he has no more breath or language at his command. But he has a full and discerning appreciation of you all and it is a joy to hear them both talk about you. *If* I ever can be with you again, I shall stick like a burr indeed! There will be no extricating and separating me from you again. We *are* such a congenial family. It seems to me no one ever understands us as we understand each other. We *do* belong together.[35]

NARRATOR: Pond described dinner at the hotel in Spokane.

POND: Our ladies dressed their best for dinner, and outshone the . . . excursionists, who occupied most of the dining hall. "Mark" didn't see it, as he never comes down to dinner [on this tour]. I know I saw it, and enjoyed a feeling of pride. I just felt and knew I was envied by the men at the other tables. Clara Clemens is a beautiful girl. As we passed out of the dining room into the great parlor, she sat down to the Chickering grand piano and began playing a Chopin nocturne. It was in the gloaming. Stealthily guests came in from dinner and sat breathlessly in remote parts of the boundless room listening to a performance that would have done credit to any great pianist. Never have I witnessed a more beautiful sight than this sweet brunette unconsciously holding a large audience of charmed listeners. If it was not one of the supreme moments of her mother's life, who saw and heard her, then I have guessed wrong. It was an incident forever fixed in my memory.[36]

SUSY: When I think of you and Mamma and Papa your superior charms and attractions make me look upon other mortals with contempt and a *profound* indifference. Oh dear, you are so lovely and I am missing you so terribly!—how, how, why, *why* did I ever let you go? I do not dare to think but rarely of going to meet you in England, for the thought makes me kind of insane. To leave Elmira and all its bores to rejoin *you*, brilliant, experienced, adorable people, to whom I belong, and to rejoin you in Europe!!! Oh, quell bonheur! *can* it ever come true?

And yet fortunately I am living in a kind of haze and do not fully take in the misfortune of this separation. I say "Is it a dream? Have they really gone and have I entered upon this strange long desolate year without them?" Generally, I cannot believe it but sometimes a ghastly wave of realization surges over me and then . . . !—it is a mistake to separate from the people we love and whom we belong to. I do not really love anybody but you dear three, and of course nobody else loves me.

NARRATOR: Susy's unhappiness was reflected in her relationships with others. Even the beloved Aunt Sue couldn't please her, and Susy wrote that Jean broke her heart when she reproved her for being disagreeable to Livy before she left. She was very lonely.

SUSY: I am thinking, thinking of you dear people . . . repining to *you* and *with you*, and not to anyone else on the face of this earth.[37]

NARRATOR: The Clemenses were given a royal reception in Australia, and they received letters from home at Ballarat.

LIVY: Susy darling, dearest child: Last evening we rec'd our first letters from you all. . . . It does make the distance seem heart breakingly long when you realize how very long ago it is since these letters were written.

I . . . often wish that you were with us for the histrionics, but quite as often I am thankful that you are escaping the discomforts.

Tuesday night we were at Horsham, a small town that has an Agricultural College. We were met at three o'clock in the morning at the train by two young men. . . . They took us on a beautiful drive out into the country the next day, where we had a cup of tea and met a number of people gathered together to meet us. Clara had candy given her and we both had flowers.

I think Papa never talked to a more enthusiastic audience than that night. They were entirely uproarious, taking a point almost before he had reached it. The house was packed, people sitting on the stage and standing around the sides of the hall. The town has only 3,000 inhabitants but many people came from neighboring towns. One man came 75 miles and went immediately back after the lecture, giving him a trip of 150 miles. . . . Well it was a most jolly house to talk to, they made me laugh most heartily, much more at them than at Papa's talk, as that really was not all new to me. A young fellow who sat next to me (he brought Clara a lovely bunch of roses next day) began to pound his sides as if troubled with stitches in them and turning to me said, "Well if it is all as funny as this I shall die!"

After the lecture twelve or fifteen people came over to the hotel and drank papa's health, sat and chatted for half or three quarters of an hour, wishing us all sorts of good things and then said good night. Four of them had to drive eight miles and two of them sixteen. And so it goes, it is constant unceasing adulation of Papa and most appreciative words about him. They know his work well out here, in fact they seem to know most of it by heart.[38]

ADELAIDE REGISTER: He has a habit of carefully holding the one side of his head up with his right hand and propping his elbow with his left palm, as though the great straggling thatch of hair had caught the wind and canted his massive head over.[39]

NARRATOR: Through Lilly Foote, Susy took up mental science seriously. She went to visit Lily Burbank in Orange, New Jersey, where she wrote Clara.

SUSY: Spider darling: I am sitting in my wee room with your friend, (now mine) Lily Burbank. It's all so strange and has been so strange from the first, this Orange experience. . . . We have had the jolliest time from the first in this home, which has been full of *histrionic* characters. We have all been congenial and have seemed to fit into each other like actors in a play. And now I feel as if I had been here perhaps all my life. It is a theatrical household and I do wish you were here. Miss Packard who made many personal speeches and combined people's psychological analyses before their faces, was the "dramatist", Miss Foote our "stay and support", I, the "star" and Miss Burbank my "manager".

NARRATOR: One evening, a number of people, including Louise Brownell and Horace Mann, came in for the dramatics. It was like the old days in Hartford.

SUSY: We had an elaborate drama planned for the base purpose of "impressing" Louise and it went off to perfection. . . . Among other achievements I did "Sarah [Bernhardt]" to this large and responsive house. . . .

I liked Lily B. so very much. I don't know when I have enjoyed a girl more. We go about a great deal together and her lectures promise to be very successful. . . .

I am staying on here . . . in the hope of singing at her lectures later.[40]

KATY: It seems she met some Christian Scientists and Spiritualists in New York and got terrible interested in them; and she got very much excited and carried away.[41]

SUSY: I have learned how to meet people with ease and comfort thro'
the help of mental science. . . . For instance, the mental scientists
say for convenience that we have a staff of being (existence) with
a positive and negative end. The negative end, which is the end
swayed and moved and effected ("a soul effected" in other words),
we are to extend toward God and the eternal truths, and the
positive end which is the firm, strong, immovable end (in other
words "the soul effecting") we must turn toward people and the
world. If this balance is kept we are not swayed and moved and
disturbed by people . . . the reason I failed with John Howells
so utterly was because I was too *negative* toward him. One doesn't
have to control one's *external* manner; it may be quiet or talkative,
but the *inner* attitude must be right and then the real poise is felt.

My relations with the people here in Orange have been more
satisfactory than any I have had at any time or with any people
in the past. My intercourse with *youths* also has been greatly
facilitated. It is all very curious and interesting. But to understand
the *law* of attracting and repelling people is a blessing.[42]

LIVY: I am very glad indeed that Susy has taken up Mental Science,
and I do hope it may do her as much good as she hopes. Last
winter we were so very anxious to have her get hold of it, and
even felt at one time that we must go to America on purpose to
have her have the treatment, so it all seems very fortunate that it
should have come about as it has this winter.[43]

NARRATOR: Clara's letters told of endless entertainments.

SUSY: Your letters are a joy forever! I think I never *read* such letters!
They are wonderful.

You monkey receiving reporters with "grace and splendor" and
having scenes with "stunners"! What *times*, what "shenshashions"
you *are* having! I feel like a country maiden as I hear of them.
Indeed *I cannot* be a part of this family!

What talks we will have when we get together again! *What*
visits! May that day hasten to us.[44]

NARRATOR: In early December Livy and Clara settled down in Pal-
merston North, in New Zealand; Sam toured with R. S. Smythe, his
Australian agent, who was to stay with them many months. Livy
wrote Susy.

LIVY: Clara and I drove along the Wanganui River to a Maori settlement. When we got there we met an old man in shawls and
mats, ragged and soiled . . . who asked if we would like to go into

the meeting house. This is not a house for religious meetings but a sort of council chamber, a gathering place for consultation, they use it between times for sleeping in. There are always some interesting curious carvings over the door and about the building. . . . When we got back to the carriage we began to feel . . . insects about us. Since we came back we have killed seven fleas. . . . In fact since I have been writing one has hopped onto my paper. I have been very much interested in the Maoris . . . but now I have had enough. . . . By the way, as we went toward the meeting house there joined us a Maori woman with her lips all tattooed.

In spite of the fact that our lives are not now all luxury we enjoy ourselves very much. I wish that I could see by reason of this trip that we were likely to soon be able to be in our house but that I cannot yet say. The debt is a heavy one to be paid off. . . . At present we feel that we shall probably reach London not before Aug. or Sept. and then spend the winter in England. . . . Now I hope and expect that you and Jean and Katy will meet us in England. . . .

Clara is sitting by me eating bread and butter and having a giggling fit.[45]

NARRATOR: Susy went back to the farm for Christmas; she wrote Clara.

SUSY: The ball here went off well and . . . thanks to mental science, I got on *finely.* . . .

I still give Susy Lewis [John Lewis' daughter] lessons, and other people mental science treatment. I cured Julie of a headache the other night before the ball. . . .

Your letters are *wonderful* and make me feel as if I were living right with you and Mamma thro' all the tremendous *and* histrionic experiences!—My goodness, it is one *triumphal march,* your progress!—it dazzles me and I can hardly take it in. But I have entirely given up *trying* to realize anything, any more. It is no use. Last night about sunset I went to Ellerslie with Ossmann and tried to believe I was *there* and that *you* were in India and that we both had been in Europe! but I didn't succeed at all. Europe has grown so vague to me I can hardly *remember* it, and being here seems neither natural or unnatural. Perhaps when I see you, I will recover some of my capacity for taking things in.

NARRATOR: In January Louise Brownell came to visit at the farm.

Susy: I go back with her to N. Y. to make a few visits before going to Hartford. If *Hartford* doesn't awaken any more "shenshations" in me, I shall be *desperate*. I am going to visit Mrs. Rice, first.

Narrator: She wrote Clara.

Susy: But, oh, I *am* so anxious to see you dear beloved crows! and it will not be so everlastingly long now. . . .

I shall be so *glad* when we are all together again, *if we ever are.*[46]

Narrator: The family sailed for India in January.

Sam: Livy and Clara enjoy this nomadic life pretty well; certainly better than one could have expected they would. They have tough experiences, in the way of food and beds and frantic little ships, but they put up with the worst that befalls with heroic endurance that resembles contentment.[47]

Clara: When we at last pressed our feet into the terra-cotta-colored soil of Ceylon, we knew that the sights before us would reward us for any number of trials in reaching them. Father seemed like a young boy in his enthusiasm over everything he saw. He kept re-iterating: "This wonderful land, this marvelous land! There can be no other like it." He loved the heat, the punkahs, the bungalows, and the continuous opportunity to wear white clothes without attracting attention.

Sam: I talked in a snow-white fulldress, swallow-tail and all, and dined in the same. It's a delightful impudence. I think I will call it my dontcareadam suit.[48]

Narrator: Sam had a splendid reception in Bombay.

Times of India: One of the most remarkable features perhaps of the crammed audience which had gathered together to give him wel-come, and which included a large party from Government House in addition to almost every prominent citizen of Bombay, was the comparatively large number of Parsee, Mahomedan, and Hindoo ladies and gentlemen who were no whit behind their European friends in the manifestation of their appreciation of the unflagging humour of the lecturer. It is a rugged and even something of a romantic figure that Mark Twain presents upon the stage, with his masses of curly hair, now nearly white, his keen, kindly eyes looking out from great shaggy brows, and his strangely magnetic smile. He was still . . . a little hoarse from his cold, and yet, notwithstanding this, nothing could have exceeded the eloquence or charm of his delivery or have been more in keeping with one's conception of the man than the deep, rugged music of his voice.

The hour and a-half during which he spoke (almost without a break) seemed little more than ten minutes, and yet it was perhaps the most delightful hour and a-half's speaking that had ever been heard by any member of that large audience.[49]

NARRATOR: They traveled all over India in their two-month stay, and everywhere Mark Twain was received royally, and as lecture halls were generally small, he would often repeat the same lecture three times to accommodate the crowds. Livy wrote Susy: "Have I written that I was surprised to see so many natives at Papa's readings, and to find that they seemed to understand everything?"[50] They were house guests of the Maharaja, Prince Kumar Shri Samatsinhji Bahadur of the Palitana State, in his exotic palace.

CLARA: On arriving . . . we three were taken to a bungalow of our own. . . . We had to take our meals alone because neither the prince nor any of his retinue would eat at the same table with white people. That was an interesting slight, tit for tat, as white people are apt to take a superior air toward the darker-skinned races, no matter how cultured and refined they may be.[51]

SAM: Livy and Clara selected presents for Susy; in Bombay, in a Parsee gentleman's house, bales of goods were sent for, by him, and they selected a dress pattern for Susy of Indian crêpe, and were so particular to get the shade of pink exactly right—the "inside of a seashell," as they described it.[52]

NARRATOR: Susy's letters about mental science were a joy to Sam.

SAM: You dear, dear Susy,[53] Mamma is busy with my pen, declining invitations. And all because we haven't you or Miss Foote or Miss Davis here to argue some of our stupid foolishnesses out of us and replace them with healthy thoughts—and by consequence physical soundness. I caught cold last night, coming from Benares, and am shut up in the hotel starving it out; and so, instead of river parties and dinners and things, all three of us must decline and stay at home. It is too bad—yes, and too ridiculous. I am perfectly certain that the exasperating colds and carbuncles came from a diseased mind, and that your mental science could drive them away, if we only had one of you three here to properly apply it. I have no language to say how glad and grateful I am that you are a convert to that rational and noble philosophy. Stick to it; don't let anybody talk you out of it. Of all earthly fortune it is the best, and most enriches the possessor. I always believed, in Paris, that if you could only get back to America and examine that system with your clear intellect you would see its truth and be saved—permanently saved from the ills which persecute life and make it a burden. Do convey my gratitude to Miss Davis and Miss Foote—I owe them a debt which would beggar my vocabulary in the expression and still leave the debt nine-tenths unpaid.[54]

Dear heart, your letter has done me good all through and through—yes, and my cold, too. I wish I hadn't declined the grand river-party down the Hoogly. . . . From him who loves you —Papa.[55]

KATY: By this time Susy got kind of lonesome staying up on the farm so she decided to go to New York for a little change.[56]

SUSY: I had a "success fou" in New York, thanks to mental science and without the help or presence of that mighty power the grey grenouille.[57]

KATY: Clara always called him [Sam] "Grenouille"—which means "frog" in French.[58]

SUSY: Perhaps I came away from there with my head a little turned. At any rate, I think I never had so perfectly delightful a time as those three weeks in New York, and I came away from there a full fledged lover of society, at least of N.Y. Society. I declare to goodness no city in the world can rival New York for brilliancy and interest, and *life,* and intelligence and all manner of resources, I think. Yes, the life there *can* be ideal, the sort of life that "Mark Twain" could attract to him. I am sure we would all *love* it.[59]

KATY: She visited Dr. Rice and she stayed with the Howells, too.[60]

SUSY: The way the Howells live seems to me quite perfect, an attractive little flat, little house keeping care, and Society on the easy and intellectual form of a foreign city, consisting of small gatherings of congenial people, little dinners and lunches and teas. I was fascinated with it. The three weeks I was there I met nothing but literary people or musicians or artists, and the atmosphere was *alive* in a wonderful *large* way. I had no idea that any part of America could afford just such an atmosphere. I felt every time I went anywhere, it was *entirely worth while.* There was an "exchange of relations". One got and gave something.[61]

AN ACQUAINTANCE: I always think of Susy as a winged creature—her motion, her look, her voice all suggested air rather than earth— sky rather than ground.[62]

SUSY'S TWENTY-FIFTH YEAR

1896

NARRATOR: From New York Susy went to Hartford, and she wrote
Clara of her disappointing meetings with old friends. She stayed
at first with the Days, who were still renting the house she grew
up in.

SUSY: Well, my beloved Spider: I am in Hartford at the Day's and
my emotions are *mixed* and have been ever since I got here. I
came as you know straight from New York, and the *real* stimulus
of being with *delightful* people. . . . The change was to say the
least, *shocking* and at first I was *absolutely* disgusted with everything I found here except our house. . . .

I came here and found I had no common ground on which to
meet . . . any of the girls and felt wretched and realized that
perhaps Mamma and Papa would blame me and yet it *did* not
seem my fault, and they actually made me feel *paralyzed* with
ennui. . . . Nevertheless there is a good side to *everything* and
altho' I think there is everything to make life in New York almost
perfect, still the *house* is beautiful and the books are beautiful
and the sky is beautiful and *you* are all *heavenly* (you and Mamma
and the grey grenouille) and when we are here together . . .
why life would be a different thing, *of course*. Then an occasional
visit to New York would be a great help too; and so I don't let
myself worry. The house is beautiful and Mamma's friends are
lovely but the *young people*,—well, there's no use talking,—they
don't *exist*, and it's hard to associate with the dead just yet. . . .

I know this letter is,—"I I I!" but never mind, you are the

black spider, and I must tell you all my adventures. When we are all together all will be well. With worlds of love, Your PIGG.[1]

NARRATOR: The Days were planning to leave Hartford so Susy went to stay with the Charles Dudley Warners. She thought of Susan Warner as her "American Mamma." Katy Leary came to Hartford and lived in a little apartment on Spring Street. The O'Neils came back to the Clemens house as caretakers and Susy spent the day-time hours there.

KATY: Susy'd come over every day to do her practicing. People used to listen to her from the street . . . for she had a wonderful voice and really we had a concert every afternoon.[2]

She had what they called a perfect soprano, and her notes was wonderful—high—without a break . . . she was in a nervous con-dition. She was trying so hard to be a singer. I think it preyed on her mind, her efforts to get strong and well, for whatever she did, she was very serious about.[3]

SAM: It is pleasant to know that while we were far away around the globe, Susy got a letter in Hartford which mightily pleased her from the great Madame Blanche Caccamesi [in Paris] saying (in substance) "I hear that the reason you did not stay and complete your vocal education is that your father was financially embarrassed and could not afford it. I would have completed it for you gratis for the sake of bringing out your noble voice and giving it to the world. I should have been repaid twice over."[4]

Her voice was not only eloquent with feeling, but of almost (particularly after she got to Hartford) unexampled power and volume.[5]

NARRATOR: She was writing, too, which interested Richard Burton, a childhood friend who was now literary editor of the Hartford *Courant*.

SUSY: I showed my poor little Allegory to Dick Burton. He was very enthusiastic about it, came over and talked with me seriously yesterday, said that he advised my going in to literature "for keeps" as he slangily expressed himself, meaning "permanently", and said he would help me place it somewhere advantageously. He also said, "I am sorry that literature is not a first interest with you and I understand it is only secondary". He told Daisy that he would be interested in helping me with so much more heart if I would only look at writing as the business of my life. Isn't this quite chic?[6]

NARRATOR: Harriet Beecher Stowe died on June 28th; Major Pond wrote Sam about the funeral.

MAJOR POND: I have just returned from Hartford with Mrs. (Henry Ward) Beecher. We attended Mrs. Stowe's funeral yesterday [July 2nd]. Mr. Twichell conducted the service. It was a pathetic incident, and I might almost say, event. There were present most of the distinguished people of Hartford, and all of your old neighbors. . . . Mr. and Mrs. Warner and Susy (Clemens) were present. . . . I received a gracious reception from everybody, having known Mrs. Stowe so long and she having been my friend for twenty years. . . . Mr. and Mrs. Twitchell had many kind inquiries and expressions for you and of you and are very very anxious that you come back sometime to live. I wonder if your ears burned yesterday.[7]

NARRATOR: While in Hartford, Pond went to call on the Charles Dudley Warners.

MAJOR POND: Mrs. Warner went with me to your house where we found Susy in possession of the old place. She, and her faithful Katy, spend their days at the house. She seemed very glad to see me. She told me that she had heard from you about two weeks ago; that you had decided to spend the winter in England (near London), and that she and Jean expected to sail in September. She seems quite happy where she is. She says it seems very much like home to her, and she wished you would come back. The place is beautiful, but there is a terrible atmosphere of lonesomeness there.[8]

NARRATOR: But Susy didn't find the house lonesome; it seemed to have a therapeutic effect upon her and she liked living at the Warners'.

SUSY: I am still at Cousin Susy's having a beautiful, happy, profitable time and getting better every day; better and stronger and more able to get on with life—which always *was* such a problem before.[9]

NARRATOR: The triumphant world tour had now reached South Africa, where they spent a long time.

CLARA: When at last we reached South Africa there was a family sigh of relief, for we realized that we were nearing the end of our world-trip and would before long be with my darling sisters again.[10]

NARRATOR: Sam gave many readings and interested himself in the political problems of the country. He was plagued with minor ailments, so, although always elated on the platform, was often privately depressed.

LIVY: Mr. Clemens has not as much courage as I wish he had, but, poor old darling, he has been pursued with colds and inabilities of various sorts. Then he is so impressed with the fact that he is sixty years old. Naturally I combat that thought all I can, trying to make him rejoice that he is not seventy. . . .

He does not believe that any good thing will come, but that we must all our lives live in poverty. He says he never wants to go back to America. I cannot think that things are as black as he paints them, and I trust that if I get him settled down for work in some quiet English village he will get back much of his cheerfulness; in fact, I believe he will because that is what he wants to do, and that is the work he loves. The platform he likes for the two hours he is on it, but all the rest of the time it grinds him, and he says he is ashamed of what he is doing. Still, in spite of this sad undercurrent, we are having a delightful trip. People are so nice, and with people Mr. Clemens seems cheerful. Then the ocean trips are a great rest to him.[11]

NARRATOR: Susy was continuing her mental science treatments.

KATY: She used to have "absent treatments" from Miss B——— every day. "Absent treatment," they called it, and when she got that treatment she'd have to be all alone by herself for about an hour. She'd just "concentrate" her mind on Miss B——— and they would do the praying for her and the thinking at the other end. . . .

There was one Spiritualist—a kind of healer—a woman, and Susy, she used to go to her, and she made passes over Susy's throat—to make it strong so she could sing good, you know. I used to go and set in the back room while Susy was in the parlor getting the treatment. One time they thought I was asleep, but I heard that Spiritualist woman tell Susy how there was a wonderful concert the night before and asked if Susy was there; then she said

"My husband was there, too, with me, and he enjoyed it so much!"

Now her husband had been dead twenty-five years, and I knew it! When I heard that I just called right out, "Rats!" and Susy said: "Oh, Katy, Katy!"

"Susy," I says, "don't you come into this house again! That woman's crazy and the worst kind of a Spiritualist!"

"Yes, maybe," says Susy, "but she's a good healer."

"There's nothing to her," I said. "She's a pirate, a regular pirate! Don't you go near her again. . . . I wouldn't go under that roof again for anything—not for any money.[12]

NARRATOR: Sam and Livy and Clara sailed for England on the 14th of July on the S.S. *Norman*. They would arrive in Southampton on the 31st.

SAM: We hope to get a house in some quiet English village away from the world and society, where I can sit down for six months or so and give myself up to the luxury and rest of writing a book or two after this long fatigue and turmoil of platform-work and gadding around by sea and land. Susy and Jean sail from New York today [August 5th], and a week hence we shall all be together again.[13]

CLARA: We thought of nothing but the pleasure of seeing Susy and Jean again. They were to be brought to London by the faithful maid, Katy, early in August. As soon as we landed we rented a small house in Guilford [Guildford], near London, where we should spend the summer.[14]

NARRATOR: At home, preparations to sail were under way.

KATY: By then we were getting letters that the family was nearing Europe, and the next thing we got a cable to come at once, to sail for London the following Saturday, Susy, Jean, and I. Well, I hurried up to Elmira to get Jean ready. I left Susy at Mr. Warner's. My! it was the hottest day we had that summer. . . . Mrs. Crane, Mr. Langdon, and Jean and myself went to New York the day before sailing, then I went back to Hartford to bring Susy down and all the trunks. Mr. Langdon had the tickets and everything was ready. I went up to the Warners' and I found Susy wasn't feeling very well. She looked very bad and says:

"Oh, Katy, did you come for me?"

I said, "Yes." Then she says: "Oh, have I got to leave now?" She was really in an awful state and I said: "Yes, Susy. We are sailing to-morrow, you know."

"Oh!" she says, "I don't think I can start now. Couldn't we wait till evening, when it's cooler?"

"Well," I said, "that's all right. It's pretty hot now and we can go in the evening when it's cooler." This was in the morning, and then I went to our own house to get a few things we needed, and when I got back in the afternoon, Susy was in a pitiful state, so sick and full of fever. I took hold of her hand and I said:

"Oh Susy! You got a fever! What shall we do? I am going to send for the doctor."

"Oh, I can't have any doctor, Katy," she said.

"You will have a doctor," I said. But she said: "No, no! I don't want any doctor or any medicine. Miss B——— will treat me." I said: "No! Nobody will treat you but the doctor. I'll get him now, myself."

So I hurried right off and got Dr. Porter right away, and he said she was coming down with spinal meningitis.[15]

CLARA: As we began to count the days before their expected arrival, a letter came saying that Susy was ill and their sailing date postponed.[16]

SAM: Susy was slightly ill—nothing of consequence. But we were disquieted and began to cable for later news. This was Friday. All day no answer—and the ship to leave Southampton next day at noon. Clara and her mother began packing, to be ready in case the news should be bad. Finally came a cablegram saying, "Wait for cablegram in the morning." This was not satisfactory—not reassuring. I cabled again, asking that the answer be sent to Southampton, for the day was now closing. I waited in the post-office that night till the doors were closed, toward midnight, in the hope that good news might still come, but there was no message. We sat silent at home till one in the morning waiting— waiting for we knew not what. Then we took the earlier morning train, and when we reached Southampton the message was there. It said the recovery would be long but certain. This was a great relief to me, but not to my wife. She was frightened. She and Clara went aboard the steamer at once and sailed for America to nurse Susy. I remained behind to search for another and larger house in Guildford.[17]

NARRATOR: Sam and R. S. Smythe, who was still with them, returned to Southampton; he wrote Livy.

SAM: My darling, you were in my mind till I went to sleep last night, and there when I woke this morning, and you have been there ever since—you have not been out of it a single waking moment since you disappeared from my vision. I hope you are not sad to-day but I am afraid you are. You and Clara are making the only sad voyage of all the round-the-world trip. I am not demonstrative; I am always hiding my feelings; but my heart was wrung yesterday. I could not tell you how deeply I loved you nor how grieved I was for you, nor how I pitied you in this awful trouble that my mistakes have brought upon you. You forgive me, I know, but I shall never forgive myself while the life is in me. If you find our poor little Susy in the state I seem to foresee, your dear head will be grayer when I see it next. (Be good and get well, Susy dear, don't break your mother's heart.) I was thinking in bed this morning, that the calamity that comes (is always the last) is never the one we had prepared ourselves for.[18]

KATY: But poor Susy got worse and worse. Mr. Langdon come to Hartford . . . and we took her over to the old home. She was very sick and she wouldn't take a bit of medicine from anybody but me.[19]

SAM: In our house after they took her there she was up and dressed and writing all the time—poor troubled head![20]

NARRATOR: She would sit and write while her fever raged. She imagined that she was with La Malibran, a famous Parisian mezzo-soprano who had died tragically young.

SUSY: My benefactress Mme Malibran Now I can better hold you. . . . In strength I bow to Mme Malibran Mr. Clemens Mr. Zola . . . to me darkness must remain from everlasting to everlasting. Forever sometimes less painful darkness but darkness is the complement of light yes tell her to say she trusts you child of great darkness and light to me who can keep the darkness universal and free from sensual taint and lead her on to strength and power and peace. . . . You will never follow far enough in her footsteps artistically to dominate the artistic world with light. Would exclude you therefore from all dominance? This is the arrogance which the Lord alone may hold.[21]

SAM: When out of her head she said many things that showed she was proud of being my daughter. "It is because I am Mark Twain's daughter." . . .

In the burning heat of those final days in Hartford she would walk to the window or lie on the couch in her fever and delirium, and when the cars went by would say: "Up go the trolley cars for Mark Twain's daughter. Down go the trolley cars for Mark Twain's daughter."[22]

At the hour when my wife and Clara set sail for America, Susy was in no danger. Three hours later there came a sudden change for the worse. Meningitis set in, and it was immediately apparent that she was death-struck. That was Saturday, the 15th of August.

"That evening she took food for the last time." (Jean's letter to me.) The next morning the brain fever was raging. She walked the floor a little in her pain and delirium, then succumbed to weakness and returned to her bed. Previously she had found hanging in a closet a gown which she had seen her mother wear. She thought it was her mother, dead, and she kissed it and cried.[23]

KATY: She wouldn't let the nurses touch her or come near her, so I sat by her night and day—night and day, I sat. Oh, it was a terrible time.[24]

SAM: And then the infection crept deeper into her brain and she could no longer see. "I am blind, Uncle Charlie, and you are blind," she told her uncle at the bedside.[25]

Susy put out her hand and stroked Katy's face and said— "Mamma." That was the last time she spoke in this life. Poor troubled heart. It turned for help and comfort in its latest consciousness to the refuge that had never failed it. If anything *could* comfort Livy, it would be the thought that she was the last image that drifted across the poor child's perishing mind and her name the last utterance that fell from the dying lips.[26]

How gracious it was that in that forlorn hour of wreck and ruin, with the night of death closing around her, she should have been granted that beautiful illusion—that the latest vision which rested upon the clouded mirror of her mind should have been the vision of her mother, and the latest emotion she should know in life the joy and peace of that dear imagined presence.

About two o'clock she composed herself as if for sleep, and never moved again. She fell into unconsciousness and so remained two days and five hours, until Tuesday evening [August 18th] at seven minutes past seven, when the release came. She was twenty-four years and five months old.[27]

Three days later, when my wife and Clara were about half-way across the ocean, I was standing in our dining-room, thinking of nothing in particular, when a cablegram was put into my hand.[28]

NARRATOR: The cable was from Sue and Charley; there were no details and no letter followed for a number of days.

SAM: I get a cablegram which I am wholly unprepared for—a message which strikes like a sword: "Susy could not stand brain congestion and meningitis and was peacefully released to-day"— and I sit back and try to believe that there are any human beings in the world, friends or foes, civilized or savage, who would close their lips *there*, and leave me these many, many, many days eating my heart out with longings for the tidings that never come. . . .

I have not a word of blame for aunt Sue—her heart and her hands were full. I have only gratitude for her. But I think that Jean could have remembered me. Or Katy or Twichell, or somebody.[29]

NARRATOR: Sam, totally crushed, wrote letter after letter to Livy.

SAM: I have spent the day alone—thinking; sometimes bitter thoughts, sometimes only sad ones. Reproaching myself for laying the foundation of all our troubles. . . . Reproaching myself for a million things whereby I have brought misfortune and sorrow to this family. And I have been re-reading Sue's letter received day before yesterday, and written three days and a half after Susy's attack of mania; reading it and feeling so thankful that you and Clara went; for I read it with a new light, now and perceive that it has warnings in it that were not before apparent. Yes, and I have been searching for letters—fruitlessly. I have no letter that Susy wrote me—oh, not so much as a line. . . . I know that if they are there you will find them. I wish she had written something to me—but I did not deserve it. You did, but I did not. You always wrote her, over burdened with labors as you were—you the most faithful, the most loyal wife, mother, friend in the earth—but I neglected her as I neglect everybody in my selfishness. Everybody but you. I have always written to you; for you are always in my heart, always in my mind.

Think of it—if she had lived and *remained* demented. For Dr. Stearns once told me that for a person whose reason is once really dethroned there is no recovery, no restoration. Poor child, her (calamity) stroke was brief. . . . The beautiful fabric of her mind did not crumble to slow ruin, its light was not smothered in slow darkness, but passed swiftly out in a disordered splendor. These are mercies. They will help us to bear what has befallen.

It rains all day—no, drizzles, and is sombre and dark. I would not have it otherwise. I could not welcome the sun today.

Shall I write again to you, I wonder. The letter would not reach you; for now there is no need to stay in America; there is but one thing to do—hide in an English village away from the sight of the human face. I think you will sail Sept. 2. I shall know presently. Though I do wish you would see that doctor in New York and take his treatment. . . .

I love you, my darling—I wish you could have been spared this unutterable sorrow.[30]

CLARA: We could not rid ourselves of a heavy depression all the way across the unending Atlantic Ocean.[31]

SAM: Oh, my heart-broken darling—no, not heart-broken yet, for you still do not know—but what tidings are in store for you! What a bitter world, what a shameful world it is. . . . My darling I will not say to you the things that are in my heart and on my tongue— they are better left unsaid. (Why are *you* visited with this calamity). . . .

I had just sent away a cheerful letter to you about the Joan reviews and such light matters when the cablegram was put into my hands in which Charley and Sue said our poor child had been "released." It was a shock. I was not dreaming of it. It seemed to make me reel. I loved Susy, loved her dearly; but I did not know how deeply, before. But—while the tears gushed I was still able to say "My grief is for the mother—for myself I am thankful; my selfish love aside, I would not have it otherwise."

You will see her. Oh, I wish I could see her, and caress the unconscious face and kiss the unresponding lips—but I would not bring her back—no, not for the riches of a thousand worlds. She has found the richest gift that this world can offer; I would not rob her of it.

Be comforted, my darling—we shall have *our* release in time. Be comforted, remembering how much hardship, grief, pain, she is spared; and that her heart can never be broken, now, for the loss of a child. . . .

I seem to see her in her coffin—I do not know in which room. In the library, I hope; for there she and Ben and I mostly played when we were children together and happy. I wish there were five of the coffins, side by side; out of my heart of hearts I wish it. You and Jean and Charley and Sue and all of you will be in that room together next Sunday, with our released and happy Susy (and no unrelated person but Katy)—and I not there in the body—but in the spirit, yes. How lovely is death; and how niggardly it is doled out.

She died in our own house—not in another's; died where every little thing was familiar and beloved; died where she had spent all her life till my crimes made her a pauper and an exile. How good it is that she got home again.[32]

NARRATOR: In Hartford Charley Langdon and Sue Crane made the decision to take Susy to Elmira.

KATY: We dressed her nice and then brought her little body to Elmira, to the Langdon house to wait for her mother.[33]

NARRATOR: Joe Twichell had come down from the Adirondacks.

SAM: It was no surprise to me to learn that you stayed by Susy long hours, careless of fatigue and heat, it was no surprise to me to learn that you could still the storms that swept her spirit when no other could; for she loved you, revered you, trusted you, and "Uncle Joe" was no empty phrase upon her lips![34]

Ah, well, Susy died at *home*. She had that privilege . . . she had you, and Sue, and Katy, and John, and Ellen. This was happy fortune—I am thankful it was vouchsafed to her.[35]

NARRATOR: Livy and Clara were due in New York on the 22nd.

SAM: All the circumstances of this death were pathetic—my brain is worn to rags rehearsing them. The mere death would have been cruelty enough, without overloading it and emphasizing it with the score of harsh and wanton details. The child was taken away when her mother was within three days of her, and would have given three decades for sight of her.[36]

CLARA: The days dragged on, but at last we could say, "Tomorrow we shall hug that darling girl and start to nurse her back to health!"[37]

SAM: Oh, poor Livy darling, at 8 tomorrow morning your heart will break, the Lord God knows I am pitying you. Smythe and I have done what we could—cabled Mr. Rogers to have Dr. Rice at the ship and keep all other friends prudently out of sight—for if you saw them on the dock you would *know;* and you would swoon before Rice could get to you to help you.

Hour by hour my sense of the calamity that has over-taken us closes down heavier and heavier upon me; and now for 48 hours there is a form of words that runs in my head with ceaseless iteration—without stop or pause—"I shall never see her again, I shall never see her again." *You* will see the sacred face once more—I am so thankful for that.

But though my heart *break* I will still say she was fortunate; and I would not call her back if I could.

I eat—because you wish it; I go on living—because you wish it; I play billiards, and billiards, and billiards, till I am ready to drop—to keep from going mad with grief and with resentful thinkings.

You will find my health perfect—for your sake—when you come.

I know where you will be, tomorrow and Sunday, and in spirit I shall be at your side and taking step by step with you.

Give my love to Clara and Jean. We have that much of our fortune left.

I love you with all my whole heart.[38]

NARRATOR: Sam spent much of his time reading.

SAM: . . . my reading being the letters, often—the letters that came from Sue and Jean and Charley, and which *now* mean so much, so *much!*[39]

If I were only with you—to be near with my breast and my sheltering arms when the ship lands and Charley's . . . tears reveal all without his speaking.[40]

KATY: We was all waiting in New York for them to land. Mr. Howells and Mr. Twichell was there too, to meet Mrs. Clemens. I'll never forget how bad Mr. Twichell felt. He said to me that day: "Oh, Katy! I don't know how I'm ever going to tell Mrs. Clemens! I don't know how I can ever talk to her about Susy!"[41]

CLARA: The morrow dawned and with the new day stalked the herald of grief. On my way to the saloon for letters, I was told the captain wished to speak to me. We met in the companionway. He handed me a newspaper with great headlines: "Mark Twain's eldest daughter dies of spinal meningitis." There was much more, but I could not see the letters. The world stood still. All sounds, all movements ceased. Susy was dead. How could I tell Mother? I went to her stateroom. Nothing was said. A deadly pallor spread over her face and then came a bursting cry, "I don't believe it!" And we never did believe it.[42]

KATY: I'll never forget Mrs. Clemens when she landed, the way she looked, and Clara, too. Oh, Clara! She was a pitiful object. I was afraid for Clara. All the time I watched her like a cat would a mouse. Such grief is terrible to see. I could hardly bear to look at Mrs. Clemens just at first. It was something awful when she turned to me and held out her hands and said, "Katy," she said, "Katy, Susy's gone—Life has killed her!" . . .

Mrs. Clemens was sitting in a big chair in the Waldorf, leaning back, just crushed with her grief. . . .

We cried together, then we'd talk again, and she wanted to know, over and over, all the things about Susy, the little things that anybody else would have forgot. And I told her everything—

every single thing, how I gave her the medicine, how she wouldn't take it from anybody else—that she wouldn't let the nurse do anything for her, and how I lay on that couch day and night, right in front of her bed where I could see her every second, and how I jumped up every time she wanted anything.

"Oh, Katy!" said Mrs. Clemens. "Oh, Katy, if it could only have been *me* instead of you! But how glad I am that you were able to do for her when I wasn't there."[43]

SAM: One year, one month, and one week later [July 14th, 1895], Livy and Clara had completed the circuit of the globe, arriving at Elmira at the same hour in the evening, by the same train and *in the same car*—and Susy was there to meet them—lying white and fair in her coffin in the house she was born in.

They were flying on the wings of steam and in the torture of dread and anxiety; and if three little days could have been spared them out of the rich hoard laid up for the building of the coming ages, poor Susy would have died in her mother's arms—and the poor three days were denied: they could not be afforded.[44]

Livy saw her in her coffin. That was denied to me.[45]

KATY: When we got to Elmira I went with her to the drawing-room where Susy lay. I was afraid to leave her alone. I hurried in after her and seen her standing there looking at Susy. Such anguish! She didn't speak, only she moaned a little bit, just like a child. Then I said, "Oh, Mrs. Clemens, come away." But she says, "Oh, Katy, can't we stay here just a little longer and look at my Susy? See how beautiful she is." And she did look beautiful. So quiet and peaceful-like and so fair.[46]

CLARA: We stumbled blindly through those black days. We saw the lonely young face forbidding in its silence—the soul removed beyond our sorrow. Susy was not moved by the heart-breaking sight of her bereaved mother. Susy was not interested. Never again would we find an answering throb from that warm heart turned cold. Mother spent day and night with the earthly form of her beloved child until even that remaining solace was wrenched from her clinging love and buried in the ground.[47]

SAM: On the 23rd her mother and her sisters saw her laid to rest— she that had been our wonder and our worship.[48]

We stand stunned as before a space where an apparently strong house has stood five minutes ago—now swept away by a cyclone— not a vestige left.[49]

CLARA: The funeral services took place in the Langdon home in Elmira, where we were shown tender sympathy and care. Susy was laid to rest in the cemetery we used to visit as children, because of its beautiful trees and tranquility.[50]

KATY: They found a little poem once that her father liked and put it on her headstone. It was lovely, I think. I copied it one time on a piece of paper. I never forgot it:

> Warm summer sun, shine brightly here,
> Warm Southern wind, blow softly here,
> Green sod above, lie light, lie light,
> Good night, dear heart; good night, good night.

Ain't that beautiful? And just what it should be for little Susy. Everything soft and kind. 'Twas just like saying good night to her, wasn't it? Perhaps that's all it was, anyway.[51]

SAM: The authorship of the beautiful lines which my wife and I inscribed upon Susy's gravestone was untraceable for a time. We had found them in a book in India, but had lost the book and with it the author's name. But in time an application to the editor of "Notes and Queries" furnished me the author's name . . . and it has been added to the verses upon the gravestone.[52]

AFTER SUSY

1896–1910

NARRATOR: The years from 1896 until Sam's death in 1910 were full of sadness; they were lightened only occasionally. Grief and remorse abated slowly. Ill health was almost constant in the family, and Sam's emergence as an international sage, as well as a writer, was matched only by his increasing bitterness. Clara, in her biography, *My Father Mark Twain,* guides us through the years after Susy.

CLARA: As soon as it was possible we sailed, with Jean and Katy, back to England.[1]

It was a long time before any one laughed in our household, after the shock of Susy's death. Father's passionate nature expressed itself in thunderous outbursts of bitterness.[2]

SAM: It is an odious world, a horrible world—it is Hell; the true one, not the lying invention of the superstitious; and we have come to it from elsewhere to expiate our sins.[3]

NARRATOR: He found comfort in writing Twichell.

SAM: Do I want you to write to me? Indeed I do. I do not want most people to write, but I do want you to do it. The others break my heart, but you will not. You have a something divine in you that is not in other men. You have the touch that heals, not lacerates. And you know the secret places of our hearts. You know our life—the outside of it—as the others do—and the inside of it—which they do not. You have seen our whole voyage. You have seen us go to sea, a cloud of sail, and the flag at the peak; and you see us now, chartless, adrift—derelicts; battered, water-logged, our sails a ruck of rags, our pride gone. For it is gone.

And there is nothing in its place. The vanity of life was all we had, and there is no more vanity left in us. We are even ashamed of that we had; ashamed that we trusted the promises of life and builded high—to come to this!

I did know that Susy was part of us; I did *not* know that she could go away; I did not know that she could go away, and take our lives with her, yet leave our dull bodies behind. And I did not know what she was. To me she was but treasure in the bank; the amount known, the need to look at it daily, handle it, weigh it, count it, *realize* it, not necessary; and now that I would do it, it is too late; they tell me it is not there, has vanished away in a night, the bank is broken, my fortune is gone, I am a pauper. How am I to comprehend this? How am I to *have* it? Why am I robbed, and who is benefited?[4]

CLARA: The pressing need for money was the greatest blessing to Father. . . . Jean and I imagined we could help earn some money; but all we were capable of was to help save it. Poor Jean was now subject to epileptic attacks—the second tragedy in our year of absence.[5]

NARRATOR: Sam wrote *Following the Equator; Joan of Arc* came out in book form, and Harper published the first five volumes of the Uniform Edition of "Mark Twain's Works."

SAM: I am working, but it is for the sake of the work—the "surcease of sorrow" that is found there. I work all the days, and trouble vanishes away when I use that magic. . . . I am well protected; but Livy! She has nothing in the world to turn to. . . . She sits solitary; and all the day, and all the days, wonders how it all happened, and why.[6]

NARRATOR: On Christmas Day Sam noted: "The family have been to breakfast. We three sat and talked as usual, but the name of the day was not mentioned. It was in our minds, but we said nothing."[7]

CLARA: Plans had been made to spend the summer in a little town called Weggis on the Lake of Lucerne.[8]

SAM: One year today [August 18th] since the great disaster fell. Livy went away to be alone. She took the steamer and spent the day solitary in an inn in an unknown town up the lake—a village. I spent the day alone under the trees on the mountain-side, writing some lines—a lament for Susy in the form of an allegory.[9]

NARRATOR: In the fall they went to Vienna, where Clara studied piano with the great Leschetizky. He brought two young Russians to dinner one night; one of them was Ossip Gabrilówitsch, a brilliant young pianist.

CLARA: Father wrote a great deal during this winter, sometimes in bed and often pacing the floor. . . . About this time he wrote his article called "What is Man?" but Mother begged him not to publish it. She thought it would have a harmful influence on many people.[10]

NARRATOR: Sam's notebook entry: "June 11, '98. Clara's birthday three days ago. Not a reference to it has been made by any member of the family in my hearing; no presents, no congratulations, no celebrations. Up to a year and ten months ago all our birthdays from the beginning of the family life were annually celebrated with loving preparations followed by a joyous and jovial outpouring of thanksgivings. The birthdays were milestones on the march of happiness. Then Susy died."[11]

In October, 1898, Livy wrote to her Hartford friend, Mary Bushnell Cheney: "There has been a great change in the work of one member of the family: Clara has left the piano and is taking singing lessons!"[12]

CLARA: We spent the summer [1899] in Sanna, a small Swedish village where Dr. [Henrick] Kellgren [an osteopath] had a sanatorium. . . .

As long as Father had a quiet place to write in he was satisfied and we all had reason to be thankful for one great good—all Father's debts were entirely paid off now through the sale of his book, *Following the Equator.* . . .

The next winter we spent in London, where Jean continued Dr. Kellgren's treatments with some slight improvement.

After spending a delightful summer [1900] in Dollis Hill, a suburb of London, Father decided that he had had enough of European life. . . . New York was selected . . . as none of us felt able to face the old Hartford home without Susy.[13]

SAM: A Hartford with no Susy in it . . . !—It is not the city of Hartford it is the city of Heartbreak.[14]

Susy is gone, George is gone . . . our house, where such warm blood and such dear blood flowed so freely, is become a cemetery. But not in any repellent sense. Our dead are welcome there; their life made it beautiful, their death has hallowed it.[15]

NARRATOR: In 1901, after a summer in the Adirondacks where Sam worked on *Double-Barrelled Detective Story,* they rented the Appleton house at Riverdale on the Hudson.

CLARA: Mother's illness had taken deeper root and she was confined to her bedroom.[16]

Most of the two years spent at Riverdale Father stuck closely to the house, hoping for permission from the doctors to pay a five-minute visit to his wife.[17]

The rigid care taken of Mother during many months bore fruit at last. And the doctors thought she might improve still more rapidly if she could live in milder climate. Therefore it was decided that the following winter should be spent in Italy after a quiet summer [1903] at Quarry Farm.[18]

NARRATOR: In Italy, at the Villa di Quarto, in Florence, Clara wrote that Livy "seemed at first to improve in the mild air and tranquil surroundings, but her illness had taken a firm grip. . . . Little notes were carried once more. . . ." Sam sent in one to Livy on their wedding anniversary.

SAM: It's a long time ago, my darling, but the 33 years have been richly profitable to us, through love—a love which has grown, not diminished, and is worth more each year than it was the year before. And so it will be always, dearest old Sweetheart of my youth.

Good night, and sleep well.[19]

CLARA: Father was courageously fighting the shadows of depression . . . for he felt that Mother's life was drawing to a close.[20]

NARRATOR: On June 5th, 1904, Livy seemed better; they were planning to buy a villa.

CLARA: Mother was better and we were going to have a home of our own once more. Later we heard Father in the next room singing "Go Chain the Lion Down." He too was happy. Suddenly the agitated voice of Katy rose above all other sounds: "Miss Clara! Miss Clara!"[21]

SAM: At a quarter past nine this evening, she that was the life of my life, passed to the relief of heavenly peace of death, after 22 months of unjust and unearned suffering. I first saw her near 37 years ago, and now I have looked upon her face for the last time. Oh, so unexpected![22]

NARRATOR: After cabling Elmira, "She passed peacefully away last night,"[23] he wrote Charley Langdon on Clara's birthday.

SAM: Thirty years ago, to-day Clara lay in the hollow of her happy mother's arm—just the top of her head showing—and Susy was admitted to see the new wonder: and said admiringly, "Lat bay got bofu' hair." And now Susy is gone, the happy mother is gone, and Clara lies motionless and wordless—and has so lain ever since Sunday night brought our irremediable disaster.[24]

NARRATOR: Sam had many problems: Livy's last gift to the children was a pair of gray mares and he sent them on a freighter with the Italian butler, Ugo, the Italian maid, Teresa, all supervised by his secretary, Isabel Lyon; Sam and the girls had to wait four days in Florence while the dressmaker finished the "mourning gowns"; Clara and Jean were far from well. He wrote Charley: "I hope to have these two safe on board the ship day after to-morrow—where their poor mother already lies lonely."[25] On June 8th he cabled the Langdons: "The ruined household undivided sail in Prince Oscar June 28 homeward bound."[26]

His notebook entry for July 14th was: "Funeral private in the house of Livy's young maidenhood. Where she stood as a bride 34 years ago, there her coffin rested; and over it the same voice [Twichell's] that had made her a wife, then, committed her departed spirit to God, now."[27]

Among the letters of condolence was one from Mary Bushnell Cheney. Sam wrote her from Tyringham, Massachusetts, where he had rented the Richard Watson Gilder house for the summer.

SAM: To her you were a being apart and lifted above the common level. You planted a seed once which blossomed and gave out a grateful fragrance for her all the months while her life continued. It was a letter in praise of Susy's little play. It was never out of reach of her hand for sixteen years till she died. It is in a little locked box wherein she kept her precious things—things which have now been sacred these eight years. It was always by her, it was familiar with her tears, it was by her when her tears were dried and she sank to rest in the Great Peace.[28]

Clara (nervously wrecked by her mother's death) is in the hands of a specialist in 69th St., and I shall not be allowed to have any communication with her—even telephone—for a year.[29]

CLARA: In the early autumn Father rented a home on Fifth Avenue, corner of Ninth Street, number 21, where he, Jean, the faithful Katy, and the secretary settled down for the winter.[30]

SAM: It has taken three months to repair and renovate our house. . . . Much of the furniture went in it today (from Hartford). . . . Katy Leary, our old housekeeper, who has been in our service more than 24 years, cried when she told me about it to-day. She said "I had forgotten it was so beautiful, and it brought Mrs. Clemens right back to me—in that old time when she was so young and lovely."[31]

CLARA: Father started *Eve's Diary* that winter.[32]

NARRATOR: He also was working on his autobiography, some chapters of which were published in the *North American Review* and *Harper's Weekly*. Susy's "Biography" was incorporated in several chapters.

SAM: As I read it *now*, after all these many years, it is still a king's message to me, and brings me the same dear surprise it brought me then—with the pathos added of the thought that the eager and hasty hand that sketched it and scrawled it will not touch mine again—and I feel as the humble and unexpectant must feel when their eyes fall upon the edict that raises them to the ranks of the noble. . . .

I cannot bring myself to change any line or word in Susy's sketch of me. . . . What comes from that source has a charm and grace of its own which may transgress all the recognized laws of literature, if it choose, and yet be literature still, and worthy of hospitality.[33]

NARRATOR: The happy camaraderie with Sue Crane continued.

SAM: Sue dear, beg for me with St. Peter if you get there first. He will remember me as the young fellow who tried for his place and couldn't pass the examination—at that time. With lots of love, Holy Samuel.[34]

NARRATOR: Clara made her concert debut in 1906, and Sam decided to build a house in Redding, Connecticut; John Howells was the architect.

CLARA: Along about this time Father took to wearing white clothes daily at all seasons of the year.[35]

He came to be a good deal more than an entertaining figure, however, for his advice was solicited . . . by all types of people. An editorial in the *Evening Mail* said:

"Mark Twain in his 'last and best of life for which the first was made' seems to be advancing rapidly to a position which makes a kind of joint Aristides, Solon and Themistocles of the American metropolis. . . .

"We must be glad that we have a public commentator always at hand and his wit and wisdom continually on tap. His sound, breezy Mississippi Americanism is a corrective to all sorts of snobbery. He cultivates respect for human rights by always making sure that he has his own."[36]

NARRATOR: In 1907 Oxford University conferred an honorary degree on Sam. It was a great moment; an English newspaper likened his reception to Voltaire's return to Paris after his exile, and the Oxford Pageant to "Mark Twain's Pageant." In 1908 the Redding house was completed and Sam moved in while Clara was on a concert tour in Europe. Jean, who had been away in sanatoriums for many months, came home in 1909.

SAM: Jean is no longer in exile; she has been with us two months, and maintains perfect health, robust health, now that she is free of the privations and irritations and captivity of the sanatoriums. She is out doors all day, riding, driving, and managing her farm. I believe she could have been with us a year ago as well as not.

Clara has virtually forsaken her New York quarters, and lives with me nearly all the time, now. So I've a family again, you see.[37]

NARRATOR: He also had a superlative cat, Tammany, whose kittens were a delight.

SAM: One of them likes to be crammed into a corner-pocket of the billiard table—which he fits as snugly as does a finger in a glove.[38]

NARRATOR: In October, 1909, Clara was married to Ossip Gabrilówitsch at "Stormfield," the Redding house.

CLARA: Only a few intimate friends were invited to the wedding. . . . Father wore his Oxford gown and looked all that he was. Jean was my beautiful maid of honor. And our beloved friend, the Reverend Joseph Twichell, came from Hartford to officiate . . . as he had done for Father and Mother so many years before.[39]

NARRATOR: On the day before Christmas, 1909, Jean was found dead.

SAM: We knew what had happened. She was an epileptic: she had been seized with a convulsion and heart failure in her bath. . . .

I lost Susy thirteen years ago; I lost her mother—her incomparable mother!—five and a half years ago; Clara has gone away to live in Europe; and now I have lost Jean. How poor I am, who was once so rich![40]

NARRATOR: Four months later, in April, 1910, Clara and Ossip were called home from Europe. Sam died on the 21st, four days after their arrival.

CLARA: He was laid in the arch of the drawing-room where he had given me away in marriage but a few months before. . . . And Halley's comet was once more shining in the sky, as it had done at his birth.[41]

REFERENCE NOTES

Reference Notes have been compiled for each chapter and follow the individual title and collection codes indicated in the bibliography. The unpublished letters are identified by collection code, initials of writer and date. Example: MTM SLC 12/19/88 refers to a letter in the Mark Twain Memorial Collection written by Samuel L. Clemens on December 19th, 1888. TS indicates typescript. Initials of letter writers are as follows:

ALS	Arthur Leffingwell Shipman
CC	Clara Langdon Clemens
CS	Clara Spaulding
CD	Caroline Dahlweiner
GHW	George Henry Warner
GWC	George Washington Cable
JC	Jane (Jean) Lampton Clemens
LGW	Elizabeth (Lilly) Gillette Warner
MBC	Mary Bushnell Cheney
MW	Margaret (Daisy) Warner
OLC	Olivia Langdon Clemens
SC	Olivia Susan (Susy) Clemens
SLC	Samuel Langhorne Clemens

BEFORE SUSY, 1835–1872

1. MT-HL I 417
2. MTA II 64-65
3. MTA II 90-92
4. MTA II 99
5. MTA II 102-103
6. MTA II 112
7. MTMF 69
8. MTA II 106
9. MTA II 112-113
10. MTM SLC 2/9/70
11. MTM SLC [Spring 1870]
12. MTM OLC [Spring 1870]
13. MTA II 113
14. MTA II 116-117
15. MTE 249-250
16. MTA II 117-118
17. MTBM 123
18. MTH 5

SUSY'S FIRST YEAR, 1872–1873

1. MTA II 117
2. BC UVA Small Fool. no. p.
3. LLMT 174
4. MTBM 97
5. LLMT 174-175
6. MTMF 162

7. MTA II 231
8. MTA II 230-231
9. MTB I 456
10. MTA II 231
11. HARPERS CXXV 6/12 104
12. MTA II 231
13. MTMF 164
14. STOWE G-WL GHW n.d.
15. MTP LGW 6/3/72
16. MTMF 163-164
17. MTL I 196
18. MTMF 163-164
19. LLMT 176-177
20. MTMF 164
21. MTB I 470
22. MTB I 461
23. MTM SLC 12/3/ [72]
24. MTBM 122

25. MTA II 269
26. MTA II 328
27. MTBM 123
28. MTM OLC 1/19/73
29. MTB I 480
30. MTBM 124
31. MTM OLC 1/19/73
32. MTB I 480
33. MTS 63
34. MTM BURPEE TS
35. MEC 3
36. MEC 5
37. MTE 241
38. HC 8/15/28
39. MTM OLC 1/19/73
40. MTB I 477
41. CORTISSOZ I 273-274

SUSY'S SECOND YEAR, 1873–1874

1. BC UVA Small Fool. n.p.
2. MTBM 123
3. MTMF 171
4. LLMT 182-183
5. MTA II 140
6. TWAINIAN XV 6 11-12/56 3
7. MTB I 482-483
8. MTM OLC 5/73
9. MTL I 207
10. MTM OLC 5/31/73
11. MTMF 177
12. BC UVA Small Fool. n.p.
13. MTP OLC Webster Coll. 6/23/73
14. MTP SLC Webster Coll. 8/73
15. MTA II 231
16. MTB I 484
17. MTA II 45-46
18. MTA II 44
19. MTB I 487
20. MTM OLC 8/2/73
21. AMT 196
22. MTP SLC Broken Idols

23. BC UVA Small Fool. n.p.
24. MTM OLC 8/2/73 and 8/6/73
25. MTM SLC 8/2/73 and 8/6/73
26. FATOUT 178
27. MTM OLC 8/11/73
28. MTM OLC 8/31/73
29. MTB I 489
30. MTL I 209
31. MTB I 494
32. MTL I 211-212
33. LLMT 189
34. MTB I 502
35. MTMF 184
36. MTE 295
37. MTE 294
38. GREENSLET 157
39. ALDRICH 143-144
40. LLMT 350
41. MT-HL I 6-7
42. MT-HL I 16
43. MTB I 502

SUSY'S THIRD YEAR, 1874–1875

1. HDT 3/23/74
2. MMT 37-38
3. HDT 3/23/74
4. MTB I 521
5. MTQ 1945 VII I 9-10

6. HDT 3/23/74
7. MTL I 218
8. CHEMUNG VI 2 12/60 773
9. MTL I 218
10. MTB I 505

11. BC UVA Small Fool. 1
12. MTL I 219
13. MT-HL I 18
14. MTL I 220
15. MFMT 59-60
16. MTB I 509
17. SJS Family Sketch 31
18. MTB I 509
19. BC UVA Small Fool. 4-5
20. SJS Family Sketch 19-20
21. MTL I 222
22. MTM BURPEE TS
23. MTMF 189
24. MTP SLC Letters 1874
25. MTB I 520-521
26. MTB I 526
27. HDT 3/23/74
28. GREENSLET 113
29. MT-HL I 43
30. MTM SLC [1874]
31. MTB I opp 536
32. SJS Family Sketch 2
33. BC UVA Small Fool. 2-3
34. MTM OLC 3/14/75

SUSY'S FOURTH YEAR, 1875–1876

1. MTL I 251-252
2. HC 9/23/85
3. MTL I 252
4. MTM OLC 3/21/75
5. BC UVA Small Fool. 1-2
6. MTMF 191
7. MTB I 541
8. MT-HL I 93
9. BC UVA Small Fool. 5-6
10. AMT 135
11. MTM ALS 1935
12. HC 8/15/28
13. MTW 4
14. MTB I 556
15. MT-HL I 98
16. MMT 14
17. MMT 7
18. MTL I 264
19. MT-HL I 103-104
20. MTB I 562
21. MFMT 36-39
22. MT-HL I 70
23. MT-HL I 127

SUSY'S FIFTH YEAR, 1876–1877

1. LEAVITT 22
2. ATLANTIC CXXX 9/22 344-346
3. STOWE G-WL LGW [1876]
4. ATLANTIC CXXX 9/22 346
5. MTB III 1660
6. ATLANTIC CXXX 9/22 346-348
7. MH 28-29
8. ATLANTIC CXXX 9/22 348
9. STOWE G-WL LGW 4/22/76
10. MT-HL I 136
11. MTA II 115-116
12. MTL I 280
13. MTA II 233-234
14. MTL I 281-282
15. BC UVA Small Fool. 13-14
16. BC UVA Small Fool. n.p.
17. BC UVA Susy's Biography 98
18. BC UVA Small Fool. 6
19. BC UVA Small Fool. 27
20. NAR DCXI 3/15/07 561-562
21. BC UVA Small Fool. 14-15
22. AMT 192-193
23. BC UVA Small Fool. 29
24. AMT 192-193
25. BC UVA Small Fool. 7
26. MTA II 242-243
27. MTM OLC 2/2/77
28. BC UVA Small Fool. 10

SUSY'S SIXTH YEAR, 1877–1878

1. BC UVA Small Fool. 28-29
2. BC UVA Small Fool. 7-8
3. MTMF 204
4. MMT 14-15
5. MTM OLC 5/6/77
6. PHELPS 62

7. MTM OLC 5/6/77
8. BC UVA Small Fool. 9
9. MTA II 54-55
10. MT-HL I 183
11. LLMT 196-197
12. LLMT 202-204
13. AMT 200
14. BC UVA Small Fool. 12-13

15. MT-HL I 194-199
16. MT-HL I 202
17. NAR DCXV 5/17/07 119-120
18. LWMT 205
19. MTA I 10
20. MT-HL I 212
21. MT-HL I 215
22. MTMF 219-220

SUSY'S SEVENTH YEAR, 1878–1879

1. MTMF 221-222
2. MT-HL I 219
3. MTMW 70
4. TWAINIAN XV 6 11-12/56
5. MT-HL I 233
6. MTN 133
7. MTM SLC 4/20/78
8. MTM OLC 4/26/78
9. MTN 135
10. MTM OLC 4/26/78
11. MT-HL I 228
12. MT-HL I 233
13. MTL I 328
14. MTN 139-140
15. MT-HL I 229
16. MTM OLC 5/7/78
17. MTB II 620
18. MTB II 622
19. MTM OLC 5/7/78
20. MT-HL I 230
21. AMT 200
22. MT-HL I 237
23. CARDWELL 23
24. MTM OLC 5/26/78
25. MTM SC 5/12/78 and 5/19/78
26. MTM OLC 5/26/78
27. HARPERS CXXV 8/12
    405
28. MTM OLC 6/9/78
29. MTM CC [June 1878]
30. MTM OLC 6/9/78
31. MTM SC 6/9/78
32. MTM OLC 7/21/78
33. SJS Family Sketch 19
34. MTM SLC [1878]
35. MTM OLC 8/4/78
36. MTM OLC 8/18/78
37. MTM SC 9/1/78
38. MTM SLC 9/13/78
39. MTM OLC 9/15/78

40. MTM OLC 9/29/78
41. MTM CC 9/29/78
42. MTL I 344
43. MTM SC 9/29/78
44. MTM OLC 10/13/78
45. MTA II 86
46. MTM OLC 9/29/78
47. MTM OLC 9/21/78
48. MTM OLC 11/10/78
49. MTN 146
50. MTM OLC 11/10/78
51. MTL I 344
52. MTL I 341
53. MTN 147
54. MTL I 340-341
55. MTM SLC 12/2/78
56. MTL I 341
57. LANGDON 9
58. MTL I 342-343
59. AMT 194
60. MTM OLC 11/20/78
61. MT-HL I 242-243
62. MTM CS 11/24/78
63. MTB II 636-638
64. MTM CS 11/24/78
65. BC UVA Small Fool. 16-17
66. MTL I 343
67. BC UVA Small Fool. 14
68. MTL I 343-344
69. MTM OLC 12/7/78
70. MTFM 32
71. MTM SC 12/7/78
72. WATKINSON CD 12/26/78
73. MTN 148
74. MTM OLC 12/22/78
75. MTM SLC [12/78]
76. LANGDON 10
77. MTM OLC 1/1/79
78. MTM SLC 2/23/79
79. BC UVA Small Fool. 17

80. MTM OLC 2/16/79
81. MTM OLC 3/2/79
82. MTB II 641-642
83. MTM OLC 3/2/79
84. MTM OLC 3/9/79

85. MTM SLC and SC 3/30/79
86. BC UVA Small Fool. 18
87. MT-HL I 262
88. MTMF 228-229
89. MTBM 138

SUSY'S EIGHTH YEAR, 1879–1880

1. SJS Family Sketch 1
2. BC UVA Small Fool. 19
3. BC UVA Small Fool. 27
4. MTM OLC 4/13/79
5. BC UVA Small Fool. 22-26
6. MTM SC [1879]
7. MTN 153
8. MTM OLC 6/79
9. MTM OLC 5/13/79
10. MTM OLC 5/28/79
11. MTM OLC 7/6/79
12. MTB II 645
13. MTN 154
14. MTM OLC 7/20/79
15. MTB II 646
16. MTL I 359-360
17. MTM ms n.d.
18. HC 9/4/79
19. MTB II 649
20. TWAINIAN XV 6 11-12/56 4

21. MTBM 139
22. MTMF 232
23. AMT 199-200
24. MTFM 40
25. BC UVA Small Fool. 27-28
26. TWAINIAN XV 6 11-12/56 4
27. SJS Family Sketch 3
28. MFMT 44
29. MH 26
30. MTM OLC 1879
31. MTM OLC 11/30/79
32. MTM OLC 12/8/79
33. MTM OLC 11/30/79
34. STOWE G-WL LGW 11/24/79
35. SJS Family Sketch 3-5
36. MTB II 650
37. BC UVA Small Fool. 20-22
38. MTB II 661
39. MTBM 140
40. MTL I 375-376

SUSY'S NINTH YEAR, 1880–1881

1. MFMT 31-32
2. MTM OLC 3/80
3. MT-HL I 305-306
4. SJS Family Sketch 6-7
5. MTM OLC 3/80
6. EC SLC n.d.
7. HC 6/7/80
8. MT-HL I 318-321
9. MT-HL I 323
10. MT-HL I 319
11. BC UVA Small Fool. 31
12. BC UVA Small Fool. 33
13. BC UVA Small Fool. 31-32
14. AMT 197-198
15. MTM SLC 8/19/80
16. MTL I 383-385
17. MTCC 2-7
18. MTCC 14
19. MTCC 18
20. NAR DCXVI 6/7/07 250

21. TWAINIAN XX 2 3-4/63 2
22. CHEMUNG VI 2 12/60 774 and 776
23. LWMT 4
24. SJS Family Sketch 28
25. MTP 1880 Bills
26. MTB II 691-692
27. MTP SLC Notebook #15 12
28. MTL I 390
29. MTMF 245
30. MTB II 696
31. SJS Family Sketch 17
32. BC UVA Small Fool. 31-32
33. BC UVA Small Fool. n.p.
34. BC UVA Small Fool. 32
35. MTB II 903-904
36. LWMT 104
37. MTBM 173
38. MTP SLC 11/30/80
39. LWMT 72

40. MTM Twichell Interview
41. LWMT 72
42. LWMT 70-71
43. MFMT 30
44. MFMT 40
45. LWMT 71-72

46. MFMT 40-42
47. SJS Family Sketch 26-27
48. LWMT 10
49. MT-HL I 351-355
50. MTL I 400-401
51. MT-HL I 357

SUSY'S TENTH YEAR, 1881–1882

1. MTBM 150
2. BELKNAP n.d.
3. STOWE G-WL LGW 3/1/81
4. MTBM 153
5. HARTWELL SLC 8/6/81
6. MTM SLC 8/8/[81]
7. MTBM 163
8. MTBM 169-170
9. BPL SLC 10/9/81 ms #532 (5)
10. MTL I 404-405
11. AMT 210-211
12. AMT 209-210
13. MTE 164
14. MTE 163-164

15. LWMT 98
16. MTB II 837
17. SJS Family Sketch 2-3
18. SJS Family Sketch 2
19. AMT 200
20. AMT 191-192
21. MFMT 75
22. MTL I 409
23. MTW 82
24. MTMF 245
25. AMT 212-213
26. TWAINIAN X 4 7-8/51 3
27. MTM ms n.d.
28. MTB II 1023-1024

SUSY'S ELEVENTH YEAR, 1882–1883

1. LWMT 343-344
2. LLMT 209
3. LIFE 242-243
4. LLMT 209
5. MFMT 188-189
6. LLMT 209-210
7. LIFE 350
8. LLMT 212-13
9. MTN 163
10. MTL I 419
11. LLMT 214
12. SJS Family Sketch 21-24
13. BC UVA Small Fool. 35
14. CARDWELL 81-82
15. BC UVA Small Fool. 35
16. MTL I 422-423
17. MT-HL II 461
18. MT-HL I 412
19. CARDWELL 84
20. MTB II 741
21. LWMT 11-12
22. MT-HL I 417
23. MT-HL I 419
24. BERG 52B 3638 SLC 9/27/82
25. MT-HL I 424
26. LWMT 72-73

27. AMT 203
28. MTN 318
29. AMT 204
30. MFMT 2-3
31. BC UVA Small Fool. 35
32. LWMT 179
33. MTA II 168-169
34. MFMT 66
35. BC UVA Small Fool. 18-19
36. MFMT 4
37. MTM SLC 12/12/82 (facsimile)
38. MFMT 33
39. TRAVELING 14
40. MFMT 33
41. TRAVELING 15
42. MFMT 33
43. LWMT 19
44. KING 94
45. LWMT 84-85
46. MFMT 27-28
47. LWMT 85
48. MFMT 29-30
49. SJS Family Sketch 5
50. MFMT 28
51. SJS Family Sketch 5-6

SUSY'S TWELFTH YEAR, 1883–1884

1. CARDWELL 92
2. MTMF 252
3. BC UVA Small Fool. 36-37
4. MTMF 252-253
5. MTMF 251-252
6. CARDWELL 93
7. MTM SLC 4/24/83
8. MTM OLC 4/24/83
9. MTMF 252
10. STOWE G-WL LGW 4/21/83
11. STOWE G-WL LGW 4/22/83
12. MT-HL I 433-434
13. MTE 165
14. LLMT 217
15. CARDWELL 95
16. MTP OLC 11/21/84
17. STOWE-DAY 42-43
18. LWMT 22-23
19. CARDWELL 95
20. ESG 12/5/35
21. MT-HL I 435
22. MFMT 59
23. MT-HL I 435-436
24. MTM OLC 1883
25. NAR DCXV 5/17/07 121
26. MTB II 752
27. MFMT 79-80
28. MTB II 752
29. LANGDON 15-16
30. MTM SLC 8/17/83
31. MTM SLC 8/19/83
32. MTM Petrie Interview
33. BM SLC Eg 2952 f 4 9/1/83
34. MTB II 774-775
35. AMT 213
36. MTB II 775
37. AMT 213
38. NAR DCXVI 6/7/07 250
39. AMT 200-201
40. MFMT 36
41. STOWE G-WL LGW 1/84
42. TURNER 28
43. BIKLÉ 116-117
44. MT-HL II 471
45. BIKLÉ 117-118
46. LWMT 81-82
47. MT-HL II 478

SUSY'S THIRTEENTH YEAR, 1884–1885

1. MTM Thompson Interview
2. GOODSPEED SLC 3/21/87
3. HOUGHTON SC 4/18/84
4. HOUGHTON CC 4/18/84
5. STOWE G-WL LGW 5/11/84
6. BC UVA Small Fool. 40
7. NF 94
8. STOWE G-WL LGW n.d.
9. MH 36-37
10. MFMT 59
11. MT-HL II 501-502
12. HC 11/9/84
13. BC UVA Small Fool. 42
14. MT-HL II 504
15. MT-HL II 506-507
16. LANGDON 14
17. NF 105
18. LANGDON 14-15
19. LWMT 73
20. MFMT 188
21. LWMT 73
22. MFMT 188
23. LWMT 73
24. MTA II 62-63
25. MTA II 62
26. LWMT 30
27. MFMT 57-58
28. HAPGOOD 204-206
29. LWMT 78
30. MT-HL II 513
31. LLMT 219-220
32. MMT 72
33. LLMT 220-223
34. FATOUT 20
35. CARDWELL 20
36. MTFM 88-89
37. MTB II 794
38. BC UVA Susy's Biog. 33
39. LWMT 29
40. BC UVA Susy's Biog. 33-36
41. MTA II 59-60
42. LANGDON 14

43. LWMT 30
44. BC UVA Susy's Biog. after 79
45. LWMT 30
46. BC UVA Susy's Biog. 36
47. MTM SC ms
48. BC UVA Susy's Biog. 38
49. MTA II 60
50. MTB II 789-790
51. BC UVA Susy's Biog. after 79
52. LWMT 30-31
53. MTB II 790
54. LWMT 31
55. BC UVA Susy's Biog. after 79
56. MTA II 61-62
57. BC UVA Susy's Biog. after 79
58. MTP DV 223 b
59. MTA II 61
60. MTM Minutes 6/37
61. LWMT 27
62. MTBM 290
63. LLMT 233
64. LLMT 239
65. MFMT 4-5
66. NAR DCXV 5/17/07 120
67. MH 47-48
68. MFMT 8
69. MFMT 44

SUSY'S FOURTEENTH YEAR, 1885–1886

1. MTN 177
2. MTA II 65
3. MTA II 68
4. MTA II 72-73
5. MTA II 81
6. MTA II 66
7. MTA II 83
8. MTA II 139-140
9. MTA II 142-144
10. MTA II 146-147
11. MTA II 146
12. MTA II 167-172
13. MTA II 170-171
14. BC UVA Small Fool. 41
15. MTP OLC JOURNAL 6/8/85
16. CHRISTIAN UNION 7/16/85
17. MTP OLC JOURNAL 6/12/85
18. AMT 204
19. MTP OLC JOURNAL 6/13/85
20. MTP OLC JOURNAL 6/16/85
21. MTP OLC JOURNAL 6/28/85
22. MTP OLC JOURNAL 7/12/85
23. BLMT 244
24. MTM ms
25. MTP OLC JOURNAL 6/28/85
26. MTP OLC JOURNAL 7/12/85
27. NAR DCXV 5/17/07 113
28. MTB II 819
29. NAR DCXV 5/17/07 113-116
30. MTB II 820
31. MTB II 819-820
32. NAR DCXV 5/17/07 116-117
33. BC UVA Susy's Biog. 44
34. MTA II 82
35. MTB II 823-824
36. BC UVA Susy's Biog. 39
37. NAR DCXXIV 9/07 327
38. CHEMUNG I 2 12/55 52
39. MTP OLC JOURNAL 8/19/85
40. MTB II 825
41. MFMT 75
42. CHEMUNG VI 2 12/60 773
43. MFMT 75-76
44. NAR DCXIV 5/3/07 1
45. NAR DCXIV 5/3/07 1-2
46. NAR DCXII 4/5/07 673-674
47. MTP OLC JOURNAL n.d.
48. MTP OLC JOURNAL 11/26/85
49. MTB I 476
50. MMT 29
51. MTP OLC JOURNAL 11/27/85
52. LLMT 246
53. MTP OLC JOURNAL 11/27/85
54. LWMT 25-26
55. MTMW 120
56. BC UVA Susy's Biog. 58
57. MTB II 826-829
58. HARPERS CXXXV No. DCCCX 9/17/ 569
59. MTB II 831
60. MT-HL II 547-548
61. MTM MW ms (envelope) [1836]
62. MTM SC ms 1/13/86
63. MT-HL II 550
64. MTM SC ms 1/13/86
65. NAR DCXV 5/17/07 120
66. BC UVA Susy's Biog. 80
67. BC UVA Susy's Biog. 84-85

68. NAR DCXX 8/2/07 691
69. NAR DCXX 8/2/07 689-690
70. **MTB II 840**
71. BC UVA Susy's Biog. 93

72. AMT 205
73. AMT 209
74. AMT 206
75. MMT 9

SUSY'S FIFTEENTH YEAR, 1886–1887

1. MT-HL II 552
2. NAR DCXVI 6/7/07 241
3. NAR DCXV 5/17/07 120-122
4. NAR DCXVI 6/7/07 247
5. BC UVA Susy's Biog. 130
6. BC UVA SLC Susy's Biog. after 130
7. BC UVA Susy's Biog. 121-122
8. NAR DCXVI 6/7/07 242
9. NAR DCXV 5/17/07 121
10. MFMT 3
11. SJS Family Sketch 7-8
12. NAR DCXIV 5/3/07 3
13. NAR DCXVI 6/7/07 245-247
14. NAR DCXV 5/17/07 119
15. MTB II 842-843
16. NAR DCXV 5/17/07 119-120
17. MTB II 842-843
18. NAR DCXV 5/17/07 120-121
19. BC UVA Susy's Biog. 47
20. MFMT 76
21. MTB II 822
22. MTN 187
23. MTB II 775-776
24. MTBM 40
25. BC UVA Susy's Biog. 130
26. MTB II 845
27. MTLW 184-185
28. MTL II 470

29. MTB II 845
30. MTLW 183-184
31. MTM SLC 7/12/86
32. MTL II 471
33. LLMT 248
34. MH 40-41
35. MTM Julia Gilman Clark Interview
36. MFMT 3
37. MTA II 63-64
38. MFMT 66
39. MTMF 258-261
40. MH 61
41. MFMT 66
42. MFMT 42-43
43. MT-HL II 575
44. HC 12/11/86
45. LWMT 28
46. MT-HL II 575
47. HC 11/1/35
48. WHEELER 325-327
49. LWMT 42
50. WHEELER 327
51. HC 11/1/35
52. MFMT 27
53. HC 11/1/35
54. MT-HL II 582
55. WHEELER 331-333

SUSY'S SIXTEENTH YEAR, 1887–1888

1. MTM MW 3/20/87
2. MMT 99
3. AMT 47
4. MTM CC 7/30/56 and 2/21/59
5. MTJ XI 2 1960 9
6. MTM BURPEE TS
7. MTN 191
8. KING 74-75
9. LWMT 239
10. KING 75
11. BC UVA OLC 7/24/87
12. MTL II 489

13. BC UVA SC 7/17/87
14. BC UVA CC 7/14/87
15. HARTWELL SLC 8/12/n.y.
16. BC UVA SC 7/17/87
17. MTBM 384
18. MTA II 57
19. MTBM 384
20. BC UVA CC 7/24/87
21. MTBM 384
22. BC UVA CC 7/24/87
23. MTA II 152-154
24. MTA II 156

25. MTN 314
26. MTA II 156-158
27. MTB II 858
28. LWMT 105-106

29. HC 3/13/88
30. HC 3/14/88
31. LLMT 249-251
32. HC 3/14/88

SUSY'S SEVENTEENTH YEAR, 1888–1889

1. MTM SLC 4/19/88
2. BM SLC 9/17/88 2952 f.6
3. KING 203
4. MTL II 499-500
5. MTB II 874-875
6. MTB II 908
7. KING 83
8. MFMT 81
9. KING 83-84
10. KING 95
11. MTMF 262-263
12. MTM OLC 11/30/88

13. MTM SLC 11/27/88
14. MTM OLC 11/30/88
15. MTBM 391
16. MTM SLC 12/19/88
17. MTM JC 12/30/88
18. MTN 205
19. MTB II 908-909
20. MTB II 910
21. LEGROS & GRANT 380
22. MTA I 78
23. MEC 6
24. MTP carbon copy in DV 223 d

SUSY'S EIGHTEENTH YEAR, 1889–1890

1. MTM OLC 3/24/89
2. MTN 208
3. MTN 318
4. NAR DCXVI 6/7/07 250
5. ST. NICHOLAS XVII 4 2/90 309
6. LWMT 25
7. ST. NICHOLAS XVII 4 2/90 309 and 312
8. MTMF 264
9. MT-HL II 604-605
10. LLMT 251
11. MFMT 44
12. LLMT 251-252
13. MTM SLC ms "Satan" [cancellation]
14. LLMT 252
15. ST. NICHOLAS XVII 4 2/90 309
16. MT-HL II 608-609
17. LWMT 158-159
18. ET 6/17/23
19. AMT 286
20. ET 6/17/23
21. AMT 286-287
22. ET 6/17/23
23. AMT 287
24. MTB II 882
25. AMT 287

26. MTB II 881-882
27. ET 6/17/23
28. LD 4/20/35 31
29. AMT 287
30. MTB II 881
31. AMT 287
32. LWMT 161
33. ST. NICHOLAS XVII 4 2/90 312
34. ST. NICHOLAS XVII 4 2/90 309
35. ST. NICHOLAS XVII 4 2/90 312-313
36. ST. NICHOLAS XVII 4 2/90 310
37. ST. NICHOLAS XVII 4 2/90 313
38. LWMT 23-24
39. MTM SLC 10/7/89
40. LWMT 24
41. MTM SLC 11/9/89
42. MFMT 57
43. MTP SLC DV 223 2-3
44. MTP SLC Broken Idols
45. MTM Minutes 6/37
46. LWMT 24
47. MFMT 57
48. AMT 193
49. STOWE G-WL LGW 12/6/89

50. STOWE G-WL GHW 12/3/89
51. MTP MBC 1/8/89 DV 223
52. MFMT 64
53. MTM SLC 12/18/89
54. MTL II 523
55. MTM SLC 12/22/89
56. MTM OLC 12/22/89
57. MTM CC 12/29/89
58. MTM OLC 2/2/90
59. MTM OLC 3/10/90

SUSY'S NINETEENTH YEAR, 1890–1891

1. MFMT 64-65
2. MTM SC [1890]
3. MTM OLC 4/20/90
4. LLMT 255-256
5. STOWE G-WL GHW 6/24/90
6. MENTOR 12 4 5/24 25
7. WHEELER 307
8. JOHNSON 324
9. WHEELER 300-301
10. JOHNSON 325
11. MTM SC [1890]
12. MTM JC [1890]
13. MTM OLC 8/24/90
14. MTM OLC 9/15/90
15. BLMT 257-258
16. HARNSBERGER SC 9/30/90 TS
17. MTP ANDREWS An Incident 1-2 TS
18. LLMT 258
19. MTP ANDREWS An Incident 2 TS
20. MTMF 265-266
21. MTM SC 10/20/90
22. MTP ANDREWS An Incident 2-3 TS
23. MTM OLC 10/26/90
24. LLMT 258
25. MTM OLC 11/3/90
26. MTM OLC 11/8/90
27. MT-HL II 633
28. LWMT 212
29. MTM OLC 10/26/90
30. MTA I 72-73
31. MTB II 901
32. MTP ANDREWS An Incident 3 TS
33. LANTERN Vol I 1891 98
34. MT-HL II 635
35. MTP ANDREWS An Incident 3-5 TS

SUSY'S TWENTIETH YEAR, 1891–1892

1. MTN 320
2. MT-HL II 645
3. MTMF 267
4. MFMT 87
5. TWAINIAN XV 5 9-10/56 3
6. MTL II 547
7. LWMT 110-111
8. MT-HL II 645
9. MTBM 395
10. MTMF 267-268
11. LWMT 110
12. MFMT 87-88
13. LWMT 112
14. TWAINIAN XV 5 9-10/56 3
15. MTN 215-216
16. EUROPE 99
17. EUROPE 108
18. EUROPE 100-101
19. LLMT 260
20. EUROPE 104-105
21. EUROPE 110
22. LWMT 113-114
23. LWMT 117-118
24. MFMT 88-89
25. EUROPE 126
26. LWMT 121
27. MTM OLC 9/23/91
28. LWMT 180
29. MTM OLC 9/23/91
30. MFMT 90-91
31. MTM OLC 9/23/91
32. LWMT 123
33. MFMT 95
34. HARNSBERGER SC 3/93 TS
35. MFMT 65
36. MTB II 934
37. MTB II 933-934
38. MFMT 96

39. MTB II 939
40. MFMT 97
41. MFMT 95

42. NAR DCXI 3/15/07 562
43. MFMT 35-36
44. BM SLC Eg 2952 f7. 1/27/92

SUSY'S TWENTY-FIRST YEAR, 1892–1893

1. MTBM 397
2. MFMT 65-66
3. MTL II 563-564
4. HARNSBERGER SC 3/26/93 TS
5. JOHNSON 320
6. MTA I 307-309
7. MTA I 311-312
8. MFMT 113
9. MTL II 566-567
10. MTSSB 16-17
11. MTL II 567
12. MTSSB 17
13. MTL II 567
14. MTB II 950-951
15. MTM SLC 8/7/[92]
16. MTP SLC 9/10/[92]
17. MTP SLC 9/17/92
18. MTL II 569
19. MTB II 953
20. MFMT 118-119
21. MTB II 955
22. MTL II 570-571
23. MTL II 570
24. MTA II 155
25. MFMT 119
26. MTL II 571
27. MTL II 567
28. MTL II 572
29. MTFM 135
30. MTL II 567
31. MFMT 119-120
32. MTL II 571
33. MFMT 120
34. MTA I 220
35. MTA I 227
36. MTMW 73
37. MTFM 139
38. HARNSBERGER SC 11/92 TS
39. MTL II 572-573
40. HARNSBERGER SC 11/92 TS
41. KING 169
42. HARNSBERGER SC 11/92 TS
43. KING 173
44. KING 176-177
45. HARNSBERGER SC 11/92 TS
46. KING 173-174
47. MTB II 959

48. KING 174
49. HARNSBERGER SC 12/22/92 TS
50. MTP SLC 12/2/92
51. MTL II 573
52. MTM OLC 1/5/93
53. HARNSBERGER SC 11/4/92 TS
54. MTM OLC 1/5/93
55. HARNSBERGER SC 11/4/ 92 TS
56. MTB II 957
57. MTFM 136
58. MENTOR XII 4 5/24 21
59. HARNSBERGER SC 12/6/92 TS
60. MTFM 136
61. MTFM 53
62. HARNSBERGER SC 12/6/92, 12/92, 12/22/92 TS
63. MTMF 268
64. MTMF 268
65. MTM OLC 1/5/93
66. HARNSBERGER SC 12/6/92 TS
67. HARNSBERGER SC 12/22/92 TS
68. HARNSBERGER SC 12/6/92 TS
69. HARNSBERGER SC 12/22/92 TS
70. MFMT 121
71. MTL II 570
72. MTFM 106
73. MFMT 121
74. MFMT 120-121
75. MTM OLC 1/5/93
76. MTMF 268-270
77. STONE 203
78. MFMT 126-127
79. MTMF 269-270
80. MTFM 140-142
81. HARNSBERGER SC 1/24/93 TS
82. HARNSBERGER SC 2/2/93 TS
83. HARNSBERGER SC 2/28/93 TS
84. HARNSBERGER SC 2/2/93 TS
85. HARNSBERGER SC 2/28/93 TS
86. MTN 228-229
87. HARNSBERGER SC 3/93 TS
88. MFMT 126-127
89. MTB II 959
90. HARNSBERGER SC 3/93 TS

SUSY'S TWENTY-SECOND YEAR, 1893–1894

1. MTM SLC 3/19/93
2. HARNSBERGER SC 3/23/93 TS
3. MTL II 580
4. HARNSBERGER SC 3/26/93 TS
5. HARNSBERGER SC 4/10/93 TS
6. HARNSBERGER SC 4/15/93 TS
7. HARNSBERGER SC 4/10/93 TS
8. MTB II 965
9. NF 231
10. HARNSBERGER SC 4/10/93 TS
11. HARNSBERGER SC 4/15/93 TS
12. LLMT 265
13. HARNSBERGER SC 4/29/93 TS
14. LLMT 266
15. MTM OLC 6/22/93
16. HARNSBERGER SC 4/29/93 TS
17. MTB II 966
18. MARCHESI 241
19. MTP SLC 7/3/93
20. HARNSBERGER SC 8/8/93 TS
21. LLMT 266
22. MFMT 121-122
23. HARNSBERGER SC 10/93 TS
24. LLMT 272
25. HARNSBERGER SC 10/5/93 TS
26. HARNSBERGER OLC (in SC) 10/5/93 TS
27. LLMT 267
28. SJS Family Sketch 11
29. HARNSBERGER OLC 10/15/93 TS
30. LLMT 269
31. MTL II 596
32. HARNSBERGER SC 11/14/93 TS
33. HARNSBERGER SLC 11/2/93 TS
34. HARNSBERGER SC 11/14/93 TS
35. MTN 320
36. MTMF 272
37. HARNSBERGER SC 11/14/93 TS
38. MARCHESI 241
39. LLMT 276-277
40. HARNSBERGER OLC 11/14/93 TS
41. HARNSBERGER SC 11/19/93 TS
42. HARNSBERGER SC 11/93 TS
43. LWMT 93
44. HARNSBERGER SC 11/93 TS
45. HARNSBERGER SC 11/23/93 TS
46. LLMT 278
47. HARNSBERGER OLC 11/27/93 TS
48. LLMT 278
49. LLMT 284-285
50. MTL II 605
51. LLMT 291
52. LLMT 290
53. MT-HL II 659
54. MFMT 131-132

SUSY'S TWENTY-THIRD YEAR, 1894–1895

1. STOWE OLC 4/1/94
2. MTB II 984
3. LLMT 301-302
4. MTA II 27
5. MTB II 986-987
6. HARNSBERGER OLC 7/1/94 TS
7. HARNSBERGER SLC 7/4/94 TS
8. HARNSBERGER OLC 7/94 TS
9. MTP SLC 6/29/84
10. HARNSBERGER SLC 7/4/94 TS
11. STOWE-DAY 44-46
12. LLMT 302-303
13. HARNSBERGER SLC 8/3/94 TS
14. HARNSBERGER SC 8/10/94 TS
15. LLMT 308
16. HARNSBERGER SC 8/10/94 TS
17. HARNSBERGER OLC 8/5/94 TS
18. MTN 316-317
19. HARNSBERGER SC 8/10/94 TS
20. MTN 317
21. HARNSBERGER SC 8/10/94 TS
22. MTB II 997

23. MTL II 615
24. STOWE-DAY 45-46
25. MTN 316
26. MTN 315
27. MTL II 617
28. MTM SLC 11/16/94
29. MFMT 127-128
30. MTA II 154-155
31. MTP SLC 11/6/[94]
32. MTN 316
33. MTM OLC 4/22/97
34. MTFM 151
35. MTFM 150
36. MFMT 130
37. MFMT 128-130
38. MFMT 136
39. MTB II 991-993
40. MTB II 995
41. MTL II 620
42. MTM SLC 1/18/95
43. STOWE-DAY 47-48
44. MTB II 996-997
45. MTMF 276
46. MTL II 624
47. EUROPE 299-300
48. MTB II 997
49. MTN 319
50. MTB II 1027
51. MTL II 624
52. MTMF 276

SUSY'S TWENTY-FOURTH YEAR, 1895–1896

1. LLMT 312
2. STOWE-DAY 48-49
3. LLMT 313
4. MFMT 136
5. MTB II 1001
6. MTL II 626-627
7. LWMT 130
8. MTN 321
9. MFMT 136
10. FOLLOWING 25
11. MTM OLC 6/18/95
12. SEP 9/29/00 6
13. MTN 320
14. LWMT 130
15. MTM OLC 6/25/95
16. MFMT 138
17. MTL II 636
18. MTB II 1006
19. HARNSBERGER SC 7/30/95 TS
20. MTFM 151
21. HARNSBERGER SC 7/30/95 TS
22. MTFM 151
23. MFMT 138-139
24. HARNSBERGER SC 7/30/95 TS
25. HARNSBERGER SC 8/10/95 TS
26. MTFM 151-152
27. SEP 9/29/00 7
28. FATOUT 249
29. MTFM 150-151
30. MTFM 150
31. HARNSBERGER SC 8/10/95 TS
32. HARNSBERGER SC 9/13/95 TS
33. MTN 320
34. HARNSBERGER SC 9/13/95 TS
35. HARNSBERGER SC 9/16/95 TS
36. POND 217
37. HARNSBERGER SC 9/16/95 TS
38. MTFM 155
39. FATOUT 256-257
40. HARNSBERGER SC n.d. before 12/30/95 TS
41. LWMT 134
42. HARNSBERGER SC n.d. before 12/30/95 TS
43. MTB II 1022
44. HARNSBERGER SC n.d. before 12/30/95 TS
45. MTFM 157-158
46. HARNSBERGER SC 12/30/95 TS
47. MTL II 630
48. MFMT 153
49. TI 1/25/96
50. MFMT 158
51. MFMT 160
52. MTN 319
53. MTFM 158
54. LLMT 316-317
55. MTFM 159
56. LWMT 132
57. HARNSBERGER SC 1896 TS
58. LWMT 72-73
59. HARNSBERGER SC 1896 TS
60. LWMT 132
61. HARNSBERGER SC 1896 TS
62. MFMT 174

SUSY'S TWENTY-FIFTH YEAR, 1896

1. HARNSBERGER SC [1896] TS
2. LWMT 132-133
3. LWMT 140
4. MTN 314
5. MTN 320
6. HARNSBERGER SC [1896] TS
7. NF 219-220
8. NF 219
9. MTP SC DV 223b 53
10. MFMT 166
11. MTB II 1017
12. LWMT 134-135
13. MT-HL II 661
14. MFMT 170
15. LWMT 135-136
16. MFMT 170
17. MTB II 1020-1021
18. LLMT 317
19. LWMT 137
20. LLMT 320
21. LLMT 319
22. MTN 318-319
23. MTA II 35-36
24. LWMT 137
25. LLMT 319
26. MTN 315
27. MTA II 36-37
28. MTB II 1021
29. LLMT 326
30. LLMT 320-321
31. MFMT 170-171
32. LLMT 321-322
33. LWMT 137
34. MTL II 635
35. MTL II 641
36. MTL II 636
37. MFMT 171
38. LLMT 323
39. LLMT 325
40. LLMT 321
41. LWMT 137
42. MFMT 171
43. LWMT 137-139
44. MT-HL II 663
45. MTN 319
46. LWMT 139
47. MFMT 171
48. MTA II 37
49. MTN 320
50. MFMT 172
51. LWMT 141
52. NAR DCXII 4/5/07 678

AFTER SUSY, 1896–1910

1. MFMT 177
2. MFMT 179
3. LLMT 328
4. MTL II 640-641
5. MFMT 177
6. MTL II 641-642
7. MTB II 1027
8. MFMT 185
9. MTN 336
10. MFMT 208
11. MTN 363
12. MTM OLC 10/7/98
13. MFMT 214-216
14. MTB II 1074
15. MTL II 697
16. MFMT 227
17. MFMT 238
18. MFMT 240
19. MFMT 247
20. MFMT 250
21. MFMT 252-253
22. MTN 387
23. MTM SLC [6/6/04]
24. MTM SLC 6/8/04
25. MTM SLC 6/26/04
26. MTM SLC 6/8/04
27. MTN 390
28. MTM SLC 7/21/04
29. MTL II 761
30. MFMT 257
31. MTL II 760-761
32. MFMT 257
33. MTA II 65-66
34. MTM SLC 3/13/05
35. MFMT 267
36. MFMT 261-262
37. MTM SLC 6/21/09
38. MTL II 821
39. MFMT 281
40. CEMT 486-487
41. MFMT 291

BIBLIOGRAPHY

Inasmuch as the style of biographical presentation calls for multitudinous reference notes, the bibliographical material has been arranged to follow the alphabetical listing of the individual title and collection codes.

BOOKS AND PERIODICALS

ALDRICH   Mrs. Thomas Bailey Aldrich. *Crowding Memories.* Boston: Houghton Mifflin Co., 1920.

AMT   [Samuel L. Clemens] Mark Twain. *The Autobiography of Mark Twain: Including Chapters Now Published for the First Time as Arranged and Edited with an Introduction and Notes by Charles Neider.* New York: Harper & Brothers, 1959.

ATLANTIC   *The Atlantic Monthly.* Boston, CXXX, September, 1922, Mrs. James T. Fields, "Bret Harte and Mark Twain in the Seventies."

BELKNAP   *Mark Twain Memorabilia.* Collected and Presented to the Connecticut State Library by Leverett Belknap, September 29, 1931, Vol. IV.

BIKLÉ   Lucy Leffingwell Cable Biklé. *George W. Cable: His Life and Letters.* New York: Charles Scribner's Sons, 1928.

BLMT   Albert Bigelow Paine. *The Boy's Life of Mark Twain: The Story of a Man Who Made the World Laugh and Love Him.* New York: Harper & Brothers, 1916.

CARDWELL   Guy A. Cardwell. *Twins of Genius.* East Lansing: Michigan State College Press, 1953.

CEMT   [Samuel L. Clemens] Mark Twain. Charles Neider, ed. *Complete Essays of Mark Twain.* Garden City, New York: Doubleday & Co., 1963.

CHEMUNG   *Chemung County Historical Journal.* Elmira, New York, Vol. I, No. 2, December, 1955, Ida Langdon, "Three Generations of the Langdon Family in Elmira"; Vol. VI, No. 2, December, 1960, Ida Langdon, "My Uncle, Mark Twain."

CHRISTIAN UNION   *The Christian Union,* Outlook Publishing Company, New York, July 16, 1885, [Samuel L. Clemens] Mark Twain, "What Ought He to Have Done?"

CORTISSOZ   Royal Cortissoz. *The Life of Whitelaw Reid.* Two vols. New York: Charles Scribner's Sons, 1921.

ESG   Elmira *Star-Gazette.* Elmira, New York, December 5, 1935.

ET   Elmira *Telegram.* Elmira, New York, June 17, 1923.

EUROPE   [Samuel L. Clemens] Mark Twain. Albert Bigelow Paine, ed. *Europe and Elsewhere*. New York: Harper & Brothers, 1923.

FATOUT   Paul Fatout. *Mark Twain on the Lecture Circuit*. Bloomington, Indiana: Indiana University Press, 1960.

FOLLOWING   [Samuel L. Clemens] Mark Twain. *Following the Equator*. Hartford, Connecticut: American Publishing Co., 1897.

GREENSLET   Ferris Greenslet. *The Life of Thomas Bailey Aldrich*. Boston: Houghton Mifflin Co., 1908.

HAPGOOD   Norman Hapgood. *The Changing Years*. New York: Farrar & Rinehart, 1930.

HARPERS   *Harper's Magazine*. New York, CXXV, No. 12, August 1912; CXXXV, September, December, 1917.

HC   Hartford *Courant*. Hartford, Connecticut, June 7, 1880; November 9, 1884; September 23, 1885; December 11, 1886; March 13 and 14, 1888; August 15, 1928; November 1, 1935.

HDT   Hartford *Daily Times*. Hartford, Connecticut, March 23, 1874.

JOHNSON   Robert Underwood Johnson. *Remembered Yesterdays*. Boston: Little, Brown & Co., 1923.

KING   Grace King. *Memories of a Southern Woman of Letters*. New York: Macmillan Co., 1932.

LANGDON   Jervis Langdon. *Samuel Langhorne Clemens: Some Reminiscences and Some Excerpts from Letters and Unpublished Manuscripts*. Privately printed, 1935.

LANTERN   *The Lantern* [Bryn Mawr College student literary publication]. Bryn Mawr, Pennsylvania, Vol. I, 1891.

LEAVITT   Michael Bennett Leavitt. *Fifty Years in Theatrical Management*. New York: Broadway Publishing Co., 1912.

LEGROS & GRANT   Lucien Alphonse Legros and John Cameron Grant. *Typographical Printing-Surfaces: The Technology and Mechanism of Their Production*. London: Longmans, Green, & Co., 1916.

LIFE   [Samuel L. Clemens] Mark Twain. *Life on the Mississippi*, Uniform Edition. New York: Harper & Brothers, 1904.

LD   *Literary Digest*. New York, Funk & Wagnalls, April 20, 1935.

LLMT   [Samuel L. Clemens] Mark Twain. Dixon Wecter, ed. *The Love Letters Of Mark Twain*. New York: Harper & Brothers, 1949.

LWMT   Mary Lawton. *A Lifetime with Mark Twain: The Memories of Katy Leary for Thirty Years His Faithful and Devoted Servant*. New York: Harcourt, Brace & Co., 1925.

MARCHESI   Blanche Marchesi. *A Singer's Pilgrimage*. London: G. Richards, Ltd., 1933.

MEC   *The List of Members of The Monday Evening Club Together with the Record of Papers Read at Their Meetings 1869-1954: With an Introduction by the Fourth Secretary [Howell Cheney] of the Club*. Hartford, Connecticut, privately printed, 1954.

MENTOR   *The Mentor*. Springfield, Ohio, Vol. 12, No. 4, Serial No. 255, May, 1924, Clara Clemens Gabrilówitsch, "My Father."

MFMT   Clara Clemens. *My Father Mark Twain*. New York: Harper & Brothers, 1931.

MH   Helen Post Chapman. *My Hartford of the Nineteenth Century*. Hartford, Connecticut: Edward Valentine Mitchell, 1928.

MMT   William Dean Howells. *My Mark Twain: Reminiscences and Criticism*. New York: Harper & Brothers, 1910.

MTA   [Samuel L. Clemens] Mark Twain. *Mark Twain's Autobiography: With an Introduction by Albert Bigelow Paine*. Two vols. New York: Harper & Brothers, 1924.

MTB   Albert Bigelow Paine. *Mark Twain: A Biography: The Personal and Literary Life of Samuel Langhorne Clemens*. Three vols. New York: Harper & Brothers, 1912.

MTBM   [Samuel L. Clemens] Mark Twain. Samuel Charles Webster, ed. *Mark Twain, Business Man*. Boston: Little, Brown & Company, 1946.

MTCC   [Samuel L. Clemens] Mark Twain. *Concerning Cats: Two Tales by Mark Twain with an Introduction by Frederick Anderson*. San Francisco: Book Club of California, 1959.

MTE   [Samuel L. Clemens] Mark Twain. Bernard De Voto, ed. *Mark Twain in Eruption: Hitherto Unpublished Papers about Man and Events*. New York: Harper & Brothers, 1940.

MTFM   Caroline Thomas Harnsberger. *Mark Twain Family Man*. New York: Citadel Press, 1960.

MTH   Henry Darbee, ed. *Mark Twain in Hartford*. Hartford, Connecticut: The Mark Twain Library and Memorial Commission,* 1958.

MT-HL   [Samuel L. Clemens and William Dean Howells] Henry Nash Smith and William M. Gibson with the assistance of Frederick Anderson, eds. *Mark Twain-Howells Letters: The Correspondence of Samuel L. Clemens and William Dean Howells, 1872-1910*. Two vols. Cambridge: Belknap Press of Harvard University, 1960.

MTJ   *Mark Twain Journal* (formerly *Mark Twain Quarterly*). Webster Groves, Missouri, Vol. VII, No. 1, 1945, Mark Lederer, "Mark Twain in Vienna"; Vol. XI, No. 2, 1960, Ernest J. Moyne, "Mark Twain Meets a Lady from Finland."

MTL   [Samuel L. Clemens] Mark Twain. *Mark Twain's Letters: Arranged with Comment by Albert Bigelow Paine*. Two vols. New York: Harper & Brothers, 1917.

MTLW   Will M. Clemens. *Mark Twain His Life and Work: A Biographical Sketch*. San Francisco: Clemens Publishing Co., 1892.

MTMF   [Samuel L. Clemens] Mark Twain. Dixon Wecter, ed. *Mark Twain to Mrs. Fairbanks*. San Marino, California: Huntington Library, 1949.

MTMW   Edward Wagenknecht. *Mark Twain: The Man and His Work*. Norman, Oklahoma: University of Oklahoma Press, New and Revised Edition, 1961.

* The name of the Mark Twain Library and Memorial Commission was changed, by an Act of the Connecticut Legislature in 1963, to the Mark Twain Memorial.

MTN   [Samuel L. Clemens] Mark Twain. *Mark Twain's Notebook:*
               Prepared for Publication with Comments by Albert Bigelow
               Paine. New York: Harper & Brothers, 1935.
MTQ   *Mark Twain Quarterly.* See MTJ.
MTS   [Samuel L. Clemens] Mark Twain. *Mark Twain's Speeches:*
               With an Introduction by William Dean Howells. New York:
               Harper & Brothers, 1910.
MTSSB   *Mark Twain's Birthday: Report of the Celebration of the*
               Sixty-Seventh Thereof at the Metropolitan Club New York
               November 28th. Privately printed, 1902.
MTW   Bernard De Voto. *Mark Twain at Work.* Cambridge: Har-
               vard University Press, 1942.
NAR   *North American Review.* New York, [Samuel L. Clemens]
               Mark Twain, "Chapters from My Autobiography"; Susy
               Clemens, "Biography of Mark Twain." DCXI, March 15,
               1907; DCXII, April 5, 1907; DCXIV May 3, 1907; DCXV
               May 17, 1907, DCXVI June 7, 1907; DCXX August 2, 1907.
NF   Kenneth R. Andrews. *Nook Farm: Mark Twain's Hartford*
               Circle. Cambridge: Harvard University Press, 1950.
PHELPS   William Lyon Phelps. *Autobiography with Letters.* New
               York: Oxford University Press, 1939.
POND   Major J. B. Pond. *Eccentricities Of Genius: Memories of*
               Famous Men and Women of Platform and Stage. London:
               Chatto & Windus, 1901.
ST. NICHOLAS   *St. Nicholas: An Illustrated Magazine for Young Folks.* New
               York, Century Co., Vol. XVII, No. 4, February, 1890 [Sam-
               uel L. Clemens and Elsie Leslie Lyde], "A Wonderful Pair
               of Slippers (With Letters Concerning Them from Mark
               Twain and Elsie Leslie Lyde)"
SEP   *Saturday Evening Post.* Philadelphia, September 29, 1900,
               James B. Pond, "Across the Continent with Mark Twain."
STONE   Albert E. Stone, Jr. *The Innocent Eye: Childhood in Mark*
               Twain's Imagination. New Haven: Yale University Press,
               1961.
STOWE-DAY   Katharine Seymour Day, "Mark Twain's First Years in Hart-
               ford, and Personal Memories of the Clemens Family" [un-
               published thesis, M.A. Trinity College, 1936].
TI   *The Times of India.* Vol. X, New Series, No. 22, Bombay,
               Saturday, January 25, 1896.
TRAVELING   [Samuel L. Clemens] Mark Twain. Daniel Morley Mc-
               Keithan, ed. *Traveling with the Innocents Abroad: Mark*
               Twain's Original Reports from Europe and The Holy Land.
               Norman, Oklahoma: University of Oklahoma Press, 1958.
TURNER   Arlin Turner. *Mark Twain and George W. Cable: The*
               Record of a Literary Friendship. Michigan State University
               Press, 1960.
TWAINIAN   *The Twainian.* Perry, Missouri, Tenth Year, No. 4, July-
               August, 1951; Fifteenth Year, No. 5, September-October,
               1956, No. 6, November-December, 1956; Twenty-second
               Year, No. 2, March-April, 1963.
WHEELER   Candace Wheeler. *Yesterdays in a Busy Life.* New York:
               Harper & Brothers, 1918.

COLLECTIONS AND LIBRARIES

BC UVA   Clifton Waller Barrett Library of American Literature, University of Virginia, Charlottesville, Virginia, [Samuel L. Clemens] "A Record of the Small Foolishnesses of Bay and Susie Clemens"; [Susy Clemens] "Biography of Mark Twain."

BERG   Henry W. and Albert A. Berg Collection, New York Public Library, New York, N.Y.

BM   Manuscript Room, British Museum, London.

BPL   Manuscript Room, Boston Public Library, Boston, Massachusetts.

EC   Elmira College Libraries, Elmira, New York.

GOODSPEED   Collection of Mrs. Charles A. Goodspeed, West Hartford, Connecticut.

HARNSBERGER   Collection of Caroline Thomas Harnsberger, Winnetka, Illinois.

HARTWELL   Collection of Mrs. Harold F. Whitmore and Mrs. Frances Whitmore Hartwell, Pasadena, California.

HOUGHTON   Houghton Library, Harvard College Library, Cambridge, Massachusetts.

MTM   Mark Twain Memorial, Hartford, Connecticut.

MTP   Mark Twain Papers, the General Library, University of California, Berkeley, California.

SJS   Estelle Doheny Collection, the Edward Laurance Doheny Memorial Library, St. John's Seminary, Camarillo, California.

STOWE
STOWE-G-WL   Stowe, Beecher, Hooker, Seymour, Day Memorial Library and Historical Foundation, Hartford, Connecticut. Gillette-Warner Letters.

WATKINSON   Charles Dudley Warner Collection, Watkinson Library, Trinity College Library, Hartford, Connecticut.

BIOGRAPHICAL DIRECTORY

Names listed here have been selected to supplement information given in the text.

ALDRICH, THOMAS BAILEY (1836–1907). Editor, writer, poet. He became managing editor of the New York *Illustrated News* 1862, editor of Boston's *Every Saturday* 1866–1874, and was editor of the *Atlantic* 1881–1890. In 1865 he married Lilian Woodman in New York. She published her memoirs, *Crowding Memories,* in 1920.

BECKWITH, JAMES CARROLL (1852–1917). Hannibal, Missouri's, second most famous citizen, who became one of New York's most popular painters. Beckwith studied in Chicago, New York and four years in Paris, where he lived and worked with John Singer Sargent. He helped to organize the Art Students League.

BEECHER, CATHARINE (1800–1878). Educator, author, antifeminist and home economist. She was a daughter of Lyman Beecher, Congregationalist preacher who had three wives and thirteen children. She was the principal of the Hartford Female Seminary.

BEECHER, HENRY WARD (1813–1889). Congregational clergyman and eloquent preacher. Son of Lyman Beecher. He was active in the Republican campaign of 1856, and enlisted sympathy for the Northern cause in England during Civil war. He became pastor of Plymouth Church, Brooklyn, New York, in 1847, and in 1874 he became center of the scandal in which Theodore Tilton charged him with adultery with Tilton's wife.

BEECHER, THOMAS KINNICUT (1824–1900). The twelfth of Lyman Beecher's thirteen children, was ordained Congregational minister in 1851; in 1854 he was invited by Jervis Langdon to assume pulpit of Park Church, Elmira, New York. He was a pioneer in the "institutional Church" movement. His second wife was Julia Jones, great-granddaughter of Noah Webster.

BLISS, ELISHA P. (1822–1880). President of the American Publishing Company, Hartford, who asked Mark Twain for a subscription book on his *Quaker City* experiences, and subsequently published all his books through 1880. In 1870 Bliss established *The Publisher,* and Mark Twain prevailed upon him to make Orion Clemens the editor.

BROWN, JOHN (1810–1882). Edinburgh physician and author of the popular and poignant tale, *Rab and His Friends.*

BROWNELL, LOUISE (d. 1961). Graduated from Bryn Mawr, where she won European fellowship to study at Oxford and Leipzig Universities. She received her Ph.D. from Bryn Mawr in 1897. In 1900 she married Arthur Percy Saunders; they had three children: Silvia, Olivia (named for Susy Clemens) and Percy Brownell.

BUNCE, WILLIAM GEDNEY (1840–1916). American impressionist painter whose master was Titian. His favorite subject was Venice; Queen Victoria ordered a Venetian landscape from him. He had a studio in Paris, where his close friend was Augustus Saint-Gaudens.

BURTON, RICHARD EUGENE (1861–1940). Son of one of Hartford's great Congregational clergymen, Nathaniel Judson Burton (successor to Horace Bushnell), he grew up in Nook Farm absorbing its attitude of genteel culture. He was a Yale graduate. He took over Mark Twain's Browning class in 1891, became literary editor of the Hartford *Courant* and later was professor of English, first at the University of Minnesota, and then at Rollins College.

BUSHNELL, REV. DR. HORACE (1802–1876). One of the great preachers of the nineteenth century, he was considered "the Emerson of Hartford." At the North Church he practiced the genial conservatism which was replacing dour Calvinism. It was Bushnell who recommended Twichell for pastor of the newly founded Asylum Hill Congregational Church in 1865. Dr. Bushnell was one of the founders of the Monday Evening Club.

CABLE, GEORGE WASHINGTON (1844–1925). American novelist known for stories of French New Orleans and the rivers, swamps and forests of Louisiana. Mark Twain's admiration of him was tempered by his irritation with Cable's sanctimoniousness (overpunctilious observance of the Sabbath).

CHAMBERLIN, FRANKLIN (1821–1896). Hartford attorney who bought several parcels of land from Hooker and Gillette in Nook Farm, and resold some of it to Mark Twain. Chamberlin built himself a large house next to the Clemens house on the corner of Farmington Avenue and Forest Street; it is now (1965) part of the Stowe-Day Foundation.

CHAMPNEY, JAMES WELLS (1843–1943). American painter and illustrator. He was born in Boston and studied in Antwerp and Paris, where he exhibited in the 1869 Salon. He taught art at Smith College and directed classes at the Hartford Society of Decorative Arts (precursor of Hartford Art School), of which Mrs. Clemens was a board member.

CHAPMAN, HELEN POST (Mrs. Thomas Brownell Chapman) (1860–1941). A neighbor of the Twichells on Woodland Street, Hartford, and an alert observer of social mores. Her husband's grandfather, Thomas Church Brownell, was the third Bishop of Connecticut and founder of Trinity College.

CHENEY, HOWELL (1870–1957). The son of Frank Woodbridge and Mary Bushnell Cheney was born and lived all his life in Manchester, Connecticut. He received his B.A. in 1892 and his M.A. in 1893 from Yale University. From 1893 to 1934 he was employed by the family firm, Cheney Brothers of Manchester. His lifelong avocation was his interest in education, especially for women. While chairman of the Board of Trustees of Mount Holyoke College in 1933, he formed Mount Holyoke in Hartford, known today (1965) as Hartford College for Women.

CHENEY, MARY BUSHNELL (Mrs. Frank Woodbridge Cheney) (1840–1917). A remarkable woman who raised twelve children, ran a large and lavish household in Manchester, Connecticut, where the normal dinner table of fourteen was generally increased by guests who were likely to be actors, lecturers, bishops or Mark Twain. She found time to write a life of her father, the Rev. Dr. Horace Bushnell, to edit and publish a shelfful of his writings, to help found the Hartford Art School and to be president of the Colonial Dames. Her husband and his brother, Knight Cheney, operated the Cheney Silk Mills in Manchester.

CLEMENS, CLARA (Mrs. Ossip Gabrilówitsch—Mrs. Jacques Samossoud) (1874–
1962). Following the birth of their daughter, Nina, at "Stormfield," on
August 18th, 1910, the Gabrilówitsches lived first in Munich and later in
Detroit. Mme. Clemens continued her concert work and appeared on the
legitimate stage, notably in *Joan of Arc,* based on her father's book.
Widowed in 1936, she moved to California and, in 1944, married Jacques
Samossoud, a Russian friend of Gabrilówitsch's. Her published works in-
cluded *My Husband Gabrilówitsch, My Father Mark Twain* and *Awake to a
Perfect Day,* her reflections on Christian Science.

CLEMENS, HENRY (1838–1858). Mark Twain's younger brother was the model
for "Sid" in *Tom Sawyer.* Mark Twain said he never knew Henry to do
a vicious thing but that "he frequently did righteous ones that cost me as
heavily." (MTA II 92)

CLEMENS, JANE LAMPTON (Mrs. John Marshall Clemens) (1803–1890). Mark
Twain's mother was born in Lexington, Kentucky, and was married there
in 1823. She and her husband moved to East Tennessee and then Missouri.
Twain wrote that the difference between his mother and the rest of the
people whom he had known was that while the rest of the people were
interested in a few things his mother felt "a strong interest in the whole
world and everything and everybody in it." (MTA I 116)

CLEMENS, JOHN MARSHALL (1798–1847). Mark Twain's father grew up in
Kentucky. With the best of intentions, he managed to fail at almost every
enterprise. The family dream involved 75,000 acres of Tennessee land
which he bought for ⅔ cent per acre, and which eventually became valuable
to later owners. The dream was a theme of Twain's *The Gilded Age.*
John and his wife, Jane, had six children: Orion, Margaret (d. 9 yrs.),
Pamela, Benjamin (d. 10 yrs.), Samuel and Henry.

CLEMENS, ORION (1825–1897). Orion, oldest child of John Marshall and Jane
Clemens, was born in Jamestown, Tennessee. When he was 15 or 16 he
learned the printer's trade in St. Louis. His wife, Mary Eleanor (Mollie)
Stotts, came from Keokuk, Iowa, where Orion eventually returned to live
after trying many jobs in various parts of the country. Twain wrote that he
"never lost a cent for anybody, and never made one for himself." (MTA II
330) Orion and Mollie had one daughter, Jennie (1855–1864).

CLEMENS, PAMELA (Mrs. William A. Moffett) (1827–1904). Mark Twain's
sister, who was an invalid all her life. Her husband was a St. Louis merchant; they had two children: Samuel, named for Mark Twain, and Annie,
who married Charles L. Webster.

COLT, ELIZABETH H. JARVIS (1826–1905). The widow of Samuel Colt, inventor
of the Colt revolver. She entertained lavishly in Hartford and lived in a spectacular house called "Armsmear."

CRANE, SUSAN LANGDON (Mrs. Theodore Crane) (1836–1924). Mrs. Clemens'
adopted sister first saw her beloved Quarry Farm when, as a little girl, her
father, Jervis Langdon, used to take her on long drives through the Elmira
countryside. Jervis Langdon bought the farm for what would be called
today a weekend retreat, and when the Cranes were married, he gave it
to them for a wedding present. Susan Crane devoted her summers to her
sister's family, and she gave generously to the community throughout her
life.

DAY, ALICE HOOKER (Mrs. John Calvin Day) (1847–1928). The daughter
of John and Isabella Beecher Hooker, she grew up in Hartford. Mark Twain
brought his fiancée to the Hooker-Day wedding in Hartford in June, 1869.

Henry Ward Beecher officiated. Olivia Langdon (Clemens) had known Alice Day for a long time as she had often visited her uncle, Thomas K. Beecher, in Elmira. Her husband, John Calvin Day (1835–1899), was a drygoods merchant with offices in New York and Hartford. They had two daughters: Katharine Seymour and Alice Hooker (1872–1920), who married Percy Jackson.

DAY, KATHARINE SEYMOUR (1870–1964). The daughter of John Calvin and Alice Hooker Day interrupted her study of painting at the Academy Julien, Paris, to be presented at three courts, the Court of Württemberg, the Court of the Khedive of Egypt and, in 1893, to Queen Victoria at the Court of St. James's. Her interest in the study of color led her, at the age of forty-seven, to enter Radcliffe College. She received an M.A. in psychology in 1922, and in 1936 she received an M.A. in history from Trinity College. Before coming to live in Hartford in her Great-Aunt Harriet Beecher Stowe's house, she was active in New York City politics and the suffragist movement. Her later years were devoted to preserving great symbols of the American heritage; she was the leader in the successful drive to save Mark Twain's Hartford house.

DEPEW, CHAUNCEY MITCHELL (1834–1928). Lawyer, U.S. Senator (1899–1911) and railroad magnate. He was born in Peekskill, New York, and graduated from Yale in 1856. He served as director and counsel for several eastern railroads, and was president of the New York Central Railroad 1885–1899.

DRUMMOND, HENRY (1851–1897). Scottish evangelist, best known for his books, *Natural Law in the Spiritual World* and *The Ascent of Man*. He attempted to connect the theory of evolution with Christian belief. He traveled in the U.S. and was inspired by Moody and Sankey.

DUFF GORDON, CAROLINE (Lina) (1872–1964). The daughter of Sir Maurice Duff Gordon (4th Baronet) and Lady Duff Gordon. Helped to found the British Institute in Florence, Italy. She was Italian correspondent for the *Observer* 1921–1935, and foreign correspondent for *The Times* 1946–1950. In 1902 she married Aubrey Waterfield, an artist. She wrote several books about Italy; the last, *Castle in Italy,* her autobiography, was recently (1964) published by John Murray. When she knew the Clemenses she was living with her aunt, Mrs. Janet Ross, at the Villa Castagnola in Settignano.

FAIRBANKS, MARY MASON (Mrs. Abel W. Fairbanks) (1828–1898). Correspondent for her husband's paper, the Cleveland *Herald,* on the *Quaker City* excursion to Europe and the Holy land in 1867. "Mother" Fairbanks received over 100 letters from Mark Twain in thirty years.

FIELDS, JAMES T. (1817–1881). Author, lecturer and partner in Ticknor & Fields, a famous Boston firm of booksellers and publishers. He was editor of the *Atlantic* from 1861 to 1870. He took Howells on as assistant editor in 1866. Mrs. Fields (Annie Adams, 1834–1915) was his second wife. She was the daughter of Zabdiel Boylston Adams, a well-known Boston physician. She was seventeen years younger than her husband and had great charm. She established a salon at her home, 148 Charles Street, Boston.

FOOTE, LILLY GILLETTE (1860–1932). The daughter of Andrew Ward Foote of Nut Plains, Guilford County, Connecticut, came to Hartford in her teens to live in Nook Farm with relatives, the Gillettes and the Hookers. She studied at Newnham College, Cambridge, and in 1880 became the Clemens children's governess.

GABRILÓWITSCH, OSSIP (1878–1936). Russian pianist who married Clara Clemens on October 6th, 1909, at "Stormfield." He was born in St. Petersburg and at the age of six began to study the piano with Anton Rubinstein. He first visited the United States in 1900. He was conductor of the Konzertverein Orchestra, Munich, 1910–1914, and the Detroit Symphony, 1918–1936.

GERHARDT, KARL (1853–1940). He was born in Boston and worked as a machinist in Chicopee, Massachusetts, and Hartford. His hobby was modeling in clay. After viewing a statue of his wife Harriet (Hattie) Josephine McClellan, the Clemenses financed three years of study for Gerhardt in Paris. His bronze bust of Mark Twain was used as a frontispiece for *Huckleberry Finn*. Among his other works were: busts of U. S. Grant and Henry Ward Beecher, statues of Nathan Hale and General Israel Putnam and the Soldiers Monument at Utica, New York. The Gerhardts named their daughter, born in Paris (1883) for Olivia Clemens.

GILDER, RICHARD WATSON (1844–1909). Editor, poet and civic crusader. He was assistant editor of *Scribner's Monthly* (1870–1881) and became editor-in-chief when it became the *Century* in 1881. He was an influential adviser to American writers and a staunch believer that Mark Twain was more than a fun-maker.

GILLETTE, FRANCIS (1807–1879). With his brother-in-law, John Hooker, he was a founder of Nook Farm; they bought the 100-acre farm from the estate of William H. Imlay in 1851. Francis Gillette was born in Bloomfield, Connecticut. He graduated from Yale in 1819; was active in state politics and later U.S. Senator. He was an abolitionist and conducted a station of the Underground Railway in his barn. He married Elizabeth Daggett Hooker in 1851; they had five children.

GILLETTE, WILLIAM HOOKER (1855–1937). Francis Gillette's youngest son became one of America's great actors. He is most remembered for his role as Sherlock Holmes. He was born and grew up in Nook Farm, where the acting profession was generally frowned on. With Mark Twain's financial help, he went to New York and returned to Hartford in 1875 playing a small part in *The Gilded Age* in which John Raymond and Kate Field starred. Opening night saw the Reverends Twichell and Burton in a box at the theater. Mark Twain, by helping Gillette, dispelled the prejudice against theatergoing by Nook Farm residents.

GILMAN, JULIA ELLEN (Mrs. Walter Haven Clark) (1873–1963). The daughter of George Shepard, one of the first directors of the Travelers Insurance Company, she was graduated from Hartford Public High School in 1892 (Clara Clemens was in the same class for a while) and from Smith College in 1896. She and her husband were both descendants of Governor John Webster, one of the founders of Hartford; they were instrumental in preserving Mark Twain's Hartford house.

GRANT, COLONEL FREDERICK DENT (1850–1912). The oldest son of Ulysses S. and Julia (Dent) Grant. A graduate of West Point, he held commands in this country, Puerto Rico and the Philippines. He married Ida M. Honoré of Chicago in 1874.

GRANT, JESSE was the second son of Ulysses S. and Julia (Dent) Grant. He was named for his grandfather, Jesse Grant, a tanner of Point Pleasant, Clermont County, Ohio.

HALL, FREDERICK J. Successor to Webster in Charles L. Webster & Company; he bought a partnership for $12,000 in 1888. He was well-meaning but was unable to pull the company out of its difficulties.

HALLEY, EDMUND (1656–1742). Distinguished English astronomer whose name was given to a bright comet which he discovered in 1682; he predicted that it would appear at regular intervals. It appeared in 1835, the year of Mark Twain's birth. Twain's biographer quotes him as saying in 1909: "It will be the great disappointment of my life if I don't go out with Halley's comet. The Almighty has said, no doubt: 'Now here are those two unaccountable freaks; they came in together, they must go out together.' Oh! I am looking forward to that." (MTB III 1511).

HAMERSLEY, WILLIAM (1838–1920). Hartford lawyer and judge who held stock in the Paige typesetter. He eventually withdrew and escaped the failure. He was a member of the Monday Evening Club.

HAPGOOD, NORMAN (1868–1937). American editor who was born in Chicago and educated at Harvard. He was a leading figure in American magazine journalism: editor of *Collier's Weekly* 1903–1912, and later *Harper's Weekly* and *Hearst's International*. He served as U.S. Minister to Denmark in 1919.

HARTE, (FRANCIS) BRET (1836–1902). American writer of short stories and poems; his "Luck of Roaring Camp" brought him fame in 1868. He was born in Albany, New York, and went to San Francisco when he was 17. He became editor of the *Californian* with Mark Twain on the staff. Their friendship was stormy, and Bret Harte was only tolerated in Nook Farm. Isabella Beecher Hooker was distressed with Mr. Harte's bottles of spirits and felt she should have given warning to the Clemenses; she wrote: ". . . . yet I dread to lose the friendship of that house which is but a slender thread already I fancy." (NF 87)

HARRIS, JOEL CHANDLER (1848–1908). American author famous for his "Uncle Remus" stories, who began his career as a newspaperman. He recognized the importance of *Huckleberry Finn*, writing, "I think that its value as a picture of life and as a study in philology will yet come to be recognized by those whose recognition is worth anything. It is the most original contribution that has yet been made to American literature." (NF 267n. 135)

HAWLEY, JOSEPH ROSWELL (1826–1905). Civil War general, Governor of Connecticut, co-editor, with Charles Dudley Warner, of the Hartford *Courant* and U.S. Senator (1881–1895). A Nook Farm resident, he brought Charles Dudley Warner to Hartford and became a friend of Mark Twain's in 1869, although he and Warner had rebuffed Mark Twain's idea of buying into the *Courant*. He married, as his second wife, Harriet Ward Foote, Isabella Beecher Hooker's cousin from Guilford, Connecticut. He was a member of the Monday Evening Club.

HOOKER, ISABELLA BEECHER (Mrs. John Hooker) (1822–1907). A born leader with interests in the great social problems of the day, with women's suffrage paramount. She was largely guided by spiritualism and believed she would become president of a matriarchal government. She called the first women's rights convention in Hartford in 1869 (its accomplishments were adversely affected by her brother Henry's alleged-adultery scandal) and after a seven-year fight managed to get a bill through the Connecticut legislature establishing the legal right of women to hold property. Her life in Nook Farm was complicated by feuds with family and friends and enlivened by spiritualistic sessions where the mediums were usually visited by spirits of Indian warriors. She had four children: Edward Beecher, Alice, Thomas and Mary.

HOOKER, JOHN (1816–1901). The sixth in direct descent from Thomas Hooker, who founded Hartford in 1636. After graduating from Yale, he opened a law office in Farmington, Connecticut, and in 1841 married Isabella Beecher.

He was patient and long-suffering with his wife's projects. The move to Nook Farm in 1851 marked the beginning of Hartford's period as a literary center. It was John Hooker's house where Mark Twain visited first in Hartford in 1868, and it was the same house which the Clemenses rented (1871–1874) while the Hookers traveled abroad or lived with the Gillettes.

HOUSE, EDWARD H. (1836–1901). An early newspaper friend of Mark Twain's who eventually settled in Japan and adopted Koto, the daughter of a Japanese woman and an Englishman. He dramatized *The Prince and the Pauper* and brought suit in 1890 to enjoin Frohman's production of Abby Sage Richard's dramatization, resulting in a bitter quarrel with Mark Twain.

HOWELLS, ELINOR MEAD (Mrs. William Dean Howells) (1837–1910). The daughter of Larkin G. Mead and Mary Jane Noyes; her brother, William Rutherford Mead, was an architect (McKim, Mead and White); another brother, Larkin, was a sculptor. Elinor Howells was a delightful woman and a good conversationalist. She and her husband and the Clemenses were a congenial foursome. The Howellses had three children: Winifred, who died young, John Mead and Mildred (Pilla).

HOWELLS, JOHN MEAD (1868–1959). American architect who was an exponent of the Gothic spirit in skyscraper design. He collaborated on the New York Daily News Building and, with Raymond Hood, won the $100,000 prize for the Tribune Tower in Chicago.

HOWELLS, MILDRED H. (Pilla) (1872–   ). The daughter of Elinor Mead and William Dean Howells is the editor of *Life in Letters of William Dean Howells,* published in 1928. She has also published poetry. She traveled a great deal and was in Bermuda at the time of Mark Twain's last trip in 1910.

HOWELLS, WILLIAM DEAN (1837–1920). Novelist, poet, editor and literary critic, he was known as the "Dean of American letters." In 1871 Howells became assistant editor of the *Atlantic,* and in 1886 he joined *Harper's Magazine* conducting a column called "The Editor's Easy Chair." He was the first president of the American Academy of Arts and Letters. The friendship between Howells and Mark Twain was significant not only for the exchange of literary ideas, but for the rapport between them which enabled each man to bring out the best in the other.

JEFFERSON, JOSEPH (1829–1905). An eminent American actor, he played his famous part of Rip in *Rip Van Winkle* for forty years. He was born in Philadelphia of a family of actors, and started his career at the age of 3. His great-grandfather was a member of Garrick's Company at the Drury Lane Theater, London.

JOHNSON, ROBERT UNDERWOOD (1853–1937). An associate editor of the *Century* he persuaded Mark Twain to write of his two weeks' experience in 1861 as a Confederate officer in the Missouri Rangers. Mark Twain responded with an imaginative sketch picturing a wartime meeting between U. S. Grant and his future publisher.

KEITH, DORA WHEELER (Mrs. Elisha Keith) (1857–1934). Portrait painter and illustrator. She was the daughter of Candace Wheeler; she studied in Paris and with William Chase. In 1906 she was elected an associate member of the National Academy. Her portraits of Mark Twain and Warner hang in the Mark Twain Memorial, Hartford.

KING, GRACE (1851–1932). One of several young women writers "discovered" by Charles Dudley Warner. Grace was fascinated by Nook Farm and became one of Isabella Beecher Hooker's quick converts; Isabella never failed to expose everyone's guests to her latest enthusiasm.

LANGDON, CHARLES JERVIS (1849–1916). Mrs. Clemens' brother, who was a passenger on the *Quaker City*. He showed Mark Twain a miniature of Livy Clemens, whereupon Mark Twain fell in love. When Charles Langdon was 21 his father, Jervis Langdon, died and Charles, Theodore Crane and J. D. F. Slee took over the management of the Langdon coal company. Charles Langdon married Ida Clark, daughter of Jefferson B. and Julia Clark, the same year. They had three children: Jervis, Julia (Julie) and Ida. There was a close relationship between the Elmira family and the Clemenses.

LANGDON, IDA (1881–1964). The youngest daughter of Charles Jervis and Ida (Clark) Langdon. She went to Bryn Mawr, received her doctorate from Cornell and taught English at Bryn Mawr, Wellesley and Elmira College. Surviving her brother and sister, she helped to perpetuate, in Elmira and in the eastern part of the country, the image of her uncle as he was known to family and friends. Two articles in the *Chemung County Historical Journal* attest to Ida Langdon's affectionate understanding of her uncle, Mark Twain.

LANGDON, JERVIS (1809–1870). Born at Vernon, Oneida County, New York, he moved with his wife, Olivia, and adopted daughter, Susan, to Elmira in 1845. Jervis Langdon started life as a country storekeeper and became a wealthy coal mine owner. A great part of his time and money was devoted to acts of justice. He was a friend of William Lloyd Garrison and Frederick Douglass. He was responsible for establishing the Park Congregational Church and securing Thomas K. Beecher as its minister.

LANGDON, JULIA (Julie) (1871–1948). The oldest daughter of Charles J. and Ida Clark Langdon was married in 1902 to Edward Eugene Loomis, Vice President of the Lackawanna Railroad. They had two daughters: Olivia and Virginia, who married, respectively, Eugene Lada-Mocarski and Bayard Schieffelin.

LANGDON, OLIVIA LEWIS (Mrs. Jervis Langdon) (1810–1890). Mrs. Clemens' mother was born in Lenox, New York; she married Jervis Langdon July 23rd, 1832. A dynamic and fascinating woman (she received her last proposal of marriage when she was seventy-eight), she was extremely well-read and a good conversationalist.

LEARY, KATY (1863–1941). Katy was 17 years old when she came to work for the Clemenses. Except for a period in the nineties when she came back to Elmira from Europe, she was with the family till Mark Twain died in 1910.

LESCHETIZKY, THEODOR (1830–1915). Polish-Austrian pianist. In 1878 he established his own school in Vienna. Among his pupils were Brailowsky and Paderewski as well as Gabrilówitsch and Clara Clemens.

LEWIS, JOHN T. (1835–1906). The tenant farmer at Quarry Farm was born in Carroll County, Maryland, and escaped from slavery in 1877. He was the only Dunkard in the vicinity of Elmira.

LYDE, ELSIE LESLIE (Mrs. Edwin Milliken) (1881–   ). A child actress known professionally as Elsie Leslie, at the age of five she played "Little Meenie" in *Rip Van Winkle* with Joseph Jefferson. She played the original "Little Lord Fauntleroy" at the age of eight. In 1889 she was cast to play both the "Prince" and the "Pauper" in Abby Sage Richardson's dramatization of Mark Twain's book. After three years in the play, she retired to school. She returned to the stage as "Lydia Languish" in the all-star cast of *The Rivals* with Jefferson. She retired from the stage in 1912 after playing opposite George Arliss in *Disraeli*.

LYON, ISABEL V. (1868–1958). Mark Twain's secretary, 1903–1909. Isabel Lyon was recommended to the Clemenses when they were living in Riverdale by Mrs. Franklin G. Whitmore of Hartford; she had been the Whitmore children's governess. After Mrs. Clemens' death she took charge of the household as well as serving as Mark Twain's secretary. She took down some of his autobiographical dictation in longhand. In 1909 she married Ralph W. Ashcroft, whom Mark Twain had hired in 1907 as special secretary and business manager. They left his employ after an unpleasant episode concerning finances and were divorced shortly after. Mrs. Ashcroft resumed her maiden name.

MATTHEWS, BRANDER (1852–1929). Literary critic, essayist and dramatist. He taught at Columbia and was president of the National Institute of Arts and Letters, 1913–1914.

McALEER, PATRICK (1846–1906). The Clemens' coachman from 1869 to 1891; he returned to work for Mark Twain the summer of 1905 in Dublin, New Hampshire. He was born in County Tyrone, Ireland, and came to the United States when he was 16.

MILLER, CINCINNATUS HINER (Joaquin) (1839–1913). An American poet who took the pen name of Joaquin from a Mexican bandit, Joaquin Muriette, about whom he had written an article. He lived for a time with the Modoc Indians in northern California. He is best remembered for his poem "Columbus." His spectacular appearance in a western outfit in London made him very popular.

MILLET, FRANCIS (Frank) D. (1846–1912). American artist and newspaperman. A graduate of Harvard, he traveled widely, reporting for newspapers and magazines. He lived for a while with the painters, Sargent and Abbey, in Broadway, England. In 1879 he married Elizabeth Greely Merrill in Paris. He became director of the American Academy in Rome in 1911; he went down with the *Titanic* in 1912.

MODJESKA, MADAME HELENA OPID (1844–1899). Polish actress who came to America in 1876 because of political difficulties at home. She was famous for her Shakespearean roles although she never learned to speak English with ease. She was a favorite with the Nook Farm residents and stayed with the Charles Dudley Warners when in Hartford.

MOMMSEN, THEODOR (1817–1903). An eminent German historian and archaeologist. He was secretary of the Berlin Royal Academy of Sciences 1874–1895 and was a factor in every liberal movement.

MOSKOWSKI, MORITZ. Clara Clemens's famous piano teacher in Berlin, 1892.

NAST, THOMAS (1840–1902). Nast was born at Landau, Bavaria, and came to America when he was 6 years old. He became a great political cartoonist and was a lifelong friend of Mark Twain's. He originated the political symbols, the Republican elephant and the Democratic donkey, and is said to have originated the modern conception of Santa Claus. For many years he published *Nast's Almanac*. His best work was considered to be the drawings he did for *Harper's Weekly* during the Civil War; his drawings for Dickens' *Pickwick Papers* were famous.

O'NEILL, JOHN. The Clemens' gardener for many years. He and his wife, Ellen, lived nearby on Forest Street; in 1891 when the family went abroad, they moved to the Clemens' place as caretakers. He stood anxiously by when Susy died; Mrs. Clemens was devoted to him.

OSGOOD, JAMES R. (1826–1892). Boston publisher who began his career as a clerk in Ticknor & Fields in 1855. In 1868 he became a partner and the firm was known as Fields, Osgood & Company. It was succeeded by James R. Osgood & Company, which in 1878 was merged with Henry Houghton's publishing firm to become Houghton, Osgood & Company. He was Mark Twain's publisher for a while before Charles L. Webster & Company came into existence. Osgood became bankrupt in 1885; he later served as Harper's London representative.

PERKINS, MARY BEECHER (Mrs. Thomas C. Beecher) (1805–1900). Sister of Harriet Beecher Stowe, she staunchly defended Henry Ward Beecher, breaking off relations with her sister, Isabella Beecher Hooker. Like other Nook Farm residents, she traveled a great deal. She accompanied her sister, Harriet, to England when Harriet called on Lady Byron and heard the revelations of Byron's incest, which she published in the *Atlantic* for September, 1869 (*Lady Byron Vindicated*). Mary defended Harriet, who was vilified by the press.

PERKINS, THOMAS CLAP (1798–1870). Hartford lawyer who married Lyman Beecher's daughter, Mary Foote Beecher. One of their daughters, Emily, married the Rev. Edward Everett Hale, author of "The Man Without a Country."

PHELPS, WILLIAM LYON (1865–1943). American educator and literary critic; he was on the faculty of Yale 1892–1933. Phelps pioneered in presenting to his students Russian novelists and modern fiction and drama.

POND, JAMES B. (1838–1903). Impresario who managed Mark Twain's and Cable's tour in 1885 and Mark Twain's world tour 1895–1896. He learned the printer's trade in Wisconsin and was a major in the Union cavalry in the Civil War. He became a newspaperman in Salt Lake City, which led to his managing a lecture tour for Ann Eliza, nineteenth wife of Brigham Young, when she renounced Mormonism. He joined Redpath's Boston Lyceum, and in 1879 opened his own agency in New York.

POTTER, EDWARD TUCKERMAN (1831–1904). The son of Bishop Alonzo Potter of New York, he was the architect of many important residences and ecclesiastical buildings, including the Church of the Heavenly Rest, New York City.

REDPATH, JAMES (1833–1891). A Scotsman who was on Greeley's *Tribune*, he became correspondent for the Union forces, and in 1868 founded the Boston Lyceum. He managed tours for Mark Twain, Emerson, Greeley, Thoreau, Sumner, Phillips and many others. In 1886 he became editor of the *North American Review*.

REID, WHITELAW (1837–1912). Newspaperman who was with the New York *Tribune* 1868–1905; he became editor in 1872. He was U.S. Minister to France (1889–1892) and a member of the American Commission to negotiate peace with Spain in 1898. From 1905 to 1912 he was U.S. Ambassador to Great Britain.

RICE, CLARENCE C. Mark Twain's physician and friend who lived in East 19th Street, New York. Through Dr. Rice, he met Henry Rogers. Mark Twain stayed with Dr. Rice in 1893, and Susy visited him in 1896.

ROGERS, HENRY HUDDLESTON (1840–1909). Wealthy oil man who grew up in Fairhaven, Massachusetts. Starting his career as newsboy, he then worked as a railroad brakeman, a job which took him to Pennsylvania, where he became a partner in one of the first refineries in the oil fields. He devised the first effective machinery to separate naphtha from crude oil. From that point, he rose rapidly to become vice president of Standard Oil in 1890. He had many interests and became one of the great tycoons of the later nineteenth century.

SALVINI, TOMMASO (1829–1916). Italian actor who became known for his interpretations of Hamlet and Othello, playing them as cruel and heartless characters.

SHIPMAN, ARTHUR LEFFINGWELL (1864–1937). Hartford lawyer, son of Judge

Nathaniel Shipman (1828–1906) and Mary Caroline (Robinson) Shipman. He and his father were members of the Monday Evening Club, as is his son, Arthur L. Shipman, Jr. His daughter-in-law, Mary Dana Shipman, great-granddaughter of Longfellow and Richard Dana, is a trustee of both the Harriet Beecher Stowe House and the Mark Twain Memorial in Hartford.

SLEE, J. D. F. An agent for the Langdon coal business in Buffalo when the Clemenses were married. In 1870, after Jervis Langdon's death, he became manager of J. Langdon & Company.

SPAULDING, CLARA L. (1849–1935). The daughter of Henry Clinton and Clara Wisner was born in Elmira, New York. She attended Vassar College for a year and a half, and married John B. Stanchfield, a lawyer, in 1886. They lived in New York City and Islip, Long Island. They had two children: Alice Spaulding Stanchfield and John B. Stanchfield, Jr.

STANLEY, SIR HENRY MORTON (1841–1904). The great explorer was born in Wales and baptized John Rowlands. His youth was spent in an orphanage until he worked his way to New Orleans, where he was adopted by Henry Morton Stanley. He was taken prisoner while in the Confederate Army and later joined the Navy and was an ensign on the *Ticonderoga*. He became a newspaperman, and in 1869 was sent by the New York *Herald* to find Livingstone in Africa. After Livingstone's death he continued Livingstone's explorations in Africa.

STODDARD, CHARLES WARREN (1843–1909). Poet and essayist whom Mark Twain met when they were contributors to the San Francisco *Golden Era* in the sixties. He became professor of English at Notre Dame and later at the Catholic University of America, Washington, D.C.

STOWE, CALVIN ELLIS (1802–1886). Professor of Biblical literature at Lane Theological Seminary, Cincinnati, Ohio, where Lyman Beecher was president. Following the death of his first wife, Eliza Tyler, he married Harriet Beecher in 1836. They had seven children: Harriet and Eliza (twins), Georgiana May, Samuel Charles, Henry, Frederick and Charles Edward.

STOWE, HARRIET BEECHER (Mrs. Calvin E. Stowe) (1811–1896). The author was born in Litchfield, Connecticut, the seventh child of Lyman Beecher by his first wife, Roxanna Ward Foote. Harriet Beecher first heard of the brutalities of slavery from an aunt who lived in the West Indies. Living in Cincinnati as a young woman, she was exposed to the problems in the neighboring slave states. In 1850 Harriet and her husband, Calvin Stowe, moved to Brunswick, Maine, where he taught at Bowdoin College. It was in Brunswick that Harriet wrote *Uncle Tom's Cabin*. They came to Hartford to live in 1864. She died in her Nook Farm home, now a museum operated by the Stowe-Day Foundation.

TAFT, CINCINNATUS A. (1822–1884). A descendant of Robert Taft (b. Ireland 1640), he was born in Dedham, Massachusetts, and graduated from the College of Physicians and Surgeons, New York, in 1846. He joined his brother, a homeopathic physician, in Hartford, but Cincinnatus Taft believed in the cure rather than the creed and did not confine himself to any one school. His large practice was his life; in twenty-eight years he was not absent from Hartford forty-eight consecutive hours. He married Ellen Teresa Clark in 1854. His daughter, Laura, was the mother of Robert H. Schutz, trustee (1965) and past president of the Mark Twain Memorial, Hartford.

TAYLOR, BAYARD (1825–1878). A prolific writer and indefatigable traveler.

He was born in Kennett Square, Pennsylvania, and was sent to Europe as New York *Tribune* correspondent when he was 19. He was secretary to the American Legation at St. Petersburg during the Civil War. His two-volume translation of Goethe's *Faust* earned him a wide reputation and an appointment as professor of German at Cornell, 1870–1877. In 1878 he became U.S. Minister to the German Court.

TIFFANY, LOUIS COMFORT (1848–1933). American glass and jewelry designer and painter. He was born in New York, the son of Charles Lewis Tiffany from Killingly, Connecticut, who established the Tiffany jewelry firm. Louis Tiffany studied painting with George Inness and later in Paris. He turned to the decorative arts, forming Louis C. Tiffany, Associated Artists in 1879. His great field was glass, and his stained-glass windows were installed in private homes and public buildings. His chapel designed for the World Columbian Exposition in 1893 was later installed in the Cathedral of St. John the Divine in New York. His blown-glass vases, bowls and small objects of iridescent brilliant color were widely imitated by the glassmakers of Bohemia.

TRUMBULL, ANNIE ELIOT (1857–1949). Witty, lively daughter of James Hammond Trumbull, Hartford philologist and historian who created the multilingual chapter headings for *The Gilded Age*. Mark Twain said he was the most learned man in Hartford and that he could swear in twenty-seven languages. Miss Trumbull published a number of novels and a volume of verse. In the nineties she and Mark Twain carried on a correspondence in German.

TWICHELL, JOSEPH HOPKINS (1838–1918). Pastor of the Asylum Hill Congregational Church, Hartford. He was born at Southington, Connecticut, educated at Yale, Union Theological Seminary and Andover Theological Seminary. Handsome and friendly, Twichell charmed his parishioners, preaching always of brotherliness and man's relation to a God of love. His wife was Julia Harmony Cushman of New Jersey; they had nine children.

VEDDER, ELIHU (1836–1923). American painter, illustrator and author. Vedder was born in New York, studied in Paris and made his permanent home in Rome from 1867. He was noted for his symbolic and decorative work.

VON GRIPENBERG, BARONESS ALEXANDRA. Swedish woman suffragist leader, writer and member of the Swedish Diet. Her book on her travels was entitled *A Half Year in the New World: Miscellaneous Sketches of Travels in the United States* (1888).

VON TAUCHNITZ, CHRISTIAN BERNHARD (1816–1895). European publisher who founded his business in Leipzig in 1837. He is best known for the Tauchnitz paperback editions of British and American authors for sale on the European continent. Mark Twain and Tauchnitz were very friendly; Tauchnitz paid royalties to his authors although the existing copyright treaties did not compel him to do so.

VON VERSEN, GENERAL. A German officer attached to the Emperor's Court who had married a relative of Mark Twain's from St. Louis. Von Versen gave the dinner party in Berlin, in February, 1892, where Twain was the guest of honor and sat at the Emperor's right. Mark Twain's style of conversation was constrained by imperial etiquette; he heard, years later, that the Emperor had wondered why he didn't do more talking at the dinner.

WARD, JOHN QUINCY ADAMS (1839–1910). American sculptor, born in Urbana, Ohio, he studied under Kirke Brown; he had no European training. His work included the statue of Washington on the steps of the Subtreasury

Building, New York, a series of emblematic figures in the cupola of the Capitol, Hartford, and "The Freedman," a statuette which sold thousands of copies.

WALKER, EVANGELINE (Mrs. Charles M. Andrews) (1870–1962). Susy Clemens' friend at Bryn Mawr, married Professor Charles M. Andrews, who was the head of the history department at Bryn Mawr in 1890. Her sister, Ethel, founded the Ethel Walker School at Simsbury, Connecticut. Mrs. Andrews' daughter, Ethel, is the wife of Supreme Court Justice John Marshall Harlan.

WARNER, CHARLES DUDLEY (1829–1900). American editor, novelist and essayist, he was born in Plainfield, Massachusetts, and graduated from Hamilton College. A prolific writer himself, he sought and encouraged numerous young writers. With Joseph Roswell Hawley, he was editor of the Hartford *Courant*. He edited the *Library of the World's Best Literature* in thirty volumes. He and his wife, Susan Lee, lived on Hawthorne Street, across from the Hooker house, where the Clemenses lived in 1871; it was the setting for his book, *My Summer in a Garden*. They later moved into the house designed by Edward Tuckerman Potter for George Warner, next door to the Clemens' house. Susan Warner was the leader of Hartford's musical activities.

WARNER, GEORGE HENRY (1833–1919). Brother of Charles Dudley Warner, he married Elizabeth (Lilly) Hooker Gillette. Their first child, Silvia, died when a baby; Margaret (Daisy) and Frank G. grew up with the Clemens girls. George Warner worked for many years for the American Land Emigrant Company, an organization with offices in New York and Des Moines which negotiated emigrant land purchases. He was a connoisseur of Oriental rugs and, through connections with importers, supplied Nook Farm residents, particularly Mrs. Clemens, who was very much interested in rugs.

WARNER, ELIZABETH (LILLY) GILLETTE (Mrs. George Henry Warner) (1838–1915). Daughter of Francis and Elizabeth Hooker Gillette, and Mrs. Clemens' close friend. She wrote for the *St. Nicholas* magazine and did some professional illustrating. She concerned herself with the education and entertainment of children, particularly her own and the Nook Farm children. Her blond beauty and gracious manner endeared her to everyone.

WEBSTER, CHARLES L. (1851–1891). Husband of Mark Twain's niece, Annie Moffett, Twain brought him to New York in 1881 to supervise one of his projects, the manufacture of the Kaolatype process for casting brass bookbinder dies. In 1884 Mark Twain made Webster manager of Charles L. Webster & Company. Webster's business life was complicated by having to serve as errand boy for endless Clemens family commissions. The firm published all Mark Twain's books from *Huckleberry Finn* to *Tom Sawyer Abroad*, as well as Grant's *Memoirs* and an unsuccessful *Life of Pope Leo XIII*. The Websters had three children: Alice Jane (Jean), author of *Daddy Longlegs*, William Walter and Samuel Charles. The latter was the editor of *Mark Twain Business Man* (1946), in which he defended with documentary evidence Mark Twain's often unwarranted criticism of Webster's handling of the publishing business.

WHEELER, CANDACE THURBER (1828–1923). The mother of the artist, Dora Wheeler Keith, Mrs. Wheeler was an artist in the field of the design and weaving of textiles. She became a partner in Associated Artists with Coleman, De Forest and Louis Tiffany. She was in charge of the decoration of the Woman's Building at the Chicago World's Fair. She was one of the founders of the Woman's Exchange and the Onteora Club. She advised Mrs. Clemens on the décor of her Hartford house in 1881.

WHITMORE, FRANKLIN GRAY (1846–1926). The son of a New York business-
man, Isaiah C. Whitmore, he entered Columbia College in 1862. In 1864 he
was a member of the Seventh Regiment which was detailed to guard the
body of Lincoln in New York City. He married Harriet Gould in 1867. In
1880 they moved to West Hartford, where he opened a real estate office.
He was Mark Twain's business agent for a number of years; he and Mrs.
Whitmore were close personal friends of the Clemenses.

INDEX

The index is necessarily selective for the Clemens family and their close associates. General family concerns and activities are listed under individual subject headings. The dialogists have not been indexed except where substantive information about them appears.

[437]